A MIRROR

for

AMERICANS

IMMIGRANTS CROSSING THE PLAINS

A MIRROR
for
AMERICANS

Life and Manners in the United States
1790–1870
as Recorded by American Travelers

III. THE FRONTIER MOVES WEST

Compiled and Edited by
WARREN S. TRYON

THE UNIVERSITY OF CHICAGO PRESS

THE UNIVERSITY OF CHICAGO PRESS, CHICAGO 37

Cambridge University Press, London, N.W. 1, England

To

My Mother

LUCY TRYON

Contents

Contents

Part III

THE VALLEY OF DEMOCRACY

Writing in 1888, Lord Bryce, author of the distinguished *American Commonwealth,* declared that "the West may be called the most distinctively American part of America, because the points in which it differs from the East are the points in which America as a whole differs from Europe." Although he admitted that "it is impossible to draw a line between the East and the West, because the boundary is always moving westward," it is clear that he was referring primarily to the great area watered by the Upper Mississippi and its tributaries. Certain fringes of that area are less easily allocated—Kentucky or Missouri, for example—because as border states, and before 1865, connected as they were by slavery and its concomitants with the South, they did not wholly share the cultural outlook of the great valley. Yet, compared to South Carolina or Louisiana, they seem alien to the dominant developments of the Cotton Kingdom and appear to be, as actually they were, more "western" than southern.

Without falling into the excesses of the frontier historians, the comment of Lord Bryce remains intrinsically true. Many of those institutions, such as democracy, nationalism, and reform, which one thinks of as so distinctly American found either their origin in or a sympathetic development through the inhabitants of the Middle West. To an even greater though less tangible degree, such attributes as practicality, materialism, aggressive optimism, the go-getter spirit, or kindly hospitality, which comprise so much of the "American character," found their chief development in the West.

Foreigners were quick to observe this fact that Europe extended to the Alleghenies and that beyond them lay America. Americans, even more, were aware of the distinction between the eastern and western sections; and, as the great tide of emigration crossed the mountains, native travelers promptly commenced their tours to report back to the curious at home what this new life was like. They did an amazingly thorough job of it and in the totality of their accounts left little unvisited or unrecorded.

In thinking of Ohio, of Illinois, or of Minnesota, one largely conceives this frontier as a farming community and pictures log cabins, Indian wars, fields of corn, and unending, boundless prairies. To a large degree the Middle West, especially in the earlier period, was true to this notion, and American travelers duly described precisely these elements. However, it is worthy of especial note that they did not make the mistake of assuming that this was all there was to the record. They were perfectly well aware that urban movements were developing rapidly on this frontier and that many emigrants had no intention of becoming farmers and proposed, rather, to build towns. They were aware, too, that towns implied problems of transportation and culture, to cite but two; and so travelers took equally in their stride cities as well as farms, canals and railways as well as prairies, and colleges and churches as well as Indians and fur-traders.

While the West was western, these travel books are filled with significant and pertinent observation. As the valley commenced to lose its distinctive character and to take on increasingly the economic and social patterns of the older East, the Middle West became less interesting alike to travelers and to the readers of their accounts. Its drabness of life, the uniformity of its towns, and the monotony of its flat countryside were increasingly emphasized, until by the close of the century one has the impression that the entire region between the Appalachians and the Rockies was just so much to be endured until the transcontinental trains reached really "interesting" scenery on the Pacific Coast.

26

Religious Ecstasy on the Frontier, 1804–5

*A*mong *the most famous characteristics associated with the frontier were its frenetic religious revivals, and among the most celebrated preachers connected with these revivals was Lorenzo Dow. He was born in 1777 in Coventry, Connecticut. If he was a dynamic character, he was also a strange and stormy one as well. In and out of the Methodist persuasion, he did much to spread the tenets of that sect, though in the end he attacked them as "badly tainted with popery"! He traveled widely on his preaching expeditions through New England, Canada, Ireland, and England and the mountain areas of the South and West. Indeed, so much a man of God was he that he left his first wife on the next morning after his wedding to continue his itinerant preaching. History does not record what his wife thought of this. Self-centered and self-interested, for all his seeming humility, he wrote much, though, except for his* Travels (1806), *little of it is readable today. His record is pedestrian, dry, and matter of fact; yet, as a participant in the events he describes, it is not without interest or importance. His description of the religious ecstasies he encountered makes somewhat different reading from that which Mrs. Royall observed with such irony and distaste. After his second marriage he settled down, mostly in Connecticut, though his death occurred in Maryland in 1834.*

ON THE JERKS

I had heard about a singularity called the *jerks* or *jerking exercise* which appeared first near Knoxville, Tennessee, in August last, to the great alarm of the people, which reports at first I considered as vague and false; but at length, like the Queen of Sheba, I set out, to go and see for myself.

When I arrived in sight of that town, I saw hundreds of people collected in little bodies; and observing no place appointed for meeting, before I spoke to any, I got on a log, and gave out a hymn; which caused them to assemble round, in solemn attentive silence: I observed several involuntary motions in the course of the meeting, which I considered as a specimen of the jerks.

Thus I got on to meeting; and after taking a cup of tea gratis, I began to speak to a vast audience, and I observed about thirty to have the *jerks,* though they strove to keep still as they could; these emotions were involuntary and irresistible, as any unprejudiced eye might discern.

Hence to Mary's-ville, where I spoke to about fifteen hundred, and many appeared to feel the word, but about fifty felt the jerks; at night, I lodged with one of the Nicholites, a kind of Quakers who do not feel free to wear coloured cloaths; I spoke to a number of people at his house that night. Whilst at tea, I observed his daughter, (who sat opposite to me at the table,) to have the jerks, and dropped the teacup from her hand, in the violent agitation: I said to her, "young woman, what is the matter?" she replied, "I have got the jerks." I asked her how long she had it? she observed, "a few days," and that it had been the means of the awakening and conversion of her soul, by stirring her up to serious consideration about her careless state, &c.

Soon after I spoke again in Knoxville, to hundreds more than could get into the Court house, the Governor being present; about one hundred and fifty appeared to have the jerking exercise, amongst whom was a circuit preacher, who had opposed them a little before, but he now had them powerfully; and I believe that he would have fallen over three times had not the auditory been so crowded that he could not, unless he fell perpendicularly.

After meeting, I rode eighteen miles, to hold meeting at night: The people of this settlement were mostly Quakers: and they had said, (as I was informed) the Methodists and Presbyterians have the jerks, because they *sing* and *pray* so much, but we are still peaceable people, wherefore we do not have them: However, about twenty of them came to meeting, to hear one, as was said, somewhat in a Quaker line; but their usual stillness and silence was interrupted; for about a dozen of them had the jerks as keen and powerful as any I had seen, so as to have occasioned a kind of grunt or groan when they would jerk. It appears, that many have undervalued the great revival, and attempted to account for it altogether on natural principles; therefore it seems to me, (from the best judgment I can form), that GOD hath seen proper to take this method, to convince people that he will work in a way to shew his power; and had sent the *jerks* as a sign of the times, partly in judgment for the people's unbelief, and yet as a mercy to convict people of divine realities.

I have seen Presbyterians, Methodists, Quakers, Baptists, Church of England, and Independents, exercised with the *jerks;* Gentleman and Lady, black and white, the aged and the youth, rich and poor, without exception; from which, I infer, as it cannot be accounted for on natural principles, and carries such marks of involuntary motion, that it is no trifling matter: I believe that those who are the most pious and given up to GOD, are rarely touched with it; and also those naturalists, who wish and try to get it to philosophize upon it, are excepted; but the lukewarm, lazy, half-hearted, indolent professor, is subject to it; and many of them I have seen, who when it came upon them, would be alarmed and stirred up to redouble their diligence with GOD; and after they would get happy, were thankful it ever came upon them. Again, the wicked are frequently more afraid of it than the small-pox or yellow fever; these are subject to it; but the persecutors are more subject to it than any, and they have sometimes cursed, and swore, and damned it, whilst jerking. There is no pain attending the jerks, except they resist it, which if they do, it will weary them more in an hour than a day's labour; which shews that it requires the *consent* of the *will* to avoid suffering.

I passed by a meeting house, where I observed the undergrowth had been cut up for a camp-meeting, and from fifty to an hundred saplings left breast high; which appeared to me so slovenish, that I could not but ask my guide the cause, who observed they were topped so high, and left for the people to jerk by; this so excited my attention, that I went over the ground, to view it; and found where the people had laid hold of them, and jerked so powerfully, that they had kicked up the earth as a horse stamping flies. I observed some emotion, both this day and night, among the people; a Presbyterian minister (with whom I stayed,) observed, "yesterday, whilst I was preaching, some had the jerks, and a young man from N. Carolina mimicked them out of derision, and soon was seized with them himself, (which was the case with many others) he grew ashamed, and on attempting to mount his horse to go off, his foot jerked about so, that he could not put it into the stirrup; some youngsters seeing this, assisted him on, but he jerked so that he could not sit alone, and one got up to hold him on, which was done with difficulty; I observing this, went to him, and asked him what he thought of it? said he, 'I believe GOD sent it on me for my wickedness, and making so light of it in others'; and he requested me to pray for him."

I observed his wife had it; she said, she was first attacked with it in bed. Dr. Nelson said, he had frequently strove to get it, (in order to philosophize upon it,) but could not; and observed they could not account for it on natural principles.

Next day, a gentleman gave me some money, and sent a horse with me several miles; and then I took to my feet, and went on to Greenville, and so on to Abington, in Viriginia. The last jerks that I saw, was a young woman, who was severely excercised during meeting; she followed me into the house, I observed to her the indecency and folly of such public gestures and grunts; and requested, (speaking sternly, to make impression on her mind) if she had any regard for her character, to leave it off; she replied, "I will, if I can." I took her by the hand, looking her in the face, and said, "do not tell lies." I perceived, (by the emotion of her hand) that she exerted every nerve, to restrain it, but instantly she jerked as if it would have jerked her out of her skin, if it were possible; I did this to have an answer to others on the subject.

A TRAVELING PREACHER

I spoke in Culpepper court-house, Virginia, and then rode fifty miles or more to Charlottesville, near the President's seat in Albermarle County; I spoke to about four thousand people, and one of the President's daughters who was present, died a few days after.

Hence I went circuitously to Lynchburg, where I spoke in the open air, in what I conceived to be the seat of satan's kingdom.

From thence, to New-London, where I began speaking in the court-house. I fell in with Brother *Stith Mead,* and we went on to the camp-meeting which I had appointed last August.

March 22nd.—Several families came about twenty miles, and encamped on the ground, though there were but few Methodists any where short of that distance; the weather was chilly, the clouds appeared threatening, and the prospects before us very gloomy; however, we poured out our complaint to GOD, who graciously heard our cry; sent off the clouds, and gave us a beautiful sun.

23rd.—About fifteen hundred people appeared on the ground, and the LORD began a gracious work that day, which I trust hell shall never be able to extinguish. One soul found peace before night, and another in the night.

24th.—About three thousand people attended; the solemnity and tenderness, and prospect of good increased.

25th. Sunday.—About five thousand on the ground, and in general, good attention. Colonel Callaway, and a number of respectable gentlemen, used their endeavours to protect our peaceable privileges.

Monday, 26th.—About three thousand appeared on the ground, and the rejoicing of old saints, the shouts of young converts, and the cries of the distressed for mercy, caused the meeting to continue all night, until we parted on Tuesday morning, 27th.

About fifty during this meeting professed to have found the pardoning love of GOD; from hence, the work went home with the people, and spread over the country.

28th.—I rode in great misery eleven miles, and spoke to hundreds, an hour, by sun in the morning. Thence to Franklin court-house at twelve o'clock, and some were offended; but good I trust was done. In the evening, I spoke twelve miles off; but was grieved with the family: could not eat with them, but next morning quitted them betimes, and went to Henry court-house; spoke to about one thousand five hundred people; and stayed with General Martin at night, where we had a good time.

30th.—I started this morning an hour before day, and rode 30 miles to Pittsylvania court-house. Here were several of my spiritual children, amongst whom was Polly Callaway; whom I once had pointed at whilst preaching, the first time she ever saw me, and GOD struck her under conviction; she ran away thirty miles to the camp-meeting, where GOD set her soul at liberty; and almost the whole of her father's family have been brought to GOD; and her brother is become an itinerant preacher. One soul was set at liberty today, some mocked and caused interruption, but good was done during three meetings.

31st.—I held meeting, sun half-hour high, and then rode eighteen miles to Wilson's meeting-house; these were tender times; eight miles hence, I spoke at night.

Sunday, April 1st.—I spoke at Rockingham court-house, N. Carolina, to fifteen or sixteen hundred people, who appeared in general solemn and well behaved, considering the inconvenience of standing in the freezing air, and falling snow, more than two hours. I rode twelve miles, and spoke at night.

2nd.—I spoke in Danville to about two thousand, this was the seat of satan's kingdom; yet, I believe, I shall one day see good times in this quarter. Some children were brought forward for me to pray for them, instead of offering them up in baptism, which I had never seen before.

3rd.—I rode thirty miles to Halifax, Virginia, where I spoke to about two thousand, and in general good attention.

April 5th.—A Presbytery was sitting at Prince-Edward, and many Lawyers were here; (it being Court time,) I spoke to about three thousand people, (standing upon the stocks or pillory,) on the subjects of predestination and deism, shewing the one to be the foundation of the other.

The first time I visited Cartersville I sent to an Inn-keeper to preach in his house, who replied, (as was said) he would first meet me in hell; he shortly after died, shocking to relate—

No one offered a place, except one man a room, which would contain about a dozen; at length, I got the liberty of a tobacco shed or ware-house where I spoke to about five hundred. One man rode into the company, and continued on his horse about two hours, until I had done; it rained so tremendously, that the people who were mostly excited by curiosity, were compelled to stay until I finished. So I left the town without eating or drinking; but now there was a stage erected for me, and I spoke to about two thousand.

8th.—I spoke under some shades at Powhatan, about two thousand present; we had a good time, except one drunken man, and some few took offence.

10th.—I spoke in Richmond to about two thousand. Here the posts of the gallery sunk some inches, crushing the bricks on which they stood, and two inches more would have let down hundreds of people upon those beneath.

I spoke under the federal oaks to about seventeen hundred; we had a melting time.

Friday, June 1st.—Camp-meeting commenced near Poplar-spring Church, in Gloucester county. No preachers were on the ground, and hundreds of people were assembled; this, indeed, was a trial of my faith among the strange people; however, in the *Name of the Lord,* I went up the stage and began the meeting, and besought GOD for a token for good; and soon a poor woman who had come thirty miles on foot under distress, was delivered, and clapping her hands, shouted for joy. Upon this, three or four preachers appeared. These things began to revive my heart, but a shower of rain expelled us from the woods into the Church, where six or eight souls found peace. The next day was a good time also.

Sunday, 3rd.—Some thousands assembled, and whilst I was speaking from a stage, a storm seemed coming up, which put the people in motion, but I requested the people to be still and raise their hearts to GOD, if perhaps He would send off the clouds; and soon the threatening grew favourable, and the clouds went round.

Monday 4th.—Our meeting broke up; about thirty found peace; and a number of backsliders were reclaimed; scores were awakened, and good was done.

Six hundred found peace, and five hundred and twenty were taken into the society, and the flame was still going on.

Friday 8th.—Camp-meeting came on at Charity chapel, Powhatan county: The Lord was precious; but the wicked strove to trouble us.

Sunday 10th.—About five or six thousand were on the ground: The work went on, and the opposition increased. Twenty-five combined together to give me a flogging—They ransacked the Camp to find me, whilst I was taking some repose. This was the first discovery of their project: as I went out of the tent, one was seen to cock a pistol towards me, whilst a voice was heard, "there he is! there he is!" My friends forced me into the tent: next day I had one of the young men arrested, and two others fled before they could be taken. The young man acknowledged his error, and promised never to do the like again: so we let him go.

What enraged them so, was my shewing their improper behaviour in their striking the blacks, &c.

Friday 15th.—I arrived on the Camp-ground, about an hour by sun in the evening: three found peace; some attempted interruption, but the Magistrates were on our side. I continued on the ground until Monday the 18th, in which time, about sixty professed to have found peace, and about one hundred awakened.

August 31st.—Camp-meeting began, and the people were entirely strangers to the quality and magnitude of this kind of meeting. Several methodist preachers came as spectators, intending, if the meeting did well to take hold, heart and hand with me, but if ill to leave it as they found it, and let the blame devolve on me. A stage being erected, I addressed the people thereon, from Luke xxi. 19. An awful solemnity came over the people; several mourners came forward to be prayed for, and some shortly found comfort, and the Lord began to move in the camp; however, the preachers were minded we should disband to private habitations; but I replied, "if I could get twenty to tarry on the ground, I would not go off until the meeting broke." Soon the Lord began to move among the people, and many were detained on the ground, and souls were born to God. Next day the congregation and work increased, and so in the course of the night likewise.

Sunday, Sept. 2nd.—It rained, (I was sick). I got on a log in the triangle, and began relating a story concerning a bird's nest. Several of them desired I should pray with them: soon nine were sprawling on the ground, and some were apparently lifeless. The Doctors supposed they were fainted, and desired water and fans to be used. I replied, "Hush!" then they to shew the fallacy of my ideas, attempted to determine it with their skill, but to their surprise, their pulse was regular. Some said, "it is fictitious, they make it." I answered, "the weather is warm, and we are in a perspiration, whilst they are cold as corses, which cannot be done by human art."

Here some supposing they were dying, whilst others suggested, "it is the work of the devil." I observed, "if it be the devil's work, they will use the dialect of hell when they come to." Some watched my words, in great solemnity, and the first and second were soon brought through, happy, and all in the course of the night; except a young woman who had come under good impression, much against her father's will, thirty miles. She continued shrieking for mercy, for eight hours, sometimes on the borders of despair, until near sun-rise, when I exhorted her if she had a view of her Saviour, to receive Him as appearing for her: here hope revived; faith sprang up; joy arose; her countenance was an index of her heart to all beholders; she uttered a word, and soon she testified the reality of her mental sensation, and the peace she had found.

We held quarterly-meeting on Clarke's creek; some supposed I would get no campers, but at this Q.-M I wanted to know if there were any backsliders in the auditory, and if there were, and they would come forward, I would pray with them: an old backslider, who had been happy in the old settlements, with tears, came forward, and fell upon his knees, and several followed his example. A panic seized the congregation, and an awful awe ensued: we had a cry and shout; it was a weeping, tender time. The devil was angry, and some, without, persecuted, saying, "is GOD deaf, that they cannot worship Him without such a noise?" though they perhaps would make a greater noise when drinking a toast. This prepared the way for the Camp-meeting, and about thirty from this neighbourhood went thirty miles upwards, and encamped on the ground. The Camp-meeting continued four days: the devil was angry at this also, and though his emissaries contrived various projects to raise a dust, their efforts proved ineffectual; in general, there was good decorum, and about fifty were awakened, and five professed justifying faith; so that it may now be said, the country which was a refuge for scape-galloweses, a few years since, in Spanish times, is in a hopeful way, and the wilderness begins to bud and blossom as the rose, and the barren land becomes a fruitful field.

27

An Early View of the Missouri Country, 1810–11

*H*enry M. Brackenridge (1786–1871) *was the distinguished son of a distinguished father, Hugh Henry Brackenridge, the author of* Modern Chivalry. *The son, born in Pittsburgh, Pennsylvania, voyaged often and extensively through the western country, came to know it well, and left many valuable observations about it. By profession he was a lawyer and, sufficiently active in public and political matters, achieved the no mean distinction of incurring the hostility of both John Quincy Adams and Andrew Jackson. The former dismissed him as "a mere enthusiast," and the latter was the subject of an attack by Brackenridge in* Letters to the Public (1832).

During the years 1810–14 Brackenridge lived in the newly acquired Territory of Louisiana, and, in the course of gathering many facts about it, he journeyed in 1811 up the Missouri River to the Missouri Fur Company's post. The Journal *of that expedition he published both separately and as a part of the more extensive* Views of Louisiana (1814). *The* Journal *is on the whole the more interesting, though the* Views, *which is somewhat in the nature of a compendium, is valuable. In 1834 Brackenridge published his most famous work,* Recollections of Persons and Places in the West, *which is hardly a travel book, though it partakes of the nature of one. It affords valuable historical material on the West and autobiographical information about the author.*

A MISSOURI FRONTIER FAMILY

On leaving St. Genevieve, I drew near a settlers cabin, and discovered a group of persons seated by a large fire, which was burning under an enormous tree. "Here he comes," several voices cried out at once; and the settler coming forward requested me to alight, with an appearance of good will which made me feel that it was sincere. The dogs who were at first very noisy, now whined a kind of welcome as if they would second the hospitality of their master. I gladly excepted the invitation, having been a good deal chilled by the cold night dews. The family consisted of the mother and fourteen children, the eldest apparently about eighteen years of age a blooming girl; the youngest an infant. They were all glowing with health. I made up an acquaintance in a few moments with a half a dozen young rogues, and passed the time agreeably. The innocence, the cheerfulness and content, which prevailed in this charming family, almost seemed to be without alloy. The scene will never fade from my recollection. They were neatly dressed in new cotton cloth, and had nothing of that wretchedness or poverty, or stupid ignorance, which is but too common in the unfortunate peasantry of most countries. Looking around, I found myself in the midst of the woods; a few trees were felled round the house, which was built of unhewn logs, the interstices not closed up.

The good man having secured my horse in a kind of shed, and given him a bundle of reeds which he had cut, returned to the fire and resumed his seat. I conversed with him on various subjects, and was much impressed at the good sense as well as various information which he possessed. He gave me a brief account of his reasons for settling here. He was a native of Connecticut, had sold a small property, which he owned in the vicinity of Hartford, and had removed to Ohio, with the intention of purchasing a tract of land on which to support his increasing family. But on his arrival, he had found the price beyond his means, after the expenses he was obliged to incur in transporting his family. He had therefore come to the resolution of proceeding to the extreme frontier, and a few months before had reached New Madrid. Here he had followed the example of others, and selected a spot on the public lands, in the hope of being able to make as much by the cultivation of the soil, as would pay for it by the time the office for the sale of the public domain, should be opened. If it should not prove successful, the improvements on the land would render it more valuable to some one else, and in the meanwhile, he would be able to support his family. Supper being now announced, we all entered the cabin, where the table was spread, and rough

benches placed around it. A tin cup filled with rich milk, was placed before each of us, and cakes of the Indian meal were smoking on the board.
The good man said grace in a reverend manner, and we did ample justice
to the simple and wholesome fare provided for us. Surrounded by health,
innocence, and benevolence, who could complain?

After supper, we returned to the fire underneath the spreading tree, and
whiled away the time in sprightly and mirthful conversation; the Yankee
girls were very talkative, the whole family appeared to be delighted with our
company in this lonely place, where they so seldom saw any strangers but
their neighbours, the bears and wolves. The hour for retiring at length arrived. My host arose. "Gentlemen," said he, "it is the practice of our family
to give a half an hour to religious devotion every evening: should you
think proper to join us, we will be glad, if not, keep your seats, and excuse
us for the present." Who could have declined such an invitation? I, with
shame it is confessed, far from being as good as I ought to be, felt a desire
to join in the good man's devotions, if not for the first time, at least never
with so much sincerity. We again entered the house, where they sung one
of Watts' pious hymns, after which, our host poured out a prayer that
seemed to flow from the very bottom of his heart. The evening service was
concluded by another hymn, after which, it being time to retire to rest, we
were shewn up to the loft, to which we ascended by a ladder. A few blankets
and bear skins had been provided for us; we resigned ourselves to sleep, in
the consciousness that even such wretches as we could not fail of experiencing
the care of the protecting angel, set once to guard this charming family from
the approach of guile.

Truth compels me to relate some further particulars respecting this interesting family, which will be painful to the reader. The autumn following,
I had to visit New Madrid, and anticipated much pleasure in seeing these
worthy people. But alas! as I drew near the house, every thing appeared still
about it, and on my making a noise, the good man, emaciated to a skeleton,
crawled out, and after recognizing, informed me in the most pathetic, yet
composed manner, of a train of misfortunes which had befallen him. His
whole family had been assailed by violent bilious fevers, his wife and five of
his children were no more, and the rest, with the exception of two boys, who
were then extremely ill, had been kindly taken away by some of the old
settlers, that they might be the better attended to; but, said he, "God's will
be done—it is all for the best."—I could have wept like Niobe.

I must also add, that the season was more unhealthy than had been known
for twenty years, and that the settler had unfortunately built his cabin on the
border of a pond, which became stagnant in summer.

AN EARLY IMPRESSION OF ST. LOUIS

St. Louis is the seat of government of the territory, and has always been considered the principal town.

This place occupies one of the best situations on the Mississippi, both as to site and geographical position. In this last respect, the confluence of the Ohio and the Mississippi, has certainly much greater natural advantages, but the ground is subject to inundation, and St. Louis has taken a start, which it will most probably retain. It is perhaps not saying too much, that it bids fair to be second to New Orleans in importance, on this river.

The ground on which St. Louis stands is not much higher than the ordinary banks, but the floods are repelled by a bold shore of limestone rocks. The town is built between the river and a second bank, three streets running parallel with the river, and a number of others crossing these at right angles. It is to be lamented that no space has been left between the town and the river; for the sake of the pleasure of the promenade, as well as for business and health, there should have been no encroachment on the margin of the noble stream. The principal place of business ought to have been on the bank. From the opposite side, nothing is visible of the busy bustle of a populous town; it appears closed up. The site of St. Louis is not unlike that of Cincinnati. How different would have been its appearance, if built in the same elegant manner: its bosom opened to the breezes of the river, the streams enlivened by scenes of business and pleasure, and rows of elegant and tasteful dwellings, looking with pride on the broad wave that passes!

From the opposite bank, St. Louis, notwithstanding, appears to great advantage. In a disjoined and scattered manner it extends along the river a mile and a half, and we form the idea of a large and elegant town. Two or three large and costly buildings (though not in the modern taste) contribute in producing this effect. On closer examination, the town seems to be composed of an equal proportion of stone walls, houses, and fruit trees: but the illusion still continues.

On ascending the second bank, which is about forty feet above the level of the plain, we have the town below us, and a view of the Mississippi in each direction, and of the fine country through which it passes. When the curtain of wood which conceals the American bottom shall have been withdrawn, or a vista formed by opening farms to the river, there will be a delightful prospect into that rich and elegant tract. The bottom at this place is not less than eight miles wide, and finely diversified with prairie and woodland.

There is a line of works on this second bank, erected for defence against the Indians, consisting of several circular towers, twenty feet in diameter, and fifteen in height, a small stockaded fort, and a stone breast work. These are at present entirely unoccupied and waste, excepting the fort, in one of the buildings of which, the courts are held, while the other is used as a prison. Some distance from the termination of this line, up the river, there are a number of Indian mounds, and remains of antiquity; which, while they are ornamental to the town, prove, that in former times, those places had also been chosen as the site, perhaps, of a populous city.

Looking to the west, a most charming country spreads itself before us. It is neither very level nor hilly, but of an agreeable waving surface, and rising for several miles with an ascent almost imperceptible. Except a small belt to the north, there are no trees; the rest is covered with shrubby oak, intermixed with hazels, and a few trifling thickets, of thorn, crab apple, or plumb trees. At the first glance we are reminded of the environs of a great city; but there are no country seats, or even plain farm houses: it is a vast waste, yet by no means a barren soil. Such is the appearance, until turning to the left, the eye again catches the Mississippi. A number of fine springs take their rise here, and contribute to the uneven appearance. The greater part fall to the S.W. and aid in forming a beautiful rivulet, which a short distance below the town gives itself to the river. I have been often delighted in my solitary walks, to trace the rivulet to its sources. Three miles from town, but within view, amongst a few tall oaks, it rises in four or five silver fountains, within short distances of each other: presenting a picture to the fancy of the poet, or the pencil of the painter.

Close to the town, there is a fine mill erected by Mr. Choteau on this streamlet; the dam forms a beautiful sheet of water, and affords much amusement in fishing and fowling, to the people of the town.

The common field of St. Louis was formerly enclosed on this bank, consisting of several thousand acres; at present there are not more than two hundred under cultivation; the rest of the ground looks like the worn common, in the neighbourhood of a large town; the grass kept down and short, and the loose soil in several places cut open into gaping ravines.

St. Louis contains according to the last census one thousand four hundred inhabitants. One fifth Americans, and about four hundred people of color. There are a few Indians and metiffs, in the capacity of servants, or wives to boatmen. This town was at no time so agricultural as the other villages;

being a place of some trade, the chief town of the province, and the residence of a number of mechanics. It remained nearly stationary for two or three years after the cession; but is now beginning to take a start, and its reputation is growing abroad. Every house is crowded, rents are high, and it is exceedingly difficult to procure a tenement on any terms. Six or seven houses were built in the course of last season, and probably twice the number will be built the next. There is a printing office, and twelve mercantile stores. The value of imports to this place in the course of the year, may be estimated at two hundred and fifty thousand dollars. The outfits for the different trading establishments, on the Mississippi or Missouri, are made here.—The lead of the Sac mines is brought to this place; the troops at Belle Fontaine put sixty thousand dollars in circulation annually. The settlers in the vicinity on both sides of the river, repair to this place as the best market for their produce, and to supply themselves with such articles as they may need.

The price of marketing does not differ much from the towns of the western country; every thing appears to be approximating to the same standard. Game of all kinds is brought in by the neighbouring Indians; or the poorer inhabitants, and sold for a mere trifle; such as venison, turkeys, geese, ducks, swans, prairie hens, &c. Upon the whole, provisions are no higher than in the towns of the Ohio.

The manners of the inhabitants are not different from those in other villages; we distinctly see the character of the ancient inhabitants, and of the new residents, and a compound of both. St. Louis, however, was always a place of more refinement and fashion, it is the residence of many genteel families, both French and American.

A few American mechanics, who have settled here, within a short time, are great acquisitions to the place; and there is still ample room for workmen of all kinds. There is a French school and an English one.

St. Louis will probably become one of those great reservoirs of the valley between the Rocky mountains and the Allegheny, from whence merchandise will be distributed to an extensive country. It unites the advantages of the three noble rivers, Mississippi, Illinois and Missouri. When their banks shall become the residence of millions, when flourishing towns shall arise, can we suppose that every vender of merchandise, will look to New Orleans for a supply, or the Atlantic cities? There must be a place of distribution, somewhere between the mouth of the Ohio and Missouri. Besides a trade to the northern parts of New Spain[1] will be opened, and a direct communication to the East Indies, by way of the Missouri, may be more than dreamt: in this case, St. Louis will become the *Memphis* of the American Nile.

1. [I.e., California.—ED.]

THE OLD FRENCH AFTER THE PURCHASE OF LOUISIANA

The French inhabitants of the Mississippi have little resemblance to the gay, and perhaps frivolous, Frenchmen of Louis the fifteenth and sixteenth, and still less to those who have felt the racking storm of the revolution.

The present inhabitants are chiefly descendents of the settlers who were induced to remove hither from Canada. In consequence of the misfortunes of France, the settlements of the Illinois experienced a sudden and rapid decay; which was again accelerated by the conquest of General Clark for the United States, in 1779. The greater number of the wealthy and respectable inhabitants descended the Mississippi, and settled in New Orleans, and the lower country. Others crossed the Mississippi, and established St. Louis and St. Genevieve. Scarcely any but natives of the country remained. The foreigners chiefly returned to the countries from whence they first emigrated.

Such is the origin of the greater part of that class of the population of this territory, which I have denominated the ancient inhabitants. They are chiefly natives of the country; but few families are immediately from France, or even from New Orleans or Canada.

In the character of these people, it must be remembered, that they are essentially Frenchmen; but, without that restlessness, impatience and fire, which distinguishes the European. There is, even in their deportment, something of the gravity of the Spaniard, though gay, and fond of amusements. From the gentle and easy life which they led, their manners, and even language, have assumed a certain degree of softness and mildness: the word *paisible* expresses this characteristic. In this remote country, there were few objects to urge to enterprise, and few occasions to call forth and exercise their energies. The necessaries of life were easily procured, and beggary was unknown. Hospitality was exercised as in the first ages. Ambition soared far hence, for here there was no prey. Judges, codes of law, and prisons, were of little use, where such simplicity of manners prevailed, and where every one knew how far to confide in his neighbour. In such a state of things, to what end is learning or science? The schools afforded but slender instruction; the better sort of people acquired in them reading, writing, and little arithmetic. The number of those who were lovers of knowledge, and make it a profession, was small. From the habits of these people, it would naturally be expected, that they would have been unaccustomed to reason on political subjects; they were in fact, as ignorant of them, as children are of life and manners. These inhabitants were as remarkable for their tame and peaceable disposition, as the natives of France are for the reverse.

Amongst their virtues, we may enumerate honesty and punctuality in their dealings, hospitality to strangers, friendship and affection amongst relatives and neighbours. Instances of abandonment on the female side, or of seduction, are extremely rare. The women make faithful and affectionate wives, but will not be considered secondary in the matrimonial association. The advice of the wife is taken on all important, as well as on less weighty concerns, and she generally decides. In opposition to these virtues, it must be said, that they are devoid of public spirit, of enterprise, display but little ingenuity or taste, and are indolent and uninformed.

They are catholics, but, very far from being bigoted or superstitious. They were perhaps more strict observers, formerly, of the rules and discipline of their church, and of the different holy days in the calendar. Their *fetes,* or celebration of these days, were considered, as the most interesting occasions; the old and young engaged in them with the greatest delight, and certainly contributed to their happiness. Of late, this attention to the ceremonies of their religion is considerably relaxed, since other objects of pursuit and interest have been opened to their view. The catholic worship is the only one yet known in the territory, except in private families, and in a few instances of itinerant preachers.

There was scarcely any distinction of classes in the society. The wealthy and more intelligent, would of course be considered as more important personages, but there was no difference clearly marked. They all associated, dressed alike, and frequented the small ball room. They were in fact nearly all connected by the ties of affinity or consanguinity: so extensive is this that I have seen the carnival, from the death of a common relation, pass by cheerless and unheeded. The number of persons excluded was exceedingly small. What an inducement to comport ones self with propriety and circumspection! The same interest at stake, the same sentiments that in other countries influence the first classes of society, were here felt by all its members. Perhaps as many from unmerited praise have been formed into valuable characters, as others from having been unjustly despised have become truly despicable.

Their wealth consisted principally in personal property, lands were only valuable when improved. Slaves were regarded in the light of *bien foncier,* or real property, and in fact, as the highest species. Lead and peltry were frequently used as the circulating medium.

There was but little variety in their employments. The most enterprising and wealthy were traders, and had at the same time trifling assortments of merchandise for the accommodation of the inhabitants, but there were no open shops or stores, as in the United States. There were no tailors or shoemakers; such as pursue these occupations at present, are from the United States. The few mechanics, exercising their trades, principally carpenters and smiths, scarcely deserved the name. The lead mines, I have already observed, engaged a considerable number. The government gave employment to but few, and those principally at St. Louis. By far the greater proportion of the population was engaged in agriculture; in fact, it was the business of all, since the surplus of produce of the country was too inconsiderable to be depended upon. A number of the young men for some time, embraced the employment of boatmen, which was by no means considered degrading; on the contrary, it was desirable for a young man to have it to say, that he had made a voyage in this capacity: and they appeared proud of the occupation, in which they certainly are not surpassed by any people in dexterity. It is highly pleasing to see them exerting themselves, and giving encouragement to each other, by their cheering songs.

But this occupation, amongst many other changes, has been reduced to the same footing as with the Americans. Arising probably from the simple cause, of there having arisen objects of more generous emulation.

What is somewhat strange, there were no domestic manufactures among them; the spinning wheel and the loom were alike unknown. So deficient were they in this respect, that although possessed of numerous herds, they were not even acquainted with the use of the churn, but made their butter by beating the cream in a bowl, or shaking it in a bottle.

Their amusements, were cards, billiards, and dances: this last of course the favourite. The dances were cotillions, reels, and sometimes the minuet. During the carnival, the balls follow in rapid succession. They have a variety of pleasing customs, connected with this amusement. Children have also their balls, and are taught a decorum and propriety of behaviour, which is preserved through life. They have a certain ease and freedom of address, and are taught the secret of real politeness, *self denial;* but which by the apes of French manners, is mistaken for an affected grimace of complaisant regard, and a profusion of bows, scrapes and professions.

Their language, every thing considered, is more pure than might be expected; their manner of lengthening the sound of words, although languid, and without the animation which the French generally possess, is by no means disagreeable. They have some new words, and others are in use, which in France have become obsolete.

In their persons, they are well formed, of an agreeable pleasant countenance; indicating cheerfulness and serenity. Their dress was formerly extremely simple; the men wore a blanket coat, of coarse cloth or coating, with a cape behind, which could be drawn over the head; from which circumstance it was called a *capote*. Both sexes wore blue handkerchiefs on their heads: but no hats, or shoes, or stockings; mockasins, or the Indian sandals, were also used. The dress of the females was generally simple and the variations of fashion, few: though they were dressed in a much better taste than the other sex. These manners will soon cease to exist, but in remembrance and description: every thing has changed. The American costume is generally introduced into the best families, and among the young girls and young men universally. I never saw any where greater elegance of dress than at the balls of St. Louis. We still see a few of both sexes in their ancient habiliments; capots, mockasins, blue handkerchiefs on their heads, a pipe in the mouth, and the hair tied up in a long queue. These people exhibit a striking difference when compared with the unconquerable pertinacity of the Pennsylvania Germans, who adhere so rigidly to the customs, manners and language of their fathers. A few years have effected a greater change with the inhabitants of this territory than has been brought about amongst the Germans in fifty years.

The Americans have communicated to them, their industry and spirit of enterprize, and they in turn, have given some of their more gentle and amiable customs. Upon the whole, the American manners, and even language, begin to predominate. The young men have already been formed by our government, and those growing up will have known no other. A singular change has taken place, which, one would think, ought not to be the result of a transition from a despotism to a republican government: luxury has increased in a wonderful degree, and there exists something like a distinction in the classes of society. On the other hand, more pains are taken with the education of youth; some have sent their sons to the seminaries of the United States, and all seem anxious to attain this desirable end. Several of the young men have entered the army of the United States, and have discovered talents. The females are also instructed with more care, and the sound of the piano is now heard in their dwellings for the first time.

It may be questioned, whether the poorest class has been benefitted by the change. Fearless of absolute want, they always lived in a careless and thoughtless manner: at present the greater part of them obtain a precarious subsistence. They generally possess a cart, a horse or two, a small stock of cattle, and cultivate some spots of ground. At St. Louis they have more employment than in the other villages; they make hay in the prairies, haul wood for sale, and are employed to do trifling jobs in town; some are boatmen or patrons. At St. Genevieve, they depend more upon their agriculture, and have portions in the great field, but this will probably soon be taken from them by the great industry of the American cultivators, who are continually purchasing, and who can give double the sum for rent; they are sometimes employed in hauling lead from the mines, but it will not be sufficient for their support. A number have removed to the country, and, in imitation of the Americans, have settled down on public lands, but here they cannot expect to remain long. Those who live in the more remote villages, are less affected by the change, but there is little prospect of their being better situated.

If I am asked, whether the ancient inhabitants are more contented, or happy, under the new order of things, or have reason to be so, I should consider the question a difficult one, and answer it with hesitation. It is not easy to know the secret sentiments of men, and happiness is a relative term. It is true, I have heard murmurings against the present government, and something like sorrowing after that of Spain, which I rather attributed to momentary chagrin, than to real and sincere sentiment: besides, this generally proceeds from those who were wont to bask in the sunshine of favour. Yet I have not observed those signs which unequivocally mark a suffering and unhappy people. The principal source of uneasiness arises from the difficulties of settling the land claims by the commissioners on the part of the United States. The principal inhabitants have lost much of that influence which they formerly possessed, and are superseded in trade and in lucrative occupations by strangers; their land claims, therefore, constitute their chief dependence. The subject on which the claimants are feelingly alive. This anxiety is a tacit compliment to our government, for under the former, their claims would be scarcely worth attention. The general complaint is, the want of sufficient liberality in determining on them. Six years have passed away without the final adjustment of the claims, and even those that have been decided upon, will give rise to lawsuits; it is probable there will be as copious a harvest of these as ever was furnished by any of the states.

The lower class have never been in the habit of thinking beyond what immediately concern themselves; they cannot, therefore, be expected to foresee political consequences. They were formerly under a kind of dependence, or rather vassalage, to the great men of villages, to whom they looked up for their support and protection. Had they been more accustomed to think it possible, that by industry it was in their power to become rich, and independent also, the change would have been instantly felt in their prosperity. But they possess a certain indifference and apathy, which cannot be changed till the present generation shall pass away. They are of late observed to become fond of intoxicating liquors. There is a middle class, whose claims or possessions were not extensive, but sure, and from the increased value of their property, have obtained since the change of government, a handsome competence. They, upon the whole, are well satisfied; I have heard many of them express their approbation of the American government, in the warmest terms. They feel and speak like freemen, and are not slow in declaring that formerly the field of enterprize was occupied by the monopolies of a few, and it is now open to every industrious citizen.

There are some things in the administration of justice, which they do not yet perfectly comprehend; the trial by jury, and the multifarious forms of our jurisprudence. They had not been accustomed to distinguish between the slow and cautious advances of *even handed justice,* and the despatch of arbitrary power. In their simple state of society, when the subjects of litigation were not of great value, the administration of justice might be speedy and simple; but they ought to be aware, that when a society becomes extensive, and its occupations, relations and interests, more numerous, people less acquainted with each other, the laws must be more complex. The trial by jury is foreign to the customs and manners of their ancestors; it is therefore not to be expected that they should at once comprehend its utility and importance.

The chief advantages which accrued from the change of government, may be summed up in a few words. The inhabitants derived a security from the Indians; a more extensive field, and a greater reward was offered to industry and enterprize; specie became more abundant, and merchandise cheaper. Landed property was greatly enhanced in value. In opposition, it may be said, that formerly they were more content and had less anxiety; there was more cordiality and friendship, living in the utmost harmony, with scarcely any clashing interests. This, perhaps, is not unlike the notions of old people, who believe that in their early days every thing was more happily ordered.

The idea of their becoming extinct, by dissolving before a people of a different race, and of losing their *moeurs cheries,* might excite unhappy sensations. Already the principal villages look like the towns of the Americans. Are not the customs and manners of our fathers, and of our own youth, dear to us all? Would it not fill our hearts with bitterness, to see them vanish as a dream? Sentiments like these, doubtless sometimes steal into their hearts.

THE INDIANS OF THE UPPER MISSOURI

The men are large and well proportioned, complexion somewhat fairer than that of Indians generally—usually go naked:—the dress they put on seems intended more for ornament than as essential; this consists of a sort of cassoc or shirt, made of the dressed skin of the antelope, and ornamented with porcupine quills, died a variety of colors; a pair of leggings, which are ornamented in the same way. A buffaloe hide dressed with the hair on, is then thrown over the right shoulder, the quiver being hung on the other, if armed with a bow.[2] They generally permit their hair to grow long; I have, in one or two instances, seen it reach to their heels, when increased by artificial locks of horse hair; and is then usually divided into several braids, matted at intervals, with a white tenacious clay; sometimes it is rolled up in a ball, and fixed on the top of the head. They always have a quantity of feathers about them; those of the black eagle are most esteemed. They have a kind of crown made of feathers, such as we see represented in the usual paintings of Indians, which is very beautiful. The swan is in most estimation for this purpose. Some ornament the neck with necklaces made of the claws of the white bear. To their heels they sometimes fasten foxes' tails, and on their leggings suspend deers' hoofs, so as to make a rattling noise as they move along. On seeing a warrior dressed in all this finery, walking with his wife, who was comparatively plain in her dress or ornaments, I could not but think this was following the order of nature, as in the peacock, the stag, and almost all animals, the male is lavishly decorated, while the female is plain and unadorned. I intend this as a hint to some of our petit maitres.

The dress of the female consists of a long robe made of the dressed skins of the elk, the antelope, or the agalia, and ornamented with blue beads, and stripes of ermine, or in its place, of some white skin. The robe is girded round the waist with a broad zone, highly ornamented with porcupine quills, and beads. They are no better off than were the Greeks and Romans, in what we deem at present so essential, but like them they bathe themselves regularly, twice a day. The women are much fairer than the men; some might be considered handsome any where; and exceed the other sex in point of numbers; the dreadful consequence of the wars in which the nation is constantly engaged.

Polygamy is general, they have often four or five wives. Their courtship and marriage resemble that of most of the Indian nations; if the parties are mutually agreeable to each other, there is a consultation of the family; if this be also favourable, the father of the girl, or whoever gives her in marriage, makes a return for the present he had received from the lover—the match is then concluded.

Their government is oligarchical, but great respect is paid to popular opinion. It is utterly impossible to be a great man amongst them without being a distinguished warrior; and though respect is paid to birth, it must be accompanied by other merit, to procure much influence. They are di-

2. A warrior is seldom seen without his arms, even in the village.—His bow, spear, or gun, is considered part of his dress, and to appear in public without them, is in some measure disgraceful.

INDIAN CHILDREN AT SCHOOL

vided into different banks or classes; that of the pheasant, which is composed of the oldest men; that of the bear, the buffaloe, the elk, the dog, &c.
Each of these has its leader, who generally takes the name of the class, exclusively. Initiation into these classes, on arriving at the proper age, and after
having given proofs of being worthy of it; is attended with great ceremony.
The band of dogs is considered the most brave and effective in war, being
composed of young men under thirty.

War parties are usually proposed by some individual warrior, and according to the confidence placed in him, his followers are numerous or otherwise. In these excursions they wander to a great distance, seldom venturing
to return home without a scalp, or stolen horses. Frequently when unsuc-
cessful they "cast their robes," as they express it, and vow to kill the first
person they meet, provided he be not of their own nation. In crossing the
river, they use canoes made of the buffaloe hide, or a few pieces of wood
fastened together. They usually leave some token, as a stake, which is
marked so as to convey some idea of their numbers, the direction which
they have taken, &c. To avoid surprise, they always encamp at the edge of a
wood; and when the party is small, they construct a kind of fortress, with
wonderful expedition, of billets of wood, apparently piled up in a careless
manner, but so arranged as to be very strong, and by this means to with-
stand an assault from a much superior force.

Their weapons consist of guns, war clubs, spears, bows, and lances. They
have two kinds of arrows, one for the purpose of the chase, and the other for
war; the latter differs in this particular, that the barb or point is fastened so
slightly, that when it enters the body, it remains in, and cannot be drawn
out with the wood; therefore, when it is not in a vital part, the arrow is
pushed entirely through. They do not poison them. Their bows are generally
very small; an elk's horn, or two ribs of a buffaloe, often constitute the
materials of which they are made. Those of wood are of willow, the back
covered with sinews.

With respect to their religion, it is extremely difficult, particularly from
the slight acquaintance I had with them, to form any just idea. They have
some notion of a supreme being, whom they call the "Master of Life," but
they offer him no rational worship, and have but indistinct ideas of a future
state. Their devotion manifests itself in a thousand curious tricks of slight of
hand, which they call magic, and which the vulgar amongst them believe to
be something supernatural. They are very superstitious. Beside their magic,
or medicine lodge, in which they have a great collection of magic, or sacred
things, every one has his private magic in his lodge, or about his person.
Any thing curious is immediately made an amulet, or a talisman; and is

considered as devoted or consecrated, so as to deprive the owner of the power of giving it away.

During my short stay amongst them, I endeavored to form a vocabulary of such words as are most likely to be primitive. I found a great diversity in the pronunciation, which I discovered to be partly owing to the circumstance of the present population being composed of the fragments or remains of different tribes; but I was also informed by the chief, that amongst the principal families there was a better language than that in use with the common people. The slaves, of whom there is a much greater number than I had supposed, and those of foreign tribes who have domiciliated themselves here, speak also an inferior dialect.

To give an account of the vices of these people, would only be to enumerate many of the most gross which prevail amongst us, with this difference, that they are practised in public without shame. The savage state, like the rude uncultivated waste, is contemplated to most advantage at a distance. Mr. Bradbury had been an enthusiast, as most philanthropic Europeans are, on the subject of Indian manners, and I was myself not a little inclined to the same way of thinking, but now both agreed that the world would lose but little, if these people should disappear before civilized communities. In these vast plains, throughout which are scattered so many lovely spots, capable of supporting thousands such nations as the Arikara, or wandering Sioux, a few wretches are constantly roaming abroad, seeking to destroy each other. To return to the subject of their moral characters—they have amongst them their poor, their envious, their slanderers, their mean and crouching, their haughty and overbearing, their unfeeling and cruel, their weak and vulgar, their dissipated and wicked; and they have also, their brave and wise, their generous and magnamimous, their rich and hospitable, their pious and virtuous, their kind, frank, and affectionate, and in fact, all the diversity of characters that exists amongst the most refined people; but as their vices are covered by no veil of delicacy, their virtues may be regarded rather as the effect of involuntary impulse, than as the result of sentiment. In some respects they are extremely dissolute and corrupt; whether this arises from refinement in vice, or from the simplicity of nature, I cannot say; but much are they mistaken who look for primitive innocence and simplicity in what they call the state of nature. It is true that an intercourse with the whites, never fails to render these people much worse than before; this is not by imparting any new vices, but by presenting temptations which easily overcome those good qualities, which "sit so loosely about them." Want of constancy, and uniformity of character, is the defect universally remarked with regard to the Indians, and this naturally arises from the want of fixed principles of virtue.

One thing I remarked as constituting the great difference between the savage and the civilized state, *their youth undergo no discipline,* there are no schools, and the few instructions which are given by parents, are directed only to the mere physical man, and have little to do with the mind, unless it be to inculcate fortitude and courage, or rather ferocity and thirst for blood: no genuine virtues are *cultivated* and the evil propensities of the individual are suffered to mature without correction, while he wanders about a vagabond, responsible to no one for the waste of time; like a young colt, he is considered as unfit for employment until he attains his growth. The lessons of morality are never taught either in public or in private; at least of that morality which instructs us how to fulfil all the duties attached to our social relations, and which regard us as candidates for a future and more happy existence. Instead of such lessons of morality, the precepts first instilled into their hearts, are cruelty, murder, and rapine. The first step the young savage is taught to take, is in blood; and is it any wonder that when manhood nerves his arm, we should see him grasp the tomahawk and the scalping knife, and his savage heart thirst for blood!

Amongst others of their customs which appeared to me singular, I observed that it was a part of their hospitality, to offer the guest, who takes up his residence in their lodges, one of the females of the family as a bedfellow; sometimes even one of their wives, daughters, or sisters, but most usually a maid-servant, according to the estimation in which the guest is held, and to decline such offer is considered as treating the host with some disrespect; notwithstanding this, if it be remarked that these favours are uniformly declined, the guest rises much higher in his esteem. Self control, in the midst of temptations which overpower the common mind, being thought, even amongst these people, to indicate a superior character. Our common boatmen soon became objects of contempt, from their loose habits and ungovernable propensities. To these people, it seemed to me that the greater part of their females, during our stay, had become mere articles of traffic; after dusk, the plain behind our tents, was crowded with these wretches, and shocking to relate, fathers brought their daughters, husbands their wives, brothers their sisters, to be offered for sale at this market of indecency and shame. I was unable to account for this difference from any people I had ever heard of; perhaps something may be attributed to the inordinate passion which had seized them for our merchandize. The silly boatmen, in spite of the endeavors of the leaders of our parties, in a short time disposed of almost every article which they possessed, even their blankets, and shirts. One of them actually returned to the camp, one morning entirely naked, having disposed of his last shirt—this might truly be called *la derniere chemisse de l'amour*.

Seeing the chief one day in a thoughtful mood, I asked him what was the matter—"I was wondering," said he, "whether you white people have any women amongst you." I assured him in the affirmative. "Then," said he, "why is it that your people are so fond of our women, one might suppose they had never seen any before?"

About two miles on this side of the first village, my attention was attracted by a number of small scaffolds, distributed over several acres of ground on the slope of a hill. I soon discovered that this was a depository of the dead. The scaffolds were raised on forks about ten feet, and were sufficiently wide to contain two bodies; they were in general covered with blue and scarlet cloth, or wrapt in blankets and buffaloe robes; we did not approach near enough to examine closely, this frightful Golgotha, or place of human skeletons, but we could see a great number of valuable articles which had been left as offerings to the manes of the deceased. Several crows and magpies were perched upon them; we could not but experience a sensation of horror, when we thought of the attraction which brought these birds to this dismal place. Some of the scaffolds had nearly fallen, perhaps overturned by the wind, or the effect of decay, and a great number of bones were scattered on the ground underneath. This mode of exposing the dead has something peculiarly horrible in it. The wolves of the prairie, the birds of the air, and even the Indian dogs, are attracted to the place, and taught to feed on human flesh.

A few days after our arrival, a great commotion was heard in the village, before daylight. The interpreter, shortly after came to us with the information, that it was a party of three hundred men, on their return, after a battle with a party of Sioux the day before, in which they had been victorious, with the loss of two or three killed, and ten or twelve wounded, and that they were then within a few miles of the village, none but the chief of the party having come in. We waited with anxiety for their approach to the village, which we were informed would be made with considerable ceremony; that they had halted within a few miles of the place, to prepare themselves for a formal and splendid entry, and that a great deal of Indian finery had been sent, to enable the warriors to decorate themselves to the best advantage.

It was nearly eleven o'clock in the day, before their approach was announced; in the meanwhile a stilly suspense reigned throughout the village, all sports and business suspended, and resembling a holiday in one of our towns. We discovered them at length, advancing by the sound of their voices over a hill, about a mile below our encampment. In a short time they made their appearance; at the same time, the inhabitants of the town moved out on foot to meet them. I accompanied them for some distance, and then took a favorable position where I might have a full view of this singular scene. They advanced in regular procession, with a slow step and solemn music, extending nearly a quarter of a mile in length, and separated in platoons, ten or twelve abreast, the horsemen placed between them, which contributed to extend their line. The different bands, of which I have spoken, the buffaloe, the bear, the pheasant, the dog, marched in separate bodies, each carrying their ensigns, which consisted of a large spear, or bow, richly ornamented with painted feathers, beads, and porcupine quills. The warriors were dressed in a variety of ways, some with their cincture and crown of feathers, bearing their war clubs, guns, bows and arrows, and painted shields: each platoon having its musicians, while the whole joined in the song and step together, with great precision. In each band there were scalps fastened to long poles: this was nothing more than the few scalps they had taken, divided into different locks of hair, so as to give the semblance of a greater number. The appearance of the whole, their music, and the voices of so many persons, had a pleasing and martial effect.

The scene which took place, when their friends and relations from the village, mingled with them, was really affecting. These approached with song and solemn dance, as the warriors proceeded slowly through their ranks. Fathers, mothers, wives, brothers, sisters, caressing each other, without interrupting for a moment, the regularity and order of the procession, or the solemnity of the song and step! As they drew near the village, the old people, who could barely walk, withered by extreme age, came out like feeble grasshoppers, singing their shrill songs, and rubbing the warriors with their hands. The day was spent in festivity by the village in general, and in grief by those who had lost their relatives. We saw a number of solitary females, on the points of the hills round the village, lamenting in mournful wailings, the misfortunes which had befallen them. For the two succeeding days the village exhibited a scene of festivity; all their painted shields and trophies were raised on high poles near the lodges, and all the inhabitants dressed out in their finery—all their labors and sports were suspended, and the whole joined in the public demonstrations of joy, while music, songs, and dances were hardly intermitted for a moment.

28

Connecticut's Canaan in the Western Reserve, 1821

The details of the life of Zerah Hawley are meager. He was born in 1781, apparently in Connecticut, where he received an excellent education. Yale conferred a Bachelor's degree on him in 1803 and a Master's degree in 1808. By profession he was a physician. When nearly forty years of age, he undertook an extended journey across New England and New York to Ohio, where in Ashtabula County, in the northeastern corner of the Western Reserve, he remained for a year during 1820–21. He thereupon returned home to Connecticut, published the account of his experiences, A Journal of a Tour *(New Haven, 1822), lived out the remainder of an uneventful life, and died in 1856.*

A Journal of a Tour is not an unbiased account of life in northeastern Ohio, and it must be regarded in the light of the author's own prejudices. That he regarded westerners much in the same manner as President Dwight of Yale is apparent. Their manners were bad and their morals little better. The fabled account of wealth and prosperity was hugely overdrawn. It is apparent that the good doctor wished he had never gone West and that his fellow-citizens in Connecticut would be well advised not to go either. Certainly his strict Calvinist opinions viewed the more lax religion of the frontier with dismay, and life in the land of steady habits had not prepared him for raw frontier settlements. Possibly forty years of age was too old to make the necessary adjustments. Nevertheless, despite Hawley's querulousness, his account was a valuable antidote to some of the overexuberant "frontier fever,"

and he noted and jotted down many observations which did not ordinarily
find their way into print.

On Sept. 30, I crossed the State line and entered Ohio, the *fabled region*
of the West. I say *fabled region,* because more, much more has been said
about the State, than has any foundation in truth. It has been compared to
Canaan, and even extolled above it. It has been called the *Garden* of America,
and many other high sounding titles have been given to it, which it is needless and superfluous to mention.

Today I rode to Harpersfield to see a sick woman, through the woods
about a mile; the road so bad in consequence of the abundance of stumps,
roots and mud, that I could only ride upon a slow walk; and entered for
the first time in my life into a log-house with one room without any fireplace, the log being laid against the logs of the house and the fire built in
front.

In consequence of this manner of building the fire, some of the logs were
entirely burnt in two, and many were much injured by the fire. The furniture of the house consisted of a bed, laid upon a bedsted made of saplings
of suitable size, (having bark on) with holes bored to receive the legs which
were made of the same materials.—Three or four indifferent chairs, a chest
or two, a few articles of hollow ware, two or three shelves made by boring
holes into the logs of the house, into which were inserted pins of wood upon
which rough boards were laid, forming the whole pantry of the house, containing a few articles of crockery. Furniture for the fire consisted of two
stones which answered the purpose of andirons, and a wooden poker which
performed the double office of shovel and tongs. A large hole through the
roof, answered the two-fold purpose of a vent for the smoke, and the admission of light. The house was also lighted and ventilated by many large
cracks or spaces between the logs, which in winter are sometimes filled with
clay, and many times are left without filling through the year, for the purpose (perhaps) of preventing pestilential diseases, as in many cases little
pain is taken to keep their habitations cleanly, and in all it is utterly impossible that neatness should exist in consequence of the continual falling of
clay from the crevices between the logs, and of bark with which the roof is
in many instances covered, and the constant accumulation of mud which is
brought into the only room in the house in great profusion. This is not an
exaggerated picture; but a reality, and will in most particulars answer for a
general description of most of the houses in this part of the country; others
there are, a few comfortable framed houses, and some far worse than what I
have described, as I shall presently show.

Most of the log houses which have two rooms, more resemble two houses standing near to each other, and covered by one roof, than one house, having a space of about six feet between them, so that in passing from one to the other, you have always to go into the open air, which every one may imagine to be very pleasant and comfortable, especially in a cold stormy winter night. In this hall are usually placed the *swill-barrel, tubs, pots, kettles, &c.* Here the hogs almost every night dance a hornpipe to a swinish tune, which some one or more musicians of their own number play upon the pots and kettles, while others regale themselves at the swill-barrel, and add to the music, by upsetting it, which produces *liquid* music by the discharge of its contents into the Hall! To this music the whole assembly join in a grunting chorus. Now the whole Assembly leave their dancing, and repair to the feast, which is widely and profusely spread upon the ground of the Hall.

I will add that almost all of the houses, whether log or framed, are built without a cellar, and the framed houses are, in this case, built on large piles, as stones are not sufficiently plenty in many towns on the Reserve for this purpose.

A block-house differs from a log one in this particular; in the former the logs are hewn square, so that they are smooth within and without, and the latter are hewn only within, having the bark on the outside. In general also blockhouses are shingled in the ordinary manner, but most of the log houses are covered with long shingles, which are kept in place by means of three or four large poles laid from one end of the roof to the other, which are prevented from slipping off, by small billets of wood placed at right angles with them at certain intervals.

A shanty is a tenement (if it may be so called) built of logs split through the centre, having the plain surface inwards, and the bark without. They are generally about ten or twelve feet square, with a roof on one side, in the manner that horse-sheds are frequently built; consequently they have no chamber at all. In some there is a chimney, in others none, the smoke escaping through an opening at one corner of the roof, or else diffusing itself through the whole apartment, and finding its exit through the large openings between the logs. The door, in order that all the room in the building may be saved for use, always opens outwards, and is hung on wooden hinges, and is usually fastened when the family goes abroad, by a stick of wood leaning against it. This is as full a description of such a building as it merits.

I will finish by giving you some account of *titled men and their habitations.* In riding through the country, you come to a log or block house; on enquiring to whom it belongs, you are surprised to hear that it belongs to Judge ——. The whole establishment consists of one room, in which all the family, with their guests, eat, sleep, and perform all the domestic operations. You proceed a little farther, and arrive at a similar mansion, and are informed that it belongs to Esquire ———, who you find is a miller, and a man who has had no other advantage for acquiring information than an ordinary school education.

Soliciting information respecting another residence, you are told that it is the property of a Representative or a Senator of the Legislature of the State of Ohio. In this villa, containing also but one room, is found a bed in two corners, in another a cup-board, in the fourth a swill-barrel, and on one side of the room a wooden clock without a case, and by one window a three-cornered piece of a looking-glass, set in a little wooden frame of domestic manufacture and on the other side may be seen the Major Z—— at work at shoes. You will find another similar residence belonging to Colonel such a one.

These things are all well enough; but if such are the residences of the Honourable, what must be those of the vulgar.

The furniture of most houses is scanty. Few families have more than one indifferent table, and chairs of the plainest kind, and most of them either broken or worn out, just sufficient to accommodate the family; so that, should company call to see them, the guests or some part of the family must either stand, or sit on the bed, or some stool or block of wood which is most convenient.

The furniture for the table is equally scanty and inconvenient. I once had occasion to dine with a family in Harpersfield, in Ashtabula county, where six of us set at the table. There was a plate for each of us, a large dish in the middle of the table contained the food. I had the good fortune to obtain a decent knife and fork, one of the family had a shoe-knife and a fork, another (if I mistake not) an old raisor-blade with a wooden handle, and the other three were content with forks only. This was a family which has been here for *seventeen* years, and have had time to be in a better condition.

The articles of crockery are also very few and indifferent. Many people brought here with them, a good supply of good crockery, which is mostly broken, and its place partially supplied with very indifferent ware. Many broken-nosed tea-pots are to be seen, and others without a handle, the use of which is supplied by means of a bail made of iron wire, which is inserted into holes drilled through the earthen pot at opposite sides.

For want of a glass, or other convenient vessel, from which to drink, if you are offered whiskey, (which is the principle drink here,) the bottle is presented to you, or a bowl, or tea-cup containing the liquor.

Iron ware is no less scarce than other articles, sometimes a pot answering the four-fold purpose of pot, dish-kettle, tea-kettle, and brass-kettle. In other cases the tea-kettle or the dish-kettle answer the same purposes. In some cases the only tea-kettle, which is to be found in a house is destitute of lid, and one ear, so that the bail applies to the inside of the kettle, which is used in this manner. All articles of iron manufactured in this part of the country are very heavy, and easily broken.

I was made to understand, before I came to the Reserve that vegetation was wonderfully luxuriant here, almost beyond a parallel; so that grass growing by the road-side, was equal, if not superiour to the best pastures in Connecticut. But to my surprise, I found not only roads, but the pastures almost destitute of vegetation. Some allowance must be made for the drought, which has continued for a number of weeks. But making all the concession of this kind which the nature of the circumstances require, I do not think that vegetation is much more if any more luxuriant than in the old settled Eastern States. Indeed, I know many towns in Massachusetts and Connecticut, which naturally produce as much, and by the present mode of cultivation, more than the best lands in this part of the country.

On the whole there is no difficulty in procuring enough to eat, if people are industrious; but in many towns here, industry is not so much the order of the day, as it is generally, in the Eastern States. Some instances, I know, of men who have no profession or trade but farming, who, instead of raising their provisions as they might, buy almost all of them, and pay for them by letting themselves out by the day.

Clothing is vastly more difficult to obtain. If persons can obtain sheep sufficient, and can raise flax enough for their own consumption, they may have plain clothes, which will be good enough for this part of the country. But sheep are yet scarce, and must be carefully penned from the wolves, as they still continue to destroy many.

From this and other causes, sheep are less numerous than the necessities of the people require, so that the present inhabitants are in general but indifferently clothed, both in summer and winter; so much so, that except when dressed in their holiday clothes, (which in general are none of the most fashionable, convenient or comfortable,) a great proportion of the inhabitants are clothed in such garments as the poorest class of people at the East would hardly think comfortable.

This is not an exaggeration, nor what I have heard; but it is what I have myself seen, and can prove if it is necessary, by many witnesses.

I was myself told before I came here, that woollen cloths were plenty and cheap, so that I had no need to supply myself with flannel or fulled cloth, nor trouble myself with the transportation of such articles. But I find the contrary, as I have not by much inquiry found one yard, either of flannel or dressed cloths to sell since I arrived in this country. You will remark that I mean domestic cloths by what I have said above. There are a few flannels and dressed foreign cloths, all which are excessively dear, costing twice or three times as much as in New England, and can be had only for money, which to most people amounts to prohibition, as they have not, (if one may believe their own words,) any money with which they may buy any thing. "Money, (say they,) is out of the question, as nothing they have to sell will bring money at any price."

Shoes are, if possible, still more difficult to be obtained. Leather cannot be had without the cash, so that here is the same difficulty as exists respecting cloths; and besides this, here is but one shoemaker for three towns! so that most children are *literally barefoot,* and cannot attend school till the middle of winter, and others cannot go at all, and some men and women are no better, as I have seen, and *many* are but a *little* removed from the same situation. This arises partly from the want of leather, and partly from the want of shoemakers.

One case I will relate, because it is fresh in my mind. I was at the house of a Mr. W——r, of Harpersfield, a local preacher in the Methodist society, a few days since, whose wife I had attended some time previous. I found him at home, and enquired after his health. "Oh," said he, "I am shuffling about, almost barefoot," looking down upon his feet, upon which he had the soles of shoes, and the quarters, bound on his feet with tow strings. He remarked farther, "I cannot get leather without money, and of that I have none, and can buy none with any thing that I have to sell." I enquired how his wife was, and he said, "Oh! she's well enough, but *barefoot* and has not had a pair of shoes for six months," and added, "she almost wishes herself back again to the State of New-York, for there she could have tea, coffee, shoes, and whatever she wanted except wheat bread." I afterwards saw her, and she also assented to what I have written above.

Many more sigh for the land of their nativity, some of whom *cannot* get back, and others are ashamed to return in their ragged state, having spent almost their all in moving to the Land of Promise, and since they have arrived here.

I will give you a description of the dress of the females in this part of the country. It is of necessity almost all home-spun, and comfortable enough; (when whole) which is not too frequently the case, but the fashion thereof is very ancient, similar to the fashion of our grandmothers.

Caps are very little worn by the women, either old or young, except on

Sabbaths and other high days, and they are such as were used to be worn as long ago, as I can remember. As to the bonnets, I can hardly give you a correct idea of them: but will describe them as well as I can. I have seen three or four, imported from New-York, of the Dunstable kind, and quite in fashion; and as to the rest, they are something like the parson's wig, and it would hardly be considered as Idolatry to worship them, as they are "in the likeness of nothing in Heaven above, in the earth beneath, or in the waters under the earth"; therefore you see there are no ideas existing in the minds of men, by which they can be accurately described. The stuff of which they are made you may know, when I tell you it is every kind of cloth from silk to flannel. I have just seen one made of yellow flannel quilted, and trimmed with the fur of the Muskrat, (as I suppose) and it is made to set close to the head, well answering the purpose of an ordinary skull-cap.

Some are made of dark mixed Chambray, and trimmed with bright *orange-coloured* ribbon; others are *black,* trimmed with *scarlet, crimson, yellow, green,* or any coloured ribbons which the wearer either fancies, or can procure: Some are white, trimmed with green, or with any of the vast varieties which can be made by a composition of all the colours of the rainbow.

The gowns worn by women, as dress-gowns in winter, are either light-coloured calico, or new domestic flannel of any colour which may please the wearer.

Crapes, silks, or even bombazetts, are seldom seen here, although there are a few, which are occasionally worn by the wealthiest people.

The dress of Misses on *gala* days is in many instances a yellow-flannel frock, with a small ruffle, sometimes of muslin, but more frequently of some coloured cotton stuff, with one of the above described bonnets, and a stout pair of cow-hide shoes when they have them.

The men generally dress in homespun cloth, and in many cases appear quite decent on days of exhibition; but their every day wardrobe is most miserably deficient. It is much the custom here to overlay pantaloons on the seat and the inside and front of the legs with sheep-skin. Some wear a semi-leathern apron ending in half legs, covering the fore part of the legs, and fastened behind by leathern straps and buttons.

Some females, sixty years or more, wear their hair plaited, and depending behind, very much in the manner of the Chinese gentlemen, and might not inaptly be styled Bashaweses with *one* tail.

Others who are very gray, comb the hair in front from one side to the other perfectly smooth. Many of the young females twist the hair, and fasten it on the top of the head with nicely polished *brass combs,* and others, for the want of these or any other combs, dock the hair square behind, leaving it about six inches long, which gives them a very uncouth and forbidding appearance.

Some infants not six weeks old, are dressed with a black, and others with a dark-checked cotton cap, with trimmings of the same.

A small part of the community, both male and female, dress with some good degree of taste and neatness.

I will now attempt to give as accurate an account of the manners of the people as is in my power.

In general, the manners of the inhabitants are very rude and uncultivated. To this remark there are a few exceptions, though not numerous. But to be more particular; when any man or boy enters a house, he does it almost invariably with his hat on, and forgets to take it off his head during his stay, unless you ask him, and then generally excuses himself from so doing, by saying, *"it is no matter about it."* This is the mode in which ninety-nine in a hundred always enter an house. Whether they do not know enough to think it is proper to take off their hats when they enter a house, or suppose that the head is the most convenient place to hang their hats, it is not for me to determine.

When the person is seated, it is as likely as any way, even if he come on urgent business, that he will say nothing for the space of half an hour, unless to answer a question, laconically, by the monosyllables, yes or no, and many times you have to learn his business by asking it directly. During all this time of silence, there is a vacant kind of stare about every part of the room and the furniture, as if they would say when there is any article of furniture which they have not been accustomed to see, "what do you call that?"

When persons have got within the door, it is common for them to stand as near it as they can, till they are invited forward, staring wildly upon every article in the house, some, especially of the children, turning quite round to see if there is nothing behind them which they have not already discovered.

When leaving the room, after the business on which they came is dispatched, upon arriving at the door, they will, in many instances, turn round again, to take another survey, very frequently departing without any ceremony or inclination of the head. For this perhaps they are not to blame, as for aught I will assert, they may be troubled with a stiffness of the back.

When females enter a room, it is in much the same manner, frequently coming in without knocking, especially on the Sabbath after meeting, when half a dozen come in upon you without any previous notice, or being bid to enter, huddling in and standing behind each other, till you have time to dispose of them in some orderly manner. They have the same stare of astonishment as the male part of the community.

A stranger is to them as much an object of curiosity, to appearance, as would be any common animal.

These manners and customs, perhaps you will say, are innocent and harmless, as they do not affect the morals of the people. To this I agree; but there are others not so free from censure. One custom in particular I shall mention, which cannot be denied or excused, which is very indelicate, and has a very demoralizing tendency. It is this. Sleeping *promiscuously* in one room. In almost every house, parents and children, brothers and sisters, brothers and sisters-in-law, strangers and neighbours, married and unmarried, all ages, sexes and conditions, lodge in the same room, with out any thing to screen them from the view of each other. This I affirm, is not the case in a solitary instance; but it is a general practice, not in the poorest families only, but among the richest and most respectable, as the inhabitants themselves will tell you. And this is done in some cases which I could particularize, where there is not the slightest shadow of necessity; even in houses where there are apartments sufficient to accommodate each sex separately, adult brothers and sisters, and young men and women, no ways related, sleep in the same bed-chamber.

Of the indelicacy of this practice, every one who has been accustomed to a more polished mode of living, will, I think, agree in opinion.

Of the immoral tendency, I think also, every one is well satisfied. Those who are in the practice of this custom, where there is no existing necessity, I think could hardly say in sincerity, "Lead us not into temptation." Of its immoral effects I could mention some instances, if it were advisable. Of the existence of this practice, I do not write from report; but from my own knowledge, and I do not exaggerate in the description.

People here possess a great share of curiosity, especially in one particular, *i.e.* a great desire to be acquainted with the business of others; so much so, that any thing uttered in a manner supposed to be secret, will, some how or other, be known in a few days time to almost every individual, in a dozen towns, and you are wholly at a loss to determine in what manner, the information could have been communicated. Frequently when a person has mounted his horse, and has set out on some business of his own, he is, without ceremony, bluntly asked, "where are you going?" If he inform the inquirer, he will add, "what are you going there for?" If he satisfies him in this particular, he proceeds to inquire, "what are you about to do?" &c.&c. appearing to feel as much or more interest in his affairs than he does himself, or than he does in his own.

If one could be convinced that this solicitude, concerning his affairs, originated in a desire to promote his interest, or from any motives of friendship, it would be gratifying enough; but when it is known that curiosity is the cause of all this apparent solicitude, it is extremely disgusting and odious, and highly reprehensible. There is still another thing. I never knew, so far as my recollection serves me, a person in *haste*. All appear at ease, whether their business drives or not, and it is a notorious fact, that people (in many towns) are very deficient in industry. It is not an uncommon circumstance, but happens to many, I believe, every year, that a part at least, of their pumpkins, corn, and potatoes, remain in the fields, until snow falls, and thus are lost, for the want of a little more industry.

Instead of preparing wood for the summer, in winter, as is the custom in the Eastern States, men frequently meet in considerable numbers, and spend half the day in idle chit-chat, or invidious remarks concerning their neighbours, each of whom, if you were to believe the assertions of some one individual, is either a *debauchee, a drunkard, a cheat,* or a *swindler.*

The people here in general are very fond of *borrowing,* it is no matter what, is it any thing you have which they fancy they want, so that you must expect to lend all your crockery, should it chance to be wanted, and if it is broken, they will be *very* sorry, and in a short time, you will have neither any to lend or use yourself. They are, in turn, very good to lend also, and are not in the habit of refusing you any thing you need, if they can spare it as well as not.

It is evident to any impartial observer, that one generation after another, degenerate in a wonderful manner. You may in many cases observe, that the grandparents are people of good manners, and generally improved minds. These, it must be remembered, are immigrants from various parts of the old Atlantic States, and have brought all their improvements with them, which they still retain.

The children of these immigrants, who came into the country with their parents, partake, in some degree, of the manners of their progenitors, although gentility of behaviour is much adumbrated. The grand children, for want of the example and instruction which their parents enjoyed, are degenerated still more, so much so, that politeness, ease of manners, and every kind of grace, is almost entirely lost or obliterated.

Whiskey is the principal drink used in all this western country, and is drunk in great abundance, and is more generally used in liberal portions, than any or all kinds of spirituous liquors, in any other part of the country with which I am acquainted. The principal reason of this is, probably, the want of a market for their surplus quantity of grain, which induces the inhabitants to convert it into whiskey, which is very cheap in consequence of its great abundance.

If we are to judge of the characters of men, by the report of their neighbours, I do not know of more than two or three honest men among all those whom I am acquainted with, or concerning whom I have received any information; but almost all, according to fame, have been guilty of some heinous transaction, and it is remarked by some, that "when people get here, they appear to think that they have got away from all restraint of law and conscience."

Two days ago, I was conversing with a gentleman, who was lately justice of the peace in Ashtabula county, respecting the state of society and morals, who remarked to me, "that when he was on the grand jury about two years since, that it was proved before them, that there were in this county, *twenty-eight* men married to women here, who had left their wives living in the Eastern States, and afterwards he learnt that there were a number more, that they did not know of at that time," so that probably the number of men living in this state of adultery, may not be less than fifty. You will remark that the population of this county, according to the census of last year, is less than seven thousand two hundred.

Schools in this part of the country, are necessarily, very indifferent. Young men and women, in many cases, can read and write, but very badly.

I knew two young men, one of nineteen, the other twenty-one years old, conversing with each other respecting the points used in writing. One remarked to the other, that "that is a comma," "the semicolon is the pause between two syllables," &c. &c. which, by their manner of speaking, they appeared to have just learned, and expressed as much pleasure in knowing these things, as children of eight years old would have done. These were the sons of one of the most wealthy farmers in the town where they resided.

If you inquire of the people, if they have seen or read such and such books, which are most common in New-England, they will reply in most cases, that they have never heard of them, and the library of most families, consists of, (at most,) three or four volumes.

Schools in this part of the country are taught, (if kept up at all,) by females about three months for the Summer term, who teach merely the rudiments of reading, writing, and plain sewing. In many cases these schools are not taught more than eight weeks, and some not more than six, and compensation for teaching is made in almost all cases in such articles as the country affords, and not in money, so that teachers of much erudition, cannot be prevailed upon to undertake the business of teaching the rising generation.

In the winter term, men teach the same branches as are taught by the females in the summer, with the addition of a little Arithmetic, and the exclusion of sewing during about three months.

From this method of teaching, and the short time the schools are kept, and the long intervals that intervene between the terms, it will readily be conceived, that the children forget nearly as much as they learn, and it is very common to meet with young men and women, who cannot read, better than children in Connecticut, of six years of age, and even with less propriety than some with which I am acquainted.

Their knowledge of Geography, Grammar &c. is confined to a few, who may have the privilege of occasionally attending the few academies which are established here; or to those very few, who have property sufficient to send their children abroad. Yet those who have property sufficient to give their children a good education, and are disposed to do so, cannot at this time procure cash sufficient to pay the expense of such an education.

On the subject of Religion and religious education, much might be said; but I shall make but few remarks on this head.

In a few towns on the Reserve, Clergymen are settled for four or six months in the year, and the remainder of the time they ride as missionaries, through the townships which lie contiguous to them. In a *very* small number of towns, ministers are settled for the whole year.

These remarks apply to Presbyterians and Episcopalians. The other Preachers are illiterate Baptist Elders, and still more illiterate Itinerant Methodists. From this view of the subject, it will easily be seen, that the situation of the inhabitants of this country is most deplorable with regard to religious privileges.

It may farther be remarked that many families are without the Word of God, and are groping in almost Heathenish darkness, and are unable to procure the Word of Life to make them wise unto Salvation. This is not all; at least eleven months in twelve, the great body of the people have no better oral instruction, than what they receive from the most uninformed and fanatical methodist Preachers, who are the most extravagant Ranters, of which any one can form an idea, who bawl forth one of their incoherent rhapsodies in one township in the morning, in another township in the afternoon, and a third in a third place in the evening. Thus they run through the country, "leading captive at their will, silly women," and men equally unwise.

Their sermons are without plan or system, beginning with *ignorance,* and ending in *nonsense,* interlarded with something nearly approaching blasphemy in many cases.

Many of the inhabitants in this part of our country are very sensible of their want of religious privileges, and earnestly desire to enjoy the rationally preached gospel, and say, "come over and help us." Missionaries are, as appears to me, almost as much needed here as in the Islands of the Seas; and as these people are our own brethren according to the flesh, there appears to be a duty incumbent on those who possess the means, an *urgent necessity,* to send them well instructed teachers, who may lead them in the way of heaven.

29

An Artist among the Indians, 1832–39

Two great passions motivated the life of George Catlin: a desire to paint and a will to preserve for posterity the vanishing life of the American Indian. Catlin was born in Wilkes-Barre, Pennsylvania, in 1796. Though trained for the law, it was not long before he was devoting his time to the portrayal of noted political figures, a work in which he had considerable success. To this kind of portraiture he joined, when he was still a young man of about thirty-three, his absorption with Indian life. He traveled, especially during the sum-

mers, year after year, among even the most remote Indian tribes, learning their habits, their manners, and their customs. What he observed as a traveler among them he recorded, not without encountering difficulties from their primitive superstitions, in a noble series of paintings which comprised ultimately a collection of over six hundred pictures. He drew warriors and squaws, their costumes and their hunts, the scenery among which they dwelt, and their villages. Indeed, hardly an aspect of Indian life escaped him. The collection, which he exhibited widely in Europe and America, brought him, if not riches, a considerable renown.

Less skilful, perhaps, with his pen than with his brush, he likewise wrote extensively about his experiences among the Indian tribes. Of the half-dozen books he published, only one, a volume on European travel (1848), was not on this favourite subject of Indian life. The following extracts are from one of the best of his volumes, the Letters and Notes on the Manners, Customs, and Condition of the North American Indians *(1841), which is illustrated with some four hundred engravings from his paintings. His literary style was somewhat diffuse, but that he knew the subject whereof he wrote is evident on every page. It is, consequently, of significance to note that Catlin took a very different attitude toward the Indian than did most of his white contemporaries, viewing them with enthusiasm and believing that, except where they were in contact with American civilization, they possessed attributes of nobility. That there was "no good Indian but a dead Indian" was not Catlin's point of view. Among the Indians, he came into contact with traders and trappers as well; their life and the transcription of their dialect he caught with skill and imagination.*

IN PRAISE OF INDIANS

The reader, to understand me rightly, and draw from these Letters the information which they are intended to give, must follow me a vast way from the civilized world; he must needs wend his way from the city of New York, over the Alleghany, and far beyond the mighty Missouri, and even to the base and summit of the Rocky Mountains, some two or three thousand miles from the Atlantic Coast. He should forget many theories he has read in the books of Indian barbarities, of wanton butcheries and murders; and divest himself, as far as possible of the deadly prejudices which he has carried from his childhood, against this most unfortunate and most abused part of the race of his fellow-man.

He should consider, that if he has seen the savages of North America without making such a tour, he has fixed his eyes upon and drawn his conclusions (in all probability) only from those who inhabit the frontier; whose habits have been changed—whose pride has been cut down—whose country has been ransacked—whose wives and daughters have been shamefully abused—whose lands have been wrested from them—whose limbs have become enervated and naked by the excessive use of whiskey.

So great and unfortunate are the disparities between savage and civil, in numbers—in weapons and defences—in enterprise, in craft, and in education, that the former is almost universally the sufferer either in peace or in war; and not less so after his pipe and his tomahawk have retired to the grave with him, and his character is left to be entered upon the pages of history, and that justice done to his memory which from necessity, he has intrusted to his enemy.

Some writers, I have been grieved to see, have written down the character of the North American Indian, as dark, relentless, cruel and murderous in the last degree; with scarce a quality to stamp their existence of a higher order than that of the brutes:—whilst others have given them a high rank, as I feel myself authorized to do, as honourable and highly-intellectual beings; and others, both friends and foes to the red men, have spoken of them as an "anomaly in nature"!

From what I have seen of these people I feel authorized to say, that there is nothing very strange or unaccountable in their character; but that it is a simple one, and easy to be learned and understood, if the right means be taken to familiarize ourselves with it. Although it has its dark spots, yet there is much in it to be applauded, and much to recommend it to the admiration of the enlightened world. And I trust that the reader, who looks through these volumes with care, will be disposed to join me in the conclusion that the North American Indian in his native state, is an honest, hospitable, faithful, brave, war-like, cruel, revengeful, relentless,—yet honourable, contemplative and religious being.

There is no difficulty in approaching the Indian and getting acquainted with him in his wild and unsophisticated state, and finding him an honest and honourable man; with feelings to meet feelings, if prejudice and dread can be laid aside, and any one will take the pains, as I have done, to go and see him in the simplicity of his native state, smoking his pipe under his own humble roof, with his wife and children around him, and his faithful dogs and horses hanging about his hospitable tenement.—So the world *may* see him and smoke his friendly pipe, which will be invariably extended to them; and share, with a hearty welcome, the best that his wigwam affords for the appetite, which is always set out to a stranger the next moment after he enters.

MR. CATLIN PAINTS THE INDIAN CHIEFS

As evidence of the hospitality of these ignorant and benighted people, and also of their honesty and honour, there will be found recorded many striking instances in the following pages. And also, as an offset to these, many evidences of the dark and cruel, as well as ignorant and disgusting excesses of passions, unrestrained by the salutary influences of laws and Christianity.

I have roamed about from time to time during seven or eight years, visiting and associating with, some three or four hundred thousand of these people, under an almost infinite variety of circumstances; and from the very many and decided voluntary acts of their hospitality and kindness, I feel bound to pronounce them, by nature, a kind and hospitable people. I have been welcomed generally in their country, and treated to the best that they could give me, without any charges made for my board; they have often escorted me through their enemies' country at some hazard to their own lives, and aided me in passing mountains and rivers with my awkward baggage; and under all of these circumstances of exposure, no Indian ever betrayed me, struck me a blow, or stole from me a shilling's worth of my property that I am aware of.

This is saying a great deal, (and proving it too, if the reader will believe me) in favour of the virtues of these people; when it is borne in mind, as it should be, that there is no law in their land to punish a man for theft—that locks and keys are not known in their country—that the commandments have never been divulged amongst them; nor can any human retribution fall upon the head of a thief, save the disgrace which attaches as a stigma to his character, in the eyes of his people about him.

And thus in these little communities, strange as it may seem, in the absence of all systems of jurisprudence, I have often beheld peace and happiness, and quiet, reigning supreme, for which even kings and emperors might envy them. I have seen rights and virtue protected, and wrongs redressed; and I have seen conjugal, filial and paternal affection in the simplicity and contentedness of nature. I have unavoidably, formed warm and enduring attachments to some of these men which I do not wish to forget—who have brought me near to their hearts, and in our final separation have embraced me in their arms, and commended me and my affairs to the keeping of the Great Spirit.

LIFE AT THE FORT OF THE AMERICAN FUR COMPANY

I arrived at the mouth of the Yellowstone, Upper Missouri, yesterday in the steamer "Yellow Stone," after a voyage of nearly three months from St. Louis, a distance of two thousand miles, the greater part of which has never before been navigated by steam; and the almost insurmountable difficulties which continually oppose the *voyageur* on this turbid stream, have been by degrees overcome by the indefatigable zeal of Mr. Chouteau, a gentleman of great perseverance, and part proprietor of the boat. To the politeness of this gentleman I am indebted for my passage from St. Louis to this place.

The Missouri is, perhaps, different in appearance and character from all other rivers in the world: there is a terror in its manner which is sensibly felt, the moment we enter its muddy waters from the Mississippi. From the mouth of the Yellow Stone River, which is the place from whence I am now writing, to its junction with the Mississippi, a distance of 2000 miles, the Missouri, with its boiling, turbid waters, sweeps off, in one unceasing current; and in the whole distance there is scarcely an eddy or resting place for a canoe. Owing to the continual falling in of its rich alluvial banks, its water is always turbid and opaque; having, at all seasons of the year, the colour of a cup of chocolate or coffee, with sugar and cream stirred into it. To give a better definition of its density and opacity, I have tried a number of simple experiments with it at this place, and at other points below, at the results of which I was exceedingly surprised. By placing a piece of silver (and afterwards a piece of shell, which is a much whiter substance) in a tumbler of its water, and looking through the side of the glass, I ascertained that those substances could not be seen through the eighth part of an inch; this, however, is in the spring of the year, when the freshet is upon the river, rendering the water, undoubtedly, much more turbid than it would be at other seasons; though it is always muddy and yellow, and from its boiling and wild character and uncommon colour, a stranger would think, even in its lowest state, that there was a freshet upon it.

For the distance of 1000 miles above St. Louis, the shores of this river (and, in many places, the whole bed of the stream) are filled with snags and raft, formed of trees of the largest size, which have been undermined by the falling banks and cast into the stream; their roots becoming fastened in the bottom of the river, with their tops floating on the surfaces of the water, and pointing down the stream, forming the most frightful and discouraging prospect for the adventurous voyageur.

Almost every island and sand-bar is covered with huge piles of these floating trees, and when the river is flooded, its surface is almost literally covered with floating raft and drift wood which bid positive defiance to keel-boats and steamers, on their way up the river.

The scene is not, however, all so dreary; there is a redeeming beauty in the green and carpeted shores, which hem in this huge and terrible deformity of waters. There is much of the way though, where the mighty forests of stately cotton wood stand, and frown in horrid dark and coolness over the filthy abyss below; into which they are ready to plunge headlong, when the mud and soil in which they were germed and reared have been washed out from underneath them, and with the rolling current are mixed, and on their way to the ocean.

The greater part of the shores of this river, however, are without timber, where the eye is delightfully relieved by wandering over the beautiful prairies; most of the way gracefully sloping down to the water's edge, carpeted with the deepest green, and, in distance, softening into velvet of the richest hues, entirely beyond the reach of the artist's pencil. Such is the character of the upper part of the river especially; and as one advances towards its source, and through its upper half, it becomes more pleasing to the eye, for snags and raft are no longer to be seen; yet the current holds its stiff and onward turbid character.

The poor and ignorant people for the distance of 2000 miles, had never before seen or heard of a steam-boat, and in some places they seemed at a loss to know what to do, or how to act; they could not, as the Dutch did at Newburgh, on the Hudson River, take it to be a *"floating saw-mill"*—and they had no name for it—so it was, like every thing else (with them), which is mysterious and unaccountable, called *medicine* (mystery). We had on board one twelve-pound cannon and three or four eight pound swivels, which we were taking up to arm the Fur Company's Fort at the mouth of Yellow Stone; and at the approach to every village they were all discharged several times in rapid succession, which threw the inhabitants into utter confusion and amazement—some of them laid their faces to the ground, and cried to the Great Spirit—some shot their horses and dogs, and sacrificed them to appease the Great Spirit, whom they conceived was offended—some deserted their villages and ran to the tops of the bluffs some miles distant; and others, in some places, as the boat landed, in front of their villages, came with great caution, and peeped over the bank of the river to see the fate of their chiefs, whose duty it was (from the nature of their office) to approach us, whether friends or foes, and to go on board. Sometimes, in this plight, they were instantly thrown 'neck and heels' over each other's heads and shoulders—men, women and children, and dogs—sage, sachem, old and young—all in a mass, at the frightful discharge of the steam from the escape-pipe, which the captain of the boat let loose upon them for his own fun and amusement.

There were many curious conjectures amongst their wise men, with regard to the nature and powers of the steam-boat. Amongst the Mandans, some called it the "big thunder canoe"; for when in distance below the village, they "saw the lightning flash from its sides, and heard the thunder come from it"; others called it the "big medicine canoe with eyes"; it was *medicine* (mystery) because they could not understand it; and it must have eyes, for said they, "it sees its own way, and takes the deep water in the middle of the channel." They had no idea of the boat being steered by the man at the wheel, and well they might have been astonished at its taking the deepest water.

The American Fur Company have erected here, for their protection against the savages, a very substantial Fort, 300 feet square, with bastions armed with ordnance; and our approach to it under the continued roar of cannon for half an hour, and the shrill yells of the half affrighted savages who lined the shores, presented a scene of the most thrilling and picturesque appearance.

The Fort in which I am residing was built by Mr. M'Kenzie, who now occupies it. It is the largest and best-built establishment of the kind on the river, being the great or principal head-quarters and depot of the Fur Company's business in this region. A vast stock of goods is kept on hand at this place; and at certain times of the year the numerous out-posts concentrate here with the returns of their season's trade, and refit out with a fresh supply of goods to trade with the Indians.

The site for the Fort is well selected, being a beautiful prairie on the bank near the junction of the Missouri with the Yellow Stone rivers; and its inmates and its stores well protected from Indian assaults.

Mr. M'Kenzie is a kind-hearted and high-minded Scotchman; and seems to have charge of all the Fur Companies' business in this region, and from this to the Rocky Mountains. He lives in good and comfortable style, inside of the Fort, which contains some eight or ten log-houses and stores, and has generally forty or fifty men, and one hundred and fifty horses about him.

He has, with the same spirit of liberality and politeness with which Mons. Pierre Chouteau treated me on my passage up the river, pronounced me welcome at his table, which groans under the luxuries of the country; with buffalo meat and tongues, with beavers' tails and marrow-fat; but *sans* coffee, *sans* bread and butter. Good cheer and good living we get however, and good wine also; for a bottle of Madeira and one of excellent Port are set in a pail of ice every day, and exhausted at dinner.

At the hospitable board of this gentleman I found also an Englishman, by the name of Hamilton, of the most pleasing and entertaining conversation, whose mind seems to be a complete store-house of ancient and modern literature and art; and whose free and familiar acquaintance with the manners and men of his country gives him the stamp of a gentleman.

We three *bons vivants* form the group about the dinner-table, of which I have before spoken, and crack our jokes and fun over the bottles of Port and Madeira; and a considerable part of which, this gentleman has brought with great and precious care from his own country.

This post is the general rendezvous of a great number of Indian tribes in these regions, who are continually concentrating here for the purpose of trade; sometimes coming, the whole tribe together, in a mass. There are now here, and encamped about the Fort, a great many, and I am continually at work with my brush; we have around us at this time the Knisteneaux,

THE BUFFALO HUNT

Crows, Assinneboins and Blackfeet, and in a few days are to have large accessions.

At present, I will give a little sketch of a bit of fun I joined in yesterday, with Mr. M'Kenzie and a number of his men, without the company or aid of Indians.

I mentioned the other day, that M'Kenzie's table from day to day groans under the weight of buffalo tongues and beavers' tails, and other luxuries of this western land. He has within his Fort a spacious ice-house, in which he preserves his meat fresh for any length of time required; and sometimes, when his larder runs low, he starts out, rallying some five or six of his best hunters (not to hunt, but to "go for meat"). He leads the party, mounted on his favourite buffalo horse (*i.e.* the horse amongst his whole group which is best trained to run the buffalo), trailing a light and short gun in his hand, such an one as he can most easily reload whilst his horse is at full speed.

Such was the condition of the ice-house yesterday morning, which caused these self-catering gentlemen to cast their eyes with a wishful look over the prairies; and such was the plight in which our host took the lead, and I, and then Mons. Chardon, and Ba'tiste Defonde and Tullock (who is a trader amongst the Crows, and is here at this time, with a large party of that tribe), and there were several others whose names I do not know.

As we were mounted and ready to start, M'Kenzie called up some four or five of his men, and told them to follow immediately on our trail, with as many one-horse carts, which they were to harness up, to bring home the meat; "ferry them across the river in the scow," said he, "and following our trail through the bottom, you will find us on the plain yonder, between the Yellow Stone and the Missouri rivers, with meat enough to load you home. My watch on yonder bluff has just told us by his signals, that there are cattle a plenty on that spot, and we are going there as fast as possible." We all crossed the river, and galloped away a couple of miles or so, when we mounted the bluff; and to be sure, as was said, there was in full view of us a fine herd of some four or five hundred buffaloes, perfectly at rest, and in their own estimation (probably) perfectly secure. Some were grazing, and others were lying down and sleeping; we advanced within a mile or so of them in full view, and came to a halt. Mons. Chardon "tossed the feather" (a custom always observed, to try the course of the wind), and we commenced "stripping" as it is termed (*i.e.* every man strips himself and his horse of every extraneous and unnecessary appendage of dress, &c. that might be an incumbrance in running): hats are laid off, and coats—and bullet pouches; sleeves are rolled up, a handkerchief tied tightly around the head, and another around the waist—cartridges are prepared and placed in the waistcoat pocket, or a half dozen bullets "throwed into the mouth," &c., &c., all of which takes up some ten or fifteen minutes, and is not, in appearance or in effect, unlike a council of war. Our leader lays the whole plan of the chase, and preliminaries all fixed, guns charged and ramrods in our hands, we mount and start for the onset. The horses are all trained for this business, and seem to enter into it with as much enthusiasm, and with as restless a spirit as the riders themselves. While "stripping" and mounting, they exhibit the most restless impatience; and when "approaching"—(which is, all of us abreast, upon a slow walk, and in a straight line towards the herd, until they discover us and run), they all seem to have caught entirely the spirit of the chase, for the laziest hag amongst them prances with an elasticity in his step—champing his bit—his ears erect—his eyes strained out of his head, and fixed upon the game before him, whilst he trembles under the saddle of his rider. In this way we carefully and silently marched, until within some forty or fifty rods; when the herd discovering us, wheeled and laid their course in a mass. At this instant we started! (and all *must* start, for no one could check the fury of those steeds at that moment of excitement,) and away all sailed, and over the prairie flew, in a cloud of dust which was raised by their trampling hoofs. M'Kenzie was foremost in the throng, and soon dashed off amidst the dust and was out of sight—he was after the fattest and the fastest. I had discovered a huge bull whose shoulders towered above the whole band, and I picked my way through the crowd to get alongside of him. I went not for "meat," but for a *trophy;* I wanted his head and horns. I dashed along through the thundering mass, as they swept away over the plain, scarcely able to tell whether I was on a buffalo's back or my horse— hit, and hooked, and jostled about, till at length I found myself alongside of my game, when I gave him a shot, as I passed him. I saw guns flash in several directions about me, but I heard them not. Amidst the trampling throng, Mons. Chardon had wounded a stately bull, and at this moment was passing him again with his piece levelled for another shot; they were both at full speed and I also, within the reach of the muzzle of my gun, when the bull instantly turned and receiving the horse upon his horns, and the ground received poor Chardon, who made a frog's leap of some twenty feet or more over the bull's back, and almost under my horse's heels. I wheeled my horse as soon as possible and rode back, where lay poor Chardon, gasping to start his breath again; and within a few paces of him his huge victim, with his heels high in the air, and the horse lying across him. I dismounted instantly, but Chardon was raising himself on his hands, with his eyes and mouth full of dirt, and feeling for his gun, which lay about thirty feet in advance of him. "Heaven spare you! are you hurt, Chardon?" "hi—hic—hic—hic—hic —hic——no,—hic——no—no, I believe not. Oh! this is not much, Mons. Cataline—this is nothing new—but this is a d——d hard piece of ground here—hic—oh! hic!" At this the poor fellow fainted, but in a few moments arose, picked up his gun, took his horse by the bit; which then opened *its* eyes, and with a *hic* and a *ugh*—UGHK! sprang upon its feet—shook off the dirt—and here we were, all upon our legs again, save the bull, whose fate had been more sad than that of either.

I turned my eyes in the direction where the herd had gone, and our companions in pursuit, and nothing could be seen of them, nor indication, except the cloud of dust which they left behind them. At a little distance on the right, however, I beheld my huge victim endeavouring to make as much head-way as he possibly could, from this dangerous ground, upon three legs. I galloped off to him, and at my approach he wheeled around—and bristled up for battle; he seemed to know perfectly well that he could not escape from me, and resolved to meet his enemy and death as bravely as possible.

I found that my shot had entered him a little too far forward, breaking one of his shoulders, and lodging in his breast, and from his very great weight it was impossible for him to make much advance upon me. As I rode up within a few paces of him, he would bristle up with fury enough in his *looks* alone, almost to annihilate me; and making one lunge at me, would fall upon his neck and nose, so that I found the sagacity of my horse alone enough to keep me out of reach of danger.

No man on earth can imagine what is the look and expression of such a subject before him as this was. I defy the world to produce another animal that can look so frightful as a huge buffalo bull, when wounded as he was, turned around for battle, and swelling with rage;—his eyes bloodshot, and his long shaggy mane hanging to the ground,—his mouth open, and his horrid rage hissing in streams of smoke and blood from his mouth and through his nostrils, as he is bending forward to spring upon his assailant.

Meanwhile M'Kenzie and his companions came walking their exhausted horses back from the chase, and in our rear came four or five carts to carry home the meat. The party met from all quarters around me and my buffalo bull, whom I then shot in the head and finished. And being seated together for a few minutes, each one took a smoke of the pipe, and recited his exploits, and his "coups" or deaths; when all parties had a hearty laugh at me, as a novice, for having aimed at an old bull, whose flesh was not suitable for food, and the carts were escorted on the trail, to bring away the meat. I rode back with Mr. M'Kenzie, who pointed out five cows which he had killed, and all of them selected as the fattest and slickest of the herd. This astonishing feat was all performed within the distance of one mile—all were killed at full speed, and every one shot through the heart. In the short space of time required for a horse under "full whip," to run the distance of one mile, he had discharged his gun five, and loaded it four times—selected his animals, and killed at every shot! There were six or eight others killed at the same time, which altogether furnished, as will be seen, abundance of freight for the carts; which returned, as well as several packhorses, loaded with the choicest parts which were cut from the animals, and the remainder of the carcasses left a prey for the wolves.

Such is the mode by which white men live in this country—such the way in which they get their food, and such is one of their delightful amusements —at the hazard of every bone in one's body, to feel the fine and thrilling exhilaration of the chase for a moment, and then as often to upbraid and blame himself for his folly and imprudence.

From this scene we commenced leisurely wending our way back; and dismounting at the place where we had stripped, each man dressed himself again, or slung his extra articles of dress, &c. across his saddle, astride of which he sat; and we rode back to the Fort, reciting as we rode, and for twenty-four hours afterwards, deeds of chivalry and chase, and hair's-breadth escapes which each and either had fought and run on former occasions. M'Kenzie, with all the true character and dignity of a leader, was silent on these subjects; but smiled, while those in his train were reciting for him the astonishing and almost incredible deeds of his sinewy arms, which they had witnessed in similar scenes; from which I learned (as well as from my own observations), that he was reputed (and actually *was*) the most distinguished of all the white men who have flourished in these regions, in the pursuit and death of the buffalo.

On our return to the Fort, a bottle or two of wine were set forth upon the table, and around them a half dozen parched throats were soon moistened, and good cheer ensued. Ba'tiste Défonde, Chardon, &c., retired to their quarters, enlarging smoothly upon the events of our morning's work; which they were reciting to their wives and sweethearts; when about this time the gate of the Fort was thrown open, and the procession of carts and pack-horses laden with buffalo meat made its entrée; gladdening the hearts of a hundred women and children, and tickling the noses of as many hungry dogs and puppies, who were stealing it and smelling at the tail of the procession. The door of the ice-house was thrown open, the meat was discharged into it, and I being fatigued, went to sleep.

WHAT IS "THE WEST"?

Notwithstanding all that has been written and said, there is scarcely any subject on which the *knowing* people of the East, are yet less informed and instructed than on the character and amusements of the West: by this I mean the "Far West." Few people even know the true definition of the term "West"; and where is its location?—phantom-like it flies before us as we travel.

In the commencement of my Tour, several of my travelling companions from the city of New York, found themselves at a frightful distance to the West, when we arrived at Niagara Falls; and hastened back to amuse their friends with tales and scenes of the West. At Buffalo a steamboat was landing with 400 passengers, and twelve days out—"Where from?" "From the West." In the rich state of Ohio, hundreds were selling their farms and going—to the West. In the beautiful city of Cincinnati, people said to me, "Our town has passed the days of its most rapid growth, it is not far enough West."—In St. Louis, 1400 miles west of New York, my landlady assured me that I would be pleased with her boarders, for they were nearly all merchants from the "West." I there asked, "Whence come those steam-boats, laden with port, honey, hides, &c.?"

From the West.

Whence those ponderous bars of silver, which those men have been for hours shouldering and putting on board that boat?

They come from Santa Fee, from the West.

Where goes this steam-boat so richly laden with dry goods, steam-engines, &c.?

She goes to Jefferson city.

Jefferson city?—Where is that?

Far to the West.

And where goes that boat laden down to her gunnels, the Yellow Stone?

She goes still farther to the West—"Then," said I, "I'll go to the West."

I went on to the Yellow Stone——*** Two thousand miles on her, and we were at the mouth of Yellow Stone river—at the West. What! invoices, bills of lading, &c., a wholesale establishment so far to the West! And those strange looking, long-haired gentlemen, who have just arrived, and are re-lating the adventures of their long and tedious journey. Who are they?

Oh! they are some of our merchants just arrived from the West.

And that keel-boat, that Mackinaw-boat, and that formidable caravan, all of which are richly leaden with goods.

These, Sir, are outfits starting for the *West*.

Going to the *West,* ha? "Then," said I, "I'll try it again. I will try and see if I can go to the West."

***What, a Fort here, too?

Oui, Monsieur—oui, Monsieur (as a dauntless, and *semibarbarian*—look-ing, jolly fellow, dashed forth in advance of his party on his wild horse to meet me.)

What distance are you west of Yellow Stone here, my goodfellow?

Comment?

What distance?—(stop)—quel distance?

Pardon, Monsieur, je ne sais pas, Monsieur.

Ne parlez vous l'Anglais?

Non, Monsr. I speaks de French and de Americaine; mais je ne parle pas l'Anglais.

"Well then, my good fellow, I will speak English, and you may speak Americaine."

Pardón, pardón, Monsieur.

Well, then we will both speak Americaine.

Val, sare, je suis bien content, pour for I see dat you speaks putty coot Americaine.

What may I call your name?

Ba'tiste, Monsieur.

What Indians are those so splendidly dressed, and with such fine horses, encamped on the plain yonder?

Ils sont Corbeaux.

Crows, ha?

Yes, sare, Monsieur.

We are then in the Crow country?

Non, Monsieur, not putty éxact; we are in de coontrae of de dam Pieds noirs.

Blackfeet, ha?

Oui.

What blue mountain is that which we see in the distance yonder?

Ha, quel Montaigne? cela est la Montaigne du (pardón).

Du Rochers, I suppose?

Oui, Monsieur, de Rock Montaigne.

You live here, I suppose?

Non, Monsieur, I comes fair from de West.

What, from the West! Where under the heavens is that?

Wat, diable! de West? well you shall see, Monsieur, he is putty fair off, súppose. Monsieur Pierre Chouteau can give you de histoire de ma vie—il bien sait que je prends les castors, very fair in de West.

You carry goods, I suppose, to trade with the Snake Indians beyond the mountains, and trap beaver also?

Oui, Monsieur.

Do you see anything of the "Flat-heads" in your country?

Non, Monsieur, ils demeurent very, *very* fair to de West.

Well, Ba'tiste, I'll lay my course back again for the present, and at some future period, endeavour to go to the "West."

AN INDIAN INITIATION

The *annual religious ceremony,* of four days, of which I have so often spoken, and which I have so long been wishing to see, has at last been enacted in this village; and I have, fortunately, been able to see and to understand it in most of its bearings, which was more than I had reason to expect; for no white man, in all probability, has ever before been admitted to the *medicine-lodge*[1] during these most remarkable and appalling scenes.

I shudder at the relation, or even at the thought of these barbarous and cruel scenes, and am almost ready to shrink from the task of reciting them after I have so long promised some account of them. I entered the *medicine-house* of these scenes, as I would have entered a church; but alas! little did I expect to see the interior of their holy temple turned into a *slaughter-house,* and its floor strewed with the blood of its fanatic devotees.

The *"Mandan religious ceremony"* then, as I believe it is very justly denominated, is an annual transaction, held in their *medicine-lodge* once a year, as a great religious anniversary, and for several distinct objects; during and after which, they look with implicit reliance for the justification and approval of the Great Spirit.

The chiefs having seated themselves on one side of the lodge, dressed out in their robes and splendid head-dresses—the band of music seated and arranged themselves in another part; and the old master of ceremonies having placed himself in front of a small fire in the centre of the lodge with his "big pipe" in his hands, and having commenced smoking to the Great Spirit, with all possible vehemence for the success of these aspirants, presented the subject which they call "pohk-hong," the cutting scene. Two men take their positions near the middle of the lodge, for the purpose of inflicting the tortures—the one with a scalping-knife, and the other with a bunch of splints in his hand; one at a time of the young fellows, already emaciated with fasting, and thirsting, and waking, for nearly four days and nights, advanced from the side of the lodge, and placed himself on his hands and feet, or otherwise, as best suited for the performance of the operation, where he submitted to the cruelties in the following manner:—An inch or more of the flesh on each shoulder, or each breast was taken up between the thumb

1. I must needs explain the word "medicine," and "medicine-bag"; and also some *medicine operations.* "Medicine" is a great word in this country. In its common acceptance here it means *mystery* and nothing else.

The Fur Traders in the country, are nearly all French; and in their language, a doctor or physician, is called "Medicin." The Indian country is full of doctors; and as they are all magicians, and skilled, or profess to be skilled, in many mysteries, the word "medicin" has become habitually applied to every thing mysterious or unaccountable; and the English and Americans have easily and familiarly adopted the same word, with a slight alteration, conveying the same meaning; and to be a little more explicit, they have denominated these personages *"medicine-men,"* which means something more than merely a doctor or physician. These physicians, however, are all *medicine-men,* as they are all supposed to deal more or less in mysteries and charms, which are aids and handmaids in their practice. Yet it was necessary to give the word or phrase a still more comprehensive meaning—as there were many personages amongst them, and also among the white men who visit the country, who could deal in mysteries, though not skilled in the application of drugs and medicines; and they all range now, under the comprehensive and accommodating phrase of "medicine-men."

The Indians do not use the word medicine, however; but in each tribe they have a word of their own construction, synonymous with mystery or mystery-man.

and finger by the man who held the knife in his right hand; and the knife, which had been ground sharp on both edges, and then hacked and notched with the blade of another, to make it produce as much pain as possible, was forced through the flesh below the fingers, and being withdrawn, was followed with a splint or skewer, from the other, who held a bunch of such in his left hand, and was ready to force them through the wound. There were then two cords lowered down from the top of the lodge (by men who were placed on the lodge outside, for the purpose), which were fastened to these splints or skewers, and they instantly began to haul him up; he was thus raised until his body was suspended from the ground where he rested, until the knife and a splint were passed through the flesh in a similar manner on each arm below the shoulder, below the elbow, and below the knees.

In some instances they remained in a reclining position on the ground until this painful operation was finished, which was performed, in all instances, exactly on the same parts of the body and limbs; and which, in its progress, occupied some five or six minutes.

Each one was then instantly raised with the cords, until the weight of his body was suspended by them, and then, while the blood was streaming down their limbs, the bystanders hung upon the splints each man's appropriate shield, bow and quiver, &c.; and in many instances, the skull of a buffalo with the horns on it, was attached to each lower arm and each lower leg, for the purpose, probably, of preventing by their great weight, the struggling, which might otherwise have taken place to their disadvantage whilst they were hung up.

When these things were all adjusted, each one was raised higher by the cords, until these weights all swung clear from the ground, leaving his feet, in most cases, some six or eight feet above the ground. In this plight they at once became appalling and frightful to look at—the flesh, to support the weight of their bodies, with the additional weights which were attached to them, was raised six or eight inches by the skewers; and their heads sunk forward on the breasts, or thrown backwards, in a much more frightful condition, according to the way in which they were hung up.

The unflinching fortitude, with which every one of them bore this part of the torture surpassed credulity; each one as the knife was passed through his flesh sustained an unchangeable countenance.

When raised to the condition above described, and completely suspended by the cords, the sanguinary hands, through which he had just passed, turned back to perform a similar operation on another who was ready, and each one in his turn passed into the charge of others, who instantly introduced him to a new and improved stage of their refinements in cruelty.

Surrounded by imps and demons as they appear, a dozen or more, who seem to be concerting and devising means for his exquisite agony, gather around him, when one of the number advances towards him in a sneering manner, and commences turning him around with a pole which he brings in his hand for the purpose. This is done in a gentle manner at first; but gradually increased, when the brave fellow, whose proud spirit can control its agony no longer, burst out in the most lamentable and heart-rending cries that the human voice is capable of producing, crying forth a prayer to the Great Spirit to support and protect him in this dreadful trial; and continually repeating his confidence in his protection. In this condition he is continued to be turned, faster and faster—and there is no hope of escape from it, nor chance for the slightest relief, until by fainting, his voice falters, and his struggling ceases, and he hangs, apparently, a still and lifeless corpse! When he is, by turning, gradually brought to this condition, which is generally done within ten of fifteen minutes, there is a close scrutiny passed upon him among his tormentors, who are checking and holding each other back as long as the least struggling or tremour can be discovered, lest he should be removed before he is (as they term it) "entirely dead."

When brought to this alarming and most frightful condition, and the turning has gradually ceased, as his voice and his strength have given out, leaving him to hang entirely still, and apparently lifeless; when his tongue is distended from his mouth, and his *medicine-bag,* which he has affectionately and superstitiously clung to with his left hand, has dropped to the ground; the signal is given to the man on top of the lodge, by gently striking the cord with the pole below, when they very gradually and carefully lower him to the ground.

In this helpless condition he lies, like a loathesome corpse to look at, though in the keeping (as they call it) of the Great Spirit, whom he trusts will protect him, and enable him to get up and walk away. As soon as he is lowered to the ground thus, one of the bystanders advances, and pulls out the two splints or pins from the breasts and shoulders, thereby disengaging him from the cords by which he has been hung up; but leaving all the others with their weights, &c. hanging to his flesh.

In this condition he lies for six or eight minutes, until he gets strength to rise and move himself, for no one is allowed to assist or offer him aid, as he is here enjoying the most valued privilege which a Mandan can boast of, that of "trusting his life to the keeping of the Great Spirit," in this time of extreme peril.

As soon as he is seen to get strength enough to rise on his hands and feet, and drag his body around the lodge, he crawls with the weights still hanging

INDIANS AT HOME

to his body, to another part of the lodge, where there is another Indian sitting with a hatchet in his hand, and a dried buffalo skull before him; and here, in the most earnest and humble manner, by holding up the little finger of his left hand to the Great Spirit, he expresses to Him, in a speech of a few words, his willingness to give it as a sacrifice; when he lays it on the dried buffalo skull, where the other chops it off near the hand, with a blow of the hatchet!

Nearly all of the young men whom I saw passing this horrid ordeal, gave in the above manner, the little finger of the left hand; and I saw also several, who immediately afterwards (and apparently with very little concern or emotion), with a similar speech, extended in the same way, the *fore*-finger of the same hand, and that too was struck off; leaving on the left hand only the two middle fingers and the thumb; all which they deem absolutely essential for holding the bow, the only weapon for the left hand.

One would think that this mutilation had thus been carried quite far enough; but I have since examined several of the head chiefs and dignitaries of the tribe, who have also given, in this manner, the little finger of the right hand, which is considered by them to be a much greater sacrifice than both of the others; and I have found also a number of their most famous men, who furnish me incontestible proof, by five or six corresponding scars on each arm, and each breast, and each leg, that they had so many times in their lives submitted to this almost incredible operation, which seems to be optional with them; and the oftener they volunteer to go through it, the more famous they become in the estimation of their tribe.

No bandages are applied to the fingers which have been amputated, nor any arteries taken up; nor is any attention whatever, paid to them or the other wounds; but they are left (as they say) "for the Great Spirit to cure, who will surely take good care of them." It is a remarkable fact (which I learned from a close inspection of their wounds from day to day) that the bleeding is but very slight and soon ceases, probably from the fact of their extreme exhaustion and debility, caused by want of sustenance and sleep, which checks the natural circulation, and admirably at the same time prepares them to meet the severity of these tortures without the same degree of sensibility and pain, which, under other circumstances, might result in inflammation and death.

During the whole of the time of this cruel part of these most extraordinary inflictions, the chiefs and dignitaries of the tribe are looking on, to decide who are the hardiest and "stoutest hearted"—who can hang the longest by his flesh before he faints, and who will be soonest up, after he has been down; that they may know whom to appoint to lead a war-party, or place at the

most honourable and desperate post. The four old men are incessantly beating upon the sacks of water and singing the whole time, with their voices
strained to the highest key, vaunting forth, for the encouragement of the
young men, the power and efficacy of the *medicine-pipe,* which will be sure
to protect them and watch over them through their present severe trial.

As soon as six or eight had passed the ordeal as above described, they
were led out of the lodge, with their weights hanging to their flesh, and
dragging on the ground, to undergo another, and still more appalling mode
of suffering in the centre of the village, and in the presence of the whole
nation.

The young men who were further to suffer were led forward and being
placed at equal distances apart, in a ring, each one was taken in charge of
two athletic young men, fresh and strong, who stepped up to him, one on
each side, and by wrapping a broad leather strap around his wrists, without
tying it, grasped it firm underneath the hand, and stood prepared for what
they call *Eh-ke-nah-ka-nah-pick* (the last race). This, the spectator looking
on would suppose was most correctly named, for he would think it was the
last race they could possibly run in this world.

In this condition they stand, pale and ghastly, from abstinence and loss of
blood, until all are prepared, and the word is given, when all start and run
around; and each poor fellow, with his weights dragging on the ground, and
his furious conductors by his side, who hurry him forward by the wrists,
struggles in the desperate emulation to run longer without "dying" (as they
call it) than his comrades, who are fainting around him and sinking down,
like himself, where their bodies are dragged with all possible speed, and
often with their faces in the dirt. In the commencement of this dance or race
they all start at a moderate pace, and their speed being gradually increased,
the pain becomes so excruciating that their languid and exhausted frames
give out, and they are dragged by their wrists until they are disengaged from
the weights that were attached to their flesh, and this must be done by such
violent force as to tear the flesh out with the splint, which (as they say) can
never be pulled out endwise, without greatly offending the Great Spirit and
defeating the object for which they have thus far suffered. The splints or
skewers which are put through the breast and the shoulders, take up a part
of the pectoral muscle, which is necessary for the support of the great weight
of their bodies, and which, as I have before mentioned, are withdrawn as
soon as he is lowered down—but all the others, on the legs and arms, seem
to be very ingeniously passed through the flesh and integuments without
taking up the muscle, and even these, to be broken out, require so strong a
force that most of the poor fellows fainted under the operation, and when

they were freed from the last of the buffalo skulls and other weights, (which was often done by some of the bystanders throwing the weight of their bodies on to them as they were dragging by on the ground) they were in every instance dropped by the persons who dragged them, and their bodies were left, appearing like nothing but a mangled and a loathesome corpse! At this strange and frightful juncture, the two men who had dragged them, fled through the crowd and away upon the prairie, as if they were guilty of some enormous crime, and were fleeing from summary vengeance.

Each poor fellow, having thus patiently and manfully endured the privations and tortures devised for him and torn himself loose from them and his tormentors, he lies the second time, in the "keeping (as he terms it) of the Great Spirit," to whom he issues his repeated prayers, and entrusts his life: and in whom he reposes the most implicit confidence for his preservation and recovery.

In this frightful scene the whole nation was assembled as spectators, and all raised the most piercing and violent yells and screams they could possibly produce, to drown the cries of the suffering ones, that no heart could even be touched with sympathy for them. I have mentioned before, that six or eight of the young men were brought from the medicine-lodge at a time, and when they were thus passed through this shocking ordeal, the medicine men and the chiefs returned to the interior, where as many more were soon prepared, and underwent a similar treatment; and after that another batch, and another, and so on, until the whole number, some forty-five or fifty had run in this sickening circle, and, by leaving their weights, had opened the flesh for honourable scars.

WILD HORSES

The tract of country over which we passed, between the False Washita and the Red River of the South, is stocked, not only with buffaloes, but with numerous bands of wild horses, many of which we saw every day. There is no other animal on the prairies so wild and so sagazious as the horse; and none other so difficult to come up with. So remarkably keen is their eye, that they will generally run "at the sight," when they are a mile distant; being, no doubt, able to distinguish the character of the enemy that is approaching when at that distance; and when in motion, will seldom stop short of three or four miles. I made many attempts to approach without ever having been more than once able to succeed.

The usual mode of taking the wild horses, is, by throwing the *laso,* whilst pursuing them at full speed, and dropping a noose over their necks, by which their speed is soon checked, and they are "choked down." The laso is a thong of rawhide, some ten or fifteen yards in length, twisted or braided, with a noose fixed at the end of it; which, when the coil of the laso is thrown out, drops with great certainty over the neck of the animal, which is soon conquered.

The Indian, when he starts for a wild horse, mounts one of the fleetest he can get, and coiling his laso on his arm, starts off under the "full whip," till he can enter the band, when he soon gets it over the neck of one of the number; when he instantly dismounts, leaving his own horse, and runs as fast as he can, letting the laso pass out gradually and carefully through his hands, until the horse falls from want of breath, and lies helpless on the ground; at which time the Indian advances slowly towards the horse's head, keeping his laso tight upon its neck, until he fastens a pair of hobbles on the animal's two forefeet, and also loosens the laso (giving the horse chance to breathe), and gives it a noose around the under jaw, by which he gets great power over the affrighted animal, which is rearing and plunging when it gets breath; and by which, as he advances, hand over hand, towards the horse's nose, he is able to hold it down and prevent it from throwing itself over on its back, at the hazard of its limbs. By this means he gradually advances, until he is able to place his hand on the animal's nose, and over its eyes; and at length to breathe in its nostrils, when it soon becomes docile and conquered; so that he has little else to do than to remove the hobbles from its feet, and lead or ride it into camp.

This "breaking down" or taming, however, is not without the most desperate trial on the part of the horse, which rears and plunges in every possible way to effect its escape, until its power is exhausted, and it becomes covered with foam; and at last yields to the power of man, and becomes his willing slave for the rest of its life. By this very rigid treatment, the poor animal seems to be so completely conquered, that it makes no further struggle for freedom; but submits quietly ever after, and is led or rode away with very little difficulty. Great care is taken, however, in this and in subsequent treatment, not to subdue the spirit of the animal, which is carefully preserved and kept up, although they use them with great severity; being, generally speaking, cruel masters.

The wild horse of these regions is a small, but very powerful animal; with an exceedingly prominent eye, sharp nose, high nostril, small feet and delicate leg; and undoubtedly, have sprung from a stock introduced by the Spaniards, at the time of the invasion of Mexico; which having strayed off upon the prairies, have run wild, and stocked the plains from this to Lake Winnepeg, two or three thousand miles to the North.

This useful animal has been of great service to the Indians living on these vast plains, enabling them to take their game more easily, to carry their burthens, &c.; and no doubt, render them better and handier service than if they were of a larger and heavier breed. Vast numbers of them are also killed for food by the Indians, at seasons when buffaloes and other game are scarce. They subsist themselves both in winter and summer by biting at the grass, which they can always get in sufficient quantities for their food.

Racing horses, it would seem, is a constant and almost incessant exercise, and their principle mode of gambling; and perhaps, a more finished set of jockeys are not to be found. The exercise of these people, in a country where horses are so abundant, and the country so fine for riding, is chiefly done on horseback; and it "stands to reason," that such a people, who have been practicing from their childhood, should become exceedingly expert in this wholesome and beautiful exercise. Amongst their feats of riding, there is one that has astonished me more than anything of the kind I have ever seen, or expect to see, in my life:—a stratagem of war, learned and practiced by every young man in the tribe; by which he is able to drop his body upon the side of his horse at the instant he is passing, effectually screened from his enemies' weapons as he lays in a horizontal position behind the body of his horse, with his heel hanging over the horse's back; by which he has the power of throwing himself up again, and changing to the other side of the horse if necessary. In this wonderful condition he will hang whilst his horse is at fullest speed, carrying with him his bow and his shield, and also his long lance of fourteen feet in length, all or either of which he will wield upon his enemy as he passes; rising and throwing his arrows over the horse's back, or with equal ease and equal success under the horse's neck.[2] This astonishing feat which the young men have been repeatedly playing off to our surprise as well as amusement, whilst they have been galloping about in front of our tents, completely puzzled the whole of us; and appeared to be the result of magic, rather than of skill acquired by practice. I had several times great curiosity to approach them, to ascertain by what means their bodies could be suspended in this manner, where nothing could be seen but the heel hanging over the horse's back. In these endeavours I was continually frustrated, until one day I coaxed a young fellow up within a little distance of me, by offering him a few plugs of tobacco, and he in a moment solved the difficulty, so far as to render it apparently more feasible than before; yet

2. Since writing the above, I have conversed with some of the young men of the Pawnees, who practice the same feat, and who told me they could throw the arrow from under the horse's belly, and elevate it upon an enemy with deadly effect!

This feat I did not see performed, but from what I did see, I feel inclined to believe that these young men were boasting of no more than they were able to perform.

leaving it one of the most extraordinary results of practice and persevering endeavours. I found on examination, that a short hair halter was passed around under the neck of the horse, and both ends tightly braided into a mane, on the withers, leaving a loop to hang under the neck, and against the breast, which, being caught up in the hand, makes a sling into which the elbow falls, taking the weight of the body on the middle of the upper arm. Into this loop the rider drops suddenly and fearlessly, leaving his heel to hang over the back of the horse, to steady him, and also to restore him when he wishes to regain his upright position on the horse's back.

AN INDIAN BALL GAME

Monday afternoon at three o'clock, I rode out with Lieutenants S. and M., to a very pretty prairie, about six miles distant, to the ball-play-ground of the Choctaws, where we found several thousand Indians encamped. There were two points of timber about a half mile apart, in which the two parties for the play, with their respective families and friends, were encamped; and lying between them, the prairie on which the game was to be played. My companions and myself, although we had been apprised, that to see the whole of a ball-play, we must remain on the ground all the night previous, had brought nothing to sleep upon, resolving to keep our eyes open, and see what transpired through the night.

During the afternoon, we loitered about amongst the different tents and shantees of the two encampments, and afterwards, at sundown, witnessed the ceremony of measuring out the ground, and erecting the "byes" or goals which were to guide the play. Each party had their goal made with two upright posts, about 25 feet high and six feet apart, set firm in the ground, with a pole across at the top. These goals were about forty or fifty rods apart; and at a point just half way between, was another small stake, driven down, where the ball was to be thrown up at the firing of a gun, to be struggled for by the players. All this preparation was made by some old men, who were, it seems selected to be the judges of the play, who drew a line from one bye to the other; to which directly came from the woods, on both sides, a great concourse of women and old men, boys and girls, and dogs and horses, where bets were to be made on the play. The betting was all done across this line, and seemed to be chiefly left to the women, who seemed to have martialled out a little of everything that their houses and their fields possessed. Goods and chattels—knives—dresses—blankets—pots and kettles—dogs and horses, and guns; and all were placed in the possession of stake-holders, who sat by them, and watched them on the ground all night, preparatory to the play.

The sticks with which this tribe play, are bent into an oblong hoop at the end, with a sort of slight web of small thongs tied across, to prevent the ball from passing through. The players hold one of these in each hand, and by leaping into the air, they catch the ball between the two nettings and throw it, without being allowed to strike it, or catch it in their hands.

In every ball-play of these people, it is a rule of the play, that no man shall wear moccasins on his feet, or any other dress than his breech-cloth around his waist, with a beautiful bead belt, and a "tail," made of white horsehair or quills, and a *"mane"* on the neck, of horsehair dyed of various colours.

The game had been arranged and "made up," three or four months before the parties met to play it, and in the following manner:—The two champions who led the two parties, and had the alternate choosing of the players through the whole tribe, sent runners, with the ball-sticks most fantastically ornamented with ribbons and red paint, to be touched by each one of the chosen players; who thereby agreed to be on the spot at the appointed time and ready for the play. The ground having been all prepared and preliminaries of the game all settled, and the bettings all made, and goods all "staked," night came on without the appearance of any players on the ground. But soon after dark, a procession of lighted flambeaux was seen coming from each encampment to the ground where the players assembled around their respective byes; and at the beat of the drums and chaunts of the women, each party of players commenced the "ball-play dance." Each party danced for a quarter of an hour around their respective byes, in their ball-play dress; rattling their ball-sticks together in the most violent manner, and all singing as loud as they could raise their voices; whilst the women of each party, who had their goods at stake, formed into two rows on the line between the two parties of players, and danced also, in an uniform step, and all their voices joined in chaunts to the Great Spirit; in which they were soliciting his favour in deciding the game to their advantage; and also encouraging the players to exert every power they possessed, in the struggle that was to ensue. In the mean time, four old *medicine-men,* who were to have the starting of the ball, and who were to be judges of the play, were seated at the point where the ball was to be started; and busily smoking to the Great Spirit for their success in judging rightly, and impartially, between the parties in so important an affair.

This dance was one of the most picturesque scenes imaginable, and was repeated at intervals of every half hour during the night, and exactly in the same manner; so that the players were certainly awake all the night, and arranged in their appropriate dress, prepared for the play which was to commence at nine o'clock the next morning. In the morning, at the hour,

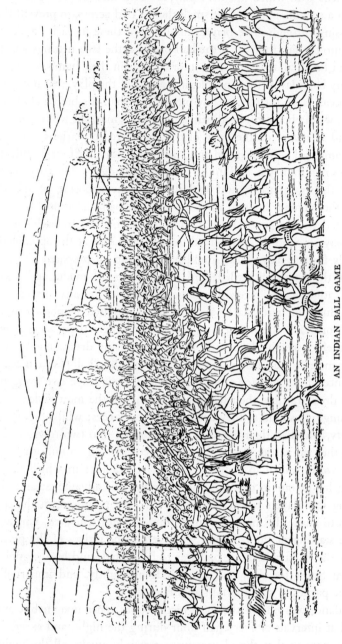

AN INDIAN BALL GAME

the two parties and all their friends, were drawn out and over the ground; when at length the game commenced, by the judges throwing up the ball at the firing of a gun; when an instant struggle ensued between the players, who were some six or seven hundred in numbers, and were mutually endeavouring to catch the ball in their sticks, and throw it home and between their respective stakes; which, whenever successfully done, counts one for game. In this game every player was dressed alike, that is, *divested* of all dress, except the girdle and the tail, which I have before described; and in these desperate struggles for the ball, when it is *up,* (where hundreds are running together and leaping, actually over each other's heads, and darting between their adversaries legs, tripping and throwing, and foiling each other in every possible manner, and every voice raised to the highest key, in shrill yelps and barks)! there are rapid succession of feats, and of incidents, that astonish and amuse far beyond the conception of any one who has not had the singular good luck to witness them. In these struggles, every mode is used that can be devised, to oppose the progress of the foremost, who is likely to get the ball; and these obstructions often meet desperate individual resistance, which terminates in a violent scuffle, and sometimes in fisticuffs; when their sticks are dropped, and the parties are unmolested, whilst they are settling it between themselves; unless it be by a general *stampedo,* to which they are subject who are down, if the ball happens to pass in their direction. Every weapon, by a rule of all ball-plays, is laid by in their respective encampments, and no man allowed to go for one; so that the sudden broils that take place on the ground, are presumed to be as suddenly settled without any probability of much personal injury; and no one is allowed to interfere in any way with the contentious individuals.

There are times, when the ball gets to the ground, and such a confused mass rushing together around it, and knocking their sticks together, without the possibility of any one getting or seeing it, for the dust that they raise, that the spectator loses his strength, and everything else but his senses; when the condensed mass of ball-sticks, and shins, and bloody noses, is carried around the different parts of the ground, for a quarter of an hour at a time, without any one of the mass being able to see the ball; and which they are often thus scuffling for, several minutes after it has been thrown off, and played over another part of the ground.

For each time that the ball was passed between the stakes of either party, one was counted for their game, and a halt of about one minute; when it was again started by the judges of the play, and a similar struggle ensued; and so on until the successful party arrived to 100, which was the limit of the game, and accomplished at an hour's sun, when they took the stakes;

and then, by a previous agreement, produced a number of jugs of whiskey, which gave all a wholesome drink, and sent them all off merry and in good humour, but not drunk.

EXPOSURE OF THE AGED

When we were about to start on our way up the river from the village of the Puncahs, we found that they were packing up all their goods and preparing to start for the prairies, farther to the West, in pursuit of buffaloes, to dry meat for their winter's supplies. They took down their wigwams of skins to carry with them, and all were flat to the ground and everything packed up ready for the start. My attention was directed by Major Sanford, the Indian Agent, to one of the most miserable and helpless looking objects that I ever had seen in my life, a very aged and emaciated man of the tribe, who he told me was to be *exposed*.

The tribe were going where hunger and dire necessity compelled them to go, and this pitiable object, who had once been a chief, and a man of distinction in his tribe, who was now too old to travel, being reduced to mere skin and bones, was to be left to starve, or meet with such death as might fall to his lot, and his bones to be picked by the wolves! I lingered around this poor old forsaken patriarch for hours before we started, to indulge the tears of sympathy which were flowing for the sake of this poor benighted and decrepit old man, whose worn-out limbs were no longer able to support him; their kind and faithful offices having long since been performed, and his body and his mind doomed to linger into the withering agony of decay, and gradual solitary death. I wept, and it was a pleasure to weep, for the painful looks, and the dreary prospects of this old veteran, whose eyes were dimmed, whose venerable locks were whitened by an hundred years, whose limbs were almost naked, and trembling as he sat by a small fire which his friends had left him, with a few sticks of wood within his reach and a buffalo's skin stretched upon some crotches over his head. Such was to be his only dwelling, and such the chances for his life, with only a few half-picked bones that were laid within his reach, and a dish of water, without weapons or means of any kind to replenish them, or strength to move his body from its fatal locality. In this sad plight I mournfully contemplated this miserable remnant of existence, who had unluckily outlived the fates and accidents of wars to die alone, at death's leisure. His friends and his children had all left him, and were preparing in a little time to be on the march. He had told them to leave him, "he was old," he said, "and too feeble to march." "My children," said he, "our nation is poor, and it is necessary that you should all go to the country where you can get meat,—my eyes are dimmed and my strength is no more; my days are nearly all numbered, and I am a burthen to my children—I cannot go, and I wish to die. Keep your hearts stout, and think not of me; I am no longer good for anything." In this way they had finished the ceremony of *exposing* him, and taken their final leave of him. I advanced to the old man, and was undoubtedly the last human being who held converse with him. I sat by the side of him, and though he could not distinctly see me, he shook me heartily by the hand and smiled, evidently aware that I was a white man, and that I sympathized with his inevitable misfortune. I shook hands again with him, and left him, steering my course towards the steamer which was a mile or more from me, and ready to resume her voyage up the Missouri.[3]

This cruel custom of exposing their aged people, belongs, I think, to all the tribes who roam about the prairies, making severe marches, when such decrepit persons are totally unable to go, unable to ride or to walk,—when they have no means of carrying them. It often becomes absolutely necessary in such cases that they should be left; and they uniformly insist upon it, saying as this old man did, that they are old and of no further use—that they left their fathers in the same manner—that they wish to die, and their children must not mourn for them.

3. When passing by the site of the Puncah village a few months after this, in my canoe, I went ashore with my men, and found the poles and the buffalo skin, standing as they were left, over the old man's head. The firebrands were lying nearly as I had left them, and I found at a few yards distant the skull, and others of his bones, which had been picked and cleaned by the wolves; which is probably all that any human being can ever know of his final and melancholy fate.

30

A Winter in the West, 1833–34

*M*isfortune, both physical and mental, trailed Charles Fenno Hoffman. *In 1817, eleven years after his birth in New York City, his right leg was amputated above the knee. Though worse misfortunes were in store for him, they did not immediately appear. After study at Columbia and a brief fling at the law, he turned to the profession of letters, which was always his abiding interest and in which his chief talents lay. In the fall of 1833, despite his handicap, he started on a tour of what was then the West, writing back letters to* the New York American *describing what he saw. He crossed Pennsylvania to Pittsburgh and made a circuit of the Old Northwest, Cleveland, the Great Lakes, Chicago, and thence southward to St. Louis. By steamboat up the Ohio, he progressed to Cincinnati, journeyed across Kentucky, the Blue Ridge to Virginia, and home. The account was published as his first book in 1835. It is one of the most charming accounts of the Middle West which exists for the period. He was alert to the color and romance of strange and different scenes; he possessed humor and a poetic nature; on the whole, he wrote well, both entertainingly and with discrimination; and his keen and alert spirit gives to his descriptions a wealth of detail.*

Upon his return to New York he pursued a literary career both as editor and as author. There are no other travel works, unless Wild Scenes in the Forest and Prairie *(1839) may be so described; but there were many songs, in which he excelled; much poetry, in which his talents were above average; and a popular novel,* Grayslaer *(1839). He belonged clearly to the Knicker-bocker group of writers in New York, and his writings still possess both charm and interest. Just past forty, his health gave way, his mind became dis-ordered, and after 1850 he was confined to the state asylum at Harrisburg, Pennsylvania, incurably insane, until his death in 1884.*

THE NATIONAL ROAD AND ITS TRAVELERS

About thirty miles from Wheeling we first struck the national road. It ap-pears to have been originally constructed of large, round stones, thrown with-out much arrangement on the surface of the soil, after the road was first lev-elled. These are now being ploughed up, and a thin layer of broken stones is in many places spread over the renovated surface. I hope the roadmakers have not the conscience to call this Macadamizing. It yields like snow-drift to the heavy wheels which traverse it, and the very best parts of the road that I saw are not to be compared with a Long Island turnpike. Two-thirds indeed of the extent traversed were worse than any artificial road I ever travelled, except perhaps the log causeways among the new settlements in northern New-York. The ruts are worn so broad and deep by heavy travel, that an army of pigmies might march into the bosom of the country under the cover they would afford. Perhaps I was the more struck with the appearance of this celebrated highway from the fact of much of the road over the mountains having been in excellent condition.—There is one feature, however, in this national road which is truly fine,—I allude to the massive stone bridges which form a part of it. They occur, as the road crosses a winding creek, a dozen times within as many miles. They consist either of one, two, or three arches; the centre arch being sprung a foot or two higher than those on either side. Their thick walls projecting above the road, their round stone buttresses, and carved key-stones combine to give them an air of Roman solidity and strength. They are monuments of taste and power that will speak well for the country when the brick towns they bind together shall have crumbled in the dust.

These frequently recurring bridges are striking objects in the landscape, where the road winds for many miles through a narrow valley. They may be seen at almost every turn spanning the deep bosom of the defile, and reflected with all their sombre beauty in the stream below.

Though your true western man generally journeys on horseback, yet one meets numbers of pedestrians on this side of the Alleghanies. They generally have a tow-cloth knapsack, or light leathern valise, hung across their backs, and are often very decently dressed in a blue coat, gray trousers, and round hat. They travel about forty miles a day.

The horsemen almost invariably wear a drab great-coat, fur-cap, and green cloth leggins; and in addition to a pair of well-filled saddle-bags, very often have strapped to their crupper a convenience the last you would expect to find in the wardrobe of a backwoodsman, videlicet, an umbrella. The females of every rank, in this mountainous country, ride in short dresses. They are generally wholly unattended, and some times in large parties of their own sex. The saddles and housings of their horses are very gay; and I have repeatedly seen a party of four or five buxom damsels, mounted on sorry-looking beasts, whose rough hides, unconscious of a currycomb, contrasted oddly enough with saddles of purple velvet, reposing on scarlet saddle-cloths, worked with orange-coloured borders. I have examined the manufacture of these gorgeous trappings at the saddleries in some of the towns in passing. They much re-semble those which are prepared in New-York for the South American mar-ket, and are of a much cheaper make, and far less durable, than those which a plainer taste would prefer. Still the effect of these gay colours, as you catch a glimpse of them afar off, fluttering through the woods, is by no means bad. They would show well in a picture, and be readily seized by a painter in re-lieving the shadows of a sombre landscape.

But by far the greatest portion of travellers one meets with, not to mention the ordinary stage-coach passengers, consists of teamsters and the emigrants. The former generally drive six horses before their enormous wagons—stout, heavy-looking beasts, descended, it is said, from the famous draught horses of Normandy. They go about twenty miles a day. The leading horses are often ornamented with a number of bells suspended from a square raised frame-work over their collars, originally adopted to warn these lumbering machines of each other's approach, and prevent their being brought up all standing in the narrow parts of the road.

As for the emigrants, it would astonish you to witness how they get along. A covered one-horse wagon generally contains the whole worldly substance of a family consisting not unfrequently of a dozen members. The tolls are so high along this western turnpike, and horses are so comparatively cheap in the region whither the emigrant is bound, that he rarely provides more than one miserable Rosinante to transport his whole family to the far west. The strength of the poor animal is of course half the time unequal to the demand upon it, and you will, therefore, unless it be raining very hard, rarely see any one in the wagon, except perhaps some child overtaken by sickness, or a mother nursing a young infant. The head of the family walks by the horse, cheering and encouraging him on his way. The good woman, when not engaged as hinted above, either trudges along with her husband, or, leading some weary little traveller by the hand behind, endeavours to keep the rest of her charge from loitering by the wayside. The old house-dog—if not chained beneath the wagon to prevent the half-starved brute from foraging too freely in a friendly country—brings up the rear. I made acquaintance with more than one of these faithful followers in passing, by throwing him a biscuit as I rode by, and my canine friend, when we met at an inn occasionally afterward, was sure to cultivate the intimacy. Sometimes these invaluable companions give out on the road, and in their broken-down condition are sold for a trifle by their masters. I saw several fine setters which I had reason to suspect came into the country in this way; and the owner of a superb brindled greyhound which I met among the mountains, told me that he had bought him from an English emigrant for a dollar. He used the animal with great success upon deer, and had already been offered fifty dollars for him.

The hardships of such a tour must form no bad preparatory school for the arduous life which the new settler has afterward to enter upon. Their horses, of course, frequently give out on the road; and in companies so numerous, sickness must frequently overtake some of the members. Nor should I wonder at serious accidents often occurring with those crank conveyances among the precipices and ravines of the mountains. At one place I saw a horse, but recently dead, lying beneath a steep, along the top of which the road led; and a little farther in advance, I picked up a pocketbook with some loose leaves floating near the edge of the precipice.

These mountains, though occasionally thus cut up by precipitous glens, are still by no means rocky—as would appear from the fact of the inhabitants hunting deer on horseback, through woods which would be almost impervious to a pair of city-bred legs. The modus operandi is very simple. The hunters collect in a troop—drive the deer in a circle—and then shoot from the saddle. The soil must in general be indifferent, according to what was told us by the keeper of the turnpike-gate, who claimed to be the father of twenty-seven children! I asked this worthy *paterfamilias* if the country was healthy.

"Healthy, sir!" he replied, "that it is—healthy and poor—ten people run away where one dies in it."

The soil improves much after leaving the mountains; and we crossed some rich bottom lands when fording the Youghioghany and Monongahela Rivers,—the former a branch of the latter, and both fine pebbly streams.

PITTSBURGH AND THE CITIES OF THE OLD NORTHWEST

It was nearly dark when we got fairly into Pittsburg, where the dust and smoke, with the rattling of drays along the streets, returning from their day's work to the suburbs, reminded me not a little of New York at night-fall. There is one sound, however, in the streets of Pittsburg, which utterly forbids a stranger mistaking them for those of any other town on the continent—it is the ceaseless din of the steam-engines. Every mechanic here, of any pretension, has one of these tremendous journeymen at work in his establishment. They may be purchased for what would be the price of a pair of horses in New-York; and it costs a mere trifle to keep them in fuel. These machines must do the work of a great many thousand men at Pittsburg.

There is no place in the Western country, "which can more justly boast of its small beginnings, its rapid but solid growth, and its future greatness," as Judge Baldwin observed, than this. Situated two thousand miles from New-Orleans, by the aid of steam she supplies the whole of the intermediate region with hardware, machinery, and cutlery. But it is not for this manufacture alone that Pittsburg, often called the "Birmingham of America," is celebrated. Her extensive glass-works are well known even beyond the Alleghanies; and this fragile production of her workshops finds its way alike to the borders of Lake Erie and of the Atlantic, and may be met in the elegant mansions of Baltimore and the remote shantees of the Arkansaw.

The timber-trade is another great feature in the business relations of Pittsburg; the boards and scantling measured within the city in 1830 amounted to more than five millions of feet; of this a great deal was floated down the branches of the Alleghany River from the south-western counties of New-York. The romantic hills of Chatauque county supply not a few of the stately trunks which, after being hewn into shape at Pittsburg, subsequently float the varied products of Northern industry through many a stranger climate to the rich markets of Louisiana. You will not wonder, therefore, that the freight exported from Pittsburg in 1830 amounted to upwards of 18,000 tons, its imports for the same year being more than 14,000 tons. The city is now, with the adjacent villages of Alleghany-town and Lawrenceville on the Alleghany, and Birmingham and Manchester on the Monongahela, the third town in population, wealth, and importance in the Mississippi valley. Next to its admirable situation, the flourishing condition of the place is no doubt to be mainly attributed to the inexhaustible quantities of fine bituminous coal which may be had for the digging in all the adjacent hills. Pittsburg is, however, indebted to the character of her early settlers for her present eminence; they were chiefly mechanics, enterprising, industrious, practical men; the improvements they commenced were based upon utility, and every path of trade they struck out led to some immediate and tangible good. The result shows itself in one of the most substantial and flourishing, but least elegant, cities on the continent. The site of the town is one of the most beautiful that can be imagined. The want of beauty in the place itself is to be attributed entirely to the manner in which it is laid out, for the streets, though by no means wide, are well and substantially built upon with brick; and a species of yellow freestone found in the vicinity is coming into use, which, for elegance as a building-material, is not surpassed by marble itself. The great defect in the town is the total want of public squares, and, indeed, of an agreeable promenade of any kind; this is the more remarkable, I might almost say provoking, as Pittsburg boasts of one spot which, if converted into a public place, would, from the view it commands, be unrivalled by any thing of the kind in the Union, unless it be the Battery of New-York. I allude to a triangular piece of ground, at the confluence of the two rivers, at the end of the town. It is the site of the old forts, and commands the first view of the Ohio, and the finest of its waters I have yet seen. Had but the ancient fortifications been preserved, this would have been one of the most interesting spots upon the continent; of Fort Du Quesne there remains now but a small mound, containing, perhaps, a couple of loads of earth; Fort Pitt may be more easily traced, part of three bastions, about breast-high, stand within different private enclosures, and a piece of the curtain, which, within a few years, was in complete preservation, may still be discovered among the piles of lumber in a steam saw-mill yard. The commandant's quarters, a steep-roofed brick dwelling, in the form of a pentagon, is, however, the only perfect remnant of these old military structures. I expected to have seen the magazine of the fort, which I was told was an admirable piece of masonry, and still endured in the shape of a porter-cellar; but upon arriving at the spot where it had stood but a few weeks before, a pile of rough stones was all that we could discover. In a country like ours, where so few antiquities meet the eye, it is melancholy to see these interesting remnants thus destroyed, and the very landmarks where they stood effaced for ever.

There is yet another place in Pittsburg which at some future day should be appropriated as a public square; a triangular bluff about one hundred feet high stretches like a huge promontory far into the town, and overlooks the whole place. The Pittsburgers, however, I fear, are more bent upon increasing their "fathers' store" than on beautifying the favoured spot in which they dwell; and it requires all the cordial hospitality of the place to reconcile a stranger to the few city improvements he sees going forward, in a community so pre-eminent for its individual enterprise. I wish we could lend them our "improving" corporation for a few weeks,—they would be really of service here, and could easily be spared at home; they might, too, learn more than one thing of the Pittsburgers, and especially how to supply the city with pure water; we have it here in the greatest abundance. The water is pumped up from the Alleghany by a steam-engine, into a large open basin, situated on an eminence known as Grant's Hill, from the signal defeat of that rash but gallant officer at its base, during the old French war. From this ample reservoir pipes conduct the fluid to every part of the city. A large Gothic cathedral is now about to be erected near the water-works.

I took an opportunity, while a lady of the party stopped to visit a pensioner in a cottage by the road-side, to examine a coal-pit just beneath the brow of the hill. Dismounting on a small platform some two hundred feet above the river, from which a railway empties the coal into the *coke*-kilns upon its bank and the freight-boats upon the shore, I entered an aperture in the rock, about six feet in height and four in breadth. A guide preceded me with a candle, and after penetrating under his escort a few hundred yards, I turned aside to explore some of the adjacent shafts: they lie like the streets of one main avenue,—the veins of a grand artery, which, after winding through the body of the hill, for the distance of half a mile, finds its way again to the light. In one of these cavernous passages, in a ledge of the rock, lay a sleeping man, the water trickling from the black walls around was the only sound to disturb his slumbers; a long-wicked candle stuck in a crevice above his head, shining over thickly-matted locks, and features begrimmed with coal-dust, revealed a figure of gigantic mould. The mattock on which his ponderous arm reposed told that it was only a miner at his noonday nap; but he might have been mistaken, by one coming suddenly upon his singular place of repose, for a slumbering Titan.

I took my passage in the stage-coach early in the evening and retired to my chamber to catch a nap before my morning's ride. The clock was striking three, when at the call of the porter I rose and descended to the bar-room. The attentive landlord, himself in waiting, was ruminating before a large coal-fire; and stretched upon the floor in a corner lay the tired domestic, who, having just fulfilled a part of his duty, in awakening the various passengers, was catching a dog-nap before the stage-coach should drive to the door. My own proper vehicle came at last, and by the light of the stage lamps,—the only ones, by-the-by, which shone through the sleeping city,—I climbed to the coachman's box, and took the traveller's favourite seat by his side. I could distinguish nothing of the city opposite but the red glare of a furnace which shot out from the bank of the river, and flowed an inverted pyramid of light upon its waters. Keeping on our way, the massive walls of the state-prison, with their circular towers and octangular area, frowned like some old Moorish castle over our path, as we drove beneath their dun-coloured battlements, and passed the last environs of Pittsburg. It was, I confess, with some soberness of spirit that I bade a last adieu to a spot where the politeness and hospitality of the inhabitants had made my time pass so pleasantly. I must, however, have been *de trop* among my new acquaintances, had I remained much longer; for in Pittsburg every one is so occupied with business, that the time bestowed in attentions to a stranger is a sacrifice of some importance.

We reached Cleaveland during a heavy shower long after nightfall. The roar of the surf reminded me of Rockaway; and the first view of Lake Erie, the next morning, was really grateful to my eyes. I felt, while walking along the high esplanade of turf which here forms its banks, and upon which the town is built, like one who has just come out of a pent-up chamber into the full and free air of heaven. The effect of coming on such a wide expanse of water when just emerging from the forest is much greater than when, after long riding through an open country, you view the ocean stretched beyond its shining beach.

Cleaveland is very prettily situated upon the lake. The Cayuhoga makes a bend around a high bluff as it passes into the inland sea which receives its waters, and on the level peninsula thus formed is built the town. The harbour, naturally an indifferent one, has been much improved by running out a pier from either side of the river, where it debouches into Lake Erie; and there being now few better ports on this side of the lake, Cleaveland must become one of the most important places on its waters. The adjacent region is, I believe, not remarkably well suited to agricultural purposes; but there is an immense tract of the most fertile country inland, which looks to Cleaveland for the chief outlet of its products. This will account for the rapid rise of property here, which is almost incredible; building-lots in some places commanding now as many thousands as they did hundreds of dollars five years since. The town, which can already boast of a public library, a fine church, two capital taverns, and many handsome private dwellings, is laid out with broad streets and a spacious square in the centre. The business part is as yet beneath the bluff, where a single winding street runs along the bank of the river towards the lake; but the main street above is already the scene of much bustle, and bears about the same relation to that below as Broadway does to Southstreet in New-York city.

I had just left the reading-room of the Franklin Hotel, in Cleaveland, and was making myself at home for the rest of the evening, in my own neat chamber, when the sound of a steamboat-bell, about nine o'clock, gave note that one of these vessels, which at this stormy season cannot navigate the lake with any regularity, had touched at Cleaveland. No time was to be lost, and huddling my clothes, &c. into my trunk as quickly as possible, I jumped into a vehicle, waiting at the tavern door, and in a few minutes was upon the quay. Here I witnessed a scene of indescribable confusion. The night was dark and somewhat gusty, and the boat and the wharf were both crowded with boxes, bales, and the effects of emigrants, who were screaming to each other in half as many languages as were spoken at Babel. Lanterns were flashing to and fro along the docks, and hoarse orders and countermands, mingled with the harsh hissing of the steam on every side. At length we pushed from the shore, and escaping in a moment from the head of the mole, stood fairly out into the lake, while the bright beacon of the Cleaveland lighthouse soon waned in the distance, and was at last lost entirely. I found myself, upon looking around, on board of the fine steamboat "New-York," Captain Fisher, to whose politeness I was much indebted for showing me about the boat before turning in for the night. Taking a lantern in his hand, and tucking my arm under his, he groped about among his motley ship's company like Diogenes looking for an honest man.

Our course first led us through a group of emigrants collected around a stove, mid-ships, where an English mother nursing her infant, a child lying asleep upon a mastiff, and a long-bearded German smoking his meerchaum on the top of a pile of candle-boxes, were the only complete figures I could make out from an indefinite number of heads, arms, and legs lying about in the most whimsical confusion. Passing farther on, we came to two tolerable cabins on either side of the boat just forward of the wheels, both pretty well filled with emigrants, who were here more comfortably bestowed. We next passed the forward bar-room (there being another abaft for cabin-passengers), and finally came to the bow, of which a horse and several dogs had already been the occupants for so many days,—the New-York having been twice driven into port and delayed by stress of weather,—that it might have been mistaken for either stable or kennel. We next ascended a steep stairway to the upper deck of all, and I here spent some moments rather amusingly in survey-ing the furniture of the emigrants with which it was crowded. They differed according to the origin of their owner. The effects of the Yankee were gen-erally limited to a Dearborn wagon, a feather-bed, a saddle and bridle, and some knickknack in the way of a machine for shelling corn, hatchelling flax, or, for aught I know, manufacturing wooden nutmegs for family use. Those of the Englishman are far more numerous; for John Bull, when he wanders from home, would not only, like the roving Trojan, carry his household gods with him into strange lands, but even the fast-anchored isle itself, could he but cut it from its moorings. Whenever, therefore, you see an antique-fashioned looking-glass, a decrepit bureau, and some tenderly-preserved old china, you will probably, upon looking further, have the whole house-keeping array of an honest Briton exposed to your view.

But still further do the Swiss and Germans carry their love of family relics. Mark that quaint-looking wagon which lumbers up a dozen square feet of the deck. It might be worth something in a museum, but it has cost five times its value in freight to transport it over the Atlantic. What an indignity it is to overwhelm the triumphal chariot with the beds and ploughs, shovels, saddles, and sideboards, chairs, clocks, and carpets that fill its interior, and to hang those rusty pots and kettles, bakepans, fryingpans, and saucepans, iron candlesticks, old horse-shoes, and broken tobacco-pipes, like trophies of conquest over Time, along its racked and wheezing sides. That short man yonder, with square shoulders and a crooked pipe in his mouth, is the owner; he, with the woollen cap, that is just raising his blue cotton frock to thrust hand into the fob of his sherrivalleys.[1] That man had probably not the slightest idea of the kind of country he was coming to. His eyes are but now just opening to his new condition; nor will he sacrifice a particle of his useless and expensive trumpery until they are completely open. That man has not yet a thought in common with the people of his new abode around him. He looks, indeed, as if he came from another planet. Visit him on his thriving farm ten years hence, and, except in the single point of language, you will find him (unless he has settled among a nest of his countrymen) at home among his neighbours, and happily conforming to their usages; while that clean-looking Englishman next to him will still be a stranger in the land.

I subsequently looked into the different cabins and compartments of the boat not yet visited, and had reason to be gratified with the appearance of all. I may say, that fine as our Atlantic boats are, I do not recollect any on the Atlantic waters, for strength and beauty united, equal to this. A great mistake, however, I think, exists here in building the boats for these waters with cabins on deck, like the river boats. In consequence of such a large part of the hull being above water, they are rendered dangerous during the tremendous gales which sweep Lake Erie, and are often compelled to make a port of safety several times during a passage.

It was during a shower, shortly after noon, when some low wooded islands on the American side of the lake, with a tall flag-staff peering above the haze from the little town of Amherstburg on the British shore, indicated that we had entered the mouth of the Detroit River.

The city of Detroit itself stands upon an elevated piece of tableland, extending probably for some twenty miles back from the river, and being per-

1. [I.e., in the pocket of his overalls.—ED.]

fectly unbroken for at least two miles along its margin. Beneath the bluff—
for the plain is so high as almost to deserve the name—is a narrow bustling
street of about half a mile in length, with the wharves just beyond it; and fifty
yards inboard runs a spacious street called Jefferson Avenue, parallel with the
lower street and the river; the chief part of the town extends for a mile or two
along the latter. The dwelling-houses are generally of wood, but there are a
great many stores now building, or already erected, of brick, with stone base-
ments. The brick is generally of an indifferent quality; but the stone, which
is brought from Cleaveland, Ohio, is a remarkably fine material for building
purposes. It is a kind of yellow freestone, which is easily worked when first
taken from the quarry, and hardens subsequently upon exposure to the
air. There are at this moment many four-story stores erecting, as well as
other substantial buildings, which speak for the flourishing condition of the
place.

The want of mechanics is so great, however, that it is difficult as yet to carry
on these operations upon the scale common in our Atlantic cities, although
the demand for houses in Detroit, it is said, would fully warrant similar out-
lays of capital. The public buildings are the territorial council-house, situated
upon an open piece of ground, designated on an engraved plan of the city as
"The Campus Martius," a courthouse, academy, and two banks. There are
also five churches, a Catholic, an Episcopal, a Presbyterian, Baptist, and
Methodist. The Catholic congregation is the largest; their stone church, after
remaining several years in an unfinished state, is soon, it is said, to be completed with funds derived from Rome; it will make an imposing appearance
when finished. The population of Detroit is, I believe, between three and
four thousand—it increases so rapidly, however, that it is difficult to form
an estimate. The historical associations, the safety, and commodiousness of
the harbour, with its extensive inland commercial advantages, must ever
constitute this one of the most interesting and important points in the
Union.

We had not been in Chicago an hour before an invitation to a public ball
was courteously sent to us by the managers; and though my soiled and travel-
worn riding-dress was not exactly the thing to present one's self in before
ladies of an evening, yet, in my earnestness to see life on the frontier, I easily
allowed all objections to be overruled by my companions, and we accordingly
drove to the house in which the ball was given.

It was a frame-building, one of the few as yet to be found in Chicago;
which, although one of the most ancient French trading-posts on the Lakes,
can only date its growth as a village since the Indian war, eighteen months

since.[2] When I add that the population has *quintupled* last summer and that but few mechanics have come in with the prodigious increase of residents, you can readily imagine that the influx of strangers far exceeds the means of accommodations; while scarcely a house, however comfortable looking outside, contains more than two or three finished rooms.

We were ushered into a tolerably sized dancing-room, occupying the second story of the house, and having its unfinished walls so ingeniously covered with pine-branches and flags borrowed from the garrison, that, with the white-washed ceiling above, it presented a very complete and quite pretty appearance. It was not so warm, however, that the fires of cheerful hickory, which roared at either end, could have been readily dispensed with. An orchestra of unplaned boards was raised against the wall in the centre of the room; the band consisting of a dandy negro with his violin, a fine military-looking bass drummer from the fort, and a volunteer citizen who alternately played an accompaniment upon the flute and triangle. As for the company, it was such a complete medley of all ranks, ages, professions, trades, and occupations, brought together from all parts of the world, and now for the first time brought together, that it was amazing to witness the decorum with which they commingled on this festive occasion. The managers (among whom were some officers of the garrison) must certainly be *au fait* at dressing a lobster and mixing regent's punch, in order to have produced a harmonious compound from such a collection of contrarieties. The gayest figure that was ever called by quadrille playing Benoit never afforded me half the amusement that did these Chicago cotillions. Here you might see a veteran officer in full uniform balancing to a tradesman's daughter still in her short frock and trousers, while there the golden aiguillette of a handsome surgeon flapped in unison with the glass beads upon a scrawney neck of fifty. In one quarter, the high-placed buttons of a linsey-woolsey coat would be *dos a dos* to the elegantly turned shoulders of a delicate-looking southern girl; and in another, a pair of Cinderella-like slippers would chassez cross with a brace of thick-soled broghans, in making which, one of the lost feet of the Colossus of Rhodes may have served for a last. Those raven locks, dressed *a la Madonne,* over eyes of jet, and touching a cheek where blood of a deeper hue, mingling

2. Alterations have taken place since the writer left there, not yet a year ago. Chicago, which but eighteen months since contained but two or three frame-buildings, and a few miserable huts, has now five hundred houses, four hundred of which have been erected this year, and two thousand two hundred inhabitants. A year ago there was not a place of public worship in the town; there are now five churches and two school-houses, and numerous brick stores and warehouses. A line of four steamboats of the largest class of lake-boats, and regular lines of brigs and schooners, are now established between this port and the principal ports of the lower lakes.

with the less glowing current from European veins, tell of a lineage drawn from the original owners of the soil; while these golden tresses, floating away from eyes of heaven's own colour over a neck of alabaster, recall the Gothic ancestry of some of "England's born." How piquantly do these trim and beaded *leggins* peep from under that simple dress of black, as its tall nut-brown wearer moves, as if unconsciously, through the graceful mazes of the dance. How divertingly do those inflated gigots, rising like windsails from that little Dutch-built hull, jar against those tall plumes which impend over them like a commodore's pennant on the same vessel. But what boots all these incongruities, when a spirit of festive good-humour animates every one present. "It takes all kinds of people to make a world" (as I hear it judiciously observed this side of the mountains), and why should not all these kinds of people be represented as well in a ball-room as in a legislature? At all events, if I wished to give an intelligent foreigner a favourable opinion of the manners and deportment of my countrymen in the aggregate, I should not wish a better opportunity, after explaining to him the materials of which it was composed, and the mode in which they were brought together from every section of the Union, than was afforded by this very ball. "This is a scene of enchantment to me, sir," observed an officer to me, recently exchanged to this post, and formerly stationed here. "There were but a few traders around the fort when I last visited Chicago, and now I can't contrive where the devil all these well-dressed people have come from!"

It has been so cold, indeed, as almost to render writing impracticable in a place so comfortless. The houses were built with such rapidity, during the summer, as to be mere shells; and the thermometer having ranged as low as 28 below zero, during several days it has been almost impossible, notwithstanding the large fires kept up by an attentive landlord, to prevent the ink from freezing while using it, and one's fingers become so numb in a very few moments when thus exercised, that, after vainly trying to write in gloves, I have thrown by my pen, and joined the group, composed of all the household, around the bar-room fire. This room, which is an old log-cabin aside of the main house, is one of the most comfortable places in town, and is, of course, much frequented; business being, so far as one can judge from the concourse that throng it, nearly at a stand still. Several persons have been severely frost-bitten in passing from door to door; and not to mention the quantity of poultry and pigs that have been frozen, an ox, I am told, has perished from cold in the streets at noonday. An occasional Indian, wrapped in his blanket, and dodging about from store to store after a dram of whiskey, or a muffled-up Frenchman, driving furiously in his cariole on the river, are almost the only human beings abroad; while the wolves, driven in by the deep snows which preceded this severe weather, troop through the town after nightfall, and may be heard howling continually in the midst of it.

The situation of Chicago, on the edge of the Grand Prairie, with the whole expanse of Lake Michigan before it, gives the freezing winds from the Rocky Mountains prodigious effect, and renders a degree of temperature which in sheltered situations is but little felt, almost painful here.

The town lies upon a dead level, along the banks of a narrow forked river, and is spread over a wide extent of surface to the shores of the lake, while vessels of considerable draught of water can, by means of the river, unload in the centre of the place. I believe I have already mentioned that four-fifths of the population have come in since last spring; the erection of new buildings during the summer has been in the same proportion; and although a place of such mushroom growth can, of course, boast of but little solid improvement in the way of building, yet contracts have been made for the ensuing season which must soon give Chicago much of that metropolitan appearance it is destined so promptly to assume. As a place of business, its situation at the central head of the Mississippi Valley will make it the New-Orleans of the north; and its easy and close intercourse with the most flourishing eastern cities will give it the advantage, as its capital increases, of all their improvements in the mode of living.

It was a still sunny morning, when, in rounding one of those beautiful promontories which form so striking a feature in the scenery of the Ohio, we came suddenly upon a cluster of gardens and villas, which indicated the vicinity of a flourishing town; and our boat taking a sudden sheer from the shore, before the eye had time to study out their grouping and disposition, the whole city of Cincinnati, imbosomed in its amphitheatre of green hills, was brought at once before us. It rises on two inclined planes from the river, the one elevated about fifty feet above the other, and both running parallel to the Ohio. The streets are broad, occasionally lined with trees, and generally well built of brick, though there are some pretty churches and noble private dwellings of cut stone and of stucco. Of the latter there are several with greater pretensions to architectural beauty than any which I remember in New-York. The first impression upon touching the quays at Cincinnati, and looking up its spacious avenues terminating always in the green acclivities which bound the city, is exceedingly beautiful; and your good opinion of the town suffers no diminution when you have an opportunity to examine its well-washed streets and tasteful private residences. Of the rides and walks in the suburbs I cannot speak too warmly; the girdle of green hills already spoken of, on some of which the primeval growth of the forest still lingers in a clump of aged trees, command some of the most beautiful views you can imagine of the opposite shores of Kentucky, with the two pretty manufacturing villages on either side of the Licking River, which debouches opposite to Cincinnati. Cincinnati herself, with her twenty gilded spires gleaming among gardens and shrubbery, lies as if spread upon a map beneath you; while, before attaining this commanding height, you have already been rewarded, when winding up the steep ascent, by a hundred charming glimpses of groves and villas, scattered along the banks of the beautiful Ohio. Verily, if beauty alone confer empire, it is in vain for thriving Pittsburg or flourishing Louisville, bustling and buxom as they are, to dispute with Cincinnati her title of "Queen of the West."

The population of the place is about 30,000. Among them you see very few but what look comfortable and contented, though the town does not wear the brisk and busy air observable at Louisville. Transportation is so easy along the great western waters, that you see no lounging poor people about the large towns, as, when business languishes in one place, and it is difficult to find occupation, they are off at once to another, and shift their quarters whither the readiest means of living invite them. What would most strike you in the streets of Cincinnati would be the number of pretty faces and stylish figures one meets in a morning. A walk through Broadway here rewards one hardly less than to promenade its New-York namesake. I have had more than one opportunity of seeing these western beauties by candle-light, and the evening display brought no disappointment to the morning promise. Nothing can be more agreeable than the society which one meets with in the gay and elegantly furnished drawing-rooms of Cincinnati; the materials being from every State in the Union, there is a total want of *caste;* a complete absence of *settishness* (if I may use the word). If there be any characteristic that might jar upon your taste and habits, it is, perhaps, a want of that harmonious blending of light and shade, that repose both of character and manner, which, distinguishing the best circles in our Atlantic cities, so often sinks into insipidity, or runs into a ridiculous imitation of the impertinent nonchalance which the pseudo pictures of English "high life" in the novels of the day impose upon our simple republicans as the height of elegance and refinement. There is a common phrase in the new settlements of the West—"We all come from some place or another,"—which you may imagine to be particularly applicable to a place that only dates from the year of our Lord 1808; and it is therefore in the highest degree absurd to speak of the Cincinnatians as a provincial people in their manners, when the most agreeable persons that figure here hail originally from New-York or Philadelphia, Boston and Baltimore, and are very tenacious of the style of living in which they have been educated.

The New-Yorker, for instance, plumes himself upon placing a bottle of Lynch's best before you; the Philadelphian on having a maître de cuisine who adds to his abstruser knowledge of the sacred mysteries the cunning art of putting butter into as tempting rolls as ever sported their golden curl upon a Chestnut-street breakfast-table; the centre table of the Bostonian is covered with new publications fresh from the American Athens; and you may be sure to find the last new song of Bayley on the music-stand of the fair Baltimorean. I need hardly add, that the picture of life and manners here by an exceedingly clever English caricaturist has about as much vrai-semblance as if the beaux and belles of Kamschatka had sat for the portraits.[3]

I have been here now nearly ten days, and scarcely an hour has passed without some gay and agreeable engagement. The acquaintance of Mr. K——— and Mr. P———, both formerly of New-York, and now distinguished members of the Ohio bar, inducted me at once into all the society of the place; my table was covered with cards on the morning after my arrival, and I see no end to the polite hospitalities of the place, should I prolong my stay.

The principal buildings of Cincinnati, besides more than twenty churches, some of which are very pretty, and several fine hotels, one of which, the Pearl-street House, would rival the best in New-York, are the Cincinnati College, a couple of Theatres, four Market-houses, one of which is five hundred feet in length, a Court-house, United States' Branch Bank, Medical College, Mechanics' Institute, the Catholic Atheneum, the Hospital, and High-School, and two Museums. The collection of one of these museums is exceedingly interesting, from embracing a number of enormous organic remains among its curiosities, with antique vases and various singular domestic utensils, excavated from some of the ancient mounds in Ohio. In the upper story of the same building there is another exhibition, which, from the accounts I have had of it, I should hardly expect to be patronised in so enlightened a community:—it is nothing less than a nightly representation of the final place of torment in the other world, with all the agreeable accompaniments that the imaginations of the vulgar delight in conceiving as belonging to it. A very respectable man, whom I chanced to meet with long before reaching here, mentioned to me the existence of this piece of charlatanism, and dwelt upon it with great unction, from the "good moral effect it would produce!" Now, is it not surprising that the very persons who condemn theatrical representations are the ones of all others to countenance such gross and impious humbug? The success of such disgraceful mummery is, perhaps, the strongest argument that could be adduced in favour of a well-regulated stage.

3. [Apparently a reference to Frances Trollope's *Domestic Manners of the Americans* (New York, 1832).—ED.]

The most remarkable, however, of all the establishments of Cincinnati are those immense slaughter-houses, where the business of butchering and packing pork is carried on. The number of hogs annually slaughtered is said to exceed one hundred and twenty thousand; and the capital employed in the business is estimated at two millions of dollars. Some of the establishments cover several acres of ground; and one of the packing-houses, built of brick, and three stories high, is more than a hundred feet long, and proportionably wide. The minute division of labour and the fearful celerity of execution in these swinish workshops would equally delight a pasha and a political economist; for it is the mode in which the business is conducted, rather than its extent, which gives dignity to hog-killing in Cincinnati, and imparts a tragic interest to the last moments of the doomed porkers, that might inspire the savage genius of a Maturin or a Monk Lewis. Imagine a long narrow edifice, divided into various compartments, each communicating with the other, and each furnished with some peculiar and appropriate engine of destruction. In one you see a gory block and gleaming axe; a seething caldron nearly fills another. The walls of a third bristle with hooks newly sharpened for impalement; while a fourth is shrouded in darkness, that leaves you to conjure up images still more dire. There are forty ministers of fate distributed throughout these gloomy abodes, each with his particular office assigned him. And here, when the fearful carnival comes on, and the deep forests of Ohio have contributed their thousands of unoffending victims, the gauntlet of death is run by those selected for immolation. The scene commences in the shadowy cell, whose gloom we have not yet been allowed to penetrate. Fifty unhappy porkers are here incarcerated at once together, with bodies wedged so closely that they are incapacitated from all movement. And now the grim executioner—like him that battled with the monster that wooed Andromeda—leaps with his iron mace upon their backs, and rains his ruthless blows around him. The unresisting victims fall on every side; but scarcely does one touch the ground, before he is seized by a greedy hook protruded through an orifice below. His throat is severed instantly in the adjacent cell, and the quivering body is hurried onward. The mallet,—the knife,—the axe,—the boiling caldron,—the remorseless scraping-iron,—have each done their work; and the fatted porker, that was but one minute before grunting in the full enjoyment of bristling hoghood, now cadaverous and "chap-fallen," hangs a stark and naked effigy among his immolated brethren.

The whole number of hogs killed last year, in Cincinnati and vicinity, is ascertained to be a little rising *one hundred and twenty-three thousand*. Deer Creek is a stream running into the Ohio River on the eastern suburb of the city. About a half a mile up this stream the slaughter-houses of Mr. Coleman are situated; and during the whole "hog-season," this stream, from the houses to the river, is running blood, and generally goes by the name of "Bloody River."

From the slaughter-houses, the hogs are conveyed in large wagons, that hold from twenty-five to forty, to the various packing-houses, where they can pack, and have ready for shipment, *two hundred and fifty barrels of pork in one day*. It is, indeed, astonishing, the rapidity with which they put a hog out of sight, when once they get fair hold of him. As at the slaughter-houses, a perfect system is kept up; every man has his allotted duty to perform. When the hogs are received, they are first weighed by the weigher, then passed to the "blocking-men, who place them on the several blocks (two are generally used), when they are received by the "cutters," and are very quickly des-patched,—the various qualities separated and thrown into their respective places. One man weighs for the barrels (two hundred pounds), and throws the meat into a "salt-box," from which the "packer" receives it; and when the barrel is packed, it is handed over to the "cooper," who heads it. It is then bored, filled with strong brine, plugged, branded, and ready for shipment.

There is more of eastern than of western genius—of the Yankee rather than the Kentuckian—in this systematic establishment, where the coarsest employment is thus reduced to mathematical precision. Indeed, the mechani-cal regularity, the neatness, and the enterprise of New-England characterise the people of Ohio generally, and constitute a marked difference between them and their neighbours over the river. The Kentuckians are chiefly de-scended from military men and hunters, who settled the broad and fertile tracts now so populous during and shortly subsequent to the Revolution; and wheresoever they wander in the far west, they are still distinguished by the traits that would naturally spring from such an origin. There is an off-handedness—if I may use the term—a fearless ardour, a frankness and a self-possession about them that engages your good-will at once; while you are both interested and amused at the exaggerated tone of sentiment, half-roman-tic, half vain-glorious, which their ideas and expressions betray. Judging, how-ever, from the occasional specimens I have seen, I should think that though individually the most characteristic and interesting people in the Union, they are by no means such useful members of society as the New-Englanders.

ACROSS HOSPITABLE KENTUCKY TO THE BLUE RIDGE

Travelling on horseback is the best mode of seeing both the scenery and the people of the western country; and having bought a good hackney at Cincinnati, I promise myself much pleasure from this part of my western tour. My route will lead south-westwardly through Kentucky as far as the mountainous parts of Tennessee, from which State I shall enter Virginia on its south-west corner.

I struck down the side of a grassy slope, and crossing a brook, soon found myself riding through a tall wood on the high-road to Lexington. I was over-taken by a young man of genteel appearance, who at once drew up by my side and entered into easy conversation, according to the custom of the country. After riding a mile or two together, he asked me if I would eat an apple, and, upon expressing assent, instead of drawing the fruit from his pocket, or sad-dle-bags, as I expected, I was not a little surprised to see him stop in front of a respectable-looking house, and halloo till half a dozen negroes made their appearance from the log-cabins around the door.

"Aunty," cried my companion, to an active-looking wench who advanced before the rest, "has your master got any apples in the house?"

"Only a few barrels left, young master."

"Well, then, bring us a dozen."

A large basket, containing as many of the finest pippins as we could stow about our persons, was, a moment after, brought to the road-side and held up to us, as we sat on horseback; and, after dividing up the contents between us, I was very naturally anxious to pay for them, but the young gentleman told me that I would only insult a decent farmer's family (not a soul to whom was known to him) by paying for what "no Kentuckian would be brute enough to refuse a stranger."

The evening had completely settled down in upon the lower grounds, as I looked from an eminence down into the little valley whence rose the white chimneys of the house where I was to pass the night. It stood in straggling and broken form, one story in height, on the margin of a lively brook, which rattled along the base of the hill; the various buildings comprehended in the mansion making quite an imposing appearance as they extended their low and irregular front along the roadside.

A limping gray-headed negro received my horse at the door, while the landlord took my saddle-bags, and ushered me into a wainscotted and white-washed chamber, where another traveller, who had arrived but a few minutes before me, was comforting himself with the contents of a pitcher of cider, which stood at his elbow.

"Come, sir, come," he exclaimed upon my entrance; "come, sir, take a drink; this cider goes very well after an evening ride."

"Help yourself, stranger," added the landlord, "while I tote your plunder into the other room."

Then, while I rejoined the cider-drinker in his thin potations, the landlord returned, and finding that my immediate destination was Lexington, he told me, with an air of great satisfaction, that, "I would have company all the way, for that gentleman was going on in the morning."

The other, a plain farmer, with whom I had now exchanged some commonplaces about agriculture, which nearly exhausted my stock of information on that subject, rejoined with animation that he was very glad I was going his way, as "he allowed the gentleman to be right good company, and he did not mistrust but what we'd have a tip-top time of it."

The next morning our road lay chiefly through a level fertile country, in a very good state of cultivation; and my companion, who is one of the most prominent planters and agriculturists in this section of the country, took great pleasure in pointing out to me the most flourishing farms, and the peculiar growth of different soils, as we rode along; recalling at the same time, most agreeably—as the railroad, now constructing between Lexington and Frankfort, occasionally intersected our route,—his early recollections of this region before such a convenience was dreamed of.

About noon, passing the gate of an extensive planter, who was personally known to Mr.——, he, much to my gratification, proposed a call upon his friend. Leaving the road, we entered at once upon a large and beautiful park. It was enclosed by a common worm-fence, but afforded some charming vistas among its noble clumps of trees, where a large herd of deer were browsing unmolested. This was the grazing portion of the farm, and the hardy *blue* grass, even thus early, afforded a rich sward beneath the boughs that were just putting forth their young leaves. Passing completely through this wooded pasture, we entered a square enclosure of some eight or ten acres of garden, lawn, and orchard combined, but not doing much credit to the characteristics of either, having a rectangular brick house placed formally in the midst, with several negro-hovels about a stone's throw from the door.

In the mean time half a dozen slaves, young and old, made their appearance, our horses were disposed of, and two tall and well-made Kentuckians, either of whom had counted, perhaps, five or six-and-twenty summers, saluted us at the door. My companion was received with a great deal of cordiality; and I was made at once at home. We dined with the young gentlemen, who, in the absence of the older members of the family, were keeping bachelor's hall together; and a half dozen plans were at once projected by them for making my time pass agreeably for a month to come. Nor would they harken to the idea of my proceeding on with Mr.—— immediately after dinner. Most unwillingly, however, I was obliged to insist upon going. Our horses were saddled, while theirs, too, were brought to the door; and descending, under the escort of our entertainers, a slight knoll back of the house, where a lively brook came singing from a rocky cave within a few yards of the door, we entered a wooded enclosure of about a hundred acres, separated by a fence from the woodland pasture around. My hospitable entertainers took the opportunity to press me again to remain at least a few days with them, adding the strong temptation of an elk-hunt on horseback, as one of these fellows when turned out in the range would afford superb sport: but I had already, before leaving Lexington, entered into engagements with my friend L——, of the Transylvania University, an accomplished young German, which compelled me to forego the pleasure. The attentive young Kentuckians accompanied us through the plantation until we came out on the highway; and finally, with one more attempt to detain us, we were dismissed upon our journey, after a promise was exacted from me that I would not return that way without at least passing a night with them.

After fording a number of fine brooks, whose full currents more than once washed our saddle-girths, L—— and I came at last to the Forks of the Kentucky River, our destination for the night. A spacious old-fashioned building, erected during the early settlement of Kentucky, and now in a state of considerable dilapidation, stood upon an eminence. Our black guide, who was an old family-servant, was our only letter of introduction; but the hospitable manner in which we were received and made at once at home showed that we needed no more. The young planter, our host, was of an old Virginia family, and the room in which I slept was decorated with several family pictures in the costume of Charles the Second's time, whose faded colours and tarnished frames were in better keeping with the ancient exterior of the dwelling than the neat apartment wherein I passed the night.

After an early breakfast, our horses were led to the door by three slaves; our entertainer's, a fine blooded gelding, having his saddle covered by a bear-skin, of which his master's rifle had robbed the original owner. All being ready for mounting, it was not yet without considerable difficulty that we got permission to start—our friendly host, who the night before would scarcely hear of our leaving him in the morning, still insisting upon our "giving him at least a few days."

An hour after we saw for the first time a blue line of mountains darkening the horizon. From this point we rode for a short distance over a very indifferent soil, through a wood of oaks. The day was half-spent, by this time, and our host of the night before, having out of politeness accompanied us thus far on our way, was compelled to return. He insisted, however, upon piloting us out of the wood, and then taking a kind farewell, he struck the rowels in his blooded horse, who, unembarrassed by the baggage which encumbered our patient roadsters, wheeled with a snort upon his hind legs, and was instantly lost in the forest from which we had just emerged.

Turning the heads of our unwilling horses, we descended into the bed of a deep and rapid brook; and climbing a precipitous bank, after proceeding about a hundred yards, a rugged path, through a thick wood of stunted growth, brought us, after dodging about half an hour in its defiles, to a cabin on the brow of the hill along whose rough sides we had been for some time riding. A lad of sixteen, lightly dressed in loose drawers and a hunting-shirt, came to the door with evident unwillingness, after we had exercised our lungs for some time in stirring up the establishment. He stood in the entrance with one hand upon the half-open door, while the other seemed to be employed in keeping back a very pretty girl about his own age, who stood peering curiously over his shoulder, while she shielded with an old bonnet the flaring tallow candle that "shed its light" with any thing but "hospitable ray" across the humble threshold. All our suing for admission was vain; the lad's father and mother were absent, and had told him to admit no strangers to sleep in the house. We offered him money most liberally, and urged that the night was such as it would be cruel to turn a dog from the door, but it produced not the least effect; he only told us that the house we had passed was better able to take us than his father's; and that there was still one about a mile ahead, where we might get in; winding up every time with, "It don't signify, strangers, anyhow; if this was my house, I'd try and accommodate you, and so would father; but father's not here, and you can't come in."

I admired the boy's firmness, even while cursing the occasion of his constancy; but there was no help for us, unless we took the house by storm; and with some difficulty urging our horses from the door, we descended a steep bank, as the lad had directed us, and found ourselves in a few moments floundering in a swamp at the bottom. The night was pitchy dark, and the rain and wind seemed utterly to confuse our horses, to whose sagacity we surrendered ourselves, in tracking out the way.

Choosing the rocky hill-side in preference to the tangled swamp at the bottom, we bounced about among broken cliffs and fallen trees. We could no more; but seeking a faint light gleaming through the trees on a high bank bank above us, we shouted lustily for a light. We were answered by the lad who an hour before had denied us admission to his house, and in a few minutes a dozen pine-torches, in the hands of as many half-naked children, showered their red light from the steep bank, and flashed upon a broad rivulet that crept through the heavy underwood beneath it.

"Stranger," shouted the noble boy, "hold on till I come below. I haven't been able to sleep since I turned you from the door; and, come what may, you shall share what we've got to-night."

A single toss of his torch threw the light, as he finished speaking, upon a bold rock below him, and leaping upon the narrow but firm foothold, he let himself down into the copse below, bounded over the brook, and was by our side in a moment. The other children, approaching the edge of the bank, threw the glare of their blazing pine-knots over a narrow and more circuitous pathway; while, marshalled by their elder brother, we scrambled up the ascent, and soon gained the house. A few moments sufficed to secure our horses in the miserable collection of logs that served as a stable. There was nothing but a bundle or two of dried fodder for them to eat, but we rubbed them well with corncobs. The warmth created by the exercise did not make a share of the children's beds less acceptable, when, stripping off our wet clothing, we bestowed ourselves supperless beneath the covering.

Weary as we were, we could not help lying awake for some time. But at last the wooden clock, which through Yankee enterprise had found its way to this remote glen, struck the hour of ten, and the whole household being long since asleep, we suppressed the murmur of our voices, and were soon dreaming with the rest.

The lad to whom we had been indebted for a night's shelter made every possible apology, the next morning, for our meagre entertainment, by pleading extreme poverty; notwithstanding which, we found it very difficult to force any remuneration upon him. The day was unfavourable for travelling, but, we were compelled by the want of forage to change our quarters.

The post-town of Manchester (what a contemptible poverty of invention is displayed everywhere throughout the Union in borrowing the names of places fifty times over) consists of about half a dozen indifferently-built houses pitched here and there upon a pretty knoll. The paint—if it were ever there—has long been worn off the houses. The regular outlay of small sums for the little necessaries required by some hundred labourers employed in the salt-works keeps life flickering in one or two small stores; and the same quantum of capital is probably the circulating medium of the whole place.

It is now about ten o'clock, and looking out of the window, in the house of which I am writing, I can see a dozen industrious burghers dawdling about a bar-room opposite. No sound of riot or obstreperous mirth comes thence; and were it not for the guttural chuckle that gurgles now and then from the burly person of my landlord, you would hardly know that they were talking. They are just now changing their position, to study the points of that sorry-looking nag, whose gummy lips, green with half-chewed grass, seems sagging to the sand as his hollow neck droops to the full length of his bridle. An hour hence the steed will stand where he is still, but the group around him will have advanced with the shadows some five yards beyond the eaves: you may then see them curiously grouped upon the clump of logs which form a primitive kind of stile to the fence before the door, and the morning mist, which still hangs upon the hills around, having by that time disappeared, they will be in less doubt about the weather.

The appearance of two well-mounted and thoroughly-equipped travellers has caused quite a sensation in the village. The idea of persons travelling from motives of liberal curiosity cannot enter into the brains of the inhabitants: they insist upon setting down my companion and myself as Yankee pedlers; and as the familiarity of the people has already afforded us a good deal of quiet diversion, we are at no pains to dispel the illusion. A villager asked me yesterday, while looking at my fowling-piece, if I had "no more of them left"; while another inquired what price I "set upon the remaining one": the first question implying, I suppose, that we had been driving a trade in guns through the country; and the last presuming, as a matter of course, that a Yankee had no use for fire-arms.

"Are there any gentlemen, sir, among the Yankees?" asked quite a decent-looking man of me this morning. I *looked* at the fellow—"I hope no offence, sir," he added; "I mean by gentlemen, planters and such-like, that live as gentlemen do here."—"If you ask for information, my friend, I have never lived among the Yankees, but"—"To be sure there are," interrupted an old Irishman sitting by; "and two gentlemen to one to what there is here."—"Well, you see, stranger, I thought they were all pedlers; but how comes you to deny your country, if it isn't after all among the leavings of Nature's work?" I answered that I was from the State of New-York. "And what now do you call that but a part of Yankee-land?" replied this intelligent yeoman. Just then I heard mine host, calling out most lustily,—"Halloo, horse!" said old Boniface, slapping on the shoulder a broad-backed fellow that stood in the doorway, "Where's Yankee and Dutchee? the bacon and greens are smoking on the table, and I must take a glass of cool liquor with them before we sit down. Ah! there's my stout rifle-cracker; come along, Dutchee, my boy," added he, as L. made his appearance; and then to me, "Yankee, my tall fellow, a glass of old peach with us before dinner: smack! how it relishes! down with it all; it won't hurt a hair of your head; I've washed my mouth with it these forty years. And now, boys, in to dinner while the bacon's hot."

I had a long conversation this morning with a middle-aged country lawyer, upon western life and character, in which I gave my sentiments with great freedom; and though, like our countrymen in every part of the union, he was sufficiently exacting of the praise of strangers, he did not seem to take offence at some of my observations, which were not altogether palatable.

"Well, sir," he began, after bidding me good morning, "what do you think of *our country?*"

"It is a rich and beautiful one, sir."

"There's no two ways about that, sir; but aren't you surprised to see such a fine population?"

"You have certainly a fine-looking set of men, with good manners, and a great deal of natural intelligence."

"But their knowledge of things, sir, and the way in which they live,—don't you think our plain country people live in a very superior way, sir?"

"Have you ever been in the Northern or Eastern States, sir?—New-York or New-England?" I replied. While answering negatively, he gave a look of utter amazement at the idea of comparing those districts with that in which he lived. I then,—while doing justice to the many attractive points in the character of these mountaineers, their hardihood and frank courtesy to strangers, their easy address, and that terseness of expression and command of language which often strikes and interests you in the conversation of men who actually cannot read,—explained to him the superiority which greater industry and acquired knowledge of useful facts gives the northern man, of the same class, in providing comforts and conveniences for himself and family, and living in a style that approaches that of the independent planter of the west. But, countryman as he was, I could not persuade one who had probably, in western phrase, been "raised on hog and hominy," and kept all his life on "bacon and greens," of the advantages of a thoroughly-cultivated garden, a well-kept dairy, and flourishing poultry-yard; much less could I make him understand the charm which lay in neat enclosures, and a sheltered porch or piazza, with shrubbery clustering around it. He only replied, when I commented upon the fields, which I sometimes saw, that had run out from indolence or bad tillage, that "there was land enough to make new ones"; and added, as we placed ourselves at the breakfast-table, "that if the people did not live up to other people's ideas, they lived as well as they wanted to. They didn't want to make slaves of themselves; they were contented with living as their fathers lived before them."

I remembered, while passing him an old-fashioned salt-cellar over our frugal table, that he had Horace on his side, and could not but acknowledge that contentment was the all in all.

3¹

A Roving Reporter on the Frontier, 1837

Edmund Flagg appears never to have stayed in one place or at one job long. Born in Wiscasset, Maine, in 1815, and graduated from Bowdoin at twenty, he followed the course of many other New Englanders by migrating to the West. If, indeed, he had one place of residence, it was Louisville, Kentucky; and, if he worked in one capacity more than another, it was as a newspaper-man. In the course of a life which extended to 1890, he traveled much and produced plays, poems, newspaper articles, criticism, and novels. At one period he was even United States consul at Venice.

The Far-West, which he wrote for the Louisville Journal, *and published in book form in 1838, was the result of a trip, taken the year previous, down the Ohio River from Louisville into the Missouri and Illinois country. The two volumes are overconsciously "literary," and the material is often badly organized and diffuse. Unhappily, Flagg appears to have felt that, the more purple-colored adjectives were stacked against a noun, the more effective was the resulting description. Yet he undeniably did see much, especially in the more intimate life of the people; and, after an appropriate amount of blue-penciling and rearrangement, he exhibited an accurate and telling portrayal of frontier conditions.*

THE OHIO AND THE MISSISSIPPI

A drizzly, miserable rain had for some days been hovering, with prover-bial tenacity, over Louisville, the "City of the Falls," while the quay con-tinued to exhibit all that wild uproar and tumult which characterizes the steamboat commerce of the Western Valley. The landing at the time was thronged with steamers, and yet the incessant "boom, boom, boom," of the high-pressure engines, the shrill hiss of scalding steam, and the fitful port-song of the negro firemen rising ever and anon upon the breeze, gave notice of a constant augmentation to the number. Some, too, were getting under way, and their lower guards were thronged by emigrants with their household and agricultural utensils. Drays were rattling hither and thither over the rough pavement; Irish porters were cracking their whips and roaring alternate staves of blasphemy and song; clerks hurrying to and fro, with fluttering note-books, in all the fancied dignity of "brief authority"; hackney-coaches dashing down to the water's edge, apparently with no motive to the nervous man but noise; while at intervals, as if to fill up the pauses of the Babel, some incontinent steamer would hurl forth from the valves of her overcharged boilers one of those deafening, terrible blasts, echoing and re-echoing along the river-banks, and streets, and among the lofty buildings.

To one who has never visited the public wharves of the great cities of the West, it is no trivial task to convey an adequate idea of the spectacle they present. The commerce of the Eastern seaports and that of the Western Valley are utterly dissimilar; not more in the staples of intercourse than in the mode in which it is conducted; and, were one desirous of exhibiting to a friend from the Atlantic shore a picture of the prominent features which characterize commercial proceedings upon the Western waters, or, indeed, of Western character in its general outline, he could do no better than to place him in the wild uproar of the steamboat quay.

Steamers on the great waters of the West are well known to indulge no violently conscientious scruples upon the subject of punctuality. Hour after hour, therefore, still found us and left us amid the untold scenes and sounds of the public landing. It is true our doughty steamer ever and anon would puff and blow like a porpoise or a narwhale; and then would she swelter from every pore and quiver in every limb with the ponderous laboring of her huge enginery, and the steam would shrilly whistle and shriek like a spirit in its confinement, till at length she united her whirlwind voice to the general roar around; and all this indicated, indubitably, an intention to be off and away; but a knowing one was he who could determine *when*.

It was not until the afternoon was far advanced that we found ourselves fairly embarked. The finest site from which to view the city we found to be the channel of the Falls upon the Indiana side of the stream, called the *Indian* chute, to distinguish it from two others, called the *Middle* chute and the *Kentucky* chute. The prospect from this point is noble, though the uniformity of the structures, the fewness of the spires, the unimposing character of the public edifices, and the depression of the site upon which the city stands, give to it a monotonous, perhaps a lifeless aspect to the stranger.

The view of the Falls from the city, on the contrary, is one of beauty and romance. They are occasioned by a parapet of limestone extending quite across the stream, which is here about one mile in width; and when the water is low the whole chain sparkles with bubbling foam-bells. When the stream is full the descent is hardly perceptible but for the increased rapidity of the current, which varies from ten to fourteen miles an hour.[1] Owing to the height of the freshet, this was the case at the time when we descended them, and there was a wild air of romance about the dark rushing waters: and the green woodlands upon either shore; while the receding city, with its smoky roofs, its bustling quay, and the glitter and animation of an extended line of steamers, was alone necessary to fill up a scene for a limner.

Long before the dawn on the morning succeeding our departure we were roused from our rest by the hissing of steam and the rattling of machinery as our boat moved slowly out from beneath the high banks and lofty syca-mores of the river-side, where she had in safety been moored for the night, to resume her course. Withdrawing the curtain from the little rectangular window of my stateroom, the dark shadow of the forest was slumbering in calm magnificence upon the waters; and glancing upward my eye, the stars were beaming out in silvery brightness. The hated clang of the bell-boy was soon after heard resounding far and wide in querulous and deafening clamour throughout the cabins, vexing the dull ear of every drowsy man. The mists of night had not yet dispersed, and the rack and fog floated quietly upon the placid bosom of the stream.

There is not a stream upon the continent which, for the same distance rolls onward so calmly, and smoothly, and peacefully as the Ohio. Danger rarely visits its tranquil bosom, except from the storms of heaven or the reckless folly of man, and hardly a river in the world can vie with it in safety, utility, or beauty. Though subject to rapid and great elevations and depressions, its current is generally uniform, never furious. The forest-trees which skirt its banks are the largest in North America, while the variety is endless. Its allu-vial bottoms are broad, deep, and exhaustlessly fertile; its bluffs are often from three to four hundred feet in height; its breadth varies from one mile to three, and its navigation, since the improvements commenced, under the authority of Congress, by the enterprising Shreve, has become safe and easy. The classification of obstructions is the following: *snags,* trees anchored by their roots; fragments of trees of various forms and magnitude; *wreck-heaps,*

---

1. It is only at high stages of the river that boats even of a smaller class can pass over the Falls. At other times they go through the "Louisville and Portland Canal."

PUBLIC LANDING, CINCINNATI

consisting of several of these stumps, and logs, and branches of trees lodged in one place; *rocks,* which have rolled from the cliffs, and varying from ten to one hundred cubic feet in size; and *sunken boats,* principally flat-boats laden with coal. The last remains one of the most serious obstacles to the navigation of the Ohio. Many steamers have been damaged by striking the wrecks of the *Baltimore,* the *Roanoke,* the *William Hulburt,* and other craft, which were themselves snagged; while keel and flat-boats without number have been lost from the same cause.

Several thousands of the obstacles mentioned have been removed since improvements were commenced, and accidents from this cause are now less frequent. Some of the snags torn up from the bed of the stream, where they probably for ages had been buried, are said to have exceeded a diameter of six feet at the root, and were upwards of an hundred feet in length. The removal of these obstructions on the Ohio presents a difficulty and an expense not encountered upon the Mississippi. In the latter streams, the root of the snag, when eradicated, is deposited in some deep pool or bayou along the banks, and immediately imbeds itself in alluvial deposit; but on the Ohio, owing to the nature of its banks in most of its course, there is no opportunity for such a disposal, and the boatmen are forced to blast the logs with gun-powder to prevent them from again forming obstructions. The cutting down and clearing away of all leaning and fallen trees from the banks constitutes an essential feature in the scheme of improvement. The construction of stone dams, by which to concentrate into a single channel all the waters of the river, where they are divided by islands, or from other causes are spread over a broad extent, is another operation now in execution. When all improvements are completed, it is believed that the navigation of the "beautiful Ohio" will answer every purpose of commerce and the traveller, from its source to its mouth, at the lowest stages of the water.

Thump, thump, crash! One hour longer, and I was at length completely roused from a troublous slumber by our boat coming to dead stop. Casting a glance from the window, the bright flashing of moonlight showed the whole surface of the stream covered with drift-wood, and, on inquiry, I learned that the branches of an enormous oak, some sixty feet in length, had become entangled with one of the paddle-wheels of our steamer, and forbade all advance.

We were soon once more in motion; the morning mists were dispersing, the sun rose up behind the forests. We passed many pleasant little villages along the banks, and it was delightful to remove from the noise, and heat, and confusion below to the lofty *hurricane deck,* and lounge away hour after hour in gazing upon the varied and beautiful scenes which presented themselves in constant succession to the eye. Now we were gliding quietly on through the long island chutes, where the daylight was dim, and the enormous forest-trees bowed themselves over us; then we were sweeping rapidly over the broad reaches of the stream, miles in extent; again we were winding through the mazy labyrinth of islets which fleckered the placid surface of the stream, and from time to time we passed the lonely cabin of the emigrant

A STORM ON LAKE ERIE

beneath the venerable and aged sycamores. Here and there, as we glided on, we met some relic of those ancient and primitive species of river-craft which once assumed ascendency over the waters of the West.

In the early era of the navigation of the Ohio, the species of craft in use were numberless, and many of them of a most whimsical and amusing description. The first was the barge, sometimes of an hundred tons' burden, which required twenty men to force it up against the current a distance of six or seven miles a day; next the keel-boat, of smaller size and lighter construction, yet in use for the purposes of inland commerce; then the Kentucky flat, or broad-horn of the emigrant; the enormous ark, in magnitude and proportion approximating to that of the patriarch; the fairy pirogue of the French voyageur; the birch caique of the Indian, and log skiffs, gondolas, and dug-outs of the pioneer without name and number. But since the introduction of steam upon the Western waters, most of these unique and primitive contrivances have disappeared; and with them, too, has gone that singular race of men who were their navigators.

During the morning of our third day upon the Ohio we passed, among others, the villages of *Rome, Troy,* and Rockport. The latter is the most considerable place of the three, notwithstanding *imposing* titles. Here terminates that series of beautiful bluffs commencing at the confluence of the mountain-streams. A new geological formation commences of a bolder character than any before; and the face of the country gradually assumes those features which are found near the mouth of the river. Passing Green River with its emerald waters, its "Diamond Island," the largest in the Ohio, and said to be *haunted,* and very many thriving villages, among which was Hendersonville, for some time the residence of Audubon, the ornithologist, we found ourselves near midday at the mouth of the smiling Wabash, its high bluffs crowned with groves of the walnut and pecan. The confluence of the streams is at a beautiful angle; and, on observing the scene, the traveller will remark that the forests upon one bank are superior in magnitude to those on the other, though of the same species. The appearance is somewhat singular, and the fact is to be accounted for only from the reason that the soil differs in alluvial character. It has been thought that no stream in the world, for its length and magnitude, drains a more fertile and beautiful country than the Wabash and its tributaries. Emigrants are rapidly settling its banks, and a route has been projected for uniting by canal its waters with those of Lake Erie.

About ten miles below the mouth of the Wabash is situated the village of Shawneetown. The buildings, among which are a very conspicuous bank, courthouse, and a land-office for the southern district of Illinois, are scattered along upon a gently elevated bottom, swelling up from the river to the bluffs in the rear, but sometimes submerged, from this latter cause it has formerly been subject to disease; it is now considered healthy; it is the chief commercial port in this section of the state, and is the principal point of debarkation for emigrants for the distant West.

From this spot the river stretches away in a long delightful reach, studded with beautiful islands, among which "Hurricane Island," a very large one, is chief. Passing the mouth of the Cumberland River with its green island, once the rendezvous of Aaron Burr and his chivalrous band, we next reached the town of Paducah, at the outlet of the Tennessee. This is a place of importance, though deemed unhealthy.

It was sunset when we arrived at the confluence of the rivers. Though the hour was a delightful one, the scene did not present that aspect of vastness and sublimity which was anticipated from the celebrity of the streams. For some miles before uniting its waters with the Mississippi, the Ohio presents a dull and uninteresting appearance. It is no longer the clear, sparkling stream, with bluffs and woodland painted on its surface; the volume of its channel is greatly increased by its union with two of its principal tributaries, and its waters are turbid; its banks are low, inundated, and clothed with dark groves of deciduous forest-trees, and the only sounds which issue from their depths to greet the traveller's ear are the hoarse croaking of frogs, or the dull monotony of countless choirs of moschetoes. Thus rolls on the river through the dullest, dreariest, most uninviting region imaginable, until it sweeps away in a direction nearly southeast, and meets the venerable Father of the West advancing to its embrace. The volume of water in each seems nearly the same; the Ohio exceeds a little in breadth, their currents oppose to each other an equal resistance, and the resultant of the forces is a vast lake more than two miles in breadth, where the united waters slumber quietly and magnificently onward for leagues in a common bed. On the right come rolling in the turbid floods of the Mississippi; and on looking upon it for the first time with preconceived ideas of the magnitude of the mightiest river on the globe, the spectator is always disappointed. He considers only its breadth when compared with the Ohio, without adverting to its vast depth. The Ohio sweeps in majestically from the north, and its clear waters flow on for miles without an intimate union with its turbid conqueror. The characteristics of the two streams are distinctly marked at their junction and long after. The banks of both are low and swampy, totally unfit for culture or habitation. "Willow Point," which projects itself into the confluence, presents an elevation of twenty feet; yet, in unusual inundations, it is completely buried six feet below the surface, and the agitated waters, rolling together their masses, form an enormous lake. How strange that the confluence of the waters of such streams, in their onward rolling to the deep, should take place at almost the only stage in their course devoid entirely of interest to the eye or the fancy.

It was late before we had passed the confluence of the Ohio with the dark-rolling tide of the "endless river," and the darkness became gradually so dense that doubts were entertained as to the prudence of attempting to stem the mighty current of the Mississippi on such a night. These, however, were overruled; and sweeping around the low peninsula of Cairo, our steamer met the torrent and quivered in every limb. A convulsed, motionless struggle ensued, in which the heavy laboring of the engine, the shrill whistle of the safety-valve, the quick, querulous crackling of the furnaces, the tumultuous rushing of the wheels, and the stern roar of the scape-pipe, gave evidence of the fearful power summoned up to overcome the flood. At length we began very slowly to ascend the stream. Our speed was about five miles an hour, and the force of the current nearly the same, which so impeded advancement that it requires as long to ascend from the confluence to St. Louis as to descend to the same point from the Falls, though the distance is less than half. All night our steamer urged herself slowly onward against the current, and the morning found us threading a narrow channel amid a cluster of islands, from whose dense foliage the night-mists were rising and settling in dim confusion. Near the middle of the stream, above this collection, lays a very large island, comprising eight or ten thousand acres, called English Island. The stream here expands itself to the breadth of four miles.

A company of emigrants, in course of the morning, were landed from our boat at a desolate-looking spot upon the Missouri shore; men, women, and little ones, with slaves, household stuff, pots, kettles, dogs, implements of husbandry, and all the paraphernalia of the backwood's farm heaped up promiscuously in a heterogeneous mass among the undergrowth beneath the lofty trees. A similar party from the State of Vermont were, during our passage, landed near the mouth of the Wabash, one of whom was a pretty, delicate female, with an infant boy in her arms. They had been *deck-passengers,* and we had seen none of them before; yet their situation could not but excite interest in their welfare.

It was yet early in the morning of our first day upon the Mississippi that we found ourselves beneath the stately bluff upon which stands the old village of Cape Girardeau, and some thirty miles further on, the waters of the Muddy River enter the Mississippi from Illinois.

A few miles above the Big Muddy stands out from the Missouri shore a huge perpendicular column of limestone, of cylindrical formation, about one hundred feet in circumference at the base, and in heighth one hundred and fifty feet, called the "Grand Tower." Upon its summit rests a thin stratum of vegetable mold, supporting a shaggy crown of rifted cedars. This is the first of that celebrated range of heighths upon the Mississippi usually pointed out to the tourist, springing in isolated masses from the river's brink upon either side, and presenting to the eye a succession of objects singularly grotesque. There are said to exist, at this point upon the Mississippi, indications of a huge parapet of limestone having once extended across the stream, which must have formed a tremendous cataract, and effectually inundated all the alluvion above. At low stages of water ragged shelves, which render the navigation dangerous, are still to be seen. The whole region bears palpable evidence of having been subjected, ages since, to powerful volcanic and diluvial action; and neither the Neptunian or Vulcanian theory can advance a superior claim.[2]

For a long time after entering the dangerous defile in the vicinity of the *Grand Tower,* through which the current rushes like a racehorse, our steamer writhed and groaned against the torrent, hardly advancing a foot. At length, as if by a single tremendous effort, which caused her to quiver and vibrate to her centre, an onward impetus was gained, the boat shot forward, the rapids were overcome, and then, by chance, commenced one of those perilous feats of rivalry frequent upon the Western waters, A RACE. Directly before us, a steamer of a large class, deeply laden, was roaring and struggling against the torrent under her highest pressure. During our passage we had several times passed and repassed each other, either boat was delayed at the various wood-yards along the route; but now, as the evening came on, and we found ourselves gaining upon our antagonist, the excitement of emulation flushed every cheek. The passengers and crew hung clustering, in breathless interest, upon the galleries and the boiler deck, wherever a post for advantageous view presented; while the hissing valves, the quick, heavy stroke of the piston, the sharp clatter of the *eccentric,* and the cool determination of the pale engineer, as he glided like a spectre among the fearful elements of destruction, gave evidence that the challenge was accepted. A dense mist came on, and the exhausted steamers were hauled up at midnight beneath the venerable trees upon the banks of the stream. On the first breakings of dawn all was again in motion. But alas! alas! in spite of all the strivings of our valorous steamer, it soon became but too evident that her mighty rival must prevail, as she came rushing up in our wake. Like a civil, well-behaved rival, she speeded on, hurling forth a triple bob-major of curses at us as she passed, doubtless by way of salvo, and disappeared behind a point. When to this circumstance is added that a long-winded racer of a mail-boat soon after swept past us in her onward course, and left us far in the rear, I shall be believed when it is stated that the steamer on which we were embarked was distinguished for anything but speed.

As we were passing Ste. Genevieve an accident occurred which had nearly proved fatal to our boat, if not to the lives of all on board her. A race which took place between another steamer and our own has been noticed. In some unaccountable manner, this boat, which then passed us, fell again in the rear, and now, for the last hour, had been coming up in our wake under high steam. On overtaking us, she attempted, contrary to all rules and regulations

2. [A reference to two conflicting opinions among early geologists as to the causes of changes in the earth's surface.—ED.]

for the navigation of the river provided, to pass between our boat and the bank beneath which we were moving; an outrage which, had it been persisted in a moment longer than was fortunately the case, would have sent us to the bottom. For a single instant, as she came rushing on, contact seemed inevitable; and, as her force was far superior to our own, and the recklessness of many who have the guidance of Western steamers was well known to us all, the passengers stood clustering around upon the decks, some pale with apprehension, and others with firearms in their hands, flushed with excitement, and prepared to render back prompt retribution on the first aggression. The pilot of the hostile boat, from his exposed situation and the virulent feelings against him, would have met with certain death; and he, consequently, contrary to the express injunctions of the master, reversed the motion of the wheels just at the instant to avoid the fatal encounter. The sole cause for this outrage, we subsequently learned, was a private pique existing between the pilots of the respective steamers.

However this may be, our passage seemed fraught with adventure, of which this is but an incident. After the event mentioned, having composed the agitation consequent, we had retired to our berths, and were just buried in profound sleep, when crash—our boat's bow struck heavily against a snag, which, glancing along the bottom, threw her at once upon her beams, and all the passengers on the elevated side from their berths. No serious injury was sustained, though alarm and confusion enough were excited by such an unceremonious turn-out.

One bright morning, when all the others of our company had bestowed themselves in their berths because of the intolerable heat, I took occasion to visit the sooty Charon in the purgatorial realms over which he wielded the sceptre. "Grievous work this building fires under a sun like that," was the salutation, as my friend the fireman had just completed the toilsome operation once more of stuffing the furnace, while floods of perspiration were coursing down a chest hairy as Esau's and as brawny. Hereupon honest Charon lifted up his face, and drawing a dingy shirt sleeve with emphasis athwart his eyes, bleared with smut, responded, "Ay, ay, sir; it's a sin to Moses, such a trade"; and seizing incontinently upon a fragment of tin, he scooped up a quantity of the turbid fluid through which we were moving, and deep, deep was the potation which went gurgling down his throat.

It was a bright morning, on the fifth day of an exceedingly long passage, that we found ourselves approaching St. Louis. At about noon we were gliding beneath the broad ensign floating from the flagstaff of Jefferson Barracks. The site of the quadrangle of the barracks enclosing the parade is the broad summit of a noble bluff, swelling up from the water, while the outbuildings are scattered picturesquely along the interval beneath. Passing the venerable village of Carondelet, with its white-washed cottages crumbling with years, and old Cahokia buried in the forests of the opposite bank, the gray walls of the Arsenal next stood out before us in the rear of its beautiful esplanade. Sweeping onward, the lofty spire and dusky walls of St. Louis Cathedral, on rounding a river bend, opened upon the eye, the gilded crucifix gleaming in the sunlight from its lofty summit; and then the glittering cupolas and church domes, and the fresh aspect of private residences, mingling with the bright foliage of forest-trees, recalled vividly the beautiful "Mistress of the North." For beauty of outline in distant view, St. Louis is deservedly famed. The extended range of limestone warehouses circling the shore give to the city a grandeur of aspect, while the dense-rolling forest-tops stretching away in the rear, and the funereal grove of steamboat-pipes lining the quay, altogether make up a combination of features novel and picturesque. As we approached the landing all the uproar and confusion of a steamboat port was before us, and our own arrival added to the bustle.

THE ILLINOIS PRAIRIES AND THEIR SETTLERS

The afternoon has been one of those dreary, drizzly, disagreeable seasons which relax the nerves and ride like an incubus upon the spirits; and my route has conducted me over a broad-spread, desolate plain; for, lovely as may appear the prairie when its bright flowerets and its tall grass tops are nodding in the sunlight, it is a melancholy place when the sky is beclouded and the rain is falling. There is a certain indescribable sensation of loneliness, which steals over the mind of the solitary traveller when he finds himself alone in the heart of these boundless plains which he cannot away with; and the approach to a forest is hailed with pleasure, as serving to quiet, with the vague idea of *Society,* this sense of dreariness and desertion.

The celebrated "Grand Prairie," upon which I was now entering, stretched itself away to the south thirty miles, a vast, unbroken meadow; and one may conceive, not describe, the terrible fury of a storm-wind sweeping over a surface like this. As the morning advanced, the violence of the tempest lulled into fitful gusts; and, as the centre of the vast amphitheatre was attained, a scene of grandeur and magnificence opened to my eye such as it never before had looked upon. Elevated upon a full roll of the prairie, the glance ranged over a scene of seemingly limitless extent; for upon every side, for the first time in my ramble, the deep blue line of the horizon and the darker hue of the waving verdure blended into one. All was bold and impressive, reposing in the stern, majestic solitude of Nature. As the sun reached the meridian the winds went down, and the stillness of death hung over the prairie. The utter desolateness of such a scene is indescribable. Not a solitary tree to intercept the vision or to break the monotony; not a sound to cheer the ear or relieve the desolation; not a living thing in all that vast wild plain.

The relief to the picture afforded by the discovery of man's habitation can hardly be described. It was near nightfall when, wearied by the fatigue of riding and drenched with mist, I reached the log-cabin of an old pioneer from Virginia, beneath whose lowly roof-tree I am seated at this present writing; and though hardly the most sumptuous edifice of which it has been my lot to be an inmate, yet with no unenviable anticipations am I looking forward to hearty refreshment and to sound slumber upon the couch by my side.

There are few objects to be met with in the backwoods of the West more unique and picturesque than the dwelling of the emigrant. After selecting an elevated spot as a site for building, a cabin or a log-house which is somewhat of an improvement upon the first—is erected in the following manner. A sufficient number of straight trees, of a size convenient for removing, are felled, slightly hewn upon the opposite sides, and the extremities notched or mortised with the axe. They are then piled upon each other so that the extremities lock together; and a single or double edifice is constructed, agreeable to the taste or ability of the builder. Ordinarily the cabin consists of two quadrangular apartments, separated by a broad area between, connected by a common floor, and covered by a common roof, presenting a parallelogram triple the length of its width. The better of these apartments is usually appropriated to the entertainment of the casual guest, and is furnished with several beds and some articles of rude furniture to correspond. The open area constitutes the ordinary sitting and eating apartment of the family in fine weather; and, from its coolness, affords a delightful retreat. The intervals between the logs are stuffed with fragments of wood or stone, and plastered with mud or mortar, and the chimney is constructed much in the same manner. The roof is covered with thin clapboards of oak or ash, and, in lieu of nails, transverse pieces of timber retain them in their places. Thousands of cabins are thus constructed, without a particle of iron or even a common plank. The rough clapboards give to the roof almost the shaggy aspect of thatch at a little distance, but they render it impermeable to even the heaviest and most protracted rain-storms. A rude gallery often extends along one or both sides of the building, adding much to its coolness in summer and to its warmth in winter by the protection afforded from sun and snow. The floor is constructed of short, thick planks, technically termed "puncheons," which are confined by wooden pins; and, though hardly smooth enough for a ballroom, yet well answer every purpose for a dwelling, and effectually resist moisture and cold. The apertures are usually cut with a view to free ventilation, and the chimneys stand at the extremities outside the walls of the cabin. A few pounds of nails, a few boxes of glass, a few hundred feet of lumber, and a few day's assistance of a house-carpenter, would, of course, contribute not a little to the comfort of the *shieling;*[3] but neither of these are indispensable.

In rear of the premises rise the out-buildings; stables, corn-crib, meat-house, &c., all of them quite as perfect in structure as the dwelling itself, and quite as comfortable for residence. If to all this we add a well, walled up with a section of a hollow cotton-wood, a cellar or cave in the earth for a pantry, a zigzag rail fence enclosing the whole clearing, a dozen acres of Indian corn bristling up beyond, a small garden and orchard, and a host of swine, cattle, poultry, and naked children about the door, and the *tout ensemble* of a backwoods farmhouse is complete. Minor circumstances vary, of course, with the peculiarities of the country and the origin of the settlers; but the principal features of the picture everywhere prevail. The present mode of cultivation sweeps off vast quantities of timber; but it must soon be superseded. Houses of brick and stone will take the place of log-cabins; hedgerows will supply that of rail enclosures, while coal for fuel will be a substitute for wood.

At Upper Alton my visit was not a protracted one. In a few hours, having gathered up my *fixens* and mounted my *creetur,* I was threading a narrow pathway through the forest. The trees, most of them lofty elms, in many places for miles locked together their giant branches over the road, forming a delightful screen from the sunbeams; but it was found by no means the easiest imaginable task, after once entering upon the direct route, to continue upon it. This is a peculiarity of Western roads. The commencement may be uniform enough, but the traveller soon finds his path diverging all at once in several different directions, like the radii of a circle, with no assignable cause therefor, and not the slightest reason presenting itself why he should select one of them in preference to half a dozen others, equally good or bad. And the sequel often shows him that there in reality existed no more cause of preference than was apparent; for, after a few tortuosities through the forest, for varieties sake, the paths all terminate in the same route. The obstacle of a tree, a stump, a decaying log, or a sandbank often splits the path as if it were a flowing stream; and then the traveller takes upon himself to exercise the reserved right of radiating to any point of the compass he may

3. [I.e., "shealing," a hut or cabin.—ED.]

think proper, provided always that he succeeds in clearing the obstruction.

But there was one feature of the scene through which I was passing that struck me as peculiarly imposing, and to which I have not yet referred. I allude to the enormous, almost preternatural magnitude of the wild-grape vine, and its tortuosity. I have more than once, in the course of my wanderings, remarked the peculiarities of these vast parasites; but such is the unrivalled fertility, and the depth of soil that vegetation of every kind there attains a size and proportion elsewhere almost unknown. Six or seven of these vast vegetable serpents are usually beheld leaping forth with a broad whirl from the mould at the foot of tree, and then, writhing, and twining, and twisting among themselves into all imaginable forms, at length away they start, all at once and together, in different directions for the summit, around which they immediately clasp their bodies, one over the other, and swing depending in festoons on every side. Some of these vines, when old and dried up by the elements, are amazingly strong; more so, perhaps, than a hempen hawser of the same diameter.

Endless thickets of the wild plum and the blackberry, interlaced and matted together by the young grape-vines streaming with gorgeous clusters, were to be seen stretching for miles along the plain. Such boundless profusion of wild fruit I had never seen before. Vast groves of the ruby crab-apple, the golden persimmon, the black and white mulberry, and the wild cherry, were sprinkled with their rainbow hues in isolated masses over the prairie, or extended themselves in long luxurious streaks glowing in the sun. The pawpaw, too, with its luscious, pulpy fruit; the peach, the pear, and the quince, all thrive in wild luxuriance here; while of the nuts, the pecan or Choctaw nut, the hickory, and the black walnut, are chief.

As for grapes, the indigenous vines are prolific; and the fruit is *said* to be so excellent, that wine might be, and even has been, made from them, and has been exported by the early French in such quantities to France, that the trade was prohibited lest the sale of a staple of that kingdom should be injured! But all this is undoubtedly exaggeration, if no more. Although the grape and the wine of southern Illinois have long been the theme of the traveller through that delightful region, yet from personal observation I am confident they are *now* by no means of such importance, and from good authority am inclined to think they *never* were so. As to the manufacture of wine becoming a matter interesting to commerce, there is no probability of that. A kind of liquor was formerly made in some quantities from what is called the *winter grape,* common to the same latitude in many portions of the United States, but it is said to have been a very indifferent beverage.

The early air of morning was intensely chilling as I pursued my solitary way through the old woods; but, as the sun went up the heavens, and the path emerged upon the open prairie, the transition was astonishing. It impresses one like passing from the damp, gloomy closeness of a cavern into the genial sunshine of a flower-garden.

For the first time during my tour in Illinois was my horse now severely troubled by that terrible insect, so notorious all over the West, the large green-bottle prairie-fly, called the "green-head." My attention was first attracted to it by observing several gouts of fresh blood upon the rein; and, glancing at my horse's neck, my surprise was great at beholding an orifice quite as large as that produced by the *fleam,* from which the dark fluid was freely streaming. The instant one of these fearful insects plants itself upon a horse's body, the rider is made aware of the circumstance by a peculiar restlessness of the animal in every limb, which soon becomes a perfect agony, while the sweat flows forth at every pore. The last year [1835] was a remarkable one for countless swarms of these flies; many animals were *killed* by them; and at one season it was even dangerous to venture across the broader prairies except before sunrise or after nightfall. In the early settlement of the county, these insects were so troublesome as in a great measure to retard the cultivation of the prairies; but, within a few years, a yellow insect larger than the "green-head" has made its appearance wherever the latter was found, and, from its sweeping destruction of the annoying fly, has been called the "horse-guard." These form burrows by penetrating the earth to some depth, and there depositing the slaughtered "green-heads." It is stated that animals become so well aware of the relief afforded by these insects and of their presence, that the traveller recognizes their arrival at once by the quiet tranquillity which succeeds the former agitation. Ploughing upon the prairies was formerly much delayed by these insects, and heavy netting was requisite for the protection of the oxen.

The region through which, for most of the day, I journeyed was that, of very extensive application in the West, styled "Barrens," by no means implying unproductiveness of soil, but a species of surface of heterogeneous character, uniting prairie with *timber* or forest, and usually a description of land as fertile, healthy, and well-watered as may be found. The misnomer is said to have derived its origin from the early settlers of that section of Kentucky south of Green River, which, presenting only a scanty, dwarfish growth of timber, was deemed of necessity *barren,* in the true acceptation of the term. This soil there and elsewhere is now considered better adapted to every variety of produce and the vicissitudes of climate than even the deep mould of the prairies and river-bottoms. The rapidity with which a young forest springs forward, when the annual fires have once been stopped in this species of land, is said to be astonishing; and the first appearance of timber upon the prairies gives it the character, to some extent, of barrens. Beneath the trees is spread out a mossy turf, free from thickets, but variegated by the gaudy petals of the heliotrope, and the bright crimson buds of the dwarf-sumach in the hollows. Indeed, some of the most lovely scenery of the West is beheld in the landscapes of these barrens or "oak openings," as they are more appropriately styled. For miles the traveller wanders on, through a magnificence of park scenery on every side, with all the diversity of the slope, and swell, and meadow of human taste and skill. Interminable avenues stretch away farther than the eye can reach, while at intervals through the foliage flashes out the unruffled surface of a pellucid lake. There are many of these circular lakes or "sinkholes," as they are termed in Western dialect, which, as they possess no inlet, seem supplied by subterraneous springs or from the clouds. The outline is that of an inverted cone, as if formed by the action of whirling waters; and, as sinkholes exist in great numbers in the vicinity of the rivers, and possess an outlet at the bottom through a substratum of porous limestone, the idea is abundantly confirmed.

Near nightfall one evening I found myself in the middle of a vast extended plain, where the eye roves unconfined over the scene, for miles unrelieved by a stump, or a tree, or a thicket, and meets only the deep blue of the horizon on every side, blending with the billowy foliage of the distant woodland. Descending a graceful slope, even this object is lost, and a boundless landscape of blue above and green below is unfolded to the traveller's vision; again approaching the summit of the succeeding slope, the forest rises in clear outline in the margin of the vast panorama.

I had travelled not many miles when a black cloud spread itself rapidly over the sky, and in a few moments the thunder began to bellow, the lightnings to flash, and the rain to fall in torrents. Luckily enough for me, I found myself in the neighbourhood of man's habitation. Leaping hastily from my steed, and lending him an impetus with my riding-whip which carried him safely beneath a hospitable shed which stood thereby, I betook myself, without ceremony or delay, to the mansion house itself, glad enough to find its roof above me as the first big rain-drops came splashing to the ground. The little edifice was tenanted by three females and divers flaxen-pated, sun-bleached urchins of all ages and sizes, and, at the moment of my entrance, all in high dudgeon, because, forsooth, they were not to be permitted to drench themselves in the anticipated shower.

"Well!" was my exclamation, in true Yankee fashion, as I bowed my head

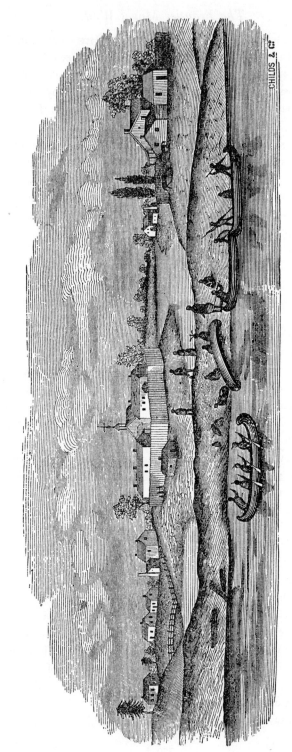

CHICAGO IN 1820

low in entering the humble postern; "we're going to get pretty considerable of a sprinkling, I guess." "I reckon," was the sententious response of the most motherly-seeming of the three women, at the same time vociferating to the three larger of the children, "Oh, there, you Bill, Sall, Polly, honeys, get the gentleman a cheer! Walk in, sir; set down and take a seat!" This evolution of "setting down and taking a seat" was at length successfully effected, after sundry manoeuvrings by way of planting the three pedestals of the uncouth tripod upon the same plane, and avoiding the fearful yawnings in the *puncheon* floor. When all was at length quiet, I improved the opportunity of gazing about me to explore the curious habitation into which I found myself inserted.

The structure, about twenty feet square, had originally been constructed of rough logs, the interstices stuffed with fragments of wood and stone, and daubed with clay; the chimney was built up of sticks laid crosswise, and plastered with the same material to resist the fire. Such had been the backwoodsman's cabin in its primitive prime; but time and the elements had been busy with the little edifice, and sadly had it suffered. Window or casement was there none, neither was there need thereof; for the hingeless door stood ever open, the clay was disappearing from the intervals between the logs, and the huge fireplace of stone exhibited yawning apertures, abundantly sufficient for all the purposes of light and ventilation to the single apartment of the building. The *puncheon* floor I have alluded to, and it corresponded well with the roof of the cabin, which had never, in its best estate, been designed to resist the peltings of such a pitiless torrent as was now assailing it. The water soon began to trickle in little rivulets upon my shoulders, and my only alternative was my umbrella for shelter. The furniture of the apartment consisted of two plank-erections designed for bedsteads, which, with a tall clothes-press, divers rude boxes, and a side-saddle, occupied a better moiety of the arena; while a rough table, a shelf against the wall, upon which stood a water-pail, a gourd, and a few broken trenchers, completed the household paraphernalia of this most unique of habitations. A half-consumed flitch of bacon suspended in the chimney, and a huge iron pot upon the fire, from which issued a savoury indication of the seething mess within, completes the "still-life" of the picture. Upon one of the beds reclined one of the females to avoid the rain; a second was alternating her attentions between her infant and her needle; while the third, a buxom young baggage, who, by-the-by, was on a visit to her sister, was busying herself in the culinary occupations of the household, much the chief portion of which consisted in watching the huge dinner-pot aforesaid, with its savoury contents.

After remaining nearly two hours in the cabin, in hopes that the storm would abate, I concluded that, since my umbrella was no sinecure *within* doors, it might as well be put in requisition *without,* and mounted my steed, though the rain was yet falling.

PRAIRIE TOWNS OF ILLINOIS

It was evening, at the close of a sultry day, that the village of Carrolton appeared before me among the trees. I was struck with the quiet air of simple elegance which seemed to pervade the place, though its general outlines are those of every other Western village I have visited. One broad, regular street extends through the town, upon either side of which stand the stores and better class of private residences; while in the back-ground, scattered promiscuously along the transverse avenues, are log-cabins surrounded by corn-fields, much like those in the villages of the French. Three sides of the town are bounded by forest, while the fourth opens upon the prairie called "String Prairie." In the centre of the village, upon the principal street, is reserved a square, in the middle of which stands the courthouse, with other public structures adjacent, and the stores and hotels along its sides. One thing in Carrolton which struck me as a little singular, was the unusual diversity of religious denominations. Of these there are not less than five or six; three of which have churches, and a fourth is setting itself in order to build; and all this in a village of hardly one thousand inhabitants. The courthouse is a handsome edifice of brick, two stories, with a neat spire. The neighbouring region is fertile and healthy. This is, indeed, strictly an agricultural village; and, so far as my own observation extended, little attention is paid or taste manifested for anything else.

About a dozen miles north of Carrolton is situated the village of White-hall, a flourishing settlement in the prairie's edge, from the centre of which, some miles distant, it may be seen. Three years ago the spot was an uncultivated waste; the town has now two houses of worship, a school, an incorporation for a seminary, two taverns, six hundred inhabitants, and a steam mill to feed them withal. A few miles from this place, on the outskirts of another small settlement, I was met by a company of emigrants from Western New-York. The women and children were piled upon the top of the household stuff with about as much ceremony as if they constituted a portion thereof, in a huge lumbering baggage-wagon, around which dangled suspended pots and kettles, dutch-ovens, and tin-kitchens, cheese-roasters and bread-toasters, all in admired confusion, jangling harsh discord. The cart-wheels themselves, as they gyrated upon the parched axles, "grated harsh thunder." In the van of the cavalcade strode soberly on the patriarch of the family, with his elder sons, axe upon shoulder, rifle in hand. For six weeks had the wanderers been travelling, and a weary, bedusted-looking race were they, that emigrant family.

The rapidity with which a Western village goes forward, and begins to assume importance among the nations, after having once been born and christened, is amazing. The mushrooms of a summer's night are but a fit parallel to the growth of the prairie-village of the Far West. Of all this I was forcibly reminded in passing through quite a town upon my route named Manchester, where I dined, and which, if my worthy landlord was not incorrect, two years before could hardly boast a log-cabin. It is now a thriving place.

The rapidity with which this state has been peopled is wonderful, especially in its northern counties. In the year 1821, that section of country embraced within the present limits of Morgan county numbered but twenty families; in 1830 its population was nearly fourteen thousand, and cannot now be estimated at less than seventeen thousand! Many of the settlers are natives of the New-England States; and with them have brought those habits of industrious sobriety for which the North has ever been distinguished.

It was near the close of the day that the extent and frequency of the farms on either side, the more finished structure of the houses, the regularity of enclosures, the multitude of vehicles of every description by which I was encountered, and the dusty, hoof-beaten thoroughfare over which I was travelling, all reminded me that I was drawing nigh to Jacksonville, the principal town in Illinois. Passing the "Diamond Grove," a beautiful forest-island of nearly a thousand acres, the traveller catches a view of the distant village stretching away along the northern horizon. He soon enters an extended avenue, perfectly uniform for several miles, leading on to the town. Beautiful meadows and harvest-fields on either side sweep off beyond the reach of the eye, their neat white cottages and palings peeping through the enamelled foliage. To the left, upon a swelling upland at the distance of some miles, are beheld the brick edifices of "Illinois College," relieved by a dark grove of oaks resting against the western sky. These large buildings, together with the other numerous public structures, imposingly situated, give to the place a dignified, city-like aspect in distant view. After a ride of more than a mile within the immediate suburbs of the town, the traveller ascends a slight elevation, and the next moment finds himself in the public square, surrounded on every side by stores and dwellings, carts and carriages, market-people, horses, and hotels.

It is only ten or twelve years since the town site of Jacksonville, now, perhaps, the most flourishing inland village in Illinois, was first *laid off;* and it is but within the past five years that its present unprecedented advancement can be dated. The public square in the centre of the town is of noble dimensions, occupied by a handsome courthouse and a market, both of brick, and its sides filled up with dwelling-houses, stores, law-offices, a church, bank, and hotel. From this point radiate streets and avenues in all directions: one through each side of every angle near its vertex, and one through the middle of every side; so that the town-plat is completely cut up into rectangles. If I mistake not in my description, it will be perceived that the public square of Jacksonville may be entered at no less than twelve distinct avenues. In addition to the spacious courthouse, the public buildings consist of three or four churches. One of these, belonging to the Congregational order, betrays much correct taste and, like the doctrines of the sect which worships here, there is an air of severe, dignified elegance about the whole structure, pleasing as it is rare. The number of Congregational churches in the West is exceedingly small.

Jacksonville is largely made up of emigrants from the North; and they have brought with them many of their customs and peculiarities. The State of Illinois may, indeed, be truly considered the New-England of the West. In many respects it is more congenial than any other to the character and prejudices of the Northern emigrant. It is not a slave state; internal improvement is the grand feature of its civil polity; and the measures for the universal diffusion of intellectual, moral, and religious culture are in active progression. In Henry county, in the northern section of the state, two town-plats have within the past year been laid off for colonies of emigrants from Connecticut, which intend removing in the ensuing fall, accompanied each by their minister, physician, lawyer, and with all the various artisans of mechanical labour necessary for such communities. The settlements are to be called Wethersfield and Andover. Active measures for securing the blessings of education, religion, temperance, etc. have already been taken.

The edifices of "Illinois College," to which I have before alluded, are situated upon a beautiful eminence one mile west of the village. During my stay at Jacksonville I visited several times this pleasant spot. Connected with the college buildings are extensive grounds; and students, at their option, may devote a portion of each day to manual labor in the workshop or on the farm. Some individuals have, it is said, in this manner defrayed all the expenses of their education. Illinois College has been founded but five or six years, yet it is now one of the most flourishing institutions west of the mountains. The library consists of nearly two thousand volumes, and its chymical apparatus is sufficient. The faculty are five in number, and its first class was graduated two years since. No one can doubt the vast influence this seminary is destined to exert, not only upon this beautiful region of country and this state, but over the whole great Western Valley. It owes its origin to the noble enterprise of seven young men, graduates of Yale College, whose names another age will enroll among our Harvards and our Bowdoins.

To the left of the college buildings is situated the lordly residence of Governor Duncan, surrounded by its extensive grounds. There are other fine edifices scattered here and there upon the eminence, among which the beautiful little cottage of Mr. C., brother to the great orator of the West, holds a conspicuous station. Society in Jacksonville is said to be superior to any in the state. It is of cast decidedly moral, and possesses much literary taste. This is betrayed in the number of its schools and churches; its lyceum, circulating library, and periodicals. In fine, there are few spots in the West, and none in Illinois, which to the *Northern* emigrant present stronger attractions than the town of Jacksonville.

At Jacksonville I tarried only a few days; but during that short period I met with a few things of tramontane origin, strange enough to my Yankee notions. It was the season approaching the annual election of representatives for the state and national councils, and on one of the days to which I have alluded the political candidates of various creeds *addressed the people;* that is—for the benefit of the uninitiated be it stated—each one made manifest what great things he had done for the people in times past, and promised to do greater things, should the dear people, in the overflowing of their kindness, be pleased to let their choice fall upon him. This is a custom of universal prevalence in the Southern and Western states, and much is urged in its support; yet, sure it is, in no way could a Northern candidate more utterly defeat his election than by attempting to pursue the same. The charge of *self-electioneering* is, indeed, a powerful engine often employed by political partisans.

The candidates, upon the occasion of which I am speaking, were six or seven in number: and though I was not permitted to listen to the *eloquence* of all, some of these harangues are said to have been powerful productions, especially that of Mr. S. The day was exceedingly sultry, and Mr. W., candidate for the State Senate, was on the *stump,* in shape of a huge meat-block at one corner of the market-house, when I entered. He was a broad-faced, farmer-like personage, with features embrowned by exposure, and hands hardened by honourable toil; with a huge rent, moreover, athwart his left shoulder-blade—a badge of democracy I presume, and either neglected or produced there for the occasion; verily, he did, in all charity, seem to have hung on his worst rigging, and that, too, for no other reason than to demonstrate the democracy aforesaid, and his affection for the *sans-culottes*. His speech, though garnished with some rhodomontade, was, upon the whole, a sensible production. I could hardly restrain a smile, however, at one of the worthy man's figures, in which he likened himself to "the *morning sun*, mounting a stump to scatter the mists which had been gathering around his fair fame." Close upon the heels of this *ruse* followed a beautiful simile— "a people free as the wild breezes of their own broad prairies!" The candidates alternated according to their political creeds, and denounced each other in no very measured terms. The approaching election was found, indeed, to be the prevailing topic of thought and conversation all over the land; insomuch that the writer, himself an unassuming wayfarer, was more than once, strangely enough, mistaken for a *candidate* as he rode through the country, and was everywhere *catechumened* as to the articles of his political faith. Internal Improvement seems now to be the order of the day in Northern Illinois. This was the hobby of most of the stump-speakers; and the projected railway from Jacksonville to the river was under sober consideration.

Before the dawn I had left the farmhouse where I had passed the night, and was thridding the dark old forest on my route to Springfield. The day which succeeded was a fine one, and I journeyed leisurely onward, until near noon, when a flashing cupola above the trees reminded me I was approaching Springfield. Owing to its unfavourable situation and the fewness of its public structures, this town, though one of the most important in the state, presents not that imposing aspect to the stranger's eye which some more inconsiderable villages can boast. Its location is the border of an extensive prairie, adorned with excellent farms, and stretching away on every side to the blue line of distant forest. This town, like Jacksonville, was laid out ten or twelve years since, but for a long while contained only a few scattered log cabins: all its present wealth or importance dates from the last six years. Though inferior in many respects to its neighbour and rival, yet such is its location by nature that it can hardly fail of becoming a place of extensive business and crowded population; while its geographically central situation seems to designate it as the capital of the state. An elegant statehouse is now erecting, and the seat of government is to be located here in 1840. The public square, a green, pleasant lawn, enclosed by a railing, contains the courthouse and a market, both fine structures of brick: the sides are lined with handsome edifices. Most of the buildings are small, however, and the humble log cabin not infrequently meets the eye. Among the public structures are a jail, and several houses of worship. Society is said to be excellent, and the place can boast much literary taste.

It was cool when I left Springfield, and now, after the fatigues of a pleasant day's ride, I am seated beneath the piazza of a neat farmhouse in the edge of the forest, looking upon a broad landscape of prairie. My landlord, a high-minded, haughty Virginia emigrant, bitterly complains, forsooth, in the absence of slave-labour, he is forced to cultivate his own farm; and though, by the aid of a Dutchman, he has made a pretty place of it, yet he vows by all he loves to lay his bones within the boundaries of the "Ancient Dominion."

After taking breakfast, I continued my journey over the undulating plains until near the middle of the afternoon, when I reached Vandalia, the capital of Illinois. The town is approached from the north, through a scattered forest, separating it from the prairies; and its unusually large and isolated buildings, few in number as they are, stationed here and there upon the eminences of the broken surface, gives the place a singularly novel aspect viewed from the adjacent heights. There is but little of scenic attraction about the place, and still less of the picturesque. Such huge structures as are here beheld, in a town so inconsiderable in extent, present an unnatural and forced aspect. Such, at all events, were my "first impressions" on entering the village.

As I drew nigh to the huge white tavern, a host of people were swarming the doors; and, from certain uncouth noises which from time to time went up from the midst thereof, not an inconsiderable portion of the worthy multitude seemed to have succeeded in rendering themselves gloriously tipsy in honour of the glorious Fourth. There was one keen, bilious-looking genius in linsey-woolsey, with a face, in its intoxicated state, like a red-hot tomahawk, whom I regarded with special admiration as high-priest of the bacchanal; and so fierce and high were his objurgations, that the idea with some force presented itself, whether he had not screamed his lean and hungry visage to its present hatchet-like proportions.

Having effected a retreat from the abominations of the bar-room, I had retired to a chamber in the most quiet corner of the mansion, and had seated myself to indite an epistle, when a rap at the door announced the presence of mine host, leading along an old yeoman whom I had noticed among the revellers; and, having given him a ceremonious introduction, withdrew. To what circumstances I was indebted for this unexpected honour, I was puzzling to divine, when the old gentleman, after a preface of clearings of the throat and scratchings of the head, gave me briefly to understand, much to my admiration, that I was believed to be neither more nor less than an "Agent for a Western Land Speculating Company of the North," etc., and then, in a confidential tone, before a syllable of negation or affirmation could be offered, that he "owned a certain tract of land, so many acres prairie, so many timber, so many cultivated, so many wild," etc. The sequel was anticipated by undeceiving the farmer forthwith, though with no little difficulty. The cause of this mistake I subsequently discovered. On the tavern register in the bar-room I had entered as my residence my native home at the North. No sooner had the traveller turned from the register than the sagacious host and his compeer brandy-bibbers turned towards it; and being unable to conceive any reasonable excuse for a man to be wandering so far from home except for lucre's sake, the conclusion at once and irresistibly followed that the stranger was a land-speculator, and it required not many moments for such a wildfire idea to run through such an inflammable mass of curiosity.

With the situation and appearance of Vandalia I was not much prepossessed; indeed, I was somewhat disappointed. Though not prepared for anything very striking, yet in the capital of a state we always anticipate something, if not superior or equal, at least not inferior to the neighbouring towns of less note. Its site is an elevated, undulating tract upon the west bank of the Kaskaskia, and was once heavily timbered, as are now its suburbs. The streets are of liberal breadth—some of them not less than eighty feet from kerb to kerb—enclosing an elevated public square nearly in the centre of the village, which a little expenditure of time and money might render a delightful promenade. The public edifices are very inconsiderable, consisting of an ordinary structure of brick for legislative purposes; a similar building originally erected as a banking establishment, but now occupied by the offices of the state authorities; a Presbyterian Church, with cupola and bell, besides a number of lesser buildings for purposes of worship and education. A handsome structure of stone for a bank is, however, in progress, which when completed, with other public buildings in contemplation, will add much to the aspect of the place.

Here also the Cumberland Road is permanently located and partially constructed. This road is projected eighty feet in breadth, with a central carriage-path of thirty feet, elevated above all standing water, and in no instance to exceed three degrees from a perfect level. The work has been commenced along the whole line, and is under various stages of advancement; for most of the way it is perfectly *direct*. The bridges are to be of limestone, and of massive structure, the base of the abutments being equal in depth to one third of their altitude. The work was for a while suspended, for the purpose of investigating former operations, and subsequently through failure of an appropriation from Congress; but a grant has since been voted sufficient to complete the undertaking so far as it is now projected. West of Vandalia the route is not yet located, though repeated surveys with reference to this object have been made. Upon this road I journeyed some miles; and even in its present unfinished condition, it gives evidence of its enormous character.

An historical and antiquarian society has here existed for about ten years, and its published proceedings evince much research and information. "The Illinois Magazine" was the name of an ably-conducted periodical commenced at this town some years since, and prosperously carried on by Judge Hall.

It is passing strange that a town like Vandalia, with all the natural and artificial advantages it possesses; located nearly twenty years ago, by state authority, expressly as the seat of government; situated upon the banks of a fine stream, which small expense would render navigable for steamers, and in the heart of a healthy and fertile region, should have increased and flourished no more than seems to have been the case. Vandalia will continue the seat of government until the year 1840; when, it is to be moved to Springfield, where an appropriation of $50,000 has been made for a state-house now in progress.

32

"We Air an Almighty People": The Old Northwest, 1848

*J*ohn L. Peyton was born near Staunton, Virginia, in 1824. He received *a degree in law from the University of Virginia in 1844. Four years later he was traveling through the Old Northwest and in 1853 took up a three-year residence in Illinois. Two books resulted from these western sojourns: A Statistical View of the State of Illinois (1855) and, much later, Over the Alleghanies (1869), from which the present excerpts are taken. When the Civil War broke, Peyton, like so many southerners, opposed secession but* *stood loyally by his state when it left the Union. He acted as agent for North Carolina in England and, after the war, chose to remain in England until 1876. His subsequent career was largely literary; he wrote no less than six works, most of which are ephemeral, though the two-volume* American Crisis *(1867) is more substantial. He died in 1896.*

Over the Alleghanies *is an excellent account of life and manners in the Old Northwest in 1848. Written with humor, it offers the comments of a good observer without any pretensions to profundity or subtlety. Despite the fact that it was written twenty years after the events described, though from notes made at the time, it captures vividly a sense of being "on the spot," at the moment of writing.*

A STAGE COACH JOURNEY ACROSS OHIO

The Xenia station, where I secured a ticket by the first train to Columbus, was a rude shed constructed of timber, and everything connected with the spot indicated the haste in which it was built. Approaching, I discovered seated upon a log a well-dressed, grey-haired gentleman of about fifty, with a florid complexion and *retroussé* nose. Saluting me with characteristic western politeness, he inquired somewhat abruptly, "where I was bound?" Replying Chicago, he seemed unexpectedly surprised and pleased, saying, "I shall be your travelling companion, as it's my own destination."

From Xenia we travelled to Columbus, the capital of the state, and thence to Tiffin, a small town which had recently sprung up like a mushroom amid the decaying logs and stumps of a forest. From this point to Sandusky on Lake Erie, there was no railway, only a stage coach. These Ohio coaches were something between a French diligence and a London omnibus, and the particular one in which we now took our seats, was neither wind nor water-tight. It was incrusted with mud until its original colour could no longer be discovered. The leather aprons, to cover the open panels in bad weather, where they are secured on buttons, were so dried and shrivelled by alternate wet and heat, that they scarcely covered half the opening. Had they been of sufficient length they could not have been buttoned—the buttons were gone, and the button-holes split. The door was an inch too small on every side for the aperture it was designed to close. This, however, was not considered important, as the four panes of glass which formed the upper half were broken. During the previous night it had rained, and the vehicle having been exposed without cover to the storm, the seats were soaked with water and were now dripping like a wet sponge. The wind being high and squally, coming over the plain, which extends from the lake shore, the curtains flapped in our faces every moment, literally giving us gratis a shower bath. In all probability we should have had a plunge bath also, but for several holes in the floor which let the water escape. The prospect was none of the pleasantest, far from cheerful, but the Illinoisian seating himself in a corner, upon the top of his carpet bag, and drawing his overcoat around his person, prepared for whatever might follow. For myself, I preferred a seat by the driver. The other passengers having made themselves "snug," according to the advice of the driver, we dashed forward to the music of his voice, the screeching of wheels, and the flapping of the aged curtains.

Pursuing what was called our road, though the traces of a road were slight, we soon found that we were in the midst of a dense forest, with no guide but the blazes, or cut spots upon the sides of the trees. After going about fifteen miles, all such slight traces as existed of the road were lost, and to add to our embarrassment the blazes forked or diverged in opposite directions. The driver now acknowledged that he had taken the wrong road.

We set off again over roots and stumps, across creeks and swamps, up hill and down hill, and by following the blazes of the trees finally returned to the main road. No sooner out of one difficulty, however, than we plunged into another. At this point one of our wheels gave way, and we were turned into the road to think of an expedient for getting on with three. The driver was not at all disconcerted, seemed quite at home in the emergency, and proceeded at once to supply the defect. Felling a small tree, he took from it a log ten feet long, one end of this was, with the assistance of the passengers, secured upon the front axle, and passed back so as to hold up the body of the coach sufficiently high to admit of the wheel on the opposite side turning upon its spindle. This done, the passengers were coolly informed that it would be necessary for them to make the residue of the journey, a distance of twenty-five miles, on foot. To my surprise, every one took this announcement with perfect good temper, whereupon the journey was resumed. At the end of three miles we came upon a farmhouse, and here the driver borrowed a wheel from the farmer's ox-cart, which was placed upon our coach, and we found ourselves unexpectedly seated once more in the vehicle. It must be confessed, too, after our walk of three miles, it seemed decidedly more comfortable. And this, though we soon entered upon "a corderoy-road," on which the jolting is truly formidable. A corderoy-road, as all Western travellers know, consists of small trees stripped of their boughs, and laid across the road, touching one another, and without any covering of earth. As the marsh underneath is of various degrees of solidity, the whole road assumed a kind of undulating appearance.

Somewhat in this fashion we made the entire journey of forty miles to Sandusky, having had three upsets and one turn-over. No lives were lost, no limbs broken, and consequently no one thought seriously of such an every-day accident. Arrived at Sandusky, we were informed that the boat from Buffalo for Detroit, in which we purposed sailing, would not be in port till the following morning. The clerk of the hotel offered us a pen, and we proceeded, in accordance with the custom of the country, to register our names, abodes, and destinations. The knight of the carpet-bag, taking the pen, wrote his name thus: *Buckner S. Morris,* Chicago, Illinois. Thus for the first time I became acquainted with the name of my travelling companion, as he with mine.

The country round about Sandusky is monotonous and uninteresting, resembling the salt marshes of the sea coast. The town itself was so new that it amounted to little more than a hamlet of scattered houses for the most part built of boards and timber. Everything about the spot looked bald, naked and raw, and there was a disagreeable angular freshness about the newly built houses. The fences round the fields in the neighbourhood were built of rails, (rifted logs) with the green, sappy bark clinging to them, the ground under tillage was still rife with trees, tall as heretofore, but shorn of their verdant tops by the process of girdling, which puts an end to vegetable life, but allows the trunk and branches to remain like so many ghosts in the wilderness: undrained swamps stagnated in the midst of corn-fields; and the roads were barely passable, except towards the centre of the town and near the port. No attention was paid to neatness and finish of any kind, and comfort, indoors or out of doors was impossible. Its chief importance arose from the harbour, where vessels navigating the lakes occasionally called. Good, firm roads however were projected, and had been commenced in town and the immediate neighbourhood. Some villas had already been erected, and others were rising, and while Sandusky was a comfortless place, it was obvious that she only awaited her share of the immense bodies emigrating west, to become a place of no small consequence. The monotonous character of the surrounding scenery, the existence during a certain portion of the year of intermittent fevers and ague, and the necessity for drainage, deterred many from stopping here, who would otherwise have been glad to cut short a western journey.

While there, for the steamer not arriving at the appointed time, we were detained two days, I walked much in the neighbourhood. On one occasion I entered the neat, comfortable house of a mechanic. Here I saw a tall handsome German, of about twenty-five years of age, trembling and shuddering with the chill which precedes the fever in the ague. He was a miserable, woebegone looking object, or rather a fine object under distressing circumstances.

In half an hour when I returned to the house, his chill had passed and his face was flushed with fever. He informed me that he had been induced to leave an excellent situation in Pennsylvania, in ignorance of the real state of things in Ohio. That he believed from the pictures drawn of it, that it was the true *El Dorado,* and had found himself a dupe, with the ague for his pains. He did not, however, intend to return, but on the opening of the next spring, when his family would join him, to proceed further west, and when he had secured a healthy situation to "squat" as a frontiersman, sports-

THE WESTERN STAGE

man and farmer. "The want of health was," he said, "the only difficulty in the way of the early improvement and rapid progress of this portion of Ohio."

"You will not find," he continued, "precious stones or metals here, but innumerable dangers, discomforts and toil; but these are inseparable from a new country, and if surmounted by industry any man can accumulate a fortune. The soil is of extraordinary fertility, and the facilities for market by the lake are all that could be desired."

I quite agreed with the young German, and saw at once that he possessed the judgment and perseverance which insure success. In the course of our conversation, he informed me that he was a native of Dresden in Saxony— that his name was Otto Paul, and that he had received a liberal education, but was so infatuated by a desire for travel, and by a fondness for hunting and shooting, and was of such an adventurous disposition that he had determined to emigrate to America. Before taking this step, he married a girl to whom he had been long attached. Sailing from Bremen they landed at Baltimore. Here he remained two years teaching in a public school, during which time his wife became the mother of two children; he then removed to Chambersburg, Pennsylvania, where his wife and children continued. In the spring they would join him, as also a brother was expected from Europe, and the party would then proceed together to the far west. Their means were small, but he had sufficient to make himself comfortable, and should make the soil contribute the rest. The history of this young man is that of thousands of others who have sought homes on the western prairies of America.

POLITICS IN DETROIT

Detroit was an ill-built, rambling town of about twelve thousand inhabitants, situated on the Straits connecting Lakes Erie, St. Clair, and Huron, and separating Canada and the United States.

As the home of General Lewis Cass, who was at this moment the democratic candidate for the Presidency, Detroit was attracting the public attention in no small degree. All eyes were turned to it. Thousands were visiting it to offer the General kind wishes, or to entice him into the expression of opinions, which might be used to damage his election. Between the crowds of friends and enemies hastening to the place, the summer tourists and the mere idlers, who came from curiosity, Detroit was decidedly lively, the theatre and music halls doing a stunning business.

An accident to the machinery of our boat caused a delay of three days. This no one seemed to regret; for said one of the passengers bound for Mackinaw, however long our detention, it is at the company's expense. I certainly did not regret the delay, as it gave me an opportunity to deliver some letters of introduction which caused me to be most kindly received.

One of my newly made friends, a Mr. L—— and himself a connection of General Cass, suggested to me that almost every stranger on a visit to Detroit called upon the General, and said if I was disposed to do so, the General would consider it a compliment, and he, as one of his personal and political friends and a connection of the family, would take pleasure in giving me an introduction. It gave me much satisfaction to accept his polite offer. Accordingly, early one morning we called—a visit at an unseasonable hour was rendered necessary by my engagements—and found the General expecting us. At the time, he was in his library, knee deep, so to speak, in letters from all parts of the country, which he had been three hours engaged, with the assistance of two secretaries, in endeavouring to answer. He gave me a hearty welcome, and we conversed with him more than an hour.

General Cass was at this time a remarkable looking man, short but of corpulent stature, with an expressive and boldly wrought countenance exhibiting great decision and firmness in lineaments. The whole face partook more of severity than mildness, though in disposition he was really most kind and generous. He was a man of fine abilities and great mental activity, with more than common skill and eloquence as a political debater.

During our interview, General Cass referred to what is called the "Monroe doctrine," and the manifest destiny of the United States, and expressed the opinion that the United States would swallow up Mexico.

At this point, somewhat surprised at the extravagance, as I then thought, of his views, I said,

"Not the whole of it, General?"

"Yes," he replied, "the whole of it, and it will not affect her digestion either. Her maw will not only contain Mexico, but Cuba and all the islands in the Atlantic and Pacific which naturally belong to this continent. It is our destiny to spread over the whole of North America, and to absorb the adjacent islands, and the sooner it is done, the better it will be for us, for the afflicted and miserably governed people of Mexico, and for the world."

The conversation continued for some time, after this manner, when the General, who knew I was from Virginia, with the prescience of an old politician, who felt that his views might be reported, and come back like bread cast upon the waters after many days, made numerous complimentary remarks about the Old Dominion.

The night before leaving Detroit, I dropped into the Court House, where there was a political meeting. It seems that before my arrival, one of the speakers had referred to a want of patriotism on the part of one of the rising politicians who was present from the country. This young gentleman was engaged in a personal vindication, and before quitting the room, expressed himself as follows:—

"Fellow-citizens, my competitor has told you of the services he rendered in the late war. I will follow his example and tell you mine. He basely insinuates that I was deaf to the voice of honour in this crisis. The truth is, I acted an humble part in that memorable contest. When the tocsin of war summoned the chivalry of the West to rally to the defence of the nation, I, fellow-citizens, animated by that patriotic spirit that glows in every American's bosom, hired a substitute for that war, and the bones of that man now lie bleaching on the plains of Mexico."

Leaving the hall, where this lively style of oratory was progressing, our attention was attracted by a kind of "guerilla" discussion between two outsiders, surrounded by their admirers. One of these men, it seems, was defending state rights doctrines, and warming in the cause, finally expressed himself in favour of slavery.

"What is that you say?" broke in a Michigander.

"Why," replied the first person, "that I not only don't oppose, but am in favour of slavery—think it the best thing for the nigger, the master, and the unhealthy climate of the South."

"Then take that for your reward," said the Michigander, who hurled a stone at his head. A yell was now raised, and the mob seized the advocate of slavery, and proceeded to cuff, kick, and beat him shamefully—in fact, were only prevented from murdering him on the spot by the intercession of Mr. Morris, myself, and a few chance passers. After great trouble we succeeded in getting the bruised and bleeding victim away. As for police, none were to be found. And this, I inquired of Mr. Morris, is what you call a free country?—a country in which a man dare not express an opinion which is unpopular, without the prospect of a bloody nose and broken head.

"The less you say on that subject, the better," responded Mr. Morris, "for you know a Yankee who went to the South and spoke against slavery, would soon be rode out of the country on a rail, clothed in a coat of tar and feathers, that is to say, if he escaped a hempen noose."

"But," said I, "there is a great difference between the two cases. If a man came South and indulged publicly in that kind of conversation, it would dissatisfy and excite ignorant slaves, and lead to insurrection and bloodshed—in the cause of peace and safety it cannot be allowed, any more than it could be tolerated for a man to teach treason, or preach immorality."

"The truth is," said Mr. Morris, "Out West we do pretty much as we please, and so do you down South. I am not going to discuss the question with you—our's is a country of free thought, free speech, and the free fight, further, this deponent saith not." Thus our evening terminated.

FRONTIER MISSOURI

An unexpected and singularly good opportunity presenting, I determined to avail myself of it to see something of the interior of Missouri, or "Misery," as disappointed emigrants call the State.

Mr. Bates was about to attend a session of the Court at Jefferson, and not only invited, but urged me to accompany him, which I consented to do. Going aboard a steamer destined for Jefferson, we found the deck crowded with passengers, consisting, in addition to a few legal gentlemen, of Indians and emigrants. One of these red-men was an Osage chief, returning with a deputation of his tribe from a visit to their great father, the President of the United States. He was an interesting and striking object, was six feet high, straight as an arrow and perfect in his proportions. On the top of his head he wore a tuft of hair, (the rest of the head was bare) with a cord tightly tied around it in which were stuck some bright coloured feathers, selected from a peacock's tail, intermixed with the bristles of the porcupine. Like the rest of his companions, he wore a dark green toga or hunting shirt, yellow leather breeches, a little the worse for wear—no stockings, and high-laced moccasins. Near him was one of his trusted companions, a chief also, dressed in the same style, and as handsome a lad of sixteen as I ever remember to have seen, his son and successor. These three chiefs constituted a separate group. The rest of the picturesque looking deputation were smoking and soon some were sleeping on the open deck, as if it were the middle of the night. Taciturn and reserved, they presented a sad picture, and no one could look on their vacant countenances without feeling that they were a melancholy and expiring race. Thus they were proceeding towards their homes, in the track of the setting sun, which, unlike their sinking fortunes, was going down to rise again.

Quite different in their countenances, but even more squalid in their poverty, was a party of savage-looking German immigrants, who had recently arrived in New York, and had been dispatched to the far West to find homes in the solitude of the prairies. The head of this party was a short, stout Bavarian, who wore a blue tail-coat, covered with grease, without a single button and only a remnant of one tail. A pair of ancient cazinet trousers, in tatters at the feet, patched in the rudest manner on the knees, and unpatched in unmentionable parts where they ought to have been—an ancient leather waistcoat and an apology for a pair of boots. Scarcely any of the men, women or children in this party were better dressed, but they had been supplied in New York and St. Louis with a few agricultural implements and carpenters' tools, and expected before winter to build themselves comfortable timber houses, and to get a considerable body of land prepared for a spring crop. Fortunately they were to join a party of their countrymen who had preceded them by two years and were prospering in their new home. Notwithstanding, therefore, their poverty and present distress, they were cheered by the hope of something better, and consequently unlike the poor Indians, their rough bearded faces shone through their dirt with cheerfulness. A half-dozen raw-boned Kentuckians, with iron constitutions and nerves apparently of whip cord, their wives and children, were also emigrating. A few natives of the West made up the list of passengers.

The Kentuckians were of the farmer class, and men of some means, of hard heads, and probably harder hearts, determined to succeed. Whittling and whistling, they passed their time in a "devil-may-care" style, which seemed to gain them admirers. It soon became evident that they would turn both German and Indian to their account. Before we had gone half the distance, two of the Germans with their families had abandoned their party and joined the Kentuckians, who promised them shelter and immediate wages. One of the Kentuckians spoke German with tolerable facility, and another managed to communicate with the Indians, and they smoked the calumet together incessantly—the calumet, too, loaded with Missouri tobacco, the most potent and, to me, the most offensive in the world. From these appearances, I did not doubt but that these children of the woods would be made in some way useful to the native-born citizens. This could not be done, however, without at the same time bettering their own condition, and advancing the common country of all.

Notwithstanding the force of the current, the numerous islands, the snags, sawyers, and other obstructions, our gallant boat, under the impetus of a high pressure engine, kept steadily upon her course, and in due time we arrived at our destination, Jefferson City, the capital of Missouri, Tuesday the 24th of October, 1848.

Landing, we proceeded to the principal hotel, and found it entirely deserted. Entering the public room, and seeing no bell, or other means of announcing our arrival, we rapped loudly upon the inner doors hoping to attract attention. Disappointed in this, we proceeded to the back yard, where we encountered a superannuated negress hastening to the rescue, who invited us to re-enter the house and make ourselves at home. She apologised for the state of affairs, saying that every one belonging to the establishment was absent at a camp meeting. The hotel was flanked by two rows of one story timber rooms, and in one of these rows we were each accommodated with a separate chamber, the negress hospitably inviting us to occupy those we liked best. About the time we had indicated our choice, the landlady appeared with her daughters—there was no landlord in the case. Information had reached her of the arrival of the boat, and she rushed home at the top of her speed. This worthy widow, with the aid of her daughters, and a negro porter, who belonged to the establishment, stowed our luggage away, lighted jocund fires on our hearths, and, in due season, placed a Missouri dinner upon the table-d'hote. This particular Missouri dinner consisted of boiled bacon and greens, a haunch of venison, and a wild turkey, with coffee for those who liked it, and whiskey for all.

Jefferson, distant from St. Louis, one hundred and forty miles, was one of those straggling Western villages where it was difficult to say when the village terminated and the country commenced. The streets were unpaved, six inches deep with dust in the summer, and knee deep with mud in the winter. Dust, dirt, and mud, and the effects of dust, dirt and mud were everywhere perceptible. The houses were spattered with thick layers of mud, and the people seemed for the most part to have wallowed in the mire. The session of Court attracted a considerable number of country people to the town, and these were principally collected about a miserable, naked-looking edifice made of mud in the form of brick, called the Court House, where a set of half educated muddy-headed lawyers, make a muddle in attempting to make the "wrong side appear the better cause." A rougher set of citizens, whether regarded with reference to dress, manners or physical appearance, separately or combined, could not be imagined. Bear-skin caps, Mackinaw blankets, leather leggings, old Bess rifles and hunting knives, entered into their dress and equipments. Tall, square-shouldered, broad-chested, stout men, made up of bone and gristle, they drank whiskey, chewed tobacco, and while waiting for the opening of Court, engaged in athletic sports in front of the temple of Thetis. These sports consisted of throwing heavy weights, jumping, wrestling, and boxing. These powerful men, thus encountering each other in trials of physical strength, recalled the athletes of old. Their general good humour, and the excellent temper with which they bore their reverses was admirable, until towards evening, when fiery liquor caused many to lose their heads.

A more cheerless, comfortless, wretched place cannot be imagined than the Court House, which, however, was soon filled after the judge took his seat. The Court was not unfrequently adjourned for a buffalo hunt, and the business of the day was always despatched, that the judge and bar might spend a part of the afternoon pitching quoits. Their evenings were passed over the whist-table, or in political discussions conducted amidst clouds of tobacco smoke. In these after dinner discussions, they often indulged in roseate views of the future of the United States, and prognosticated as time developed the power, of what the Editor of the Jefferson paper, Mr. Windett (a Yankee importation), called "our Almighty country," universal dominion for her. The general form of expression with this knight of the quill, who was leading the Western mind through his Missouri organ, was,

"Yes, sir, we *air* an Almighty *people*."

AN ILLINOIS INN

Mr. Bull's hotel was a frame building with only three rooms, and standing upon the bleak and timberless prairie, looked wretchedly cheerless and miserable. Entering the house, however, I found the temperature almost oppressive, the heat being produced by a closed stove, plied with coals taken from a surface vein passing through his garden. To counteract the effects of the heat, I divested myself of fur over-coat, gloves and cap, and taking a glass of warm whiskey and milk, settled myself in a corner while Mrs. Bull and her daughters prepared supper in the adjoining room, which was called the kitchen.

Mr. Bull now emerged with two free and independent citizens from the basement story, and the parties quickly settled themselves in the neighbourhood of the stove and proceeded to discuss the Presidential election. None of the party saluted nor took the slightest notice of my presence, nor in their vituperation and abuse of their political adversaries did they seem to care what might be my sentiments. These two free and independent citizens would in any other country but America have been called servants, but here they were styled "helps," and considered that they were conferring a very great favour upon Mr. Bull by assisting in his farming operations at thirty dollars each month, their employer finding bed and board.

I had not been long in the room, when I found that, notwithstanding the stove which was now nearly at a white heat, a certain sensation of chillness was creeping over me from having laid aside my furs. Rising to take a turn around the chamber, I inquired for my sleigh-driver. Mr. Bull now deigned to speak and said he was attending to his horses, and in the course of a few minutes he made his appearance. The free and independent citizens had pointed out the stable and the corn, and then left him to take care of his own cattle. The sleigh-driver, who was owner of the horses, knew the customs of the country too well to expect any assistance, and had proceeded with characteristic energy to groom his own stud. He now took a seat with the others, and helping himself to a quid of tobacco—they were all chewing—proceeded to give his views on the political affairs of the country.

A warm discussion arose between the *parti carré,* for the sleigh-driver turned out to be a Whig, and this was kept up till supper, which was announced in this wise—Mrs. Bull, calling from the kitchen to her lesser half, said—

"John!" (No response). "You John B-u-l-l! stop that nonsense about old Zack Tailer, and come to your supper. What does Giniril Tailer care for such chaw-bacons as you! The hominey's spili'. Fetch in the gem'man what drove the sleigh, and tell that 'er young 'un his supper's waitin'."

Mr. Bull turned his red eyes and heavy countenance upon me, and pronounced, with a growl, a single, but magic word—

"Supper!"

The party then rose and proceeded to the table, "that 'er young 'un" at the head of the file. The two ploughmen quietly took the seats of honour, to the right and left of Mr. and Mrs. Bull, a distinction I was glad to accord them, while I entered in earnest upon venison steak, fried hominy, and hot coffee, flanked by the Misses Bull, who were not bad company.

Before supper was over, our party was increased by what I suppose I ought to call Mr. Bull's calves, in the form of three stalwart sons, varying in age, from sixteen to twenty-two. These young men had been all day, not-withstanding the weather, working in a piece of wood, getting out fencing timber to enclose ground for a spring crop.

During the winter months, the boys, as old Bull called these young giants, expected to prepare, and in the spring to put up sufficient fencing to enclose several hundred acres of land, all of which they intended to plant in Indian corn, and they estimated the crop at much more than they could gather, but after securing a supply for bread, horses, pigs, poultry, &c., they intended turning in a herd of bullocks to feed upon it, and when these were fat, to drive them to Chicago, where there were already a few butchers engaged in salting and packing beef for export. By this plan on the year's operations, these boys expected each to clear "a pile of tin," and with this to operate on, they would be prepared to commence the world as the heads of families.

The eldest son had already prepared the timber for a log hut, which was to be erected in the spring, when he was to be married to Nancy Elphinstone, the daughter of a squatter, or prairie farmer, living a half mile distant. Mrs. Bull informed me that Nannie was a strong, industrious young woman, who would attend to Jim's house and business in the best manner, and make him a capital wife. That she could cook, wash, sew, knit, milk, churn, do any and every thing required of a Western wife, and didn't want much help either. Jim, at any rate, seemed well pleased at the prospect of possessing her, and remained in the kitchen, where I also preferred stopping.

Mr. Bull, sen., the sleigh-driver, and the two free and independent voters now retired to the public room or parlour, or whatever it may have been called. In the kitchen I sat listening to the conversation of Mrs. Bull and her children, while the three young men swallowed the food before them with the avidity of persons ravenous through extreme hunger. Their work, they said, gave them an appetite, the cold another, and the last was voracious.

Before going to bed, Mrs. Bull prepared for all a strengthening draught, consisting of whiskey, maple syrup, nutmeg, and boiling water, the whole dashed with rum. It was a nice draught—no thin, miserable stuff, but a warm, generous fluid. I required no pressing invitation to partake of it. Soon after indulging in a glass, a pleasant glow was diffused through the system, and a slight flush appeared upon the countenance, a blush lighting up the nose of even Mrs. Bull. This seductive draught soon opened all the sources of their eloquence, and I enjoyed a further hour listening to their domestic stories. Soon these gleams of the inward life disappeared, and my eye-lids becoming heavy, I retired to my bed-room, which I shared with Jim Bull, jun., and his brothers, and fell to sleep.

CHICAGO

In the afternoon Mr. Shirley called with his "trap" and a pair of Morgan horses to drive me about the city, and point out the sights of Chicago. The city is situated on both sides of the Chicago river, a sluggish, slimy stream, too lazy to clean itself, and on both sides of its north and south branches, upon a level piece of ground, half dry and half wet, resembling a salt marsh, and contained a population of 20,000. There was no pavement, no macadamized streets, no drainage, and the three thousand houses in which the people lived, were almost entirely small timber buildings, painted white, and this white much defaced by mud. I now recall but a single exception to this rule, in a red brick, two story residence in the north division, surrounded by turf, and the grounds ornamented with trees and shrubbery.

The city was not yet lighted with gas, and the gardens were open fields where I often saw horses, cows and animals of inferior dignity, sunning themselves, instead of what I expected to see, shrubs and flowers. To render the streets and sidewalks passable, they were covered with deal boards from house to house, the boards resting upon cross sills of heavy timber. This kind of track is called "the plank road." Under these planks the water was standing on the surface over three-fourths of the city, and as the sewers from the houses were emptied under them, a frightful odour was emitted in summer, causing fevers and other diseases, foreign to the climate. It not unfrequently happened that from the settling or rolling of a sleeper, that a loose plank would give way under the weight of a passing cab, when the foul water would spurt into the air high as the windows.

On the outskirts of the town where this kind of road terminated, the highways were impassable, except in winter when frozen, or in summer when dry and pulverized into the finest and most penetrating of dust. At all other seasons they were little less than quagmires. As may be imagined, the communication with the interior was principally carried on in canoes and batteaux. Of architectural display there was none. The houses were built hurriedly to accommodate a considerable trade centering here, and were devoid of both comforts and conveniences. Every one in the place seemed in a hurry, and a kind of restless activity prevailed which I had seen no where else in the West, except in Cincinnati. A central point in the western route of emigrants, it was even at this inclement season animated by passing parties. In summer, I understood emigrant parties went through daily. Those whom I now saw, were wild, rough, almost savage looking men from North Germany, Denmark and Sweden—their faces covered with grizzly beards, and their teeth clenched upon a pipe stem. They were followed by stout, well-formed, able-bodied wives and healthy children. Neither cold nor storm stopped them in their journey to the promised land, on the frontiers of which they had now arrived. In most instances they followed friends who had prepared a resting place for them.

Chicago was already becoming a place of considerable importance for manufactures. Steam mills were busy in every part of the city preparing lumber for buildings which were contracted to be erected by the thousand the next season. Large establishments were engaged in manufacturing agricultural implements of every description for the farmers who flocked to the country every spring. A single establishment, that of McCormick, employed several hundred hands, and during each season completed from fifteen hundred to two thousand grain-reapers and grass-mowers. Blacksmith, wagon and coachmaker's shops were busy preparing for a spring demand, which, with all their energy, they could not supply. Brickmakers had discovered on the lake shore, near the city and a short distance in the interior, excellent beds of clay, and were manufacturing, even at this time, millions of brick by a patent process, which the frost did not hinder, or delay. Hundreds of workmen were also engaged in quarrying stone and marble on the banks of the projected canal; and the Illinois Central Railway employed large bodies of men in driving piles, and constructing a track and depot on the beach. Real estate agents were mapping out the surrounding territory for ten and fifteen miles in the interior, giving fancy names to the future avenues, streets, squares and parks. A brisk traffic existed in the sale of corner lots, and men with nothing but their wits, had been known to succeed in a single season in making a fortune—sometimes, certainly, it was only on paper.

Wishing to change a few American (gold), eagles, for I had provided myself with this kind of solid currency for my Western tour, my friend Shirley accompanied me to a timber-shed, or shanty, bespattered with mud and defaced by the sun and storm, where the great banking establishment of those days was conducted by George Smith and Co. When there, placing my eagles upon the counter, Mr. Willard, the manager, a lean, yellow, thick-skinned, but shrewd man of business from the East, though I hardly think he could be classed among the wise men, returned me notes of the denomination of one, two, three and four dollars, which read as follows:

The Bank of Atlanta, Georgia, promises to pay the bearer on demand, one dollar, when five is presented at their banking-house at Atlanta.

GEORGE SMITH, *President.*

WILLARD, *Cashier.*

I objected most decidedly to receiving this currency, because Atlanta was by the usual route of travel nearly two thousand miles distant; because when

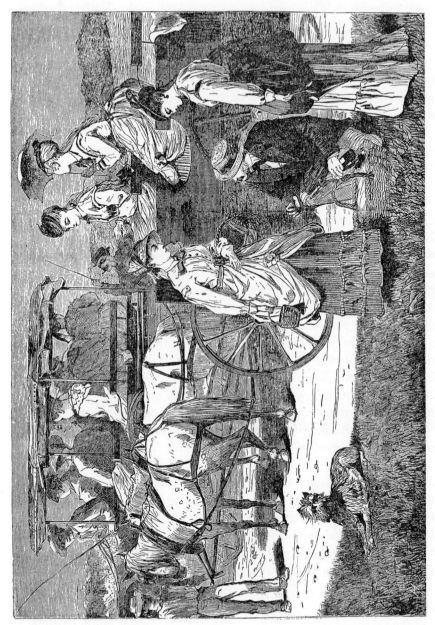

PICNIC EXCURSION

the notes were presented, the bank of Atlanta might pay them in the currency of another "wild cat" bank, probably conducted by Tom Mackenzie in Texas or New Mexico, and because they would only pay them in particular amounts of five dollars, a sum, I said ironically, which a judicious man was not likely to accumulate in his hands of this kind of currency. Stating these objections, both Messrs. Willard and Shirley smiled at my ignorance and inexperience, my "old fogyism," and explained that these notes were as current in Chicago and the State of Illinois as gold; and much more plentiful, thought I to myself. Nevertheless, on their assurances I accepted them, with a mental reservation, however, that I would divest myself of the trash before my departure.

We now left the bank for a ramble about the "Garden City," as Chicago was then and is now called, from the fact that the houses were very small and the gardens enormous. Returning to the hotel, Mr. Rossiter informed me that my bank notes (and my pocket was stuffed with them) were called "wild cat money," and such institutions as that at Atlanta "Wild Cat Banks"; but he said the circulating medium of the United States was so far below the actual wants of the people, that they were compelled to resort to such systems of credit to get on rapidly and improve the country, and as long as farmers would take the money (as they now did) there would be no difficulty.

"Why, sir," said Mr. Rossiter, looking around his establishment with pride, "this hotel was built with that kind of stuff, and what is true of 'The American,' is very nearly true of every other house in Chicago. I will take 'wild cats' for your bill, my butcher takes them of me, and the farmer from him, and so we go, making it pleasant all round. I only take care," continued Mr. Rossiter, "to invest what I may have at the end of a given time in corner lots. Then I'll be prepared, I guess, for the deluge, or crash, when it comes, and sooner or later it must come, as sure as the light of day. Mr. Smith has already in circulation six millions of his wild cat currency, and in order to be prepared for contingencies—to be out of the way of a hempen collar and Chicago lamppost, when people are ruined by his financiering devices—he remains in New York and carries on his operations through Mr. Willard and his 'lambs,' as the clerks are called. On this kind of worthless currency, based on Mr. Smith's supposed wealth and our wants, we are creating a great city, building up all kind of industrial establishments, and covering the lake with vessels—so that suffer who may when the inevitable hour of reckoning arrives, the country will be the gainer, Jack Rossiter will try, when this day of reckoning comes, to have 'clean hands' and a fair record, and I would advise you, on leaving Illinois, to do likewise—wash your hands of Smith and Co. A man who meddles, my dear sir, with wild cat banks is on a slippery spot, and that spot the edge of a precipice."

It required no persuasion to make me follow the sensible advice of my host, and when I afterwards stepped on the steamer which was to bear me across the lake on my return, I divested myself of the last note—which had come into my possession in the way of change—a note of small denomination, by presenting it to the hotel-porter as a gratuity for what one was not then likely to get from Western "helps," a little common civility. Pat was delighted to receive the shin plaster, and gave "yer 'onour" many thanks.

Mr. Shirley drove me to the Chicago Theatre, where Hamlet was played that night—a promising young Western actor, named Perry, taking the principal part. The Theatre was then owned by the manager, Mr. Rice, who was a good actor and a pleasant man. The house was well attended, and the play a decided success. After the performance, we accepted an invitation and went to Mr. Rice's residence in Wabash Avenue, where a number of his friends and some of the principal members of the company were assembled for supper. Here the evening passed rapidly amidst the sparkle of wit, humour and champagne.

The morning following my attendance at the theatre, I found Chicago covered with snow two feet deep on a level, and at places where it was drifted from thirty to forty feet deep! The population was stirring, however, like a hive of bees to open a pathway, by throwing it from the trottoirs into the streets before it became so frozen as to be immovable, except with enormous labour. By mid-day the pavements were tolerably comfortable, but we seemed to be moving in a trench—the shops on one side and the snow upon the other. The snow thrown into the streets raised their level about four feet, so that as we walked on the side-walk, the feet of the horses pulling the sleighs were almost even with our shoulders. Becoming as the season advances more and more firmly frozen and compactly beat down, the streets are smooth and slippery to a degree, forming admirable roads for sleighs, in which every one not on foot moves about, and they furnish delightful means of locomotion. Coach bodies are placed upon sleds, and ladies go to make morning calls in them as also to parties and picnics.

Picnicking was by the by one of the Chicago winter amusements, and they are sometimes very amusing. They are organised somewhat after this fashion. A hotel from ten to fifteen miles in the country is secured for a particular evening and dinner prepared for six or seven o'clock, as the case may be. By this hour sleighs arrive from Chicago, driven by the beaux and freighted with the belles and their chaperons nestling under buffalo robes and other furs. After dinner, dancing commences, the services of one of the numerous German bands in Chicago having been previously secured. Dancing is usually kept up till eleven when the sleighs reappear and taking up their "freight," one by one disappear in the night.

From our dinner table, the day following the pic-nic, we adjourned to the Tremont House, to a ball given by the bachelors. These balls occurred once a week during the winter, and were called the "Bachelors' Assembly Balls," and were intended as a return by the *brave garçons* of Chicago to the community, for the lavish hospitalities bestowed upon them by managing mammas. The rooms were large, handsomely decorated, brilliantly lighted and enlivened, and embellished by a dashing company. The music was all that could be desired, and the supper beyond praise.

Everything passed off the evening of my attendance agreeably, and as this was usually the case, these assemblies were decidedly popular. In the company there were many young married ladies, and even those who could lay claims to being "fair, fat and forty." I soon discovered that Chicago society in its freedom from restraint and easy sociability was more French than English, and more American than either. Many of the handsomest, gayest and most desirable-looking ladies were mothers, and in the same room mothers and daughters were often "tripping the light fantastic toe." This I thought entirely as it should be, and admirable evidence of the healthfulness of the north-western climate. It was also a refutation, complete and perfect of the common error—I might almost say popular superstition in England—that American ladies fade at forty and go off at fifty. Frail creatures, they are not quite so frail and fleeting in their charms as their British sisters imagine, certainly not in Chicago.

33

The American Spirit in the West, 1856

J. Milton Mackie (see p. 391), though he journeyed mostly through the West Indies and the Southern States, managed a river trip up the Mississippi to St. Louis. The following extract gives his impression of the ebullient spirit of the western country. However St. Louis may consider itself geographically today, or textbooks persist in referring to it as "border territory," the city, though it possessed southern characteristics, was essentially frontier and "western," even as late as 1856. Mackie was quite correct in thinking of it from such a point of view and in suspecting that this "western" spirit was representative of a goodly portion of the "American" spirit.

It was late on a rainy evening that I arrived at the great Western city of St. Louis. On entering the hotel which had been recommended to me, I found the hall filled like a merchant's exchange, and made my way to the office, not without some difficulty. The clerks were all too busy to notice my arrival. I was not asked to register my name in the hotel book, but did so without invitation. After waiting some little time, however, I succeeded in catching the eye of a clerk, when we held the following conversation:

"Have you a room for me?"

"Not a room in the house, sir."

"Well, give me a cot, then."

"Not a cot in the house, sir."

"But I am ill, and can go no farther. You may give me a sofa—anything."

"Not a sofa in the house, sir. Nothing in the house, sir."

And the clerk passed on, to say the same thing to another applicant for hospitality—and to another—until he was so tired of refusing, that he did it without pity, or even politeness. I turned toward one of the bystanders, a good Samaritan, who picked me up in my hour of need, and gave me a cot in his empty parlor.

I then learned that I had arrived at the wrong hour in the day. In the great Western hotels, the tide of travel ebbs and flows twice in the twenty-four hours. After nine o'clock in the morning, rooms are easy to be had; after nine in the evening they can rarely be obtained for money, and never for love. The hospitality of the house ceases at nine P.M. The civility of the clerks is completely exhausted by that time. Travellers arriving later than that are a nuisance to all the officials, from landlord to chambermaid. The cold, inhospitable looks the belated comer gets all round seem to say to him, "Why did you not arrive earlier in the day, sir?" If it would do any good, you might easily account for the lateness of your getting to town, and show that the blame rested on other shoulders than your own; but it will be of no avail. You can have as many apartments as you please tomorrow morning; but to-night you must get your sleep on three chairs, or walking the hall, if you happen to be a somnambulist.

So it is year in and year out. A porter gifted with a strong pair of lungs is kept pretty constantly perambulating the halls of the house, and bawling out, loud enough to waken every sleeper and stun every waker, "all aboard! all aboard! Omnibus ready for the cars!" A person accustomed to the quiet of his own mansion may be annoyed by this; but before he has lived forty days in the hotel, he pays no more attention to them than to the hand organ which nightly grinds its grist of melodies under his windows. Not less embarrassing are the piles of luggage heaped up in the halls and passage ways, against which one is constantly liable to run his nose or bark his shins. And when the trunks are loaded on the backs of hurrying porters, the risk of a collision is still greater; for poor Paddy, with half a ton of trunks to his back, is blind as a bat, and sees nothing but the main chance of the open doorway. The traveller is more in danger of being run down in his hotel than on the river, or the rail. Porters, waiters, guests, all are in quick motion; and one or the other is pretty sure to knock him over. Indeed, the society of a Western hotel is in a constant flux. The universe, in the Hegelian philosophy, is not more fluid. Every man is either just in from Cincinnati or Chicago, or he is just starting for one of these places. Unless he makes his hundred miles between breakfast and dinner, he counts himself an idler, and talks of growing rusty. A great deal of his business he transacts "aboard the cars," or the steamboats; some of it at the hotels; and all of it on his feet, and ready to "bolt." The dinner table, too, is an exchange for him. Business before soup—it is the first course of the dinner, and the last. Between fish and pudding he will sell a prairie. With every mouthful of bread he will engage to deliver ten thousand

THE "S.S. JACOB STRADER," OF THE LOUISVILLE MAIL COMPANY

bushels of wheat. The "upset price" is knocked hard down on the table with the end of his knife handle; and the bargain is clinched by the help of the nut cracker or the sugar tongs. If he sees his next neighbor prefer mutton, he at once offers to sell him sheep by the thousand; if he dines on pork, he will invite him to go into a speculation in hogs. His railroad shares he will dispose of at the price of peanuts; and his State bonds he will give away to any one who will pay his champagne bill, and the piper generally; or rather, he would do so a few years ago.

I was not so ill as to prevent my getting down to the table at mealtime. This was the chief amusement of my day, being as good a high-low comedy as may be seen on any stage, at least west of the Alleghanies. The table groans with good things. Here are the veritable solids, and none of what the Frenchman calls *les choses maigres*. The waiters drop fatness, literally. Your plate is brought to you heaped up with roast beef. Every third man has his pudding. The waiters hand about the iced cream in slices, which suggest the resemblance of small prairies. And, finally, the dinner goes off, like the finale of a display of fireworks, with "Jenny Lind cake," "vanities," "cookeys," "lady fingers," "jelly snips," and "pecans."

The only difficulty is in getting little enough of anything you may call for. Just a bit of a thing—*un morceau*—is an impossibility. A thin cut can't be had. A man, therefore, with a delicate stomach, is entirely out of place here, where the arrangements are all designed for persons who are ready to "go the whole animal." When I came down in the evening, to get a cup of tea and a bite at a biscuit, I never could escape the everlasting "Have a beef-steak, sir?" of the waiters. 'Tis a great country out West, and the men who live in it are feeders to correspond. They want their meat three times a day, as regularly as poor Pat does when he leaves his potato island and arrives in this land of beeves and buffaloes. Even their horses have freer access to the corn crib than negroes do in Virginia. The Western man expects to see plenty around him. Nothing is too good for him. He never stops to count the cost. Corn and wine are his—honey, and the honeycomb. The cattle on a thousand acres are his also. The prairies are white with his flocks; the eye follows the waving grain to the horizon; the buffalo yields him its tongue, the bear its haunches, and the buck his saddle; the wild turkey is brought in from the forests, the canvas-back duck from the bays, and the pinnated grouse from the prairies; the salmon trout is caught at Mackinaw, the whitefish fill the lakes, and oysters "hermetically sealed" arrive by express from the seaboard, every day in their season.

The society one meets in a Western hotel consists principally of the gentlemen of the road. I mean the railroad men, so called—road builders and road owners. There are, also, the men of real estate, who deal in prairie and river bottoms. There are grain and lumber merchants. There are speculators of every kind. But all have only one thought in their minds. To buy, sell, and get gain—this is the spirit that pervades this house, and the country. The chances of making fortunes in business or speculation are so great, that everybody throws the dice. Five years hence every man expects to be a nabob. I saw in the West no signs of quiet enjoyment of life as it passes, but only of a haste to get rich. Here are no idlers. The poor—if any such there be—and the wealthy are all equally hard at work. Beyond the Alleghanies the day has no siesta in it. Life is a race, with no chance of repose except beyond the goal. The higher arts which adorn human existence—elegant letters, divine philosophy—these have not yet reached the Mississippi. They are far off. There are neither gods nor graces on the prairies yet. One sees only the sower sowing his seed. No poets inhabit the savannas of Iowa, or the banks of the Yellow Stone. These are the emigrants' homes. Life in the valley of the Mississippi is, in fact, but pioneering, and has a heavy pack to its back. At present, the inhabitants are hewing wood and drawing water—laying the foundations of a civilization which is yet to be, and such as never hath been before. This they are doing with an energy superior to that which built Carthage or Ilium. Though men do not write books there, or paint pictures, there is no lack, in our Western world, of mind. The genius of this new country is necessarily mechanical. Our greatest thinkers are not in the library, nor the capitol, but in the machine shop. The American people is intent on studying, not the beautiful records of a past civilization, not the hieroglyphic monuments of ancient genius, but how best to subdue and till the soil of its boundless territories; how to build roads and ships; how to apply the powers of nature to the work of manufacturing its rich materials into forms of utility and enjoyment. The youth of this country are learning the sciences, not as theories, but with reference to their application to the arts. Our education is no genial culture of letters, but simply learning the use of tools. Even literature is cultivated for its jobs; and the fine arts are followed as a trade. The prayer of this young country is, "Give us this day our daily bread"; and for the other petitions of the Pater Noster it has no time. So must it be for the present. We must be content with little literature, less art, and only nature in perfection. We are to be busy, not happy. For we live for futurity, and are doing the work of two generations yet unborn.

Everything is beautiful in its season. What is now wanted in this country is, that all learned black-smiths stick to their anvils. No fields of usefulness can be cultivated by them to so great advantage as the floor of their own smithy. In good time, the Western bottom lands will spontaneously grow poets. The American mind will be brought to maturity along the chain of the great lakes, the banks of the Mississippi, the Missouri, and their tributaries in the far Northwest. There, on the rolling plains, will be formed a republic of letters, which, not governed, like that on our seaboard, by the great literary powers of Europe, shall be free indeed. For there character is growing up with a breadth equal to the sweep of the great valleys; dwarfed by no factitious ceremonies or usages, no precedents or written statutes, no old super-

EXPLOSION ON BOARD THE "HELEN MCGREGOR"

stition or tyranny. The winds sweep unhindered, from the lakes to the gulf, from the Alleghanies to the Rocky Mountains; and so do the thoughts of the Lord of the prairies. He is beholden to no man, being bound neither head nor foot. He is an independent world himself, and speaks his own mind. Some day he will make his own books, as well as his own laws. He will not send to Europe for either pictures or opinions. He will remain on his prairie, and all the arts of the world will come and make obeisance to him, like the sheaves in his fields. He will be the American man, and beside him there will be none else.

Of course, one does not go to the West to study fashions or manners. The guests of a Western hotel would not bear being transported to Almack's without some previous instruction in bowing and scraping, or some important changes of apparel. Foreign critics, travelling in pursuit of the comical, do not fail of finding it here in dress, in conversation, in conduct: for men here show all their idiosyncrasies. There are no disguises. Speech is plump, hearty, aimed at the bull's eye; and without elegant phrase or compliment. On the road, one may meet the good Samaritan, but not Beau Brummell. Anything a Western man can do for you, he will do with all his heart; only he cannot flatter you with unmeaning promises. You shall be welcome at his cabin; but he cannot dispense his hospitality in black coat and white cravat. His work is too serious to be done in patent leathers. He is, in outward appearance, as gnarled as his oaks, but brave, strong, humane, with the oak's great heart and pith. The prairie man is a six-foot animal, broad shouldered and broad fore-headed; better suited to cutting up corn than cutting a figure in a dance, to throwing the bowie knife than to thrumming the guitar. In Europe, a man always betrays a consciousness of the quality of the person in whose presence he is standing. If he face a lord, it is with submission; if a tradesman, with haughtiness; if a servant, with authority; if a beggar, with indifference. At the West, two persons meeting stand over against each other like two door-posts. Neither gives signs of superiority or inferiority. They have no intention of either flattering or imposing upon each other. Words are not wasted. So is the cut of each other's coat a matter of perfect indifference. Probably the man who is "up for Congress" wears the shabbier one of the two. If disposed to make a show at all, the Western gent is more apt to be proud of his horses than his broadcloth. His tread may occasionally have something in it indicative of the lord of the prairie; but he has little or no nonsense about him. The only exception is, perhaps, a rather large-sized diamond pin in his shirt bosom.

The Western cockney differs considerably from him of New York. He has more of the "ready-made-clothing" appearance about him, and wears his hat drawn closer down over his left eye. Sometimes his cigar is in his buttonhole, and sometimes in his cheek. He chews tobacco. He vibrates between sherry cobblers and mint juleps. His stick is no slight rattan, but a thick hickory or buckeye, and has a handle large enough to allow of its being carried suspended from his shoulder. His watch chain is very heavy—lead inside, and gold out. He is learned in politics, and boasts that a United States senator from his State once put his arm around his neck, and slapped him familiarly between the shoulders. When he was in Washington, he messed and slept with the Western members of the House. He knows, personally, all the Western judges and generals in Congress; bets at all the elections; and makes money out of them, let whichever party conquer. He also goes in the steamboats whenever there is to be a race; plays "poker" on board, and lives on the profits. He has a small capital in wild lands, likewise, and owns a few corner lots in Cairo, and other cities laid down in his maps. These he will sell cheap for cash. He affects the man of business, and ignores ladies' society. His evenings are spent at a club house, having the name of "Young America" blazoned on its front in large gilt letters. He dines at the crack hotel of the town, and, having free passes over all railroads, he keeps up his importance in the world by going to and fro, and putting on the airs of a man owning half the Western country.

34

The Mingling of West and South, 1856

In 1856 Frederick Law Olmstead (see p. 348) was once more on his way south, this time to travel through Texas. His itinerary took him across the mountains on the Baltimore and Ohio Railroad to Cincinnati, and from thence, as a side excursion, across Kentucky and Tennessee, from which he returned to the Ohio to pursue his main objective in Texas. Though Kentucky and Tennessee were but a prelude to his Texan destination, true to his investigating instincts, he recorded with his usual objectivity the sights he saw there. It is clear he comprehended the phenomenon of a cultural transition in these two states. In their early days Kentucky and Tennessee had been "western" states; because of slavery, they increasingly partook of southern characteristics. What Olmstead saw was a society which had retained much of its frontier outlook and yet had added many overtones derived from the Cotton Kingdom. Five years later this cultural cleavage was to join Tennessee to the Confederacy and hold Kentucky to the Union.

We left Cincinnati, crossing the river upon a dirty little high pressure ferry-boat, and drove through the streets of Covington. This city, with its low and scattered buildings, has the aspect of a suburb, as in fact it is. It is spread loosely over a level piece of ground, and is quite lacking in the energy and thrift of its free-state neighbor. Whether its slowness be legitimately traced to its position upon the slave side of the river, as is commonly done; or only in principal part to the caprice of commerce, is not so sure. It is credible enough, that men of free energy in choosing their residence, should prefer free laws when other things are equal; but 200 miles further down the river, we find (as again at St. Louis) that things are not equal, and that the thrift and finery are upon the slave side. Leaving it behind, we roll swiftly out upon one of the few well-kept macadamized roads in America, and enter with exhilaration the gates of magnificent Kentucky.

Here spreads, for hundreds of miles before you, an immense natural park. Travel where you will for days, you find always the soft, smooth sod, shaded with oaks and beeches, noble in age and form, arranged in vistas and masses. Man has squatted here and there over the fair heritage, but his shabby improvements have the air of poachers' huts amidst this luxuriant beauty of nature. Midway of the route, the land is high and rougher in tone, and the richest beauty is only reached at the close of day, when you bowl down into the very garden of the state—the private grounds, as it were, of the demesne. Here accumulation has been easy, and wealth appears in more suitable mansions, occupied by the lords of Durham and Ayrshire herds, as well as of a black feudal peasantry, unattached to the soil. There is hardly, I think, such another coach ride as this in the world, certainly none that has left a more delightful and ineffaceable impression on my mind.

Our progress was much impeded by droves of hogs, grunting their obstinate way towards Cincinnati and a market. Many of the droves were very extensive, filling the road from side to side for a long distance. Through this brute mass, our horses were obliged to wade slowly, assisted by lash and yells. Though the country was well wooded, and we passed through now and then a piece of forest, I venture to say we met as many hogs as trees in all the earlier part of the day.

The farms we passed on the road were generally small, and had a slovenly appearance that ill accorded with the scenery. Negro quarters, separate from the family dwelling, we saw scarcely anywhere. The labor appeared about equally divided between black and white. Sometimes we saw them at work together, but generally at separate tasks on the same farm. The main crop was everywhere Indian corn, which furnishes the food for man and beast, and the cash sales evidently of hogs and beef. Many of the farms had been a great while under cultivation. Large old orchards were frequent, now loaded with apples left, in many cases, to fall and rot, the season having been so abundant as to make them not worth transportation to market. I was much surprised, on considering the richness of the soil and the age of the farms, that the houses and barns were so thriftless and wretched in aspect. They were so, in fact, to one coming from the North; but on further experience they seemed, in recollection, quite neat and costly structures compared with the average Southern dwellings.

But a very small proportion of the land is cultivated or fenced, in spite of the general Western tendency towards a horizontal, rather than a perpendicular agriculture. Immense tracts lie unused, simply parts of our Great West.

We stopped for dinner at a small and unattractive village, and at an inn to which scarcely better terms could be applied. The meal was smoking on the table; but five minutes had hardly elapsed, when "Stage's ready," was shouted, and all the other passengers bolting their coffee, and handing their half dollars to the landlord, who stood eagerly in the door, fled precipitately to their seats. We held out a few moments longer, but yielded to repeated threats that the stage was off without us, and mounted to our places amid suppressed oaths on all sides.

At this dinner I made the first practical acquaintance with what shortly was to be the bane of my life, viz., corn-bread and bacon. I partook innocent and unsuspicious of these dishes, as they seemed to be the staple of the meal, without a thought that for the next six months I should actually see *nothing else.* Here, relieved by other meats and by excellent sweet potatoes baked and in *pone,* they disappeared in easy digestion. Taken alone, with vile coffee, I may ask, with deep feeling, who is sufficient for these things?

At one of our stopping places we passed a husking bee—a circle of neighbors, tossing rapidly bright ears of corn into a central heap, with jokes and good cheer; near by, a group of idle boys looking on from a fence, and a half-a-dozen horses tied around.

We had had glowing descriptions of Lexington, and expected much. Had we come from the South we should have been charmed. Coming from the East we were disappointed in the involuntary comparison. Of all Southern towns there are scarce two that will compare with it for an agreeable residence. It is regular in its streets, with one long principal avenue, on which most of the business is done. The tone of building is more firm and quiet than that of most Western towns, and the public buildings are neat. There are well-supplied shops; many streets are agreeably shaded; but the impression is one of irresistible dullness. It is the centre of no great trade, but is the focus of intelligence and society for Kentucky, which, however, is not concentrated in the town, but spread on its environs. These have undeniably a rare charm.

The rolling woodland pastures come close upon the city, and on almost every knoll is a dwelling of cost and taste. Among these is Henry Clay's Ashland.

It is not without feeling that we could visit a spot haunted by a man who had loomed so high upon our boyhood. Nothing had been changed about the house and grounds. His old servant showed us such parts of the house as could be visited without intrusion, the portraits and the presents. The house was one of no great pretensions, and so badly built as to be already falling into decay. The grounds were simply and well retired behind masses of fine trees; the whole bearing the look of a calm and tasteful retreat.

Lexington boasts a university, well attended, and ranking among the highest Western schools in its departments of Law and Medicine. Its means of ordinary education are also said to be of the best.

With such advantages, social, atmospheric, educational, what residence more attractive for one who would fain lengthen out his summers and his days? Were it only free. In the social air there is something that whispers this. You cannot but listen. Discussion may be learned, witty, delightful, only—not free. Should you come to Lexington, leave your best thoughts behind. The theories you have most revolved, the results that are to you most certain, pack them close away, and give them no airing here. Your mind must stifle, if your body thrive. Apart from slavery, too, but here a product of it, there is that throughout the South, in the tone of these fine fellows, these otherwise true gentlemen, which is very repugnant—a devilish, undisguised, and recognised contempt for all humbler classes. It springs from their relations with slaves, "poor whites," and tradespeople, and is simply incurable. A loose and hearty blasphemy is also a weakness of theirs, but is on the whole far less repulsive. God is known to be forgiving, but slighted men and slaves hanker long for revenge. Lexington society, however, can, I believe, be said to have less of these faults so offensive to a Northern man, than any Southern city equally eligible in other respects.

But, besides the social objections, there are others of a different character. Malaria hangs over it, as over all the West, and whoever comes from the East runs double risk from its influences. Labor, other than forced, and consequently, costly, slovenly, and requiring incessant supervision, is not to be had. The summer heats are tedious and severe, and the droughts so unmitigated as that sometimes the land is nearly baked to a depth of five feet, and the richest soil is no better than the poorest.

From Lexington we went by rail to Louisville (94 miles; $3; 5 hours). On the train we could not help observing that the number of handsome persons in our car was unusual, and among the young Kentuckians we saw, were several as stalwart in form and manly in expression as any young men on whom my eyes have fallen.

A young man passing, with a pistol projecting from his pocket, some one called out with a laugh—"You'll lose your pistol, sir." This opened a little talk on weapons, in which it appeared that among young men a bowie-knife was a universal, and a pistol a not at all unusual, companion in Kentucky.

Louisville has interminable ragged, nasty suburbs, and lacks edifices—in other respects it is a good specimen of a brisk and well-furnished city. Its business buildings are large and suitable, its dwellings, of the better class, neat, though rarely elegant, its shops gay and full, its streets regular and broad, its tone active, without the whirr of Cincinnati. It has great business, both as an entrepôt and as itself, a manufacturing producer. It owes its position to the will of nature, who stopped here, with rapids, the regular use of the river. Cincinnati, by the canal around them, has, however, almost free competition with it, and it has well stood its ground. It has grown with all a Western rapidity. In 1800, population, 600; 1850, about 50,000.

Finding that the night exposure, by stage, would be too great to be voluntarily encountered at the season, we abandoned our plan of proceeding across the state to Nashville, and ordered our baggage to be sent on board the favorite steamer "Pike," up for St. Louis. The promise of steamboat speed and comfort was too seductive, and the charms of river scenery, both on the Ohio and the Cumberland, had been glowingly painted for us.

Over a deep-rutted miry road, cut up by truck loads of cotton, sugar, and iron, we were driven two or three miles to Portland, once the rival, now the port and mean suburb, of Louisville. After only a few hours more or less, not days as we feared, beyond her advertised time, the fast mail boat Pike took her departure.

It was a matter of luck, we found, that we were off so soon, and was so considered, by passengers generally—other boats, advertised as positively to sail days before, lying quietly against the bank as we moved out. Just before we left, sitting on the guards, I heard the captain say, "Yes, I guess we might as well go off, I don't believe we'll get anything more. The agent told me to start out more than an hour ago; but I held on for the chance, you know." Shortly after this a man appeared in the distance running down the levee, with a carpetbag, straight for us. The last bell had been rung with extra-terrible din, the gang-plank hauled aboard, and men were stationed at the hawsers to cast off. "Halloo, look at that chap," said the captain, "he's *hell-bent* on this boat now, ain't he. I'll have to wait for that fellow, sure." Accordingly the plank was got out again, and the individual, who proved to be a deck passenger, walked on board.

Toward night of the same day, we were steaming down the river at a fine rate, when we suddenly made a shear to the right, and, after a long sweep, steamed some distance up the river, and gently laid our nose against the bank. The passengers all gathered to see the landing. Nothing was said, but, after a few minutes, the mate, who had been dressing, appeared, with a box of raisins under his arm, and walked up to a solitary house at some distance from the shore. He was met at the door by an old gentleman and his wife, to whom he gave the box and a newspaper, and, after a moment's chat, he returned on board, gave the necessary orders, and we were soon on our way again. Think of a huge "floating palace," of 600 tons, with 200 passengers on board, spending a quarter of an hour on such an errand! But for thousands of miles here these steamers are the only means of communication, and every article, be it a newspaper or a thousand bales of cotton, must be delivered or despatched in this way.

Travelers usually make the observation in descending the Ohio, that the free side shows all the thrift and taste. It is a customary joke to call their attention to this, and encourage them to dilate upon it when the boat's head has been turned around without their notice. And I cannot say with candor, that taking the whole distance, such was our own observation. The advantage, if any, is slight on the side of the free states. They certainly have more neat and numerous villages, and I judge more improved lands along the river bank; but the dwellings, not counting negro huts, appeared to us nearly on a par, and the farms, at a rough guess, of about equal value.

What is most striking everywhere, is the immensity of the wasted territory, rather than the beauty of the improved. The river banks seem, as you glide for hours through them, without seeing a house or a field, as if hardly yet rescued from the beasts and the savages, so little is the work done compared with that which remains to do. There is soil enough here, of the richest class, to feed and clothe, with its cotton and its corn, ten-fold our whole present population.

At about 1 A.M., we found ourselves alone with a shivering boy, almost speechless with sleep, upon a wharf-boat, in Smithland, at the mouth of the Cumberland River, looking with regret on the fast-drifting lights of the Pike. Following, by a blurred lantern, his dubious guidance, we climbed a clay bank, and found ourselves shortly before our beds. At a first experience of a Western, viz., one-sheeted, bed, I was somewhat taken aback; and, determining not to abandon my hold on civilization sooner than necessary, I unconscionably caused the chambermaid, who was also the landlady, to be roused at this late hour, and had, amid much grumbling and tedium, my bed put in a normal state. Next morning I was happy to see that several panes had been put in the window in anticipation of our arrival, and some paper pasted against the walls, but no provision for personal ablutions could be discerned, though as the curtain-less window opened on a gallery, there was every opportunity for public inspection. Descending in search of these unwonted articles, we discovered, by the sour looks we met, that we had caused a family indigestion by our night attack, and, suddenly concluding to adopt the customs of the country, we were shown to the common lavabo, and why not? One rain bathes the just and unjust, why not one wash-bowl? Not twice in the next six months, away from cities or from residences we pitched for ourselves, did we find any other than this equal and democratic arrangement.

Smithland is—or was, for who knows what a Western year may bring forth—a thriving county seat, composed of about two taverns, one store, five houses and a wharf-boat. Being Thanksgiving day, we dined in company with several of our fellow-citizens, wearing full-dress shirts, but no coats, on corn-bread and pork, with sweet potatoes, and two pickles.

The prospect, in view of a long continuance of this life at Smithland, being composed of the trees and bushes of the opposite shore, and of a long, flat reach of river, was not encouraging. But, as good fortune would have it, we had scarcely begun the melancholy digestion of our dinner, when the flat, stern-wheel boat, David A Tomkins, came in sight, and made direct for Smithland. On ascertaining that she was actually bound for Nashville, with great eagerness we paid our first-class bill, and hurried our baggage on board.

The boat was a good specimen of a very numerous class on Western and Southern rivers. They are but scows in build, perfectly flat, with a pointed stem and a square stern. Behind is the one wheel, moved by two small engines of the simplest and cheapest construction. Drawing but a foot, more or less, of water, they keep afloat in the lowest stages of the rivers. Their freight, wood, machinery, boilers, hands and steerage passengers, are all on the one flat deck just above the surface of the water. Eight or ten feet above, supported by light stanchions, is laid the floor used by the passengers. The engines being, as generally in Western boats, horizontal, this floor is laid out in one long saloon eight or ten feet wide from the smoke-pipes, far forward, which stretches to the stern. It is lined upon each side with state-rooms, which open also out upon a narrow upper guard or gallery. Perched above all this is the pilot-house, and a range of state-rooms for the pilots and officers, popularly known as "Texas." To this Texas, inveterate card-players retire on Sundays, when custom forbids cards in the saloon. A few feet of the saloon are cut off by folding doors for a ladies' cabin. Forward of the saloon the upper deck extends around the smoke-pipes, forming an open space, sheltered by the pilot-deck, and used for baggage and open-air seats.

Such is the contrivance for making use of these natural highways. And really admirable it is, spite of drawbacks, for its purpose. Without it the West would have found it impossible to be the West. Roads, in countries so sparcely settled, are impracticable. These craft paddle about, at some stage of water, to almost every man's door, bringing him foreign luxuries, and taking away his own productions; running at high water in every little creek, and at low water, taking, with great profit the place of the useless steamers on the main streams.

Our captain promised we should be in Nashville the following day; but he should have added "water and weather permitting," for we had one hundred tedious hours to spend upon the narrow decks of the Tomkins. We were hardly fairly under way when we went foul of a snag, and broke, before we were clear, several buckets of our wheel. We ran on in a dilapidated state till near night, when the boat's head was put against a bank, and what timber was required was cut in the woods. Woods are common property here. With this and with planks kept on board for the purpose, the repairs were soon effected. With the twilight, however, came a thick fog down upon the river, and we remained, in consequence, tied quietly to a tree until late the next day, but a few miles from Smithland. The evening was something hard to pass: a fierce stove, a rattle of oaths and cards within, and the cold fog without. Our passengers were some twenty in number, mostly good-natured people from the neighboring country, fraternizing loudly with the officers of the boat, over their poker and brag. The ladies occupied themselves in sewing and rocking, keeping up a thin clatter of talk at their end of the cabin.

Early next day we passed a side-wheel steamer of a small class, upon a shoal, almost high and dry. She had been lying for a month where she was, all hands discharged, and the whole machine idle. We afterwards passed two or three others of a larger size, accidently locked into the river by a fall of water. Our own craft, though drawing only fourteen inches, was within an ace of a similar predicament. After many times grounding, but always getting free after more or less delay, we were at length driven hard and fast by rapids upon a heap of rocks barely covered with water.

Then it was we learned the use of those singular spars which may always be seen standing on end against the forward deck, in any picture of a Western boat. They are, in fact, steamboat crutches. One of these, or the pair, if occasion requires, is set upon the river-bottom, close to the boat's head, and a tackle led from its top to a ring in the deck. Then, by heaving on the wind-lass, the boat is lifted bodily off the ground. As soon as she swings free of the bottom, steam is applied with fury, and forward she goes until the spar slips from its place, and lets her fall. Such was the amusement we had during the greater part of our Sunday on board. Finally, having secured, by going up and down the river, two woodscows, and having got into them, lashed along-side, all our freight, having hobbled about here and there, looking for a wetter place, during many hours, we scratched over. The freight was soon restored, and the flat-boats sent adrift, to find their way home with the cur-rent, under the management, one, of an aged negro, the other of a boy and girl of tender years.

We were amused to notice of how little account the boat was considered, in comparison with the value of *time*. Whenever any part of the hull was in the way of these spars, axes were applied without a thought, other than that of leaving hull enough to keep afloat. In fact, costing little, these steamers are used with perfect recklessness. If wrecked, why, they have long ago paid for themselves, and the machinery and furniture can almost always be saved. This apparatus of stilts is used upon the largest boats, and good stories are told of their persistence in lifting themselves about, and forcing a passage over gravel banks, whenever freights are higher than steamboats. The "first boat over" sometimes wins extravagant rewards. When sugar, for instance, goes up to $1 per pound in up-river towns, after a dry season, a few hogsheads will almost pay for a cheap steamboat.

The Cumberland, flowing, after its head branches unite, through a com-paratively level and limited district, though watering an immense region, is but a small and quiet stream. Its banks, so far as navigation extends, are low, though frequently bluffs of small height come jutting down to the river. Ordinarily, the trees of the rich bottom alone are to be seen overhanging the placid surface. For miles, almost for hours, there is not a break in the line of dripping branches. Monotony is immediate. But it is not without suffering this that a traveler can receive true and fixed impressions. You turn again and again from listlessly gazing at the perspective of bushes, to the listless conversation of the passengers, and turn back again. Making a landing, or stopping to wood-up, become excitements that make you spring from your berth or your book. Two sounds remain still very vividly in my ears in think-ing of this sail—the unceasing "Choosh, choosh; choosh, choosh," of the steam, driven out into the air, after doing its work; and the "shove her up! shove her up!" of the officer of the deck, urging the firemen to their work. The first of these sounds is of course constantly heard upon high-pressure boats, and is part and parcel of Western scenery. Of a calm day it rings for miles along, announcing the boat's approach. On board, the sound is not as annoying as might be expected.

Turkeys, buzzards, and ducks make up the animated nature of the scenery. The ducks clatter along the surface, before the boat as it approaches, refusing to leave the river, and accumulating in number as they advance, until all take refuge in the first ready shelter offered by a flat shore.

The buzzards, hovering, keen-eyed, in air, swoop here and there towards whatever attracts their notice, or loiter idly and gracefully along, following the boat's motion with scarce a play of the wing, as if disdaining its fussy speed.

The turkeys sit stupidly in the trees, or fly in small or large flocks across the stream. We counted more than ninety in one frightened throng.

It is a matter of surprise to meet so few farms along the banks of such a stream. But it is the common surprise of the West. Everything almost, but land, is wanting everywhere. Except a small quantity of tobacco, hardly any-thing else than corn is here cultivated. The iron works along the river make a large market for bread-stuffs, i.e., corn-bread stuffs. The farms are carried on by slave labor on a moderate scale. The farmers, not working themselves, are generally addicted to sporting, and to an easy view of life. The spots chosen for cultivation, so far as can be seen from the river, are those where the land comes high to the bank, affording a convenient landing. A considerable item of revenue is the furnishing of wood to passing steamers—much black muscle paying thus its interest. The wood is piled in ranks along the bank, or some-times a flat is loaded ready for steamers to take in tow, so that no time may be lost in waiting. We saw the usual picturesque evening wooding-up scenes to great advantage here. An iron grating, filled with blazing chips of rich pine, is set upon the boat's guard, or upon the bank. A red glare is thus thrown over the forest, the water, the boat, and the busy group of men, run-ning, like bees, from shore to boat. A few minutes of mad labor suffice to cover the boat's spare deck-room—the torch is quenched, and, with a jerk of the bell, the steamer moves off into the darkness.

As we lay quiet one evening in the fog, we heard and listened long to the happy wordless song of the negroes gathered at firelight work, probably corn-husking, on some neighboring plantation. The sound had all the rich and mellow ring of pure physical contentment, and did one good to hear it. Like the nightingale, the performers seemed to love their own song, and to wait for its far off echo. It was long before we discovered that this was artifi-cial, and came in response from the next plantation.

It was with very great pleasure that we left the woods behind us, and emerged into the cultivated district surrounding Nashville. On a narrow boat, the berths and table must be correspondingly restricted and four days of such confinement prove a great fatigue. After an amount of excited shrieking on the part of our steam-whistle, in quite inverse proportion to our real importance, we opened the town, and in a few minutes lay beneath its noble suspension bridge, resting our crazy head upon its levee. Two negroes with carriages had answered our tremendous calls, two with handbarrows soon joined them, and we were very shortly in lodgings in the heart of the town.

The approach by the river, at a low stage of water, is anything but striking. The streets are, as usual, regular—some of them broad—but the aspect of the place, as a whole, is quite uninviting. The brick, made from adjacent clay, are of a sombre hue, and give, with many neglected frame houses, a dull character to a first impression; in fact, though there are some retired residences of taste in the town, there is little that calls out admiration from an Eastern man. It is our misfortune that all the towns of the Republic are alike, or differ in scarcely anything else than in natural position or wealth. Nashville has, however, one rare national ornament, a capitol, which is all it pretends to be or need to be.

The whole city is on high ground; but this stands at its head, and has a noble prominence. It is built of smooth-cut blue limestone, both within and without, and no stucco, sham paint, nor even wood-work, is anywhere admitted. Ornamenting its chambers are columns of a very beautiful native porphyry, fine white grains in a chocolate ground. Better laws must surely come from so firm and fit a senate house.

Like Lexington, Nashville stands in the centre of a rich district, for which it is a focus of trade and influence. Being also the state capital, and its chief town in point of size, it holds its most distinguished and cultivated society. In its vicinity are some large and well-administered estates, whose management puts to shame the average bungling agriculture of the state. The railroad to Chattanooga, connecting with the seaboard towns, was just completed at the time of our visit, and gave promise of renewing the vigorous youth and growth of the town. Perhaps the demands and condition of its society are best illustrated by one fact, which may be said to speak volumes—the city has a bookstore (Mr. Berry's), which is thought to contain a better collection of recent literature, on sale, than is to be found elsewhere in the United States. Certainly its shelves have the appearance of being more variously filled than any accessible to dollars and cents in New York, and furnished us everything we could ask at a moment's notice.

The population of the town, in 1853, was estimated at 18,000. It is a speaking fact that a state so large should show a capital so small. Nor, except

Memphis, its port, which has 10,000, is there any other town worth mentioning in the state. Servile labor must be unskilled labor, and unskilled labor must be dispersed over land, and cannot support the concentrated life nor amass the capital of cities.

35

"It's All Go Ahead in This Country":
Minnesota in 1856

*C*hristopher C. Andrews (1829–1922) was born in Hillsboro, New Hampshire. He was too restless a spirit for the law or a government clerkship in Washington, and in 1856 he journeyed to Minnesota. He liked it so well there, apparently, that he stayed, not to leave except on military service in the Civil War or as representative of the United States to Sweden and Brazil.

The account of his travels to Minnesota, which he wrote up for the Boston Post, he afterward published in book form. His good sense of humor, his lively enthusiasm, and his excellent powers of observation make a most readable volume. His adherence to the Democratic party, which appears in this record, lasted only until the Civil War. As early as 1856 he was already exhibiting an interest in lumbering and forestry which in later life made him a distinguished conservationist. Perhaps the most notable feature of his book is the ease and clearness with which he catches, even in a brief sentence, the essential manners and characteristics of people and places.

The Frontier Moves West

A NOTE ON RAILWAY FOOD AND POLITICS

I have a word to say about refreshments on railroad routes. It is, perhaps, well known that the price for a meal anywhere on a railroad in the United States is fifty cents. That is the uniform price. Would that the meals were as uniform! But alas! a man might as well get a quid of tobacco with his money, for he seldom gets a *quid pro quo*. Once in a couple of days' travel you may perhaps get a wholesome meal, but as a general thing what you get (when you get out of New England) isn't worth over a dime. You stop at a place, say for breakfast, after having rode all night. The conductor calls out, "Twenty minutes for breakfast." There is a great crowd and a great rush, of course. Well, the proprietor expects there will be a crowd, and ought to be prepared. But how is it? Perhaps you are lucky enough to get a seat at the table. Then your chance to get something to eat is as one to thirteen: for as there is nothing of any consequence on the table, your luck depends on your securing the services of a waiter who at the same time is being called on by about thirteen others as hungry as yourself. Then suppose you succeed! First comes a cup of black coffee, strong of water; then a piece of tough fried beef steak, some fried potatoes, a heavy biscuit—a little sour (and in fact everything is sour but the pickles). You get up when you have finished eating—it would be mockery to say when you have satisfied your appetite—and at the door stand two muscular men (significantly the proprietor is aware of the need of such) with bank bills drawn through their fingers, who are prepared to receive your 50¢. It is not unusual to hear a great deal of indignation expressed by travellers on such occasions. No man has a right to grumble at the fare which hospitality sets before him. But when he buys a dinner at a liberal price, in a country where provisions are abundant, he has a right to expect something which will sustain life and health. Those individuals who have the privilege of furnishing meals to railroad travellers probably find security in the reflection that their patronage does not depend on the will of their patrons. But the evil can be remedied by the proprietors and super-intendents of the roads, and the public will look for a reformation in dinners and suppers at their hands.

The ride that evening was pleasant. The cars were filled with lusty yeo-men, all gabbling politics. There was an overwhelming majority for Fremont. Under such circumstances it was a virtue for a Buchanan man to show his colors. There was a solid old Virginian aboard; and his open and intelligent countenance—peculiar, it seems to me, to Virginia—denoted that he was a good-hearted man. I was glad to see him defend his side of politics with so much zeal against the Fremonters. He argued against half a dozen of them with great spirit and sense. In spite of the fervor of his opponents, however, they treated him with proper respect and kindness.

The practice of taking a vote for presidential candidates in the cars has been run into the ground. By this I mean that it has been carried to a ridiculous excess. So far I have had occasion to vote several times. A man may be indifferent as to expressing his vote when out of his state; but a man's curiosity must have reached a high pitch when he travels through a train of cars to inquire how the passengers vote. It is not uncommon, I find, for people to carry out the joke by voting *with* their real opponents. Various devices are resorted to to get a unanimous vote. For example, a man will say, "All who are in favor of Buchanan take off their boots; all in favor of Fremont keep them on." Again, when there are several passengers on a stage-coach out west, and they are passing under the limbs of a tree, or low bridge, as they are called, it is not unusual for a Fremont man to say, "All in favor of Fremont bow their heads." We had an hour to spend at Columbus, which, after booking our names at the Neil House for dinner—and which is a capital house— we partly spent in a walk about the city. It is the capital of the state, delightfully situated on the Scioto river, and has a population in the neighborhood of 20,000. The new Capitol there is being built on a scale of great magnificence. Though the heat beat down intensely, and the streets were dusty, we were "bent on seeing the town." We—my friend B. and myself—had walked nearly half a mile down one of the fashionable streets for dwellings, when we came to a line which was drawn across the sidewalk in front of a residence, which, from the appearance, might have belonged to one of the upper-ten. The line was in charge of two or three little girls, the eldest of whom was not over twelve. She was a bright-eyed little miss, and had in her face a good share of that metal which the vulgar think is indispensable to young lawyers. We came to a gradual pause at sight of this novel obstruction. "Buchanan, Fillmore, or Fremont?" said she, in a tone of dogmatical interrogatory. B. was a fervid Fremonter—he probably thought she was—so he exclaimed, "Fremont for ever!" I awaited the sequel in silence. "Then you may go round," said the little female politician. "You may go round," and round we went, not a little amused at such an exhibition of enthusiasm. I remember very well the excitement during the campaign of 1840; and I did my share with the New Hampshire boys in getting up decoy cider barrels to humbug the Whigs as they passed in their barouches to attend some great convention or hear Daniel Webster. But it seems to me there is much more political excitement during this campaign than there was in 1840. Flag-staffs and banners abound in the greatest profusion in every village. Every farm-house has some token of its politics spread to the breeze.

CITIES IN THE WILDERNESS

How short a time it is since a railroad to the Mississippi was thought a wonder! And now within the state of Illinois four terminate on its banks. Of course I started on one of these roads from Chicago to get to Dunleith. I think it is called the Galena and Chicago Union Road. A good many people have supposed Galena to be situated on the Mississippi river, and indeed railroad map makers have had it so located as long as it suited their convenience— (for they have a remarkable facility in annihilating distance and in making crooked ways straight)—yet the town is some twelve miles from the great river on a narrow but navigable stream. The extent and importance of Rockford, Galena, and Dunleith, cannot fail to make a strong impression on the traveller. They are towns of recent growth, and well illustrate that steam-engine sort of progress peculiar now-a-days in the west. Approaching Galena we leave the region of level prairie and enter a mineral country of naked bluffs or knolls, where are seen extensive operations in the lead mines. The trip from Chicago to Dunleith at the speed used on most other roads would be performed in six hours, but ten hours are usually occupied, for what reason I cannot imagine. However, the train is immense, having on board about six or seven hundred first class passengers, and two-thirds as many of the second class. Travelling in the cars out west is not exactly what it is between Philadelphia and New York, or New York and Boston, in this respect: that in the West more families are found in the cars, and consequently more babies and carpet bags.

It may not be proper to judge of the health of a community by the appearance of people who are seen standing about a railroad station; yet I have often noticed, when travelling through Illinois, that this class had pale and sickly countenances, showing too clearly the traces of fever and ague.

But I wish to speak about leaving the cars at Dunleith and taking the steamboat for St. Paul. There is a tremendous rush for the boats in order to secure state-rooms. Agents of different boats approach the traveller, informing him all about their line of boats, and depreciating the opposition boats. For instance, an agent, or, if your please, a runner of a boat called Lucy—not Long—made the assertion on the levee with great zeal and perfect impunity that no other boat but the said Lucy would leave for St. Paul within twenty-four hours; when it must have been known to him that another boat on the mail line would start that same evening, as was actually the fact. But the activity of the runners was needless; for each boat had more passengers than it could well accommodate. I myself went aboard the "Lady Franklin," one of the mail boats, and was accommodated with a state-room. But what a scene is witnessed for the first two hours after the passengers begin to come aboard! The cabin is almost filled, and a dense crowd surrounds the clerk's office, just as the ticket office of a theatre is crowded on a benefit night. Of course not more than half can get state-rooms and the rest must sleep on the cabin floor. Over two hundred cabin passengers came up on the Lady Franklin. The beds which are made on the floor are tolerably comfortable, as each boat is supplied with an extra number of single mattresses. The Lady Franklin is an old boat, and this is said to be its last season. Two years ago it was one of the excursion fleet to St. Paul, and was then in its prime. But steamboats are short

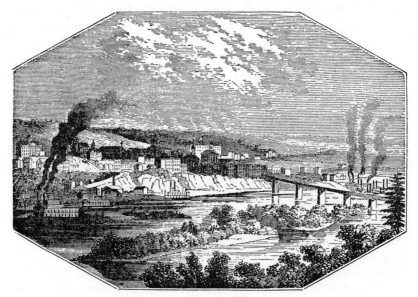

ST. PAUL IN 1865

lived. We had three tables set, and those who couldn't get a seat at the first or second sat at the third. There was a choice you may believe, for such was the havoc made with the provisions at the first table that the second and third were not the most inviting. It was amusing to see gentlemen seat themselves in range of the plates as soon as they were laid, and an hour before the table was ready. But the officers were polite—as is generally the case on steamboats till you get down to the second mate—and in the course of a day or two, when the passengers begin to be acquainted, the time wears away pleasantly. We were nearly four days in making the trip. The line of boats of which the Lady Franklin is one, carries the mail at fifty dollars a trip. During the boating season I believe the fare varies from seven to ten dollars to St. Paul. This season there have been two lines of boats running to Minnesota. All of them have made money fast; and next season many more boats will run.

But there are several thrifty and pleasant villages in Minnesota, on the river, before reaching St. Paul, but the town of Hastings eclipses everything but St. Paul. It is finely located on rising ground, and the river is there narrow and deep. The boat stopped here an hour, and I had a good opportunity to look about the place. The town appears to have considerable trade with the back country. Its streets are laid out with regularity; its stores and buildings are spacious, durable, and neat. I heard that over $2000 were asked for several of the building lots. A little way into the interior of the town I saw men at work on a stone church and approaching the spot, I determined to make some inquiries of a boy who was briskly planing boards. First, I asked how much the church was going to cost? About $3000, he replied.

"Are there any other churches in the place?"

"Yes, up there, where they are building."

"What denomination is that?"

"I don't know," he responded. "I only came into the place yesterday."

I thought he was doing well to begin to build churches so soon after his arrival. And from his countenance, I have no doubt he will do well, and become a useful citizen of the state.

St. Paul is not on the west side of the Mississippi, but on the East. Though it is rather too elevated and rough in its natural state to have been coveted for a farm, it is yet just such a spot as a pioneer would like to plant himself upon, that he might stand in his door and have a broad and beautiful view towards the south and west. And when the speculator came he saw that it was at the head of navigation of what he thought was the Upper Mississippi, but which in reality is only the Middle Mississippi. Then stores were put up, small and rude, and trade began to increase with settlers and hunters of furs. Then came the organization of the territory, and the location of the capital here, so that St. Paul began to thrive still more from the crumbs which fell from the government table, as also by that flood of emigration which nothing except the Rocky Mountains has ever stayed from entering a new territory. And now it has passed its doubtful era. It has passed from its wooden to its brick age. Before men are certain of the success of a town, they erect one story pine shops; but when its success appears certain, they build high blocks of brick or granite stores. So now it is common to see four and five story brick or stone buildings going up in St. Paul.

I believe this city numbers at present about 10,000 population. It is destined to increase for a few years still more rapidly than it has heretofore. But that it will be a second Chicago is what I do not expect. It would certainly seem that the high prices demanded for building lots must retard the progress of the place; but I am told the prices have always been as high in proportion to the business and number of population. $500 and upwards is asked for a decent building lot in remote parts of the town.

I have had an agreeable stroll down upon the bluff, south-east from the city, and near the elegant mansion of Mr. Dayton. The first engraving of St. Paul was made from a view taken at that point. As I stood looking at the city, I recalled the picture in Mr. Bond's work, and contrasted its present with the appearance it had three or four years ago. What a change! Three or four steamers were lying at the levee; steam and smoke were shooting forth from the chimneys of numerous manufactories; a ferry was plying the Mississippi, transporting teams and people; church steeples and domes and great warehouses stood in places which were vacant as if but yesterday; busy streets had been built and peopled; rows of splendid dwellings and villas, adorned with delightful terraces and gardens, had been erected. I went out Sunday morning too, and the view was none the less pleasant. Business was silent; but the church bells were ringing out their sweet and solemn melody, and the mellow sunlight of autumn glittered on the bright roofs and walls in the city. The whole scene revealed the glorious image of that ever advancing civilization which springs from well rewarded labor and general intelligence.

Like all new and growing places in the west, St. Paul has its whiskey shops, its dusty and dirty streets, its up and down sidewalks, and its never-ceasing whirl of business. Yet it has its churches, well filled; its spacious school-houses; its daily newspapers; and well-adorned mansions. There are many cottages and gardens situated on the most elevated part of the city, north and west, which would not suffer by a comparison with those cheerful and elegant residences so numerous for six to ten miles around Boston. From the parlors of these homes one may look down upon the city and upon the smooth bosom of the river. In the streets, too, you see much evidence of opulence and luxury, in the shape of handsome carriages, which are set out to advantage by a first-rate quality of horses.

One element of the success of this city is the public spirit of its leading business men. They have put their hands deep into their pockets to improve and advance the place. In all their rivalry there is an amicable feeling and boundless liberality. They help him that tries to help himself, and help each other in a way that will help them all together; and such kind of enterprises produces grand results. Why, here is a new hotel (the Fuller House) at which I stop, which is surpassed but by very few hotels in the country. It is a first-class house, built of brick, five stories high, and of much architectural beauty. The building itself cost upwards of $100,000. One can well imagine the comfort of finding such a house at the end of a long and tedious journey in a new country.

It is estimated that 28,000 people have visited and left St. Paul during the present season. During July and August the travel diminishes, but as soon as autumn sets in it comes on again in daily floods. It is really a novel and interesting state of things one finds on his arrival at the hotel. There are so many people from so many different places! There everybody is a stranger to almost everybody, and therefore quite willing to get acquainted with somebody. Everyone wants a bit of information on some point. Everybody is going to some place where he thinks somebody has been or is going, and so a great many new acquaintances are made without ceremony or delay; and old acquaintances are revived. I find people who have come from all sections of the country—from the east and the west, and from the south—not adventurers merely, but men of substance and means, who seek a healthier climate and a pleasant home. St. Anthony is on the east side of the Mississippi; Minneapolis is opposite, on the west side. Both places are now large and populous. The main street of St. Anthony is over a mile in length. One of the finest water powers in the Union is an element of growth to both towns. The lumber which is sawed there is immense. A company is undertaking to remove the obstructions to navigation in the river between St. Paul and St. Anthony, $20,000 were raised for the purpose; one-half by the Steamboat Company, and the other half by the people of St. Anthony. The suspension bridge which connects Minneapolis with St. Anthony is familiar to all. It is a fit type of the enterprise of the people. I forget the exact sum I paid as toll when I walked across the bridge—perhaps it was a dime; at any rate I was struck with the answer given by the young man who took the toll, in reply to my inquiry as I returned, if my coming back wasn't included in the toll paid going over? "No," said he, in a very good-natured way, "we don't know anything about coming back; *it's all go ahead in this country.*"

NORTH OF ST. PAUL

Between St. Paul and Crow Wing is a tri-weekly line of stages. The coaches are of Concord manufacture, spacious and comfortable; and the entire equipage is well adapted to the convenience of travellers. Next season, the enterprising proprietors, Messrs. Chase and Allen, who carry the mail, intend establishing a daily line. I left the Fuller House in the stage at about five in the morning. There was only a convenient number of passengers till we arrived at St. Anthony, where we breakfasted; but then our load was more than doubled, and we drove out with nine inside and about seven outside, with any quantity of baggage. The road is very level and smooth; and with the exception of encountering a few small stumps where the track has been diverted for some temporary impediment, and also excepting a few places where it is exceedingly sandy, it is an uncommonly superior road. It is on the eastern bank of the Mississippi, and was laid out very straight. But let me remark that everybody who travels it seems conscious that it is a *government* road. There are several bridges, and they are often driven over at a rapid rate, much to their damage.

It was midnight when we arrived at Watab, where we were to lodge. The weather had been delightful during the day, but after nightfall a high wind rose and filled the air with dust. I descended from the stage—for I had rode upon the outside—with self-satisfied emotions of having come eighty-two miles since morning. The stage-house was crowded. It is a two-story building, the rooms of which are small. I went to bed, I was about to say, without any supper. But that was not so. I didn't get any supper, it is true, neither did I get a bed, for they were all occupied. The spare room on the floor was also taken. The proprietor, however, was accommodating, and gave me a sort of a lounge in rather a small room where three or four other men, and a dog, were sleeping on the floor. I fixed the door ajar for ventilation, and with my overcoat snugly buttoned around me, though it was not cold, addressed myself to sleep.

A heavy rain had fallen during the night; the stage was but moderately loaded, and I started out from Watab, after breakfast the next morning, in bright spirits. Still the road is level, and at a slow trot the team makes better time than a casual observer is conscious of. Much of the best land on either side of the road is in the hands of speculators, who purchased it at public sale, or afterwards plastered it over with land warrants. There is evidence of this on the entire route; for, although we pass populous villages, and a great many splendid farms, the greater part of the land is still unoccupied.

Crow Wing was selected as a trading post upwards of twenty years ago. The houses here are very respectable in size, and furnished in metropolitan style and elegance. The farms are highly productive, and the grazing for stock unequalled. There is a good ferry at the upper end of the town, at a point where the river is quite narrow and deep. You can be taken over with a horse for twenty-five cents; with a carriage, I suppose, the tariff is higher.

Perhaps one cause of my favorable impression of Crow Wing is the excellent and home-like hotel accommodations which I have found. The proprietor hardly assumes to keep a public-house, and yet provides his guests with very good entertainment; and I cannot refrain from saying that there is no public-house this side of St. Paul where the traveller will be better treated. Mr. Morrison—for that is the proprietor's name—came here fifteen years ago, having first come into this region in the service of John Jacob Astor. He married one of the handsomest of the Chippewa maidens, who is now his faithful wife and housekeeper, and the mother of several interesting and amiable children. Mr. M. is the postmaster. He has been a member of the territorial legislature, and his name has been given to a large and beautiful county. I judge that society has been congenial in the town. The little church, standing on an eminence, indicates some union of sentiment at least, and a regard for the higher objects of life. Spring and summer and autumn must be delightful seasons here, and bring with them the sweetest tranquillity. Nor are the people shut out from the world in winter; for then there is travel and intercourse and traffic. So are there pleasures and recreation peculiar to the season.

But the serene and quiet age of the settlement is near its close. Enterprise and speculation, with their bustle and turmoil, have laid hold of it. The clank of the hammer, the whistle of steamboats, the rattling of carts, heaps of lumber and of bricks, excavations and gradings, short corners and rough unshapen walks, will usurp the quiet and the regularity of the place. Indeed a man ought to make a fortune to compensate for residing in a town during the first years of its rapid building. The streets appear, on the map, to be well laid out. A number of purchasers of lots are preparing to build; and a few new buildings are already going up.

In Ohio and in Michigan timber has been an encumbrance; for there was great labor to be performed by the settler in clearing the land and preparing it for the plough; and at this day we see in travelling through each of those states, as well as in Kentucky, Tennessee, and Missouri, fields planted amidst heavy timber trees which have been belted that they may wither and die. Unlike the gorgeous forests in New Hampshire, which behind high cliffs and mountain fastnesses defy the woodman, the timber of Minnesota grows in the valleys of her great rivers and upon the banks of their numerous tributaries. It is thus easily shipped to a distant market; while the great body of the land, not encumbered with it, but naked, is ready for the plough and for the seed. Most of the timber which grows in the region below this point is hard wood, such as elm, maple, oak, and ash.

The relative importance of the lumber business would hardly be estimated by a stranger. It has been carried on for at least six years; and considerable has found its way as far down as St. Louis. It will be asked, I imagine, if all this timber land, especially the pine, has been sold by the government; and if not, how it happens that men cut it down and sell it? I will answer this. The great region of pineries has not yet been surveyed, much less sold by the government. But notwithstanding this, men have cut it in large quantities, sold it into a greedy market, and made money, if not fortunes in the business. As a sort of colorable excuse for cutting timber, those employed in the business often make a preemption claim on land covered with it, and many people suppose they have the right to cut as much as they please after the incipient steps towards preemption. But this is not so. All that a claimant can do in this respect is to cut wood enough for his fuel, and timber enough for his own building purposes, until he receives a patent from the government. Of course it is altogether reasonable and proper that men should be precluded from doing so until their title in the soil is complete. Because, until a preemption claim is perfect, or, until the land has been acquired by some legal title, it is not certain that the claimant will ultimately secure it or pay any money to the government. But does not the government do anything to prevent these trespasses? Yes, but all its attempts are baffled.

For example, last spring a large quantity of splendid lumber was seized by the United States marshal and sold at public auction. It was bid off by the lumbermen themselves, who had formed a combination to prevent its falling into the hands of other purchasers. This combination had no resistance as I am aware of in the public opinion of the territory, and the timber was sold to those who had it cut at a price so far below its value that it didn't pay the expense of the legal proceedings on the part of the government. This is accounted for in the fact of the exhaustless quantity of pine timber towards the north; in the demand for it when sawed; and in the disposition to protect enterprising men, though technically trespassers, who penetrate into the forest in the winter at great expense, and whose standing and credit are some guaranty of their ultimate responsibility to the government, should they not perfect their titles. The business of getting out the timber is carried on in the winter, and affords employment for a large number of athletic young men.

Most people have seen or been told something of the lumbermen of Maine. Allowing this to be so, it will not be difficult to comprehend the condition and character of the lumbermen of Minnesota and the northwest. But if there is anybody who fancies them to be a set of laborers, such as build our railroads and dig coal and minerals, he is greatly mistaken. The difference is in birth and education; between foreigners and native-born citizens. A difference not in rights and merits, so much as in habits and character. Born on American soil, they have attended our common schools, and have the bearing and independence of sovereigns. None but very vigorous men can endure, or at least attempt to endure, the exposure of living in the woods all winter and swinging the axe; though by proper care of themselves, such exercise is conducive to health and strength. Accordingly we find the lumberman—I mean of course the practical lumberman—to be a thick-set, muscular young man, with a bright eye and florid cheek; in short, one whom we would call a double-fisted fellow. He is not one of your California boys, but more affable and domestic, with a shorter beard, and not so great a profusion of weapons. His dress is snug and plain—the regular pioneer costume of boots over the pants, and a thick red shirt in lieu of a coat. His capital stock is his health and his hands. When in employment he is economical and lays up his wages. When out of employment and in town, his money generally goes freely. As a class, the lumbermen are intelligent. They are strong talkers, for they put in a good many of the larger sort of words; and from their pungent satire and sledge-hammer style of reasoning, are by no means very facile disputants. They are preeminently jokers. This is as they appear on their way to the woods. During the season of their active labor they usually spend the evening, after a day of hard work, in story-telling or in a game of euchre. Their wages amount to about two dollars a day, exclusive of board. They have good living in the woods, the provisions, which are furnished on an ample scale, being served by male cooks.

I ought not to leave unmentioned the valuable cargoes of lumber which are floated down the Mississippi. When coming up in the boat I was astonished to see such stupendous rafts. Large logs are transported by being made into rafts. At a landing where the boat stopped, I on one occasion attempted to estimate the number of logs comprised in one of these marine novelties, and found it to be about eight hundred; the logs were large, and were worth from five to six dollars each. Here then was a raft of timber worth at least $4000. They are navigated by about a dozen men, with large paddles attached at either end of the raft, which serve to propel and steer. Often, in addition to the logs, the rafts are laden with valuable freights of sawed lumber. Screens are built as a protection against wind, and a caboose stands somewhere in the center, or according to western parlance it might be called a cabin. Sometimes the raft will be running in a fine current; then only a couple of hands are on the watch and at the helm. The rest are seen either loitering about observing the country, or reclining, snugly wrapped up in their blankets. Some of these rafts must cover as much as two acres.

OPPORTUNITIES ON THE FRONTIER

As I have looked abroad upon the vast domain of the West beyond the dim Missouri, or in the immediate valley of the Mississippi, I have wondered at the contrast presented between the comparatively small number who penetrate to the frontier, and that great throng of men who toil hard for a temporary livelihood in the populous towns and cities of the Union. And I have thought if this latter class were at all mindful of the opportunities for gain

and independence which the new territories afforded, they would soon abandon—in a great measure at least—their crowded alleys in the city, and aspire
to cultivators and owners of the soil. Why there has not been a greater emigration from cities I cannot imagine, unless it is owing to a misapprehension
of Western life. Either it is this, or the pioneer is possessed of a very superior
degree of energy.

It has been said that the frontier man always keeps on the frontier; that he
continues to emigrate as fast as the country around him becomes settled.
There is a class that do so. Not, however, for the cause which has been sometimes humorously assigned—that civilization was inconvenient to them—but
because good opportunities arise to dispose of the farms they have already improved; and because a further emigration secures them cheaper lands. The
story of the pioneer who was disturbed by society when his nearest neighbor
lived fifteen miles off, even if it be true, fails to give the correct reason for the
migratory life of this class of men.

It almost always happens that wherever we go somebody else has preceded
us. Accident or enterprise has led some one to surpass us. Many of the most
useful pioneers of this country have been attracted hither by the accounts
given of its advantages by some one of their friends who had previously located himself here. Ask a man why he comes, and he says a neighbor of his, or
a son, or a brother, has been in the territory for so many months, and he likes
it so well I concluded to come also. A very respectable gentleman from Maine,
a shipowner and a man of wealth, who came up on the boat with me to
St. Paul, said his son-in-law was in the territory, and he had another son at
home who was bound to come, and if his wife was willing he believed the
whole family would come. Indeed the excellent state of society in the territory is to be attributed very much to the fact that parents have followed
after their children.

It is pretty obvious too why men will leave poor farms in New England,
and good farms in Ohio, to try their fortunes here. The farmer in New England, it may be in New Hampshire, hears that the soil of Minnesota is rich
and free from rocks, that there are other favorable resources, and a salubrious
climate such as he has been accustomed to. He concludes that it is best to sell
out the place he has, and try ploughing where there are no rocks to obstruct
him. The farmer of Ohio does not expect to find better soil than he leaves;
but his inducements are that he can sell his land at forty or fifty dollars an
acre, and preempt as good in Minnesota for a dollar and a quarter an acre.
This operation leaves him a surplus fund, and he becomes a more opulent
man, with better means to adorn his farm and to educate his children.

Those who contemplate coming West to engage in agricultural employment should leave their families, if families they have, behind till they have selected a location and erected some kind of a habitation; provided, however, they have no particular friend whose hospitality they can avail themselves of till their preliminary arrangements are effected. It will require three months, I judge, for a man to select a good claim (a quarter section, being 160 acres), and fence and plough a part of it and to erect thereon a cabin. There is never a want of land to preempt in a new country. The settler can always get an original claim, or buy out the claim of another very cheap, near some other settlers. The liberal policy of our government in regard to the disposal of public lands is peculiarly beneficial to the settler. The latter has the first chance. He can go on to a quarter section which may be worth fifteen dollars an acre, and preempt it before it is surveyed, and finally obtain it for $1.25 an acre. Whereas the speculator must wait till the land is surveyed and advertised for sale; and then he can get only what has not been preempted, and at a price which it brings at auction, not less than $1.25 an acre. Then what land is not sold at public sale is open to private entry at $1.25 an acre. It is such land that bounty warrants are located on. Thus it is seen the pioneer has the first choice. Why, I have walked over land up here that would now bring from ten to twenty dollars an acre if it was in the market, and which any settler can preempt and get for $1.25 an acre. I am strongly tempted to turn farmer myself, and go out and build me a cabin. The speculation would be a good one. But to acquire a title by preemption I must dwell on the soil, and prove that I have erected a dwelling and made other improvements. In other words, before a man (or any head of a family) can get a patent, he must satisfy the land officers that he is a dweller in good faith on the soil. It is often the case, indeed, that men get a title by preemption who never intend to live on their quarter section. But they do it by fraud. They have a sort of mental reservation, I suppose, when they take the requisite oaths. In this way many valuable claims are taken up and held along from month to month, or from year to year, by mock improvements. A pretender will make just improvements enough to hinder the actual settler from locating on the claim, or will sell out to him at a good profit. A good deal of money is made by these fictitious claimants. It is rather hard to prevent it, too, inasmuch as it is difficult to disprove that a man intends some time to have a permanent home, or, in fact, that his claim is not his legal residence, though his usual abiding place is somewhere else. Nothing could be more delightful than for a party of young men who desire to farm to come out together early in the spring, and aid each other in preempting land in the same neighborhood. The preemptor has to pay about five dollars in the way of fees before he gets through the entire process of securing a title. It is a popular error (much like the opinion that

FIRST TRAIN THROUGH THE PALISADES

a man cannot swear to what he sees through glass) that improvements of a certain value, say fifty dollars, are required to be made, or that a certain number of acres must be cultivated. All that is required, however, is evidence that the party has built a house fit to live in, and has in good faith proceeded to cultivate the soil. The law does not permit a person to preempt 160 acres but once; yet this provision is often disregarded, possibly from ignorance, I was about to say, but that cannot be, since the applicant must make oath that he has not before availed himself of the right of preemption.

Speculators have located a great many land warrants in Minnesota. Some have been located on lakes, some on swamps, some on excellent land. Of course the owner, who, as a general thing, is a non-resident, leaves his land idle for something to "turn up" to make it profitable. There it stands doing no good, but on the contrary is an encumbrance to the settler, who has to travel over and beyond it without meeting the face of a neighbor in its vicinity. The policy of new states is to tax non-resident landholders at a high rate. When the territory becomes a state, and is obliged to raise a revenue, some of these fellows outside, who, to use a phrase common up here, have plastered the country over with land warrants, will have to keep a lookout for the tax-gatherer. Now I do not mean to discourage moneyed men from investing in Minnesota lands. I do not wish to raise any bugbears, but simply to let them know that hoarding up large tracts of land without making improvements, and leaving it to increase in value by the toil and energy of the pioneer, is a way of doing things which is not popular with the actual settler. But there is a great deal of money to be made by judicious investments in land. Buying large tracts of land I believe to be the least profitable speculation, unless indeed the purchaser knows exactly what he is buying, and is on hand at the public sale to get the benefit of a second choice. I say second choice, because the preemptor has had the first choice long ago, and it may be before the land was surveyed. What I would recommend to speculators is to purchase in some good town sites. Buy in two or three, and if one or two happen to be failures, the profits on the other will enable you to bear the loss. I know of a man who invested $6000 at St. Paul six years ago. He has sold over $30,000 worth of the land, and has as much more left. This is but an ordinary instance. The advantage of buying lots in a town arises from the rapid rise of the value of the land, the ready market, and withal the moderate prices at which they can be procured during the early part of its history.

To such persons as have a desire to come West, and are not inclined to be farmers, and who have not capital enough to engage in mercantile business, there is sufficient employment. A new country always opens up avenues of successful business for every industrious man and woman; more kinds even than I could well enumerate. Every branch of mechanics needs workmen of all grades; from the boy who planes the rough boards to the head workman. Teaming affords good employment for young men the year round. The same may be said of the saw-mills. A great deal of building is going on constantly; and those who have good trades get $2.50 per day. I am speaking, of course, of the territory in general. One of the most profitable kinds of miscellaneous business is surveying. This art requires the service of large numbers; not only to survey the public lands, but town sites and the lands of private individuals. Labor is very high everywhere in the West, whether done by men, women, or children;—even the boys, not fourteen years old, who clean the knives and forks on the steamboats, get $20 a month and *are found*. But the best of it all is, that when a man earns a few dollars he can easily invest it in a piece of land, and double his money in three months, perhaps in one month.

I have now a young man in my mind who came to a town ten miles this side of St. Paul, six months ago, with $500. He commenced trading, and has already, by good investments and the profits of his business, doubled his money. Everything that one can eat or wear brings a high price, or as high as it does in any part of the West. The number of visitors and emigrants is so large that the productions of the territory are utterly inadequate to supply the market. Therefore large quantities of provisions have to be brought up the river from the lower towns. At Swan River, 100 miles this side of St. Paul, pork is worth $35. Board for laboring men must be about four dollars a week. For transient guests at Crow Wing it is one dollar a day.

There is one drawback which this territory has in common with the greater part of the West. It is not only a drawback, but a nuisance. I mean drinking or whiskey shops. The greater proportion of the settlers are temperate men, I am sure; but in almost every village there are places where the meanest kind of intoxicating liquor is sold. There are some who sell liquor to the Indians. But such business is universally considered as the most degraded that a mean man can be guilty of. It is filthy to see men staggering about under the influence of bad whiskey, or of any kind of whiskey. Mr. Gough[1] is needed in the West.

Minnesota is not behind in education. Ever since Governor Slade, of Vermont, brought some bright young school mistresses up to St. Paul (in 1849), common school education has been diffusing its precious influences. The government wisely sets apart two sections of land—the 16th and the 36th—in every township for school purposes. A township is six miles square; and the two sections thus reserved in each township comprise 1280 acres. Other territories have the same provision. This affords a very good fund for educa-

1. [John B. Gough, a noted temperance orator.—ED.]

tional uses, or rather it is a great aid to the exertions of the people. There are some flourishing institutions of learning in the territory. But the greatest institution after all in the country—the surest protection of our liberties and our laws—is the FREE SCHOOL.

36

Hustle and Bustle in Chicago, 1871

*M*rs. *Sara Clarke Lippincott (1823–1904), better known to her thousands of readers as Grace Greenwood, was one of the most popular writers of her day and has, furthermore, the distinction of being one of the earliest women newspaper correspondents in the United States. She was born in Pompey, New York, but a large part of her life was spent in Pennsylvania, first at Pittsburgh, later at Philadelphia. In later life—except that the word connotes things which Mrs. Lippincott certainly was not—she might almost be termed a "cosmopolite," what with much travel both in America and in Europe and residence in Washington, New York, and Chicago.*

She wrote voluminously. Newspapers contained her articles, magazines her stories, while the publishing houses poured out year after year volumes of essays, poetry, juveniles, and novels. It was Grace Greenwood to whom Hawthorne referred when he spoke of the "damned mob of scribbling women." She wrote amiably and possessed a sure touch for what would take with the public. There is a certain sparkle and sprightliness about her work which is undeniable, yet withal she was superficial, and her writings for the most part merit the obscurity into which they have fallen. New Life in New Lands, *published in 1873, is no different from the rest of her work. En route across the nation, in preparation for a series of articles for the* New York Tribune, *she stopped at Chicago. Her description portrays entertainingly an impression most Americans had of that city, "independent as a hog on ice."*

I had been from Chicago some four years, and in that time its growth and improvement have been absolutely marvellous. It grows on Independence days and Sabbath days and all days. It grows o' nights. Its enterprise, daring, and vigilance storm the land and fetter the sea, defy and override physical laws, and circumvent nature. A great part of the west side of the city seems to me to have been heaved up out of the mud by a benevolent earthquake. I see beautiful and stately marble buildings where four years ago were the humble little domiciles of the Germans, or the comfortless shanties of the Irish emigrants. What were then wastes of sand and rubbish and weeds are now lovely public squares or parks, with hard, smooth drives, ponds, rocks, hillocks, rustic bridges and seats, pretty vine-shaded arbors, and the usual park accompaniments of tame bears and caged eagles.

All this rapid change and progress is as mysterious as it is marvellous, till you know a regular, genuine Chicagoan, and see him go about his business with a drive, and devotion, a matchless economy of time and means, which stop just short of hurry and greed,—of the desperate and the sordid. The very struggle which the men of Chicago have always waged against adverse natural conditions has been to a degree ennobling, and has lifted their lives above the commonplace. It is essentially heroic; it is something titanic; it is more creation than development. Foot by foot, inch by inch, they have gained on swampy flats, on oozing clay-banks, on treacherous sand-heaps. Every year has chronicled new enterprises, new triumphs. The sluggish, miasmatic waters, once all abroad, have been driven back, and headed off, and hemmed in, and at last brought to bay in the horrible little river that now creeps in a Stygian flood through the city it does its best to poison and pollute, while sullenly bearing back and forth rich burdens of commerce. But the hour has almost come when that ill-famed stream must take the back track,—double on itself,—actually run up its channel, and through the Illinois Canal into the Illinois River, and so down into the Mississippi. Then Lake Michigan, who does a great deal of mischief for lack of better employment, will have a heavier job to perform in the cleansing line than the rivers Peneus and Alpheus together accomplished for Augeas.

But for a pleasanter theme. Lincoln Park, on the north side, is perhaps the

most striking and apparently magical of all the enterprises and improvements of the city. It is already very beautiful, with a variety of surface and
ornamentation most wonderful, when we remember that scarcely five years
ago the spot was a dreary waste of drifting sand and unsightly weeds. The
manner in which these elusive sands, full of the restlessness of the waves
from which they have been rescued, are fixed and fettered is very curious.
Boards, stones, sticks, leaves, weeds, are laid on them, then clay is added, and
so soil enough created to be sown or planted. The modest elevations called
"hills," by courtesy, are also, I am told, "fearfully and wonderfully made"
out of the most unsightly refuse and rubbish; so that, if future *savans,* taking
them for Indian mounds, shall ever excavate one, they may perhaps come
upon distinct strata of oyster-shells, tin fruit-cans, old shoes, and broken
crockery, with a substratum of hoop-skirts. No means, however humble, for
breaking and elevating the surface are despised. I should not be surprised to
hear that moles were protected by game-laws. Water for ponds and fountains
comes forth into the light and the sweet, vital upper air, leaping and shouting. Those artesian wells, with the lake-tunnels, will yet make Chicago more
than the rival of Rome in fountains and baths, and in that cleanliness which
is next to godliness. The great drive on the lake shore, from Chicago to
Evanston, will be another wonder, only surpassed by the system of continuous
boulevards and parks, a complete circumvallation of the city, which at no
distant day will furnish one of the grandest drives in the world. Citizens of
Atlantic cities say they miss their grand rocks and hills, and the sea, "that
symbol of the infinite." But Lake Michigan is a respectable bit of water; and
the prairie has a beauty and even a grandeur of its own. If a cornfield of
several thousand acres is not "a symbol of the infinite," I should like to know
what is. The present entrance to Lincoln Park is a little depressing, being
through a cemetery, but those old settlers are fast being unsettled and re-
established elsewhere. Even the dead must "move on" in Chicago. It were
impossible for one to tell where in this vicinity he could take his last sleep.
Chicago houses are all liable to be moved, even the "house of worship" and
"the house appointed for all living." A moving building has ceased to be a
moving sight here. Not only do small frame cottages, that a year or two ago
were in quiet rural localities, take fright at the snort and the rush of advancing trade, and prance off to "fresh fields and pastures new," but substantial
brick edifices sometimes migrate. A few years ago a Baptist church, on Wabash Avenue, saw fit to change sides, and came over—in several pieces to be
sure—to the corner of Monroe and Morgan Streets, where it now stands,
looking as decorous and settled and close-communion as ever.

The parks of the west side, patriotically and democratically named "Union" and "Jefferson," though reminding one somewhat, by their modest dimensions, ingenious contrivances, and artifices of rock and water and hillock and bridge (with a "real flagstaff" and "real flag"), of the pious devices of John Wemmick for the amusement of "the aged,"[1] are yet sources of incalculable enjoyment and good for all who live in their pleasant vicinity. Wooden pavements, splendid macadamized roads, and the new boulevards are fast bringing the beautiful suburban settlements of Lake View, Kenwood, and Hyde Park into the municipal fold. The city is bearing down upon them at a tremendous rate, and the roar of traffic will soon drown for them through the day the deep sweet monotone of the lake. In the heart of the town Chicago is making worthy preparations to entertain the great floating population of the world setting westward. The work on the new Pacific Hotel goes bravely on. I do not quite like the location, and the court-yard seems to me too small for so immense a caravansary. I am sorry to hear that it is proposed to change its name in order to do honor to one of its most munificent proprietors. No man's name seems to me big enough for such a hotel. The old court-house has taken to itself wings to meet the great rush of business in the murder and divorce line; and I hear much of Potter Palmer's new hotel, which is to be a monster affair, capable of accommodating an old-fashioned German principality, to say the least.

In short, all is astir here. There is no such thing as stagnation or rest. Lake-winds and prairie-winds keep the very air in commotion. You catch the contagion of activity and enterprise, and have wild dreams of beginning life again, and settling—no, circulating, *whirling*—in Chicago, the rapids and wild eddies of business have such a powerful fascination for one. Chicago postmen sometimes go their rounds on velocipedes. Chicago newsboys are preternaturally clever and wide-awake.

I suppose I need hardly say that I like Chicago,—like it in spite of lake-wind sharpness and prairie flatness, damp tunnels, swinging bridges, hard water, and easy divorces. With all the distinctive characteristics of a great city, it has preserved in a wonderful degree the provincial virtues of generous hospitality, cordiality, and neighborly kindness. A lady from the East lately said of it, very charmingly, "It is New York with the heart left in." I do not deny that the genuine Chicagoan has well learned the prayer of the worthy Scotchman, "Lord, gie us a guid conceit o' oursels!" and that the prayer has been abundantly answered; but I do not think that his self-satisfaction often amounts to arrogance, or inclines him to rest on his laurels or his oars. He well knows, I think, that there is small profit in gaining the whole world to lose his own soul, and beautiful churches and beneficent mission schools,

---

1. [A reference to scenes and characters in Charles Dickens' *Great Expectations*.—Ed.]

quiet deeds of mercy and munificent charities, show that he finds ways of ascent into the higher life, even from the busy dock, the noisy factory, the grim foundry, and the tempestuous Exchange.

My memory of the journey from Washington, over the Northern Central and Pennsylvania Central, is a long panorama of surpassing summer beauty, though, like Pilgrim, after leaving the "Delectable Mountains," I had to pass through the "Valley of the Shadow of Death" at Pittsburg, and, unlike him, had a world of trouble about my baggage. But, dear me, it is so long ago,— nearly four weeks! In that time Chicago, very likely, has opened a tunnel, and stolen an acre of land from the lake, and drilled an artesian well or two, and tossed up several good-sized hills in Lincoln Park.

Part IV

WESTWARD THE COURSE
OF EMPIRE

American interest in the Far West was of long duration, as the popularity of the Lewis and Clark expedition and the fame of Dana's *Two Years before the Mast* or Parkman's *Oregon Trail* clearly testified. Yet it was an interest at first more or less sporadic and certainly never fully sustained until near the middle of the nineteenth century. This was due, in part, to the fact that the area was not originally an American possession and, in part, to the fact that the territories nearer the Mississippi were still primitive, open to occupation, and sufficiently bizarre to satisfy the longings of the romantically inclined. With the acquisition of the Oregon country (1846) and the cession of the Southwest and California from Mexico (1848), together with a population sufficient to create a tier of states in the hitherto unoccupied areas just west of the Mississippi, American concern in the Far West markedly quickened. The sensational discovery of gold in 1849 made the interest permanent.

Travelers wrote of the routes to the Pacific Coast and about what they found there on arrival. Three main routes were ordinarily followed: the Santa Fé Trail to the Southwest, the California Trail, and the Oregon Trail. Until the late forties and early fifties, accounts were largely by emigrants in company with other emigrants and are not quite "travel" books within the ordinary meaning of the word. Once population had moved in, however, the observer made a quick appearance, and thereafter travelers' accounts began to multiply.

They were interested in all manner of things and people, as good travelers should be: alkali deserts, Indians, gold and silver deposits, the mining camps, and the prospects of wealth. In a lesser degree they described cowboys, ranchers, fur-traders, and giant trees; but, more than anything else, they wrote minutely and at length of fabulous, romantic, spectacular San Francisco, of California, and of the way thither. The Oregon country, particularly the Columbia River region, received some attention; but, rather surprisingly, the Southwest came in for only minor recording. By and large, the travelers' accounts of the Far West do not deal so analytically, or probe so deeply into economic and social phenomena, as do those of the eastern states or the Cotton Kingdom. But for sheer entertainment and readability the books on this section are unsurpassed.

In the end the West became "tamed," though never by 1900 so completely as to lose its fascination. Transcontinental trains naturally brought in a different type of tourist from that which horse and coach had conveyed. Nevertheless, by the close of the century, the West commanded better observers and better observations than was the lot of the rest of the nation.

THE COURSE OF EMPIRE

37

Outfitting a Santa Fé Expedition, 1844

Josiah Gregg, who was born in Overton County, Tennessee, in 1806, is the classic historian of the Santa Fé trade. Before he was twenty-one he had settled at Independence, Missouri, from which, for motives of health, he began in 1831 his many journeys with the southwestern traders. Well educated, a keen observer, and armed with copious notes, he wrote down the sum of his experiences in his Commerce of the Prairies, *published in two volumes in New York in 1844. It went through many editions in his own day and has remained popular for a century. His last visit to Santa Fé was made in 1849, after which he engaged in an ill-fated expedition to California. Worn out from unparalleled sufferings, he died on his return in 1850.*

People who reside at a distance have generally considered St. Louis as the emporium of the Santa Fé trade; but that city, in truth, has never been a place of rendezvous, nor even of outfit, except for a small portion of the traders who have started from its immediate vicinity. The town of Franklin on the Missouri River, about a hundred and fifty miles farther to the westward, seems truly to have been the cradle of our trade; but as the navigation of the Missouri River had considerably advanced towards the year 1831, and the advantages of some point of debarkation nearer the western frontier were very evident, whereby upwards of a hundred miles of troublesome land-carriage over unimproved and often miry roads might be avoided, the new town of Independence, but twelve miles from the Indian border and two or three south of the Missouri River, being the most eligible point, soon began to take the lead as a place of debarkation, outfit, and departure, which in spite of all opposition it has ever since maintained. It is to this beautiful spot, already grown up to be a thriving town, that the prairie adventurer, whether in search of wealth, health, or amusement, is latterly in the habit of repairing about the first of May, as the caravans usually set out some time during that month. Here they purchase their provisions for the road, and many of their mules, oxen, and even some of their wagons—in short, load all their vehicles and make their final preparations for a long journey across the prairie wilderness.

As Independence is a point of convenient access (the Missouri River being navigable at all times from March till November), it has become the general port of embarkation for every part of the great western and northern "prairie ocean." Besides the Santa Fé caravans, most of the Rocky Mountain traders and trappers, as well as emigrants to Oregon, take this town in their route. During the season of departure, therefore, it is a place of much bustle and active business.

Among the concourse of travelers at this starting point, besides traders and tourists a number of pale-faced invalids are generally to be met with. The prairies have, in fact, become very celebrated for their sanative effects—more justly so, no doubt, than the more fashionable watering-places of the North. Most chronic diseases, particularly liver complaints, dyspepsias, and similar affections, are often radically cured; owing, no doubt, to the peculiarities of diet and the regular exercise incident to prairie life, as well as to the purity of the atmosphere of those elevated unembarrassed regions. An invalid myself, I can answer for the efficacy of the remedy, at least in my own case. Though, like other valetudinarians, I was disposed to provide an ample supply of such commodities as I deemed necessary for my comfort and health, I was not long upon the prairies before I discovered that most of such extra preparations were unnecessary, or at least quite dispensable. A few knick-knacks, as a little tea, rice, fruits, crackers, etc., suffice very well for the first fortnight, after which the invalid is generally able to take the fare of the hunter and teamster. Though I set out myself in a carriage, before the close of the first week I saddled my pony; and when we reached the buffalo range I was not only as eager for the chase as the sturdiest of my companions, but I enjoyed far more exquisitely my share of the buffalo than all the delicacies which were ever devised to provoke the most fastidious appetite.

The ordinary supplies for each man's consumption during the journey are about fifty pounds of flour, as many more of bacon, ten of coffee and twenty of sugar, and a little salt. Beans, crackers, and trifles of that description are comfortable appendages, but being looked upon as dispensable luxuries, are seldom to be found in any of the stores on the road. The buffalo is chiefly depended upon for fresh meat, and great is the joy of the traveler when that noble animal first appears in sight.

The wagons now most in use upon the prairies are manufactured in Pittsburg; and are usually drawn by eight mules or the same number of oxen. Of late years, however, I have seen much larger vehicles employed, with ten or twelve mules harnessed to each and a cargo of goods of about five thousand pounds in weight. At an early period the horse was more frequently in use, as mules were not found in great abundance; but as soon as the means for procuring these animals increased, the horse was gradually and finally discarded, except occasionally for riding and the chase.

Oxen having been employed by Major Riley for the baggage wagons of the escort which was furnished the caravan of 1829, they were found, to the surprise of the traders, to perform almost equal to mules. Since that time, upon an average, about half the wagons in these expeditions have been drawn by oxen. They possess many advantages, such as pulling heavier loads than the same number of mules, particularly through muddy or sandy places; but they generally fall off in strength as the prairie grass becomes drier and shorter, and often arrive at their destination in a most shocking plight. In this condition I have seen them sacrificed at Santa Fé for ten dollars the pair; though in more favorable seasons they sometimes remain strong enough to be driven back to the United States the same fall. Therefore, although the original cost of a team of mules is much greater, the loss ultimately sustained by them is usually less, to say nothing of the comfort of being able to travel faster and more at ease. The inferiority of oxen as regards endurance is partially owing to the tenderness of their feet; for there are very few among the thousands who have traveled on the prairies that ever knew how to shoe them properly. Many have resorted to the curious expedient of shoeing their animals with moccasins made of raw buffalo-skin, which does remarkably well as long as the weather remains dry; but when wet, they are soon worn through. Even mules, for the most part, perform the entire trip without being shod at all; though the hoofs often become very smooth, which frequently renders all their movements on the dry grassy surface nearly as laborious as if they were treading on ice.

The supplies being at length procured and all necessary preliminaries systematically gone through, the trader begins the difficult task of loading his wagons. Those who understand their business take every precaution so to stow away their packages that no jolting on the road can afterwards disturb the order in which they had been disposed. The ingenuity displayed on these occasions has frequently been such that after a tedious journey of eight hundred miles the goods have been found to have sustained much less injury than they would have experienced on a turnpike road, or from the ordinary handling of property upon our western steamboats.

The next great difficulty the traders have to encounter is in training those animals that have never before been worked, which is frequently attended by an immensity of trouble. There is nothing, however, in the mode of harnessing and conducting teams in prairie traveling which differs materially from that practiced on the public highways throughout the states, the representations of certain travelers to the contrary notwithstanding.

At last all are fairly launched upon the broad prairie—the miseries of preparation are over—the thousand anxieties occasioned by wearisome consultations and delays are felt no more. The charioteer as he smacks his whip feels a bounding elasticity of soul within him, which he finds it impossible to restrain; even the mules prick up their ears with a peculiarly conceited air, as if in anticipation of that change of scene which will presently follow. Harmony and good feeling prevail everywhere. The hilarious song, the *bon mot,* and the witty repartee go round in quick succession; and before people have had leisure to take cognizance of the fact, the lovely village of Independence with its multitude of associations is already lost to the eye.

It may be proper to observe here for the benefit of future travelers that in order to make a secure shelter for the cargo against the inclemencies of the weather, there should be spread upon each wagon a pair of stout Osnaburg sheets, with one of sufficient width to reach bottom of the body on each side, so as to protect the goods from driving rains. By omitting this important precaution many packages of merchandise have been seriously injured. Some preferred lining the exterior of the wagon-body by tacking a simple strip of sheeting all around it. On the outward trips especially a pair of Mackinaw blankets can be advantageously spread betwixt the two sheets, which effectually secures the roof against the worst of storms. This contrivance has also the merit of turning the blankets into a profitable item of trade by enabling the owners to evade the custom-house officers, who would otherwise seize them as contraband articles.

But after this comes the principal task of organizing. The proprietors are first notified by proclamation to furnish a list of their men and wagons. The latter are generally apportioned into four divisions, particularly when the company is large—and ours consisted of nearly a hundred wagons, besides a dozen of dear-borns and other small vehicles and two small cannons (a four and six pounder), each mounted upon a carriage. To each of these divisions a lieutenant was appointed, whose duty it was to inspect every ravine and creek on the route, select the best crossings, and superintend what is called in prairie parlance the "forming" of each encampment.

Upon the calling of the roll we were found to muster an efficient force of nearly two hundred men, without counting invalids or other disabled bodies, who, as a matter of course, are exempt from duty. There is nothing so much dreaded by inexperienced travelers as the ordeal of guard duty. But no matter what the condition or employment of the individual may be, no one has the smallest chance of evading the common law of the prairies. The amateur tourist and the listless loafer are precisely in the same wholesome predicament —they must all take their regular turn at the watch. There is usually a set of genteel idlers attached to every caravan, whose wits are forever at work in devising schemes for whiling away their irksome hours at the expense of others. By embarking in these trips of pleasure they are enabled to live without expense; for the hospitable traders seldom refuse to accommodate even a loafing companion with a berth at their mess without charge. But then these lounging attachés are expected at least to do good service by way of guard-duty. None are even permitted to furnish a substitute, as is frequently done in military expeditions, for he that would undertake to stand the tour of another besides his own would scarcely be watchful enough for the dangers of the prairies. Even the invalid must be able to produce unequivocal proofs of his inability, or it is a chance if the plea is admitted. For my own part, although I started on the sick list, and though the prairie sentinel must stand fast and brook the severest storm (for then it is that the strictest watch is necessary), I do not remember ever having missed my post but once during the whole journey.

The usual number of watches is eight, each standing a fourth of every alternate night. When the party is small the number is greatly reduced, while in the case of very small bands they are sometimes compelled for safety's sake to keep one watch on duty half the night. With large caravans the captain usually appoints eight sergeants of the guard, each of whom takes an equal portion of men under his command.

The wild and motley aspect of the caravan can be but imperfectly conceived without an idea of the costumes of its various members. The most fashionable prairie dress is the fustian frock of the city-bred merchant furnished with a multitude of pockets capable of accommodating a variety of extra tackling. Then there is the backwoodsman with his linsey or leather hunting-shirt—the farmer with his blue jean coat—the wagoner with his

CROSSING THE PECOS

flannel-sleeve vest—besides an assortment of other costumes which go to fill up the picture.

In the article of firearms there is also an equally interesting medley. The frontier hunter sticks to his rifle, as nothing could induce him to carry what he terms in derision "the scatter-gun." The sportsman from the interior flourishes his double-barreled fowling-piece with equal confidence in its superiority. The latter is certainly the most convenient description of gun that can be carried on this journey; as a charge of buck-shot in night attacks (which are the most common) will of course be more likely to do execution than a single rifle-ball fired at random. The repeating arms have lately been brought into use upon the prairies and they are certainly very formidable weapons, particularly when used against an ignorant savage foe. A great many were furnished beside with a bountiful supply of pistols and knives of every description, so that the party made altogether a very brigand-like appearance.

When caravans are able to cross in the evening they seldom stop on the near side of a stream—first, because if it happens to rain during the night it may become flooded and cause both detention and trouble; again, though the stream be not impassable after rain, the banks become slippery and difficult to ascend. A third and still more important reason is that, even supposing the contingency of rain does not occur, teams will rarely pull as well in cold collars, as wagoners term it—that is, when fresh geared—as in the progress of a day's travel. When a heavy pull is just at hand in the morning wagoners sometimes resort to the expedient of driving a circuit upon the prairie before venturing to take the bank.

For the edification of the reader, who has, no doubt, some curiosity on the subject, I will briefly mention that the kitchen and table wares of the traders usually consist of a skillet, a frying-pan, a sheet-iron camp-kettle, a coffee-pot, and each man with his tin cup and a butcher's knife. The culinary operations being finished, the pan and kettle are set upon the grassy turf, around which all take a lowly seat and crack their gleesome jokes while from their greasy hands they swallow their savory viands—all with a relish rarely experienced at the well-spread tables of the most fashionable and wealthy.

The insatiable appetite acquired by travelers upon the prairies is almost incredible, and the quantity of coffee drunk is still more so. It is an unfailing and apparently indispensable beverage, served at every meal—even under the broiling noon-day sun the wagoner will rarely fail to replenish a second time his huge tin cup. Every year large parties of New Mexicans, some provided with mules and asses, others with *carretas* or truckle-carts and oxen, drive out into these prairies to procure a supply of buffalo beef for their families. They hunt like the wild Indians, chiefly on horseback and with bow and arrow, or lance, with which they soon load their carts and mules. They find no difficulty in curing their meat even in mid-summer, by slicing it thin and spreading or suspending it in the sun; or, if in haste, it is slightly barbecued. During the curing operation they often follow the Indian practice of beating or kneading the slices with their feet, which they contend contributes to its preservation.

Here the extraordinary purity of the atmosphere is remarkably exemplified. The caravans cure meat in the same simple manner, except the process of kneading. A line is stretched from corner to corner on each side of a wagon-body and strung with slices of beef, which remains from day to day till it is sufficiently cured to be stacked away. This is done without salt, and yet it very rarely putrefies. In truth, as blow-flies are unknown here, there is nothing to favor putrefaction. While speaking of flies I might as well remark that after passing beyond the region of the tall grass between the Missouri frontier and Arkansas River, the horse-fly, also, is unknown. Judging from the prairies on our border we had naturally anticipated a great deal of mischief from these brute-tormentors; in which we were very agreeably disappointed.

Upon encamping, the wagons are formed into a hollow square (each division to a side), constituting at once an enclosure (or *corral*) for the animals when needed, and a fortification against the Indians. Not to embarrass this cattle-pen, the camp fires are all lighted outside of the wagons. Outside of the wagons, also, the travelers spread their beds, which consist, for the most part, of buffalo-rugs and blankets. Many content themselves with a single Macki-naw; but a pair constitutes the most regular pallet; and he that is provided with a buffalo-rug into the bargain is deemed luxuriously supplied. It is most usual to sleep out in the open air, as well to be at hand in case of attack as, indeed, for comfort; for the serene sky of the prairies affords the most agreeable and wholesome canopy. That deleterious attribute of night air and dews so dangerous in other climates is but little experienced upon the high plains: on the contrary, the serene evening air seems to affect the health rather favorably than otherwise. Tents are so rare on these expeditions that in a caravan of two hundred men I have not seen a dozen. In time of rain the traveler resorts to his wagon, which affords a far more secure shelter than a tent; for if the latter is not beaten down by the storms which so often accompany rain upon the prairies, the ground underneath is at least apt to be flooded. During dry weather, however, even the invalid prefers the open air.

Prior to the date of our trip it had been customary to secure the horses by hoppling them. The fore-hopple (a leather strap or rope manacle upon the fore-legs), being most convenient, was more frequently used; though the side-line (a hopple connecting a fore and hind leg) is the most secure; for with this an animal can hardly increase his pace beyond a hobbling walk; whereas, with the fore-hopple, a frightened horse will scamper off with nearly as much velocity as though he were unshackled. But better than either of these is the practice which the caravans have since adopted of tethering the mules at night around the wagons, at proper intervals, with ropes twenty-five or thirty feet in length tied to stakes fifteen to twenty inches long driven into the ground; a supply of which, as well as mallets, the wagoners always carry with them.

38

California on the Eve of Conquest, 1847

*O*ne readily believes that Henry A. Wise was a very charming man, for he *wrote a very charming book. He was born in the Brooklyn Navy Yard in 1819, and his whole life was connected with the United States Navy. During the Mexican War he was assigned to duty in California waters, and in* Los Gringos *he gives a record of his travels around the Horn, of South America, and of California. Whatever the Mexican War may have been like in other theaters, it appears to have been in California largely a matter of Mexican beauties, fandangos, and hunting expeditions. The account is told with fresh-ness and verve and portrays beautifully the idyllic character of California before it was to be turned upside down in the rush for gold two years later.*

The rain came down in a steady drizzle, as we anchored in our new haven, but as the falling water thinned, and rolled partially along the land, we discerned an endless succession of green gentle slopes and valleys, with heights of just a medium between hills and mountains, rising gradually from the shores of the bay, clothed and crowned with magnificent vegetation.

The town of Monterey, if it could be dignified by the title, we found a mean, irregular collection of mud huts, and long, low, adobie dwellings, strewn promiscuously over an easy slope, down to the water's edge. The most conspicuous was the *duana*—Custom House—a spacious frame building near the landing, which unquestionably had in times past been the means of yielding immense revenues to the Mexican exchequer, but now its roomy storehouses were empty and silent. Neither men nor merchandise disturbed its quiet precincts. Notwithstanding the rain, numbers of us resolved to dare the moisture, and I, for one, would wade about on land, up to my neck in water, at any time to get quit of a ship after forty days aquatic recreation; but here there was no resisting the gratefully green appearance of the shores around us: we were soon stowed in a boat—the oars dipped smart and strong in the water, and we went merrily towards the land. Indeed I have invariably observed that men-of-war's men are wont to use their arms with much vigor, on first pulling on shore in a strange port; a physical characteristic which I am led to attribute to a desire on their part to test the virtues of any liquid compounds to be met with in the abodes of hospitable publicans. The anchorage was barely half a mile from the shore, and in a few minutes we disembarked at a little pier, that only partially served to check the rolling swell from seaward; but what's a wet foot in a fit of enthusiasm, or a heavy shower! Nothing, certainly, so we scrambled up the slimy steps, and while on the point of giving a yell of delight, to announce our arrival in California, my pedal extremities flew upwards and down I sank, making a full length *intaglio* in the yielding mud—this was my first impression, but after getting decently scraped by Jack's knives, I became less excitable, and took intense delight during the course of the afternoon, in beholding my companions going through precisely the same performances. By cautious navigation we reached the main street, then our progress was dreadfully slow and laborious. The mud—a sticky, red pigment, lay six good inches on the dryest level, and at every step our feet were disengaged by a powerful jerk, and a deep, guttural noise from the slippy holes; occasionally, too, we were forced to climb ungainly barricades of timber, with here and there a piece of ordnance gazing ferociously out into the surrounding country. Although a casual observer might naturally have supposed that the mud would have offered a sufficient barrier to all the armies ever raised, still, as trouble had been brewing, and most of the garrison withdrawn for an expedition into the interior, these pre-cautions were quite an imposing display, which was, no doubt, all intended. At last, by dint of perserverance, we attained a firm foothold in the barracks, and then had breath and leisure to look around.

Monterey, before the war, contained about five hundred people, but on our advent there was scarcely a native to be seen: all the men had gone to join their belligerent friends in the southern provinces, leaving their property and dwellings to be guarded by their wives and dogs; even their ladies bore us no good will, and our salutations were returned by a surly *adios,* extorted from closed teeth and scowling faces. The dogs were more civil, and even when showing their fangs, were sagacious enough to keep beyond the chastening reach of Yankee arms. There were a goodly number of sentinels on the alert, prowling about, with heavy knives in their girdles, and the locks of their rifles carefully sheltered from the rain; and at night it became a matter of some bodily danger for an indifferent person to come suddenly in view of one of these vigilant gentlemen, for with but a tolerable ear for music he might detect the sharp click of a rifle, and the hoarse caution of "Look out, thar, stranger"; when if the individual addressed did not speedily shout out his name and calling, he stood the merest chance of having another eyelet-hole drilled through his skull.

All this at the first rapid glance gave us no very bright anticipations; everything looked triste and cheerless. Upon inquiring, too, we were shocked to learn there was nothing eatable to be had, nor what was yet more melan-choly, naught drinkable nor smokable: everybody was so much occupied in making war, as to have entirely lost sight of their appetites. We began to indulge the faintest suspicions that somehow or other we had gotten into the wrong place, and that California was not so charming a spot as we had been led to believe; however, there was no appeal, and fortunately for our health and spirits, as we were leaning listlessly over the piazza of the barracks, staring might and main at the little church in the distance, we beheld a body of horsemen coming slowly over the verdant plains, and soon after they drew bridles, and dismounted before us. The *cavallada*—spare horses—were driven into the corral near by, and we presented in due form to the riders. It was the most impressive little band I ever beheld; they numbered sixty, and, without exception, had gaunt bony frames like steel, dressed in skins, with heavy beards and unshorn faces, with each man his solid American rifle, and huge knife by the hip. With all their wildness and ferocious appearance they had quite simple manners, and were perfectly frank and respectful in bearing. Their language and phraseology were certainly difficult for a stran-ger to comprehend, for many of them had passed the greater portion of their lives as trappers and hunters among the Rocky Mountains; but there was an air of indomitable courage hovering about them, with powers to endure any amount of toil or privation—men who wouldn't stick at scalping an Indian or a dinner of mule meat;—and you felt assured in regarding them, that with a score of such staunch fellows at your side you would sleep soundly, even though the forests were alive with an atmosphere of Camanche yells. They were the woodsmen of our far west, who on hearing of the disturbances in California enrolled themselves for service in the Volunteer Battalion—more by way of recreation, I imagine, than for glory or patriotism. In truth, the native had good reason to regard them with terror.

We soon became quite sociable, and after a hearty supper of fried beef and biscuit, by some miraculous dispensation a five gallon keg of whiskey was uncorked, and, after a thirty days' thirst, our new found friends slaked away unremittingly. Many were the marvellous adventures narrated of huntings, fightings, freezings, snowings, and starvations; and one stalwart bronzed trapper beside me, finding an attentive listener, began,—"The last time, Captin, I cleared the Oregon trail, the Ingens fowt us amazin' hard. Pete," said he, addressing a friend smoking a clay-pipe by the fire, with a half pint of corn-juice in his hand, which served to moisten his own clay at intervals between every puff,—"Pete, do you notice how I dropped the red skin who pit the poisoned arrer in my moccasin! Snakes, Captin, the varmints lay thick as leaves behind the rocks; and bless ye, the minit I let fall old Ginger from my jaw, up they springs, and lets fly their flint-headed arrers in amongst us, and one on 'em wiped me right through the leg. I tell yer what it is, I riled, I did, though we had tolerable luck in the forenoon—for I dropped two and a squaw and Pete got his good six—barrin' that the darned villians had hamstrung our mule, and we were bound to see the thing out. Well, Captin, as I tell ye, I'm not weak in the jints, but it's no joke to hold the heft of twenty-three pounds on a sight for above ten minits on a stretch; so Pete and me scrouched down, made a little smoke with some sticks, and then we moved off a few rods, whar we got a clar peep; for better than an hour we seed nothin', but on a suddin I seed the chap—I know'd him by his paintin'—that driv the arrer in my hide; he was peerin' around quite bold, thinkin' we'd vamosed; I jist fetched old Ginger up and drawed a bee line on his cratch, and, stranger, I giv him sich a winch in the stomach that he dropped straight in his tracks; he did! in five jumps I riz his har, and Pete and me warn't troubled agin for a week." With such pleasant converse we beguiled the time until the night was somewhat advanced; when, finding a vacant corner near the blazing fire, with a saddle for pillow, I sank into profound slumber, and never woke to consciousness until the band was again astir at sunrise.

The time passed rapidly away. The rainy season had nearly ended,—we were only favored with occasional showers, and by the latter part of February, the early spring had burst forth, and nothing could exceed the loveliness of the rich, verdant landscape around us. After the treaty and capitulation had been signed by the Picos at Los Angeles, their partizans dispersed, and all who resided in Monterey shortly returned to their homes. Every day brought an addition to the place—great ox-cart caravans with hide bodies, and unwieldy wheels of hewn lumber, came screaming along the roads, filled with women and children, who had sought refuge in some secure retreat in the country. Cattle soon were seen grazing among the hills. The town itself began to look alive—doors were unlocked and windows thrown open—a café and billiards emerged—pulperias, with shelves filled with aguadiente appeared on every corner—the barricades were torn down—guns removed— and the Californians themselves rode blithely by, with heavy, jingling spurs, and smiling faces—the women, too, flashed their bright eyes less angrily upon their invaders—accepted pleasant compliments without a sneer, and even Doña Augustia Ximénes, who took a solemn oath upon her missal a few months before, never to dance again, until she could wear a necklace of Yankee ears, relented too, and not only swept gracefully through waltz and contra danza, but when afterwards one of our young officers became ill with fever, she had him carried from the tent to her dwelling, watched him with all a woman's care and tenderness, as much as though she had been the mother that bore him, until he was carried to his last home.

Gradually these good people became aware that the Yankees were not such a vile pack of demoníos as they first believed, and thus whenever guitars were tinkling at the fandangos, or meals laid upon the board, we were kindly welcomed, with the privilege of making as much love, and devouring as many *frijoles* as may have been polite or palatable. Upon visiting the residences of the townspeople, true to the old Spanish character there was no attempt made in show or ostentation—that is always reserved for the streets or alemeda, but a stranger is received with cordiality, and a certain ease and propriety to which they seem to the "manor born." With the denizens of Monterey, even the wealthiest, cleanliness was an acquirement very little appreciated or practised, and I should presume the commodity of soap to be an article "more honored in the breach than the observance." For being given to cold water as a principal of lady-like existence I was something shocked on one occasion, to find a nice little Señorita, to whom I had been playing the agreeable the night previous, with a chemisette of a chocolate hue peeping through a slit in her sleeve; her soft, dimpled hands, too, made me speculate mentally upon the appearance of her little feet, and I forthwith resolved, in the event of becoming so deeply infatuated as to induce her papa to permit a change of estate, to exact a change of raiment in the marriage contract.

The occasion of inspecting the arcana of this young woman's vestments was during a visit to her portly mamma, and I may as well, by way of example, describe my reception. The dwelling was a low, one story pile of adobies, retaining the color of the primitive mud, and forming a large parallelogram; it enclosed a huge pen, or corral, for cattle, over which guard was carefully mounted by crowds of *gallinazos*. There were divers collections of Indian families coiled and huddled about beneath the porticos and doorways, each member thereof rejoicing in great masses of wiry shocks of hair, quite coarse enough to weave into bird cages on an emergency; there were some bee-hive shaped ovens also, from the apertures of which I remarked a number of filthy individuals immersed neck deep, taking, no doubt, balmy slumber, with the rain doing what they never had the energy to perform themselves—washing their faces. This much for externals—men and beasts included, merely premising that the whole affair was situated in a quiet detachment by itself, a few hundred yards in the rear of the village. My guide, though a good pilot, and retaining a clear perception of the road, was unable to convoy me safely to the house, without getting stalled several times in the mire; however, I reached terra firma, thankful to have escaped with my boots overflowing with mud, and then we marched boldly into the domicile. We entered a large, white-washed *sala,* when, after clapping hands, a concourse of small children approached with a lighted tallow link, and in reply to our inquiries, without further ceremony, ushered us by another apartment into the presence of the mistress of the mansion. She was sitting *a la grande Turque,* on the chief ornamental structure that graced the chamber—namely, the bed, upon which were sportively engaged three diminutive brats, with a mouse-trap—paper cigarritos—dirty feet, and other juvenile and diverting toys. The Doña herself was swallowing and puffing clouds of smoke alternately—but I must paint her as she sat, through the haze. "Juana," said she, calling to a short, squat Indian girl, *"lumbrecita por el Señor,"*—a light for the gentleman—and in a moment I was likewise pouring forth volumes of smoke. I saw but little of her figure, as she was almost entirely enveloped in shawls and bed clothes; the arms, however, were visible, very large, round and symmetrical, which of themselves induced me to resign all pretensions to becoming her son-in-law. She excused herself on the plea of indisposition for not rising, and it being one I surmised she was a martyr to every year or so, I very readily coincided, but in truth I found the Señora Mariqueta sensible, good-humored, and what was far more notable, the mother of fourteen male and five female children—making nineteen the sum of boys and girls total, as she informed me herself, without putting me to the trouble of counting the brood; and yet she numbered but seven and thirty years, in the very prime of life, with the appearance of being able again to perform equally astonishing exploits for the future. After an hour's pleasant chat we took leave, with the promise on my part of teaching the eldest daughter, Teresa, the Polka, for which I needed no incentive, as she was extremely graceful and pretty.

One morning, at break of day, I left Monterey for a tramp among the hills; the natives by this time had become pacifically disposed, and there was no serious apprehensions of getting a hide necklace thrown over one's head, in shape of the unerring lasso, if per chance a Yankee strayed too far from his quarters. With a fowling-piece on my arm, and a carbine slung to the back of an attendant, we pursued a tortuous path, through a gap in the hills, to the southward, and after a four or five miles' walk we found ourselves at the Mission of Carmelo. It is within a mile of the sea, protected by a neck of land, close to a rapid clear stream of the same name. A quaint old church, falling to decay, with crumbling tower and belfry, broken roofs, and long lines of mud-built dwellings, all in ruins, is what remains of a once flourishing and wealthy settlement. It still presents a picturesque appearance, standing on a little rise, above a broad fertile plain of many acres, adjacent to the banks of the river, and at the base a large orchard of fruits and flowers. Following up the stream for some leagues, through the same rich level, crossing and re-crossing the pure running water, with noble salmon flashing their silver sides at every fathom, we soon bagged as much game as we could stagger under: wild ducks, quail, partridges, hares of a very large size, and rabbits. By this time we had penetrated so far from ravine and hill as to have completely lost our bearings, and becoming quite bewildered, I began to entertain serious ideas of seeking some place of shelter for the night but I espied a horseman slowly winding his way beneath us in the gorge. By discharging a barrel of my piece, and continued shouts, we soon attracted attention, and thus being encouraged by the sight of a fellow-being, we sprang briskly down the steep. I heard a shrill voice crying, *"Que es lo que quiere?"* "We are lost," I replied; "will you assist us?" With many a wary glance and movement, he at last came frankly towards us, and I then discovered an intelligent little fellow, about ten years of age astride a powerful animal, which he guided by a single thong of hide. On learning our situation he gladly volunteered to guide us, and told me that we had described a wide circuit around the hills, and were within a short league of the Mission. This last was highly gratifying information, and mounting my worn-out attendant on the horse, our little guide took the bridle, and led the way towards the valley. It was quite dark on reaching the stream, and I felt thoroughly knocked up, but a few minutes bathe in the chill water gave me new life, and shortly after we were housed in the great hall of the Mission.

It chanced to be Sunday evening, moreover, during carnival, and there were preparations for a more brilliant fandango than the usual weekly affair produced. A few horses were picketted about the great *patio,* and two or three ox-carts with hide bodies were serving as boudoirs to damsels, who had come from afar to mingle in the ball. But the company had not yet assembled in the old hall, that had once served the good *frayles* for a refectory; and on entering I was kindly welcomed by the Patrona Margaria, and her handsome coquettish daughter, Domatilda, who were the liege and lady hostess of the Carmelo Mission. With her own hands the jolly madre soon prepared me an *olla podrida* of tomatoes, peppers, and the remains in my game bag. Then her laughing nymph patted me some *tortillas;* and after eating ravenously, and draining a cup of aguadiente, the hospitable old lady tumbled me into her own spacious couch, which stood in an angle of the hall, and giving me a hearty slap on the back, shouted, *"Duerme usted bien hijo mio hasta la media noche"*—Sleep like a top until midnight. I needed no second bidding, and in a moment was buried in a deep sleep.

Unconscious of fleeting hours, I was at length restored to life, but in the most disordered frame of mind; suffering under a most complicated attack of nightmare, of which bear-hugs, murders, manacles and music present but a slight idea of my agony; and indeed, when after pinching myself, and tearing my eyelids fairly open, I had still great difficulty in recalling my erring faculties. I found my own individual person deluged with a swarm of babies, who were lying athwart ships, and amid ships, fore and aft, heads and toes, every way; and one interesting infant, just teething, was suckling vigorously away on the left lobe of my ear, while another lovingly entwined its little fingers in my whiskers. Nor was this half the bodily miseries I had so innocently endured. A gay youth, with a dripping link, nicely balanced against my boots, was sitting on my legs, with a level space on the bed before him, intently playing *monté,* to the great detriment of the purses of his audience. On glancing round, I beheld the lofty apartment lighted by long tallow candles melted against the walls, whose smoke clung in dense clouds around the beams of the lofty hall; the floor was nearly filled, at the lower end, with groups of swarthy Indians and paisanos, sipping aguadiente, or indulging in the same exciting amusement as the gentleman sitting on my feet. On either side were double rows of men and women, moving in the most bewildering mazes of the contra danza: turning and twisting, twining and whirling with unceasing rapidity, keeping time to most inspiriting music, of harps and guitars; whilst ever and anon, some delighted youth would elevate his voice, in a shout of ecstacy, at the success of some bright-eyed señorita in the dance. It took me but an instant to appreciate all this; and then, being fully roused to my wrongs, I gave one vigorous spring, which sent the *monté* man, candle, cards, and coppers, flying against the wall, and bounding to my feet I made a dash at the Patrona, drank all the *licores* on the tray, and seizing her round the waist, away we spun through the fandango. Long before rosy morn I had become as merry and delighted as the rest of the company. I bought a dirty pack of cards for a rial, and opened a monte bank, for coppers and paper cigars and I comprehended by their guttural exclamations that their *compadre* was not so verdant a person as they at first imagined. I busied myself swearing love, and sipping *dulces* with the brunettas; vowing friendship with the men; drinking strong waters; promising to redress all grievances, to pay all claims out of my own pocket for the government; and ending by repudiating the Yankees, and swearing myself a full-blooded Californian.

We remained two months at Monterey; and then upon the assembling of the squadron we were glad to lift the anchors, and sail for the waters of San Francisco.

The face of the coast presents the same general aspect as that southward of Monterey—one great sea-wall of mountains, split into deep ravines, and tufted with towering pines.

Near to the mouth of San Francisco the land recedes, and passing through the narrow jaws of the Straits, which are framed in by bold, precipitous, and rocky cliffs, where violent currents are sweeping and foaming in eddying whirls around their base, you soon debouch into the outer bay. It is like a great lake, stretching away right and left, far into the heart of California.

Our anchorage was near the little village of Yerbabuena, five miles from the ocean, and within a short distance from the Franciscan Mission and Presidio of the old royalists. The site seems badly chosen, for although it reposes in partial shelter, beneath the high bluffs of the coast, yet a great portion of the year it is enveloped in chilling fogs; and invariably, during the afternoon, strong sea breezes are drawn through the straits like a funnel, and playing with fitful violence around the hills, the sand is swept in blinding clouds over the town and the adjacent shores of the bay.

INDIAN BATTLE

Yet with all these drawbacks the place was rapidly thriving under the indomitable energy of our countrymen. Tenements, large and small, were running up, like card-built houses, in all directions. The population was composed of Mormons, backwoodsmen, and a few very respectable traders from the eastern cities of the United States. Very rare it was to see a native: our brethern had played the porcupine so sharply as to oblige them to seek their homes among more congenial kindred. On Sunday, however, it was not uncommon to encounter gay cavalcades of young paisanos, jingling in silver chains and finery, dashing into town, half-a-dozen abreast; having left their sweethearts at the Mission, or some neighboring rancho, for the evening fandango. Towards afternoon, when these frolicsome *caballeros* became a trifle elevated with their potations, they were want to indulge in a variety of capricious feats on horseback—leaping and wheeling—throwing the lasso over each other;—or if by chance a bullock appeared, they took delight while at full speed in the *carrara,* in catching the beasts by a dextrous twist in the tail; and the performance was never satisfactorily concluded until the bullock was thrown a complete summerset over his horns. These paisanos of California pass most of their existence on horseback; there the natural vigor of manhood seems all at once called into play, and horse and backer appear of the same piece. The lasso is their plaything, either for service or pastime; with it, the unruly wild horse, or bullock, is brought within reach of the knife. Without the horse and lasso, these gentry are helpless as infants; their horses are admirably trained, and sometimes perform under a skilful hand pranks that always cause surprise to strangers. I was amused one afternoon while passing a fandango, near Monterey, to see a drunken *vaquero*—cattle driver—mounted on a restive, plunging beast, hold at arms length a tray of glasses, brimming with aguadiente, which he politely offered to everybody within reach of his curvettings, without ever once spilling a drop. It is remarkable, too, how very long the Californian can urge a horse, and how lightly he rides, even when the beast appears thoroughly exhausted, tottering at every pace under a strange rider; yet the native will lift him to renewed struggles, and hold him up for leagues further. The saddles here, as well as those along the southern coasts, partake in build of the old Spanish high peak and croupe, and are really intended for ease and comfort to the rider. The stirrups of all are similar—weighty wooden structures—and the feet rest naturally in them.

There is nothing either pleasing or inviting in the landscape in the vicinity of Yerbabuena. All looks bare and sterile from a distance, and on closer inspection, the deep sandy soil is covered with impervious thickets of low thorny undergrowth, with none of the rich green herbage, forests or timber as in Monterey. The roads were so heavy that the horses could hardly strain, nearly knee deep, through the sand, and consequently, our rides were restricted to a league's *pasear* to the mission, or across the narrow strip of the peninsular to the old presidio; but in the town we passed the hours pleasantly, became conversant with the Morman bible and doctrine, rolled ten-pins, and amused ourselves nightly, at the monte in the *casa de bebida de Brown;* still there was a great stir and bustle going on. A large number of merchant ships had arrived, bringing the regiment of New York volunteers, and the beach was strewn with heavy guns, carriages, piles of shot, ordnance stores, wagons, tents and camp-equipage, whilst the streets were filled with troops, who belonged to the true democracy, called one another mister, snubbed their officers, and did generally as they pleased, which was literally nothing.

Sunday, the Fourth of July, we attended church. The building was oblong, painted roughly in fresco, and decorated with a number of coarse paintings, and lots of swallow-tailed, green and yellow pennants dangling from the ceiling. During service an indefatigable cannonier, outside, gave frequent *feux de joie,* from a graduated scale of diminutive culverins—made of brass in shape of pewter porter pots, half filled with powder, and the charge rammed down with pounded bricks—this with music of kettle-drums, cymbals and fiddles made a very respectable din; there were two gentlemenly priests of the order of Saint Francisco who preached each a brief sermon with eloquence and force. Among the congregation were all the belles and dandies of the valley; the former kneeled demurely on little rugs or bits of carpet in the nave of the church; but the latter were lounging near the doors—their gala costume quite in keeping with Andalusia—and one handsome fellow at my side took my eye, as I have no doubt he did that of many a brighter. He was dressed in a close-fitting blue cloth jacket; sky-blue velvet trowsers, slashed from the thigh down, and jingling with small filagree silver buttons, snow-white laced *calçoncillos,* terminated by nicely stamped and embroidered *botas;* around the waist was passed a heavy crimson silk sash; a gay woollen serapa hung gracefully over the shoulder; in one hand a sugar-loafed, glazed sombrero, bound with thick silver cords; and in the other, silver spurs of an enormous size, each spike of the rowels two inches long: all these bright colors—set off by dark, brilliant eyes, jetty black locks, and pliant figure—would have made him irresistible anywhere. Turning towards me, he asked me, smilingly, *Porque no sirve ud à la Misa?* Why don't you kneel at the Mass?—*Tengo pierna de palo,* quoth I, quite gravely: glancing at my pins with much interest, to discover if they were of timber, he seemed to relish the joke, and we then sidled out of the church, and became firm friends on the spot.

Early in September we returned to Monterey. The bright green verdure that clothed the hill sides, the beautiful mantle of green and flowers of spring had long since paled beneath the blaze of summer. No rain had fallen; the clear rills that murmured in every gully were absorbed by the parched earth. The broad lagoons near the beach were rapidly receding, and mud had been converted into dust.

Monterey was rapidly increasing, and houses of a more substantial build than the paper-like structures of Yerbabuena, were rising in the streets. A salutary system of police had also been established in the town—the Reverend Alcade was a terror to evil doers. Woe betide the pockets of those who slaughtered cattle at their door-steps, or the rollicking gentry vaulting at full speed through the streets, or drunken Indians, or quiet persons in back rooms, amusing themselves at monté—for down came that ivory-headed cane—"Alcade de Monterey"—like a talisman; and with a pleasant smile he would sweep the white and yellow dross into his capacious pockets. Others were mulcted in damages, or made to quarry stone for the school-house; but, whether native or foreigner, the rod fell impartially on their pockets, and all, more or less, contributed towards the new California college. These measures were not relished at first by the natives, but in the end they discerned the wisdom of a prompt and just administration of the laws, and became devoted admirers of the indefatigable Alcade.

On Saturday evenings, crowds of degraded Indians, of both sexes, after laboring during the week, and feeding on locusts or grasshoppers, were accustomed to congregate on the outskirts of the town, where, with gaming and arguadiente, they were enabled to remain torpid all the following day. Their favorite amusement was a game called *escondido*—hide and seek—played with little sticks; and their skill was exerted by trying to discover in whose hands they were: seating themselves on the ground, around a huge blazing fire, separate parties were ranged on opposite sides; then beginning a low, wild chaunt, moving their bodies to and fro, groping with their hands within the serapas before them, until the perspiration starts in streams down their naked sides, after a strange succession of deep, harsh, guttural grunts and aspirations, they suddenly terminate their exertions by giving a sharp yell, and pointing to one of the opposite party, who, if rightly detected, pays forfeit. When one set of players becomes exhausted, others supply their places, and thus they keep it up the live-long night.

Among the Californians an agreeable pastime, much in vogue, is the *merendar*—Anglice, pic-nic. They are usually given on the patron saint's day of some favorite señora or señorita, by their admirers. A secluded, pleasant spot is selected a few miles away from the presidio, where provisions, wine and music are collected beforehand; then each cavalier, with arm thrown affectionately around his sweetheart, on the saddle before him, seeks the rendezvous. Guitars and choral accompaniments soon are heard, and the *merenda* begins, and is kept up with the greatest possible fun and spirit: dancing, frolicking and love-making. There are two or three singular dances of the country: one, called the *Son,* where a gentleman commences, by going through a solo part, to quick, rattling music, then waving a handkerchief to a damsel, who either pays the same compliment to another favored swain, or merely goes through a few steps, without relieving the first comer, who, in turn, is obliged to continue the performance until a lady takes pity on him. It not unfrequently happens, that when a particularly graceful girl is on the floor, making her little feet rapidly pat the ground, like castanets, to the inspiriting music, that some enthusiastic *novio* will place his sombrero on her head, which can never be reclaimed without a handsome present in exchange. But, Heaven help us! the pranks and mischief indulged in on the return home; the tricks and tumbles, laughter and merriment; even the horses appear to enter into the play, and when a cluster of gay lads and lassies have jostled one another from the saddles, the waggish animals, fully appreciating the joke, stop of their own accord. The last affair of this kind I attended, was given by the best-hearted little fellow in the territory; and I am prepared to prove it—Señor Verde, he was an universal favorite, as well with old as young; for he was at different times taking a short *pasear* on every horse, laughing with the madres, and kissing the shy doncellas—*valgame dios*—but I had work in getting him into Monterey that night, for my caballo carried weight—besides a big overgrown dame and myself, Verde hung on to the tail.

We were many weeks in Monterey. But at last we began to tire of foggy mornings, damp nights, tough beef, lounging under the Consul's piazza, sweltering dust, catching fleas, playing monté, and fandangos at Carmelo. The time was drawing near for our departure.

39

California Exchanges Latin Civilization
for American, 1846–49

Joseph Warren Revere, with an ancestry as distinguished as his name, was born in Boston in 1812. Until 1850 his early years were connected with the United States Navy, and he saw service in the Pacific, the Carribean, the Mediterranean, the Baltic, the China Seas, and finally, in 1845, the California coast. He was present during the brief conflict of the Mexican War which changed the ownership of California from Mexico to the United States and himself raised the American flag at Sonoma, July 9, 1846. He returned home in 1848 but came back to California during the gold rush of 1849. His account as a traveler covers vital and significant years. He saw California when it was a sleepy, half-settled community; he witnessed its transfer to the United States; he observed the radical and swift change which occurred with the influx of the Forty-niners. In a short space of time he covers the period when Lieutenant Wise saw California to when Bayard Taylor wrote down his observations. The account possesses generally neither the geniality of the one nor the romanticism of the other. Yet there is, especially in the documents he includes, an aspect of sober and accurate reality in his volume.

When the Civil War broke out, Revere joined the army rather than the navy. He got into difficulties, however, when he removed troops without orders. Though he was a brigadier general, and his previous career had been distinguished, he was court-martialed and dismissed. Lincoln revoked the order, but Revere thereupon resigned. He died in Hoboken, New Jersey, in 1880.

SUTTER'S FORT

Emerging from the woods lining the banks of the river, we stood upon a plain of immense extent, bounded on the west by the heavy timber which marks the course of the Sacramento, the dim outline of the Sierra Nevada appearing in the distance. We now came to some extensive fields of wheat in full bearing, waving gracefully in the gentle breeze like the billows of the sea, and saw the whitewashed walls of the fort situated on a small eminence commanding the approaches on all sides.

We were met and welcomed by Capt. Sutter and the officer in command of the garrison; but the appearance of things indicated that our reception would have been very different had we come on a hostile errand.

The appearance of the fort, with its crenulated walls, fortified gateway, and bastioned angles; the heavily bearded, fierce-looking hunters and trappers, armed with rifles, bowie knives and pistols; their ornamented hunting shirts, and gartered leggins; their long hair turbaned with colored handkerchiefs; their wild and almost savage looks, and dauntless independent bearing; the wagons filled with golden grain; the arid, yet fertile plains; the "caballados" driven across it by wild shouting Indians, enveloped in clouds of dust, and the dashing horsemen, scouring the fields in every direction;—all these accessories conspired to carry me back to the romantic East. Everything bore the impress of vigilance and preparation for defense—and not without reason.

The fame of Capt. Sutter and his fort is so extended, that some account of that distinguished person may be interesting to my readers.

John A. Sutter is a Swiss by birth and a soldier by profession; and, like many of his countrymen, he early sought in the service of a foreign sovereign, that advancement in the career of arms which he was unlikely to find at home, accepting the post of Lieutenant in one of the Swiss regiments of infantry in the service of France, during the reign of Charles X. At the period of the revolution of 1830, and the consequent dethronement of that monarch, he was with his regiment in garrison at Grenoble. Even after the revolution was under full headway, and the tri-color flying in the town, the brave Swiss, with their proverbial fidelity, kept the white flag of the Bourbons displayed over the citadel; nor was it until the revolution was consummated, and Charles a fugitive, that they consented to capitulate. On the disbanding of their corps, which took place shortly afterwards. Sutter came to the United States, became a citizen, and after spending several years in different States of our Union, engaging in various pursuits, and undergoing many vicissitudes of fortune, he concluded to emigrate to Oregon, whence he went to California. With adventurous daring he resolved to take up his abode, alone and unsupported, in the midst of the savages of the frontier; for at that time not a single white man inhabited the valley of the Sacramento. His first attempt to ascend that river was a failure, he having lost his way among the interminable "slues"; but still persevering, he arrived at his present location, established alliances with several tribes of Indians in the vicinity, acquired a great ascendancy and power among them, took some of them for soldiers and instructed them in the mysteries of European drill, built his fort on the most improved frontier model, and boldly made war upon the refactory tribes in the vicinity. I doubt if a more remarkable instance of individual energy, perseverance and heroism, has ever been displayed under similar circumstances. This unceremonious way of settling down in a strange country, and founding a sort of independent empire on one's "own hook," is one of those feats which will excite the astonishment of posterity. In times past men have been deified on slighter grounds.

At length the influence and power of Sutter attracted the attention of the Mexican government; but as he was too remote, as well as too strong, to be punished or betrayed, they thought it their wisest plan to conciliate him. He was, therefore, made military commandant of the frontier, with full authority and absolute power, extending to life itself, within the limits of his jurisdiction. In this office he continued for several years, trading with the Indians, teaching them the rudiments of manufactures, agriculture and arms, and acquiring an extensive influence in the valley. He always, however, had a decided leaning towards his adopted country, and hospitably received and entertained, even to his own detriment, such parties of Americans as came near his retreat; and, I regret to add, that many of our countrymen made but a poor return for this kindness and liberality. Finally, the Mexicans seeing that the Americans, emboldened by his example, began to settle in the valley, and growing jealous of his influential position, endeavored to remove him, and as an inducement to give up his border fortress to a Mexican garrison, offered him the beautiful and improved mission lands of San José, near the pueblo of that name, and the sum of fifty thousand dollars; proving their eagerness to get rid of him by actually providing security for the money, a practice almost unknown in Mexican financiering, which generally consists of promises intended to be broken. But not an inch would Sutter budge from his stronghold, sagaciously looking forward, with the eye of faith, to the time when the United States should acquire possession of the country—a consummation which he devoutly hoped for, and hailed with delight when it came to pass.

The fort consists of a parallelogram enclosed by adobe walls, fifteen feet high and two feet thick, with bastions or towers at the angles, the walls of which are four feet thick, and their embrasures so arranged as to flank the curtain on all sides. A good house occupies the centre of the interior area, serving for officers' quarters, armory, guard and state rooms, and also for a kind of citadel. There is a second wall on the inner face, the space between it and the outer wall being roofed and divided into work-shops, quarters, &c., and the usual offices are provided, and also a well of good water. Corrals for the cattle and horses of the garrison are conveniently placed where they can be under the eye of the guard. Cannon frown (I believe that is an inveterate habit of cannon,) from the various embrasures, and the *ensemble* presents the very ideal of a border fortress.

A CALIFORNIA RANCHO

A Californian rancho or farm, of the first class, is about equal in extent to a German principality. While some are content with one, two, or three square leagues, (not miles), others luxuriate in a domain of eleven square leagues, which, according to California measure, is nearly three times the size of a township of our public lands. About the homestead a rancho presents a singularly primitive and patriarchal appearance. Job himself, hardly possessed more extensive herds of wild cattle, which are usually seen on the outskirts of the rancho, but betake themselves to the woods or the ravines among the hills at the approach of a stranger. They seem to have a vague apprehension that you intend to drive them to the *rodea,* where they are driven to be counted on particular days, or perhaps to the *matanzas* or shambles. As you advance nearer the house, you fall in with the tame milch cows and brood mares and colts, guarded by their stallion, who starts fiercely from his pasture, and regards with jealous gaze the animals of your *caballada,* keeping a wary eye, the while, on his seraglio; still approaching, you meet large herds of sheep, attended by little half-naked Indians; and when close to the house your ears are saluted with the yelping of a regiment of curs, whose melodious notes are always at a concert pitch. And now you reach the *milpa,* (kitchen garden), a horticultural appendage, which is sometimes rudely fenced with brush, "dumped" around it without excessive regard to quantity or symmetry; but oftener boasting no better enclosure than a small troop of Indians, who, with loud cries of questionable melody, warn off the profane flocks and herds which would fain trespass upon its sacred precincts.

Nor is it by day alone that these aboriginal moveable and musical fences perform their functions; for during the season when the "sarse" is ripening, the remorseless rascals bivouac near the "milpa," making night hideous with their excruciating melodies, and gambling with their *parientes* (relations) when the ranchero permits them. The house is usually a rude edifice of *adobes,* (sun-burnt bricks), with the usual farm offices around it, patched on as may be most convenient; and it is invariably flanked by a *"corral,"* (a circular fence for enclosing cattle), or by several corrals, according to the size and consequence of the rancho. Of course these houses vary in splendor and magnitude, as one star differeth from another in glory; but the best of them are not remarkable in these respects. The family is generally pretty large— consisting first, of the head of the household, usually a bland, jolly-looking old gentleman, and next, of his handsome sons, appareled in the becoming Mexican riding dress, and accomplished in all the arts and mysteries of the *campo,* such as managing and lassoing the wildest cattle and most intractable horses. Then come the women, mother and daughters, comely and buxom, and reasonably tidy, but less delicate and more robust than their Mexican sisters. The rest of the family consists of "vaqueros," and servants, male and female, of Indian blood, who inhabit the "rancheria," or small Indian village, built of rush wigwams, near the house. Although these worthy rancheros have few superfluities to offer, besides beef and mutton, the wayfaring stranger is always sure of a hearty and unaffected welcome amongst them. Hospitality is inherent in the Spanish blood. As the poorest shepherd of the Sierra Morena, or the Alpuxarras invariably offers a part of his humble dish of *"gaspacho"* to a stranger, so the honest ranchero of California places everything at his disposal; and while an offer of remuneration is received with a constrained politeness, indicating wounded sensibility, it is always met with a decided negative. How long this will be the case remains to be seen. As civilization advances it is not unlikely that putting everything "at your disposition" will mean as little in California as in Castile; and the only mortification evinced at an offer of remuneration will result from the insufficiency of the guerdon. The world is advancing; and California must keep pace with it.

The ranchero prefers the month of March for the "fundacion" or establishment of his farm. In the first place, he builds a house of boughs, a mere sylvan bower, which, for the next seven months, answers all the purposes of a more substantial lodge, besides enabling the occupant, however poor, to keep openhouse. During these seven months he enjoys, without interruption, the most charming summer weather, the skies being almost without a cloud, and occasional mists and constant dews supplying the place of rain. In this part of California thunder and lightning are unknown, but at rare intervals thunder is heard in the neighborhood of Los Angeles. Taking possession of his primitive mansion with his family, the ranchero proceeds to improve his estate. He purchases about one hundred head of cattle, at least thirty or forty horses, and usually adds a flock of sheep and a quantity of poultry. When the breeding of cattle is properly attended to, the increase in this country is astonishing. The kind of cattle most suitable for a rapid increase are "vaquillas," (heifers), the usual proportion being one hundred heifers to half a dozen bulls. To one "manada," (herd), consisting of thirty or forty mares, a single stallion is added. On a well-regulated rancho, the increase of neat cattle may be safely calculated at thirty per cent. per annum, allowing for casualties. Thus one hundred head, properly selected, nearly double at the end of the third year, at which time the first year's calves begin to produce, making, I believe, a greater ratio than is known in any other country. This estimate, however, is exceedingly moderate, fifty per cent. and even seventy per annum having been obtained under favorable circumstances. This is probably due to the favorable climate, the unequalled pasture, and the state of nature in which the animal lives.

When the ranchero procures his cattle and other animals, until they are "carenciado," or accustomed to the farm, they are driven every day or two round and round some convenient spot, by the shouting "vaqueros." Both the place and the act of driving are called "rodea," and this practice renders the cattle comparatively tame and peaceable, habituating them to the control of man, and exerting a great influence upon their increase. A "rodea" is usually held, in a well-regulated district, one day in each week, and upon every rancho alternately, the neighboring rancheros attending to reclaim their stray cattle. The several owners recognize their animals by their peculiar *"fierro"* or brand, and by the *"señal"* or ear-mark, which differ on each rancho. The brand, which is registered according to law, is usually the initial letter of the ranchero or his rancho, but is sometimes a merely arbitrary sign. The ear-mark is a peculiar slit or hole, or a combination of both. These marks are made on the young calves, and at least once a year they are renewed. To effect this, the animals must be thrown down, which feat is performed by two horsemen with their lassos. The usual time for marking is at the annual "matanzas," or slaughter, in the month of August. The cattle are then driven to the corral, or circular farmyard, and the doomed ones slaughtered; the hides are pegged out in the sun, the meat cut into strips and hung on trees and poles to dry, and the tallow, after being melted down in large try-pots or kettles, is packed in skins sewed up with thongs. The hides and tallow are the only parts exported, the dried beef being consumed in the country as well as the finer quality of tallow or "manteca," made from the fat of the intestines. The heads, horns, hoofs, bones, &c., are utterly wasted and thrown away; and, indeed, until within a few years, immense numbers of cattle were slaughtered for their hides alone, the entire carcass being left to corrupt, or to feed immense numbers of wild beasts and large vultures, which were thus greatly encouraged and augmented. Stabling for any kind of animals is entirely unknown, the nearest approach to it being a sheep-fold. A "mayor-domo" or steward, usually a white man, but sometimes an Indian, superintends a whole rancho; a couple of vaqueros are necessary to look after the cattle and horses, and an Indian family attend to the sheep and do "chores." The wages of the Indians are moderate, and are always paid in merchandise, a dollar in money being sometimes thrown in on a feast day.

A rancho is thus soon established, and if the owner be industrious and provident, he secures not only a competence, but, by cultivating his fields—which in the valleys produce one hundred bushels of wheat to the acre, and other crops in proportion—his fortune is made. In no other country was it so easy to acquire an independence. I say *was,* because the new order of things will probably raise the price of land, and prevent the occupation of such large tracts by individuals. Still, for many years to come, industrious farmers can undoubtedly become opulent on small means, without troubling themselves about gold mines. A league of land on most ranchos will support one thousand head of neat cattle, besides horses, sheep, hogs, &c. Of these, after the third year, three hundred can be killed, annually, without prejudice to the increase of the stock at a handsome rate, the females being mostly reserved from slaughter. These will yield, on an average, $10 per head; say $3000. If the rancheros are not rich, it is owing partly to the oppressive, plundering system, pursued by their late government, but chiefly to their own good-for-nothing habits. Laziness, carelessness, gambling, a low state of civilization, and a community of goods are not calculated to produce thrift, and it is not strange that their condition has been less comfortable than that of day-laborers in the Atlantic States. As an instance of their improvidence, I will state that, although cattle are so abundant, milk, butter and cheese, can scarcely ever be procured at a rancho. They will not trouble themselves to tame cows for milking; but this rule is not invariable, a few milch cows (*vacas chichiguas*) being sometimes found about a rancho. All the Californians care to eat is bovine and cereal food, and they are good judges of beef and tortillas.

After his wife and children, the darling objects of a Californian's heart are his horses. In this respect he is not surpassed by the Arab. His whole ambition centres in his horses; his livelihood depends on them; and they are the chief ministers of his pleasures. Dismount a Californian, and he is at once reduced to a perfectly helpless state, and is of no use in the world. He can neither take care of his farm, nor hunt, nor move from place to place; and is, to all intents and purposes, a wretched cripple. Even his work is done on horseback, when ingenuity can make that possible; and an American carpenter, residing in the country, assured me that an apprentice left him because he could not "shove the jack-plane" on horseback. If the Californian wishes to visit his next-door neighbor, even in town, he mounts his horse; and I have been told of a skilful and celebrated vaquero, who having occasion to walk from a gambling-house to a dram-shop across the street, and from insuetude in this mode of progression having impaired the beauty of his countenance, indignantly explained upon picking himself up, "Zounds! this it is to walk on the ground."

The trade of this country has been mostly monopolized by a few Boston houses, and Boston is better known among the natives of all kinds than any other part of the United States. These houses despatched to their agents assorted cargoes of plain cottons, prints, handkerchiefs, shoes, hats, coarse woollens, hardware, fancy goods, and, in short, specimens of all the cheapest fabrics of Lowell, Lynn, and Marblehead, and a plentiful supply of the auction trash of Boston. All these "notions" arriving at Monterey, a bargain was struck, as in Mexico, with the Governor, "Commandante General," "Administrador," &c., to lump the duties, with a sovereign contempt of the Mexican tariff, and without regard to what was contraband or non-contraband. The vessel received her permit, and forthwith opened a retail shop on board, peddling the goods from port to port at most enormous profits, justified to the awfully-shaved purchaser by well-salted invoices, and monstrous duties paid to the honest officials. Now the ranchero purchaser was already in debt to the merchant and had no money; but his credit stood high, and he took more goods on a fresh "trust," at prices which no man without a caoutchouc conscience could ask, and which no man without a naked family would ever agree to pay. Thus a piece of coarse Lowell "manta," or unbleached muslin, costing at home not over three dollars, was spared to the ranchero for twenty dollars, and other things in the same fair proportion. But the benevolent dealer sold his goods without money, if not without price, contenting himself with the note of his easy customer. Had this been the end of the joke, the ranchero would have been perfectly satisfied. But the most awful day in the calendar—pay-day—was yet to come; and the Scripture tells us that, "Where the carcass is, there shall the young eagles be gathered." So our Boston adventurers were seldom out of the way when the "matanzas" was going on. Then, or shortly afterwards, the "cuerreros," (hide-seekers), and the "cuerreritos," (the little ditto, or clerks), were on the alert, and incontinently set about riding to the ranchos, and riding down the rancheros, with urgent and fervent dunning exhortations to the effect that they would be pleased to "poney up." Various were the shifts and devices resorted to by the hard-pushed debtors— who emulated their brethren in more enlightened communities—to avoid "coming up to the Capting's office to settle." Their cattle had not yielded the expected increase, the wild Indians had proved uncommonly thievish, and a hundred other dilatory pleas were interposed. But the persevering Yankee never relaxed his efforts, never ceased to dun, dun, dun, until he had worried the debtor out of the requisite number of hides at moderate prices. Hence, perhaps, the expression common to baffled creditors, "I will take it out of your hide." Well, the hides went to Boston, and in due time a few of them came back in the shape of dressed leather and pegged shoes, which were disposed of to the original owners of the raw material at a "ruinous sacrifice," each pair of the latter probably stripping only one bull of his hide. Since the time when Queen Dido came the hide game over the natives at Carthage, it is probable that there has been no parallel to the hide-and-go-seek game between Boston and California.

THE DISCOVERY OF GOLD

It was reported that gold had been found in the valleys of the rivers which flow into the Tulé Lakes. I profess to know nothing of these gold deposits from my own observations, and perhaps Mr. Benton is right in pronouncing them a curse to California. Certain it is, that a land to which nature has been so prodigal might well dispense with them, and perhaps a hundred years hence it will be apparent that the true wealth of California did not lay in her shining sands. Whether the same eminent Senator will be right in predicting that those treasures will prove ephemeral no man can determine. The probability is, that large quantities of gold will be found for many years to come, and it is not unlikely that the value of that precious metal will be seriously affected by the vast additions which will be made to the currency of the world in the course of the next ten years.

What is to be the moral effect of this well-founded mania in the present anomolous condition of California, it is fearful to contemplate. She is without government, without laws, without a military force, while tens of thousands of adventurers from all parts of the earth are pouring into her golden valleys. Among these there must be many lawless and dangerous men; and it is to be feared that thousands who go out respectable, law-abiding citizens, will be transformed by the evil spirit of avarice and by associating on familiar terms with the vicious and depraved, into knaves and men of violence. It will not be surprising to hear at any moment of the most atrocious robberies and murders in the gold region, and it is to be hoped that the heterogeneous mass congregated in the valley of the Sacramento and elsewhere, will pause for a moment in their greedy pursuit of gold, and organize an association for the preservation of law and order. In the present state of affairs, it is apparent from the official documents, that it would be in vain to send troops to California. Our very men-of-war appear to be infected with insubordination as soon as they approach the magic shores of California, and ere this time a large fleet of merchantmen are rotting in the harbor of San Francisco. Where all this is to end, heaven only knows; and the most effective counteracting measure, would be to immediately quiet the land titles, and hold out inducements to settlers to turn their attention to the cultivation of the soil.

The most reliable and intelligent accounts of the gold deposits are to be found in the public documents, and the probability is, that they will continue to furnish the most authentic data respecting the auriferous regions. It is very certain that I could have written nothing so complete and graphic as the account furnished by the accomplished temporary governor, Col. R. B. Mason. His admirable report has been copied all over the world—published in every newspaper, and reprinted in ten thousand catch-penny pamphlets. But it still remains the most accurate and authentic history of the discovery of the gold deposits, and of the early operations of the gold collectors. It ought to be preserved in all the books which treat of California, and familiar as it is, I shall republish it in preference to any second-hand statement of my own. I shall also add the despatches of Lieut. Larkin and Commodore Jones, which will be found extremely interesting.

I begin these interesting extracts with the standard authority—the celebrated report of Col. Mason. Such valuable documents never grow stale.

> "Headquarters 10th Military Depot
> "Monterey, California
> "Aug. 17, 1848

"Sir:

"I have the honor to inform you that, accompanied by Lieutenant W. T. Sherman, I started on the twelfth of June last, to make a tour through the northern part of California. My principal purpose, however, was to visit the newly-discovered gold 'placer'[1] in the Valley of the Sacramento. We reached San Francisco on the twentieth, and found that all, or nearly all its male inhabitants had gone to the mines. The town, which a few months before was so busy and thriving, was then almost deserted.

"On the evening of the twenty-fifth, the horses of the escort were crossed to Sousolito in a launch, and on the following day we resumed the journey to Sutter's Fort, where we arrived on the morning of the second of July. Along the whole route, mills were lying idle, fields of wheat were open to cattle and horses, houses vacant, and farms going to waste. At Sutter's there was more

1. This word has now become naturalized among us. It is pronounced in the singular as if written "plarthair," and in the plural as if written "plarthair-ess."

life and business. Launches were discharging their cargoes at the river, and carts were hauling goods to the fort, where already were established several stores, a hotel, &c. Captain Sutter had only two mechanics in his employ, (a wagon-maker and blacksmith), to whom he was then paying ten dollars a day. Merchants pay him a monthly rent of one hundred dollars per room; and while I was there, a two-story house in the fort was rented as a hotel for five hundred dollars a month.

"At the urgent solicitation of many gentlemen, I delayed there to participate in the first public celebration of our national anniversary at that fort, but on the fifth resumed the journey and proceeded twenty-five miles up the American fork, to a point on it known as the Lower Mines, or Mormon Diggings. The hill-sides were thickly strewn with canvass tents and bush arbors; a store was erected, and several boarding shanties in operation. The day was intensely hot, yet about two hundred men were at work in the full glare of the sun, washing for gold—some with tin pans, some with close-woven Indian baskets, but the greater part had a rude machine, known as the cradle. This is on rockers, six or eight feet long, open at the foot, and at its head has a coarse grate, or sieve; the bottom is rounded, with small cleets nailed across. Four men are required to work this machine: one digs the ground in the bank close by the stream; another carries it to the cradle and empties it on the grate; a third gives a violent rocking motion to the machine; while a fourth dashes on water from the stream itself.

"The sieve keeps the coarse stones from entering the cradle, the current of water washes off the earthy matter, and the gravel is gradually carried out at the foot of the machine, leaving the gold mixed with a heavy fine black sand above the first cleets. The sand and gold mixed together are then drawn off through auger holes into the pan below, are dried in the sun, and afterwards separated by blowing off the sand. A party of four men thus employed at the lower mines averaged one hundred dollars a day. The Indians and those who have nothing but pans or willow baskets, gradually wash out the earth, and separate the gravel by hand, leaving nothing but the gold mixed with sand, which is separated in the manner before described. The gold in the lower mines is in fine bright scales, of which I send several specimens. .

"As we ascended the north branch of the American fork, the country became more broken and mountainous; and at the saw-mill, twenty-five miles above the lower washings, or fifty miles from Sutter's, the hills rise to about a thousand feet above the level of the Sacramento plain. Here a species of pine occurs which led to the discovery of the gold. Captain Sutter, feeling the great want of lumber, contracted in September last with a Mr. Marshall to build a saw-mill at that place. It was erected in the course of the past winter and

MINING IN CALIFORNIA

spring—a dam and race constructed—but when the water was let on the wheel, the tail race was found to be too narrow to permit the water to escape with sufficient rapidity. Mr. Marshall, to save labor, let the water directly into the race with a strong current, so as to wash it wider and deeper. He effected his purpose, and a large bed of mud and gravel was carried to the foot of the race.

"One day Mr. Marshall, as he was walking down the race to his deposit of mud, observed some glittering particles at its upper edge; he gathered a few, examined them, and became satisfied of their value. He then went to the fort, told Captain Sutter of his discovery, and they agreed to keep it secret until a certain grist-mill of Sutter's was finished. It, however, got out, and spread like magic. Remarkable success attended the labors of the first explorers, and in a few weeks hundreds of men were drawn thither. At the time of my visit, but little over three months after the first discovery, it was estimated that upwards of four thousand people were employed. At the mill there is a fine deposit, or bank of gravel, which the people respect as the property of Captain Sutter, although he pretends to no right to it, and would be perfectly satisfied with the simple promise of a pre-emption, on account of the mill, which he has built there at considerable cost. Mr. Marshall was living near the mill, and informed me that many persons were employed above and below him; that they use the same machines at the lower washings and that their success was about the same—ranging from one to three ounces of gold per man, daily. This gold, too, is in scales a little coarser than those of the lower mines.

"From the mill Mr. Marshall guided me up the mountain on the opposite, or north bank, of the south fork, where, in the bed of small streams or ravines, now dry, a great deal of coarse gold has been found. I there saw several parties at work, all of whom were doing very well; a great many specimens were shown me, some as heavy as four or five ounces in weight, and I send three pieces. You will perceive that some of the specimens accompanying this, hold mechanically pieces of quartz; that the surface is rough, and evidently moulded in the crevice of the rock. This gold cannot have been carried far by water, but must have remained near where it was first deposited from the rock that once bound it. I inquired of many people if they had encountered the metal in its matrix, but in every instance they said they had not; but that the gold was invariably mixed with washed gravel, or lodged in the crevices of other rocks. All bore testimony that they had found gold in greater or less quantities in the numerous small gullies or ravines that occur in that mountainous region.

"On the seventh of July I left the mill, and crossed to a stream, emptying into the American fork, three or four miles below the sawmill. I struck this stream (now known as Weber's creek) at the washings of Sunol & Co. They had about thirty Indians employed, whom they pay in merchandise. They were getting gold of a character similar to that found in the main fork, and doubtless in sufficient quantities to satisfy them. From this point, we proceeded up the stream, about eight miles, where we found a great many people and Indians; some engaged in the bed of the stream, and others in the small side valleys that put into it. These latter are exceedingly rich, and two ounces were considered an ordinary yield for a day's work. A small gutter, not more than a hundred yards long by four feet wide and two or three feet deep, was pointed out to me as the one where two men—William Daly and Parry McCoon—had, a short time before, obtained seventeen thousand dollars' worth of gold. Captain Weber informed me that he knew that these two men had employed four white men and about a hundred Indians, and that, at the end of one week's work, they paid off their party, and had left ten thousand dollars' worth of this gold. Another small ravine was shown me, from which had been taken upwards of twelve thousand dollars' worth of gold. Hundreds of similar ravines, to all appearances, are as yet untouched. I could not have credited these reports had I not seen, in the abundance of the precious metal, evidence of their truth.

"Mr. Neligh, an agent of Commodore Stockton, had been at work about three weeks in the neighborhood, and showed me, in bags and bottles, over two thousand dollars' worth of gold; and Mr. Lyman, a gentleman of education, and worthy of every credit, said he had been engaged, with four others, with a machine, on the American fork, just below Sutter's mill; that they had worked eight days, and that his share was at the rate of fifty dollars a day; but hearing that others were doing better at Weber's place, they had removed there, and were then on the point of resuming operations. I might tell of hundreds of similar instances; but, to illustrate how plentiful the gold was in the pockets of common laborers, I will mention a simple occurrence which took place in my presence when I was at Weber's store. This store was nothing but an arbor of bushes, under which he had exposed for sale goods and groceries suited to his customers. A man came in, picked up a box of Seidlitz powders, and asked the price. Captain Weber told him it was not for sale. The man offered an ounce of gold, but Captain Weber told him it only cost fifty cents, and he did not wish to sell it. The man then offered an ounce and a half, when Captain Weber *had* to take it. The prices of all things are high, and yet Indians, who before hardly knew what a breech-cloth was, can now afford to buy the most gaudy dresses.

"On the eighth of July I returned to the lower mines, and on the following day to Sutter's, where, on the nineteenth, I was making preparations for a visit to the Feather, Yubah, and Bear rivers, when I received a letter from Commander A. R. Long, United States Navy, with orders to take the sloop of war, Warren, to the squadron at La Paz. In consequence I determined to return to Monterey, and accordingly arrived here on the seventeenth of July. Before leaving Sutter's, I satisfied myself that gold existed in the bed of the Feather river, in the Yubah and the Bear, and in many of the smaller streams that lie between the latter and the American fork; also, that it had been found in the Cosumnes to the south of the American fork. In each of these streams the gold is found in small scales, whereas, in the intervening mountains, it occurs in coarser lumps.

"The principal store at Sutter's fort, that of Brannan & Co., had received, in payment for goods, thirty-six thousand dollars' worth of this gold, from the first of May to the tenth of July. Other merchants had also made extensive sales. Large quantities of goods were daily sent forward to the mines, as the Indians, heretofore so poor and degraded, have suddenly become consumers of the luxuries of life. I before mentioned that the greater part of the farmers and rancheros had abandoned their fields to go to the mines. This is not the case with Captain Sutter, who was carefully gathering his wheat, estimated at forty thousand bushels. Flour is already worth, at Sutter's thirty-six dollars a barrel, and soon will be fifty. Unless large quantities of breadstuffs reach the country, much suffering will occur; but as each man is now able to pay a large price, it is believed the merchants will bring from Chili and Oregon a plentiful supply for the coming winter.

"The most moderate estimate I could obtain from men acquainted with the subject, was, that upwards of four thousand men were working in the gold district, of whom more than one-half were Indians; and that from thirty to fifty thousand dollars' worth of gold, if not more, was daily obtained. The entire gold district, with very few exceptions of grants made some years ago by the Mexican authorities, is on land belonging to the United States. It was a matter of serious reflection to me, how I could secure to the government certain rents or fees for the privilege of procuring this gold; but upon considering the large extent of country, the character of the people engaged, and the small scattered force at my command, I resolved not to interfere, but to permit all to work freely, unless broils and crimes should call for interference. I was surprised to learn that crime of any kind was very infrequent, and that no thefts or robberies had been committed in the gold district.

"All live in tents, in bush arbors, or in the open air; and men have frequently about their persons thousands of dollars worth of this gold, and it was to me a matter of surprise that so peaceful and quiet state of things should continue to exist. Conflicting claims to particular spots of ground may cause collisions, but they will be rare, as the extent of country is so great, and the gold so abundant, that for the present there is room enough for all. Still the government is entitled to rents for this land, and immediate steps should be devised to collect them, for the longer it is delayed the more difficult it will become.

"The discovery of these vast deposits of gold has entirely changed the character of Upper California. Its people, before engaged in cultivating their small patches of ground, and guarding their herds of cattle and horses, have all gone to the mines, or are on their way thither. Laborers of every trade have left their work-benches, and tradesmen their shops. Sailors desert their ships as fast as they arrive on the coast, and several vessels have gone to sea with hardly enough hands to spread a sail. Two or three are now at anchor in San Francisco with no crew on board. Many desertions, too, have taken place from the garrisons within the influence of these mines; twenty-six soldiers have deserted from the post of Sonoma, twenty-four from that of San Francisco, and twenty-four from Monterey. For a few days the evil appeared so threatening, that grave danger existed that the garrisons would leave in a body. I shall spare no exertions to apprehend and punish deserters, but I believe no time in the history of our country has presented such temptations to desert as now exist in California.

"The danger of apprehension is small, and the prospect of high wages certain; pay and bounties are trifles, as laboring men at the mines can now earn in *one day* more than double a soldier's pay and allowances for a month, and even the pay of a lieutenant or captain cannot hire a servant. A carpenter or mechanic would not listen to an offer of less than fifteen or twenty dollars a day. Could any combination of affairs try a man's fidelity more than this? I really think some extraordinary mark of favor should be given to those soldiers who remain faithful to their flag throughout this tempting crisis. No officer can now live in California on his pay, money has so little value; the prices of necessary articles of clothing and subsistence are so exorbitant, and labor so high, that to hire a cook or servant has become an impossibility, save to those who are earning from thirty to fifty dollars a day. This state of things cannot last forever. Yet from the geographical position of California, and the new character it has assumed as a mining country, prices of labor will always be high, and will hold out temptations to desert. If the government wish to prevent desertions here on the part of men, and to secure zeal on the part of officers, their pay must be increased very materially.

"Many private letters have gone to the United States giving accounts of the vast quantity of gold recently discovered, and I have no hesitation now in saying that there is more gold in the country drained by the Sacramento and San

Joaquim rivers, than will pay the cost of the present war with Mexico a hundred times over. No capital is required to obtain this gold, as the laboring man wants nothing but his pick and shovel and tin pan, with which to dig and wash the gravel; and many frequently pick gold out of the crevices of the rocks with their butcher-knives, in pieces from one to six ounces.

"Mr. Dye, a gentleman residing in Monterey, and worthy of every credit, has just returned from Feather River. He tells me that the company to which he belonged worked seven weeks and two days, with an average of fifty Indians, (washers), and that their gross product was two hundred and seventy-three pounds of gold. His share, (one seventh), after paying all expenses, is about thirty-seven pounds, which he brought with him and exhibited in Monterey. I see no laboring man from the mines who does not show his two, three, or four pounds of gold. A soldier of the artillery company returned here a few days ago from the mines, having been absent on furlough twenty days. He made by trading and working during that time one thousand five hundred dollars. During these twenty days he was travelling ten or eleven days, leaving but a week, in which he made a sum of money greater than he receives in pay, clothes, and rations during a whole enlistment of five years. These statements appear incredible, but they are true.

"The 'placer' gold is now substituted as the currency in this country; in trade it passes freely at sixteen dollars per ounce; as an article of commerce its value is not yet fixed. The only purchase I made was at twelve dollars the ounce. That is about the present cash value in the country, although it has been sold for less. The great demand for goods and provisions made by the sudden development in wealth, has increased the amount of commerce at San Francisco very much, and it will continue to increase.

"I have the honor to be, your most ob't. serv't,

"R. B. MASON

"*Colonel First Dragoons, Commanding*"

"BRIGADIER GENERAL R. JONES,
  "*Adjutant General U. S. A., Washington, D.C.*"

EXTRACT FROM A LETTER FROM MR. LARKIN TO MR. BUCHANAN

"SAN FRANCISCO, UPPER CALIFORNIA
June 1, 1848

"A few men have been down to the boats in this port, spending twenty to thirty ounces of gold each—about three hundred dollars. I am confident that this town has one-half of its tenements empty, locked up with the furniture. The owners—storekeepers, lawyers, mechanics and laborers—all gone to the Sacramento with their families. Small parties, of five to fifteen men, have sent to this town, and offered cooks ten to fifteen dollars per day for a few weeks. Mechanics and teamsters, earning the year past five to eight dollars per day, have struck and gone. Several United States volunteers have deserted. United States bark Anita, belonging to the army, now at anchor here, has but six men. One Sandwich Island vessel in port lost all her men; engaged another crew at fifty dollars for the run of fifteen days to the Islands.

"One American captain having his men shipped on this coast in such a manner that they could leave at any time, had them all on the eve of quitting, when he agreed to continue their pay and food; leaving one on board, he took a boat and carried them to the gold regions—furnishing tools and giving his men one-third. They have been gone a week. Common spades and shovels, one month ago worth one dollar, will now bring ten dollars at the gold regions. I am informed fifty dollars has been offered for one. Should this gold continue as represented, this town and others would be depopulated. Clerks' wages have risen from six hundred to one thousand per annum, and board; cooks, twenty-five to thirty dollars per month. This sum will not be any inducement a month longer, unless the fever and ague appears among the washers. The *Californian,* printed here, stopped this week. The *Star* newspaper office, where the new laws of Governor Mason, for this country, are printing, has but one man left. A merchant, lately from China, has even lost his China servants. Should the excitement continue through the year, and the whale-ships visit San Francisco, I think they will lose most of their crews. How Colonel Mason can retain his men, unless he puts a force on the spot, I know not.

"I have seen several pounds of this gold, and consider it very pure, worth, in New York, seventeen to eighteen dollars per ounce; fourteen to sixteen dollars, in merchandize, is paid for it here. What good or bad effects this gold mania will have on California, I cannot foretell. It may end this year; but I am informed it will continue many years. Mechanics now in this town are only waiting to finish some rude machinery, to enable them to obtain the gold more expeditiously, and free from working in the river. Up to this time, but few Californians have gone to the mines, being afraid the Americans will soon have troubles among themselves, and cause disturbance all around. Although my statements are almost incredible, I believe I am within the statements believed by everyone here. Ten days back, the excitement had not reached Monterey.

"I have the honor to be, very respectfully,

"Thomas O. Larkin"

"Hon. James Buchanan
"*Secretary of State, Washington*"

40

Eldorado: California and the Forty-niners, 1849

*P*erhaps *the most sensational news ever to break in nineteenth-century America was the discovery of gold in California. At once—around the Horn, over the Isthmus, across the continent—poured a hungry multitude in search of the golden grains and quick riches. They came from all walks of life and from every section of the nation. Jammed in together in the gold regions of California, they transformed the sleepy Latin civilization of the natives and ratified in fact the Treaty of Guadalupe-Hidalgo written on paper two years before. If life was lawless, it was also picturesque. And to the sensation of get-rich-quickness were added lurid accounts of desperadoes, gamblers, prostitutes, and every other element that was at once damnable or interesting.*

An insatiable demand for news of California swept through the East, and the New York Tribune *could have selected no person better qualified to report the story than Bayard Taylor. Born in 1825 in Kennett Square, Pennsylvania, Taylor was by instinct and inclination a reporter and a traveler. Though he regarded himself as a poet and a novelist, the world does not today, nor did it much in his own time, regard these aspects of his career seriously. But as a wanderer with a keen eye for what was interesting, it was another matter. He had already published one travel book,* Views Afoot *(1846), with great success. He now spent some five months in California, in the first flush of the gold discoveries, and produced* Eldorado *(1850) with equal success. He added to his popularity by long lecture tours, filling many a lyceum and theater stage with verbal accounts of his experiences, often garbed in the costume of the people of whom he talked, and thus brought to the staid mid-*

dle classes a sense of romance and adventure. His account of California clearly
seeks to capture the dramatic, the sensational, and the colorful. With sober
matters of economics he was little concerned. But there is no reason to believe
that, if his picture seems one-sided, it is not also accurate, for he was, after all,
dealing with a bizarre and melodramatic society.

FIRST IMPRESSIONS OF SAN FRANCISCO

At last the voyage is drawing to a close. Fifty-one days have elapsed since
leaving New York and now we are in front of the entrance to San Francisco
Bay. The mountains on the northern side are 3,000 feet in height, and come
boldly down to the sea. As the view opens through the splendid strait, three
or four miles in width, the island rock of Alcatraz appears, gleaming white in
the distance. There is a small fort perched among the trees on our right,
where the strait is narrowest, which might be made as impregnable as Gibral-
tar. The town is still concealed behind the promontory around which the Bay
turns to the southward, but between Alcatraz and the island of Yerba Buena,
now coming into sight, I can see vessels at anchor. High through the vapor in
front, and thirty miles distant, rises the peak of Monte Diablo, which overlooks everything between the Sierra Nevada and the Ocean. On our left opens
the bight of Sousolito.

At last we are through the Golden Gate—fit name for such a magnificent
portal to the commerce of the Pacific! Yerba Buena Island is in front; southward and westward opens the renowned harbor, crowded with the shipping
of the world, mast behind mast and vessel behind vessel, the flags of all nations fluttering in the breeze! Around the curving shore of the Bay and upon
the sides of three hills which rise steeply from the water, the middle one receding so as to form a bold amphitheatre, the town is planted and seems
scarcely yet to have taken root, for tents, canvas, plank, mud and adobe
houses are mingled together with the least apparent attempt at order and du-
rability. But I am not yet on shore. The gun of the Panama has just announced our arrival to the people on land. We glide on with the tide, past the
U.S. ship Ohio and opposite the main landing, outside of the forest of masts.
A dozen boats are creeping out to us over the water; the signal is given—the
anchor drops—our voyage is over.

I left the Panama, in company with Lieut. Beale, in the boat of the U.S. ship
Ohio, which put us ashore at the northern point of the anchorage, at the foot
of a steep bank, from which a high pier had been built into the bay. A large
vessel lay at the end, discharging her cargo. We scrambled up through the
piles of luggage, and among the crowd collected to witness our arrival, picked

out two Mexicans to carry our trunks to a hotel. The barren site of the hill before us was covered with tents and canvas houses, and nearly in front a large two-story building displayed the sign: "Fremont Family Hotel."

As yet we were only in the suburbs of the town. Crossing the shoulder of the hill, the view extended around the curve of the bay, and hundreds of tents and houses appeared, scattered all over the heights, and along the shore for more than a mile. A furious wind was blowing down through a gap in the hills, filling the streets with clouds of dust. On every side stood buildings of all kinds, begun or half-finished, and the greater part of them mere canvas sheds, open in front, and covered with all kinds of signs, in all languages. Great quantities of goods were piled up in the open air, for want of a place to store them. The streets were full of people, hurrying to and fro, and of as diverse and bizarre a character as the houses: Yankees of every possible variety, native Californians in *sarapes* and sombreros, Chilians, Sonorians, Kanakas from Hawaii, Chinese with long tails, Malays armed with their everlasting creeses, and others in whose embrowned and bearded visages it was impossible to recognize any especial nationality. We came at last into the plaza, now digni- fied by the name of Portsmouth Square. It lies on the slant side of the hill, and from a high pole in front of a long one-story adobe building used as the Custom House, the American flag was flying. On the lower side stood the Parker House—an ordinary frame house of about sixty feet front—and to- wards its entrance we directed our course.

Our luggage was deposited on one of the rear porticos, and we discharged the porters, after paying them two dollars each—a sum so immense in com- parison to the service rendered that there was no longer any doubt of our having actually landed in California. There were no lodgings to be had at the Parker House—not even a place to unroll our blankets; but one of the pro- prietors accompanied us across the plaza to the City Hotel, where we ob- tained a room with two beds at $25 per week, meals being in addition $20 per week. I asked the landlord whether he could send a porter for our trunks. "There is none belonging to the house," said he; "every man is his own porter here." I returned to the Parker House, shouldered a heavy trunk, took a valise in my hand and carried them to my quarters, in the teeth of the wind. Our room was in a sort of garret over the only story of the hotel; two cots, evi- dently of California manufacture, and covered only with a pair of blankets, two chairs, a rough table and a small looking-glass, constituted the furniture. There was not space enough between the bed and the bare rafters overhead, to sit upright, and I gave myself a severe blow in rising the next morning with- out the proper heed. Through a small roof-window of dim glass, I could see the opposite shore of the bay, then partly hidden by the evening fogs. The wind whistled around the eaves and rattled the tiles with a cold, gusty sound, that would have imparted a dreary character to the place, had I been in a mood to listen.

Many of the passengers began speculation at the moment of landing. The most ingenious and successful operation was made by a gentleman of New York, who took out fifteen hundred copies of The Tribune and other papers, which he disposed of in two hours, at one dollar apiece! Hearing of this I bethought me of about a dozen papers which I had used to fill up crevices in packing my valise. There was a newspaper merchant at the corner of the City Hotel, and to him I proposed the sale of them, asking him to name a price. "I shall want to make a good profit on the retail price," said he, "and can't give more than ten dollars for the lot." I was satisfied with the whole-sale price, which was a gain of just four thousand per cent!

I set out for a walk before dark and climbed a hill back of the town, passing a number of tents pitched in the hollows. The scattered houses spread out below me and the crowded shipping in the harbor, backed by a lofty line of mountains, made an imposing picture. The restless, feverish tide of life in that little spot rendered it singularly impressive. Every new-comer in San Francisco is overtaken with a sense of complete bewilderment. One knows not whether he is awake or in some wonderful dream. Never have I had so much difficulty in establishing, satisfactorily to my own senses, the reality of what I saw and heard.

It may be interesting to give here a few instances of the enormous and unnatural value put upon property at the time of my arrival. The Parker House rented for $110,000 yearly, at least $60,000 of which was paid by gamblers, who held nearly all the second story. Adjoining it on the right was a canvas-tent fifteen by twenty-five feet, called "Eldorado," and occupied likewise by gamblers, which brought $40,000. On the opposite corner of the Plaza, a building called the "Miner's Bank," about half the size of a fire-engine house in New York, was held at a rent of $75,000. A friend of mine, who wished to find a place for a law-office, was shown a cellar in the earth, about twelve feet square and six deep, which he could have at $250 a month. A citizen of San Francisco died insolvent to the amount of $41,000 the previous Autumn. His administrators were delayed in settling his affairs, and his real estate advanced so rapidly meantime, that after his debts were paid his heirs had a yearly income of $40,000.

The prices paid for labor were in proportion to everything else. The carmen of Mellus, Howard & Co. had a salary of $6,000 a year, and many others made from $15 to $20 daily. Servants were paid from $100 to $200 a month, but the wages of the rougher kinds of labor had fallen to about $8. Yet, notwithstanding the number of gold-seekers who were returning enfeebled and disheartened from the mines, it was difficult to obtain as many workmen as the forced growth of the city demanded. A gentlemen who arrived in April told me he then found but thirty or forty houses; the population was then so scant that not more than twenty-five persons would be seen in the streets at any one time. Now, there were probably five hundred houses, tents and sheds, with a population, fixed and floating, of six thousand. People who had been absent six weeks came back and could scarcely recognize the place. Streets were regularly laid out, and already there were three piers, at which small vessels could discharge. It was calculated that the town increased daily by from fifteen to thirty houses; its skirts were rapidly approaching the summits of the three hills on which it is located.

A curious result of the extraordinary abundance of gold and the facility with which fortunes were acquired, struck me at the first glance. All business was transacted on so extensive a scale that the ordinary habits of solicitation and compliance on the one hand and stubborn cheapening on the other, seemed to be entirely forgotten. You enter a shop to buy something; the owner eyes you with perfect indifference, waiting for you to state your want; if you object to the price, you are at liberty to leave, for you need not expect to get it cheaper; he evidently cares little whether you buy it or not. One who has been some time in the country will lay down the money, without wasting words. The only exception I found to this rule was that of a sharp-faced Down-Easter just opening his stock, who was much distressed when his clerk charged me seventy-five cents for a coil of rope, instead of one dollar. This disregard for all the petty arts of money-making was really a refreshing feature of society. Another equally agreeable trait was the punctuality with which debts were paid, and the general confidence which men were obliged to place, perforce, in each other's honesty. Perhaps this latter fact was owing, in part, to the impossibility of protecting wealth, and consequent dependence on an honorable regard for the rights of others.

About the hour of twilight the wind fell; the sound of a gong called us to tea, which was served in the largest room of the hotel. The fare was abundant and of much better quality than we expected—better, in fact, than I was able to find there two months later. The fresh milk, butter and ex-cellent beef of the country were real luxuries after our sea-fare. Thus braced against the fog and raw temperature, we sallied out for a night-view of San Francisco, then even more peculiar than its daylight look. Business was over about the usual hour, and then the harvest-time of the gamblers commenced. Every "hell" in the place, and I did not pretend to number them, was crowded, and immense sums were staked at the monte and faro tables. A boy of fifteen, in one place, won about $500, which he coolly pocketed and carried off. One of the gang we brought in the Panama won $1,500 in the course of the evening, and another lost $2,400. A fortunate miner made himself conspicuous by betting large piles of ounces on a single throw. His last stake of 100 oz. was lost, and I saw him the following morning dashing through the streets, trying to break his own neck or that of the magnificent *garañon* he bestrode.

Walking through the town the next day, I was quite amazed to find a dozen persons busily employed in the street before the United States Hotel, digging up the earth with knives and crumbling it in their hands. They were actual gold-hunters, who obtained in this way about $5 a day. After blowing the fine dirt carefully in their hands, a few specks of gold were left, which they placed in a piece of white paper. A number of children were engaged in the same business, picking out the fine grains by applying to them the head of a pin, moistened in their mouths. I was told of a small boy having taken home $14 as the result of one day's labor. On climbing the hill to the Post Office I observed in places, where the wind had swept away the sand, several glittering dots of the real metal, but, like the Irishman who kicked the dollar out of his way, concluded to wait till I should reach the heap. The presence of gold in the streets was probably occasioned by the leakings from the miners' bags and the sweepings of stores; though it may also be, to a slight extent, native in the earth, particles having been found in the clay thrown from a deep well.

LAW AND ORDER

I witnessed, while in Stockton, a summary exhibition of justice. The night before my arrival, three negroes, while on a drunken revel, entered the tent of a Chilian, and attempted to violate a female who was within. Defeated in their base designs by her husband, who was fortunately within call, they fired their pistols at the tent and left. Complaint was made before the Alcalde, two of the negroes seized and identified, witnesses examined, a jury summoned, and a verdict given, without delay. The principal offender was sentenced to receive fifty lashes and the other twenty—both to leave the place within forty-eight hours under pain of death. The sentence was immediately carried into execution, the negroes were stripped, tied to a tree standing in the middle of the principal street, and in the presence of the Alcalde and Sheriff received their punishment. There was little of that order and respect shown which should accompany even the administration of impromptu law; the bystanders jeered, laughed, and accompanied every

blow with coarse and unfeeling remarks. Some of the more intelligent professed themselves opposed to the mode of punishment, but in the absence of
prisons or effective guards could suggest no alternative, except the sterner
one of capital punishment.

The history of law and society in California, from the period of the golden
discoveries, would furnish many instructive lessons to the philosopher and
the statesman. The first consequence of the unprecedented rush of emigration from all parts of the world into a country almost unknown, and but
half reclaimed from its original barbarism was to render all law virtually
null, and bring the established authorities to depend entirely on the humor
of the population for the observance of their orders. The countries which
were nearest the golden coast—Mexico, Peru, Chili, China and the Sandwich
Islands—sent forth their thousands of ignorant adventurers, who speedily
outnumbered the American population. Another fact, which none the less
threatened serious consequences, was the readiness with which the worthless
and depraved class of our own country came to the Pacific Coast. From the
beginning, a state of things little short of anarchy might have been reasonably awaited.

Instead of this, a disposition to maintain order and secure the rights of
all, was shown throughout the mining districts. In the absence of all law or
available protection, the people met and adopted rules for their mutual
security—rules adapted to their situation, where they had neither guards nor
prisons, and where the slightest license given to crime or trespass of any kind
must inevitably have led to terrible disorders. Small thefts were punished by
banishment from the placers, while for those of large amount or for more
serious crimes, there was the single alternative of hanging. These regulations, with slight change, had been continued up to the time of my visit to
the country. In proportion as the emigration from our own States increased,
and the digging community assumed a more orderly and intelligent aspect,
their severity had been relaxed, though punishment was still strictly ad-
ministered for all offences. There had been, as nearly as I could learn, not
more than twelve or fifteen executions in all, about half of which were in-
flicted for the crime of murder. This awful responsibility had not been assumed lightly, but after a fair trial and a full and clear conviction, to which
was added, I believe in every instance, the confession of the criminal.

In all the large digging districts, which had been worked for some time,
there were established regulations, which were faithfully observed. Alcaldes
were elected, who decided on all disputes of right or complaints of trespass,
and who had power to summon juries for criminal trials. When a new
placer or gulch was discovered, the first thing done was to elect officers and

extend the area of order. The result was, that in a district five hundred miles long, and inhabited by 100,000 people, who had neither government, regular laws, rules, military or civil protection, nor even locks or bolts, and a great part of whom possessed wealth enough to tempt the vicious and depraved, there was as much security to life and property as in any part of the Union, and as small a proportion of crime. The capacity of a people for self-government was never so triumphantly illustrated. Never, perhaps, was there a community formed of more unpropitious elements; yet from all this seeming chaos grew a harmony beyond what the most sanguine apostle of Progress could have expected.

The rights of the diggers were no less definitely marked and strictly observed. Among the hundreds I saw on the Mokelumne and among the gulches, I did not see a single dispute nor hear a word of complaint. A company of men might mark out a race of any length and turn the current of the river to get at the bed, possessing the exclusive right to that part of it, so long as their undertaking lasted. A man might dig a hole in the dry ravines, and so long as he left a shovel, pick or crowbar to show that he still intended working it, he was safe from trespass. His tools might remain there for months without being disturbed. I have seen many such places, miles away from any camp or tent, which the digger had left in perfect confidence that he should find all right on his return. There were of course exceptions to these rules—the diggings would be a Utopia if it were not so—but they were not frequent. The Alcaldes sometimes made awkward decisions, from inexperience, but they were none the less implicitly obeyed. I heard of one instance in which a case of trespass was settled to the satisfaction of both parties and the Sheriff ordered to pay the costs of Court—about $40. The astonished functionary remonstrated, but the power of the Alcalde was supreme, and he was obliged to suffer.

SACRAMENTO CITY

The plan of Sacramento City is very simple. It is laid out in regular right-angles, in Philadelphia style, those running east and west named after the alphabet, and those north and south after the arithmetic. The limits of the town extended to nearly one square mile, and the number of inhabitants, in tents and houses, fell little short of ten thousand. The previous April there were just four houses in the place! Can the world match a growth like this?

The original forest-trees, standing in all parts of the town, give it a very picturesque appearance. Many of the streets are lined with oaks and sycamores, six feet in diameter, and spreading ample boughs on every side. The emigrants have ruined the finest of them by building camp-fires at their bases, which, in some instances, have burned completely through, leaving a charred and blackened arch for the superb tree to rest upon. The storm which occurred a few days previous to my visit, snapped asunder several trunks which had been thus weakened, one of them crushing to the earth a canvas house in which a man lay asleep. A heavy bough struck the ground on each side of him, saving his life. The destruction of these trees is the more to be regretted, as the intense heat of the Summer days, when the mercury stands at 120°, renders their shade a thing of absolute necessity.

The value of real estate in Sacramento City is only exceeded by that of San Francisco. Lots twenty by seventy-five feet, in the best locations, brought from $3,000 to $3,500. Rents were on a scale equally enormous. The City Hotel, which was formerly a saw-mill, erected by Capt. Sutter, paid $30,000 per annum. A new hotel, going up on the levee, had been already rented at $35,000. Two drinking and gaming-rooms, on a business street, paid each $1,000, monthly, invariably in advance. Many of the stores transacted business averaging from $1,000 to $3,000 daily. Board was $20 per week at the restaurants and $5 per day at the City Hotel. But what is the use of repeating figures? These dead statistics convey no idea of the marvellous state of things in the place. It was difficult enough for those who saw to believe, and I can only hope to reproduce the very faintest impression of the pictures I there beheld. It was frequently wondered, on this side of the Rocky Mountains, why the gold dust was not sent out of the country in larger quantities, when at least forty thousand men were turning up the placers. The fact is, it was required as currency, and the amount in circulation might be counted by millions. Why, the building up of a single street in Sacramento City (J street) cost *half a million,* at least! The value of all the houses in the city, frail and perishing as many of them were, could not have been less than $2,000,000.

It must be acknowledged there is another side to the picture. Three-fourths of the people who settle in Sacramento City are visited by agues, diarrhoeas and other reducing complaints. In Summer the place is a furnace, in Winter little better than a swamp; and the influx of emigrants and discouraged miners generally exceeds the demand for labor. A healthy, sensible, wide-awake man, however, cannot fail to prosper. In a country where Labor rules everything, no sound man has a right to complain. When carpenters make a strike because they only get *twelve dollars* a day, one may be sure there is room enough for industry and enterprise of all kinds.

The city was peopled principally by New-Yorkers, Jerseymen and people from the Western States. In activity and public spirit, it was nothing behind San Francisco; its growth, indeed, in view of the difference of location, was more remarkable. The inhabitants had elected a Town Council, adopted a City Charter and were making exertions to have the place declared a port of entry. The political waters were being stirred a little, in anticipation of the approaching election. Mr. Gilbert, of the Alta California, and Col. Stewart, candidate for Governor, were in the city. A political meeting, which had been held a few nights before, in front of the City Hotel, passed off as uproariously and with as zealous a sentiment of patriotism as such meetings are wont to exhibit at home.

The city already boasted a weekly paper, the Placer Times, which was edited and published by Mr. Giles, formerly of the Tribune Office. His printers were all old friends of mine—one of them, in fact, a former fellow-apprentice—and from the fraternal feeling that all possess who have ever belonged to the craft, the place became at once familiar and home-like. The little paper, which had a page of about twelve by eighteen inches, had a circulation of five hundred copies, at $12 a year; the amount received weekly for jobs and advertising, varied from $1,000 to $2,000. Tickets were printed for the different political candidates, at the rate of $20 for every thousand. The compositors were paid $15 daily. Another compositor from the Tribune Office had established a restaurant, and was doing a fine business. His dining saloon was an open tent, unfloored; the tables were plank, with rough benches on each side; the waiters rude Western boys who had come over the Rocky Mountains—but the meals he furnished could not have been surpassed in any part of the world for substantial richness of quality. There was every day abundance of elk steaks, unsurpassed for sweet and delicate flavor; venison, which had been fattened on the mountain acorns; mutton, such as nothing but the wild pastures of California could produce; salmon and salmon-trout of astonishing size, from the Sacramento River, and now and then the solid flesh of the grizzly bear. The salmon-trout exceeded in fatness any fresh-water fish I ever saw; they were between two and three feet in length, with a layer of pure fat, quarter of an inch in thickness, over the ribs. When made into chowder or stewed in claret, they would have thrown into ecstacies the most inveterate Parisian gourmand. The full-moon face of the proprietor of the restaurant was accounted for, when one had tasted his fare; after living there a few days, I could feel my own dimensions sensibly enlarged.

The road to Sutter's Fort, the main streets and the levee fronting on the Embarcadero, were constantly thronged with the teams of emigrants, coming in from the mountains. Such worn, weather-beaten individuals I never before imagined. Their tents were pitched by hundreds in the thickets around the town, where they rested a few days before starting to winter in the mines and elsewhere. At times the levee was filled throughout its whole length by their teams, three or four yoke of oxen to every wagon. The beasts had an expression of patient experience which plainly showed that no roads yet to be traveled would astonish them in the least. After tugging the wagons for six months over the salt deserts of the Great Basin, climbing passes and cañons of terrible asperity in the Sierra Nevada, and learning to digest oak bark on the arid plains around the sink of Humboldt's River, it seemed as if no extremity could henceforth intimidate them. Much toil and suffering had given to their countenances a look of almost human wisdom. The cows had been yoked in with the oxen and made to do equal duty. The women who had come by the overland route appeared to have stood the hardships of the journey remarkably well, and were not half so loud as the men in their complaints.

The amounts of gambling in Sacramento City was very great, and the enticement of music was employed even to a greater extent than in San Francisco. All kinds of instruments and tunes made night discordant, for which harrowing service the performers were paid an ounce each. Among the many drinking houses, there was one called "The Plains," which was much frequented by the emigrants. Some western artist, who came across the country, adorned its walls with scenic illustrations of the route, such as Independence Rock, the Sweet-Water Valley, Fort Laramie, Wind River Mountains, etc. There was one of a pass in the Sierra Nevada, on the Carson River route. A wagon and team were represented as coming down the side of a hill, so nearly perpendicular that it seemed no earthly power could prevent them from making but a single fall from the summit to the valley. These particular oxen, however, were happily independent of gravitation, and whisked their tails in the face of the zenith, as they marched slowly down.

I was indebted for quarters in Sacramento City, to Mr. De Graw, who was installed in a frame house, copper-roofed, fronting the levee. I slept very comfortably on a pile of Chinese quilts, behind the counter, lulled by the dashing of the rain against the sides of the house. The rainy season had set in, to all appearances, though it was full a month before the usual time. The sky was bleak and gray, and the wind blew steadily from the south, an unfailing sign to the old residents. The saying of the Mexicans seemed to be verified, that, wherever *los Yankis* go, they take rain with them.

Sacramento City was one place by day and another by night; and of the two, its night-side was the most peculiar. As the day went down dull and cloudy, a thin fog gathered in the humid atmosphere, through which the canvas houses, lighted from within, shone with a broad, obscure gleam, that confused the eye and made the streets most familiar by daylight look strangely different. They bore no resemblance to the same places, seen at mid-day, under a break of clear sunshine, and pervaded with the stir of business life. The town, regular as it was, became a bewildering labyrinth of half-light and deep darkness, and the perils of traversing it were greatly increased by the mire and frequent pools left by the rain.

To one, venturing out after dark for the first time, these perils were by no means imaginary. Each man wore boots reaching to the knees—or higher, if he could get them—with the pantaloons tucked inside, but there were pitfalls, into which had he fallen, even these would have availed little. In the more frequented streets, where drinking and gambling had full swing, there was a partial light, streaming out through doors and crimson window-curtains, to guide his steps. Sometimes a platform of plank received his feet; sometimes he skipped from one loose barrel-stave to another, laid with the convex-side upward; and sometimes, deceived by a scanty piece of scantling, he walked off its further end into a puddle of liquid mud. Now, floundering in the stiff mire of the mid-street, he plunged down into a gulley and was "brought up" by a pool of water; now, venturing near the houses a scaffold-pole or stray beam dealt him an unexpected blow. If he wandered into the outskirts of the town, where the tent-city of the emigrants was built, his case was still worse. The briery thickets of the original forest had not been cleared away, and the stumps, trunks and branches of felled trees were distributed over the soil with delightful uncertainty. If he escaped these, the lariats of picketed mules spread their toils for his feet, threatening entanglement and a kick from one of the vicious animals; tent-ropes and pins took him across the shins, and the horned heads of cattle, left where they were slaughtered, lay ready to gore him at every step. A walk of any distance, environed by such dangers, especially when the air was damp and chill, and there was a possibility of rain at any moment, presented no attractions to the weary denizens of the place.

A great part of them, indeed, took to their blankets soon after dark. They were generally worn out with the many excitements of the day, and glad to find a position of repose. Reading was out of the question to the most of them when candles were $4 per lb. and scarce at that; but in any case, the preternatural activity and employment of mind induced by the business habits of the place would have made impossible anything like quiet thought. I saw many persons who had brought the works of favorite authors with them, for recreation at odd hours, but of all the works thus brought, I never

saw one read. Men preferred—or rather it grew, involuntarily, into a custom
—to lie at ease instead, and turn over in the brain all their shifts and
manoeuvres of speculation, to see whether any chance had been left untouched. Some, grouped around a little pocket-stove, beguile an hour or two
over their cans of steaming punch or other warming concoction, and build
schemes out of the smoke of their rank Guayaquil *puros*—for the odor of a
genuine Havana is unknown. But, by nine o'clock at farthest, nearly all the
working population of Sacramento City are stretched out on mattrass, plank
or cold earth, according to the state of their fortunes, and dreaming of
splendid runs of luck or listening to the sough of the wind in the trees.

There is, however, a large floating community of overland emigrants,
miners and sporting characters, who prolong the wakefulness of the streets
far into the night. The door of many a gambling-hell on the levee, and in
J and K streets, stands invitingly open; the wail of torture from innumerable
musical instruments peals from all quarters through the fog and darkness.
Full bands, each playing different tunes discordantly, are stationed in front
of the principal establishments, and as these happen to be near together, the
mingling of the sounds in one horrid, ear-splitting, brazen chaos, would
drive frantic a man of delicate nerve. All one's old acquaintances in the
amateur-music line, seem to have followed him. The gentleman who played
the flute in the next room to yours, at home, has been hired at an ounce a
night to perform in the drinking-tent across the way; the very French horn
whose lamentations used to awake you dismally from the first sweet snooze,
now greets you at some corner; and all the squeaking violins, grumbling
violincellos and rowdy trumpets which have severally plagued you in other
times, are congregated here, in loving proximity. The very strength, loudness
and confusion of the noises, which, heard at a little distance, have the effect
of one great scattering performance, marvellously takes the fancy of the
rough mountain men.

Some of the establishments have small companies of Ethiopian melodists,
who nightly call upon "Susanna!" and entreat to be carried back to Old
Virginny. These songs are universally popular, and the crowd of listeners is
often so great as to embarrass the player at the monte tables and injure the
business of the gamblers. I confess to a strong liking for the Ethiopian airs,
and used to spend half an hour every night in listening to them and watching
the curious expressions of satisfaction and delight in the faces of the overland
emigrants, who always attended in a body. The spirit of the music was always encouraging; even its most doleful passages had a grotesque touch of
cheerfulness—a mingling of sincere pathos and whimsical consolation, which
somehow took hold of all moods in which it might be heard, raising them to

the same notch of careless good-humor. The Ethiopian melodies well deserve to be called, as they are in fact, the national airs of America. Their quaint, mock-sentimental cadences, so well suited to the broad absurdity of the words—their reckless gaiety and irreverent familiarity with serious subjects—and their spirit of antagonism and perseverance—are true expressions of the more popular sides of the national character. They follow the American race in all its emigrations, colonizations and conquests, as certainly as the Fourth of July and Thanksgiving Day. The penniless and half-despairing emigrant is stimulated to try again by the sound of "It'll never do to give it up so!" and feels a pang of home-sickness at the burthen of the "Old Virginia Shore."

At the time of which I am writing, Sacramento City boasted the only theatre in California. Its performances, three times a week, were attended by crowds of the miners, and the owners realized a very handsome profit. The canvas building used for this purpose fronted on the levee, within a door or two of the City Hotel; it would have been taken for an ordinary drinking-house, but for the sign; "EAGLE THEATRE," which was nailed to the top of the canvas frame. Passing through the bar-room we arrive at the entrance; the prices of admission are: Box, $3, Pit, $2. The spectators are dressed in heavy overcoats and felt hats, with boots reaching to the knees. The box-tier is a single rough gallery at one end, capable of containing about a hundred persons; the pit will probably hold three hundred more, so that the receipts of a full house amount to $900. The sides and roof of the theatre are canvas, which, when wet, effectually prevents ventilation, and renders the atmosphere hot and stifling. The drop-curtain, which is down at present, exhibits a glaring landscape, with dark-brown trees in the foreground, and lilac-colored mountains against a yellow sky.

The overture commences; the orchestra is composed of only five members, under the direction of an Italian, and performs with tolerable correctness. The piece for the night is "The Spectre of the Forest," in which the celebrated actress, Mrs. Ray, "of the Royal Theatre, New Zealand," will appear. The bell rings; the curtain rolls up; and we look upon a forest scene, in the midst of which appears Hildebrand, the robber, in a sky-blue mantle. The foliage of the forest is of a dark-red color, which makes a great impression on the spectators and prepares them for the bloody scenes that are to follow. The other characters are a brave knight in a purple dress, with his servant in scarlet; they are about to storm the robber's hold and carry off a captive maiden. Several acts are filled with the usual amount of fighting and terrible speeches; but the interest of the play is carried to an awful height by the appearance of two spectres, clad in mutilated tent-covers, and holding spermaceti candles in their hands. At this juncture Mrs. Ray rushes in and throws herself into an attitude in the middle of the stage: why she does it, no one can tell. This movement, which she repeats several times in the course of the first three acts, has no connection with the tragedy; it is evidently introduced for the purpose of showing the audience that there is, actually, a female performer. The miners, to whom the sight of a woman is not a frequent occurrence, are delighted with these passages and applaud vehemently.

In the closing scenes, where Hildebrand entreats the heroine to become his bride, Mrs. Ray shone in all her glory. "No!" said she, "I'd rather take a basilisk and wrap its cold fangs around me, than be clasped in the hembraces of an 'artless robber." Then, changing her tone to that of entreaty, she calls upon the knight in purple, whom she declares to be "me'ope—me only 'ope!" We will not stay to hear the songs and duetts which follow; the tragedy has been a sufficient infliction. For her " 'art-rending" personations, Mrs. Ray received $200 a week, and the wages of the other actors were in the same proportion. A musical gentleman was paid $96 for singing "The Sea! the Sea!" in a deep bass voice. The usual sum paid musicians was $16 a night. A Swiss organ-girl, by playing in the various hells, accumulated $4000 in the course of five or six months.

The southern part of Sacramento City, where the most of the overland emigrants had located themselves, was an interesting place for a night-ramble, when one had courage to undertake threading the thickets among which their tents were pitched. There, on fallen logs about their camp-fires, might be seen groups that had journeyed together across the Continent, recalling the hardships and perils of the travel. The men, with their long beards, weather-beaten faces and ragged garments, seen in the red, flickering light of the fires, made wild and fantastic pictures. Sometimes four of them might be seen about a stump, intent on reviving their ancient knowledge of "poker," and occasionally a more social group, filling their tin cups from a kettle of tea or something stronger. Their fires, however, were soon left to smoulder away; the evenings were too raw and they were too weary with the day's troubles to keep long vigils.

SAN FRANCISCO REVISITED

When I had climbed the last sand-hill, riding in towards San Francisco, and the town and harbor and crowded shipping again opened to the view, I could scarcely realize the change that had taken place during my absence of three weeks. The town had not only greatly extended its limits, but actually seemed to have doubled its number of dwellings since I left. High up on the hills, where I had seen only sand and chapparal, stood clusters of houses; streets which had been merely laid out, were hemmed in with buildings and thronged with people; new warehouses had sprung up on the water side, and new piers were creeping out toward the shipping; the forest of masts had greatly thickened; and the noise, motion and bustle of business and labor on all sides were incessant. Verily, the place was in itself a marvel. To say that it was daily enlarged by from twenty to thirty houses may not sound very remarkable after all the stories that have been told; yet this, for a country which imported both lumber and houses, and where labor was then $10 a day, is an extraordinary growth. The rapidity with which a ready-made house is put up and inhabited, strikes the stranger in San Francisco as little short of magic. He walks over an open lot in his before-breakfast stroll—the next morning, a house complete, with a family inside, blocks up his way. He goes down to the bay and looks out on the shipping—two or three days afterward a row of storehouses, staring him in the face, intercepts the view.

A better idea of San Francisco cannot be given than by the description of a single day. Supposing the visitor to have been long enough in the place to sleep on a hard plank, in spite of the attacks of innumerable fleas, he will be awakened at daylight by the noises of building, with which the hills are all alive. The air is temperate, and the invariable morning fog is just beginning to gather. By sunrise, which gleams hazily over the Coast Mountains across the Bay, the whole populace is up and at work. The wooden buildings unlock their doors, the canvas houses and tents throw back their front curtains; the lighters on the water are warped out from ship to ship; carts and porters are busy along the beach; and only the gaming-tables, thronged all night by the votaries of chance, are idle and deserted. The temperature is so fresh as to inspire an active habit of body, and even without the stimulus of trade and speculation there would be few sluggards at this season.

As early as half-past six the bells begin to sound to breakfast, and for an hour thenceforth, their incessant clang and the braying of immense gongs drown all the hammers that are busy on a hundred roofs. The hotels, restaurants and refectories of all kinds are already as numerous as gaming-tables, and equally various in kind. The tables d'hôte of the first class, (which charge $2 and upwards the meal,) are abundantly supplied. There are others, with more simple and solid fare, frequented by the large class who have their fortunes yet to make. At the United States and California restaurants, on the plaza, you may get an excellent beefsteak, scantily garnished with potatoes, and a cup of good coffee or chocolate, for $1. Fresh beef, bread, potatoes, and all provisions which will bear importation, are plenty; but milk, fruit and vegetables are classed as luxuries, and fresh butter is rarely heard of. On Montgomery street, and the vacant space fronting the water, venders of coffee, cakes and sweetmeats have erected their stands, in order to tempt the appetite of sailors just arrived in port, or miners coming down from the mountains.

By nine o'clock the town is in the full flow of business. The streets running down to the water, and Montgomery street which fronts the Bay, are crowded with people, all in hurried motion. The variety of characters and costumes is remarkable. Our own countrymen seem to lose their local peculiarities in such a crowd, and it is by chance epithets rather than by manner, that the New-Yorker is distinguished from the Kentuckian, the Carolinian from the Down-Easter, the Virginian from the Texan. The German and Frenchman are more easily recognized. Peruvians and Chilians go by in their brown ponchos, and the sober Chinese, cool and impassive in the midst of excitement, look out of the oblique corners of their long eyes at the bustle, but are never tempted to venture from their own line of business. The eastern side of the plaza, in front of the Parker House and a canvas hell called the Eldorado, are the general rendezvous of business and amusement —combining 'change, park, club-room and promenade all in one. There, everybody not constantly employed in one spot, may be seen at some time of the day. The character of the groups scattered along the plaza is oftentimes very interesting. In one place are three or four speculators bargaining for lots, buying and selling "fifty varas square" in towns, some of which are canvas and some only paper; in another, a company of miners, brown as leather, and rugged in features as in dress; in a third, perhaps, three or four naval officers speculating on the next cruise, or a knot of genteel gamblers, talking over the last night's operations.

The day advances. The mist which after sunrise hung low and heavy for an hour or two, has risen above the hills, and there will be two hours of pleasant sunshine before the wind sets in from the sea. The crowd in the streets is now wholly alive. Men dart hither and thither, as if possessed with a never-resting spirit. You speak to an acquaintance—a merchant, perhaps. He utters a few hurried words of greeting, while his eyes send keen glances on all sides of you; suddenly he catches sight of somebody in the crowd; he is off, and in the next five minutes has bought up half a cargo, sold a town lot at treble the sum he gave, and taken a share in some new and imposing speculation. It is impossible to witness this excess and dissipation of business, without feeling something of its influence. The very air is pregnant with the magnetism of bold, spirited, unwearied action, and he who but ventures into the outer circle of the whirlpool, is spinning, ere he has time for thought, in its dizzy vortex.

But see! the groups in the plaza suddenly scatter; the city surveyor jerks his pole out of the ground and leaps on a pile of boards; the venders of cakes and sweetmeats follow his example, and the place is cleared, just as a wild bull which has been racing down Kearney street makes his appearance. Two vaqueros, shouting and swinging their lariats, follow at a hot gallop; the dust flies as they dash across the plaza. One of them, in mid-career, hurls his lariat in the air. Mark how deftly the coil unwinds in its flying curve, and with what precision the noose falls over the bull's horns! The horse wheels as if on a pivot, and shoots off in an opposite line. He knows the length of the lariat to a hair, and the instant it is drawn taut, plants his feet firmly for the shock and throws his body forward. The bull is "brought up" with such force as to throw him off his legs. He lies stunned a moment, and then, rising heavily, makes another charge. But by this time the second vaquero has thrown a lariat around one of his hind legs, and thus checked on both sides, he is dragged off to slaughter.

The plaza is refilled as quickly as it was emptied, and the course of business is resumed. About twelve o'clock, a wind begins to blow from the north-west, sweeping with most violence through a gap between the hills, opening towards the Golden Gate. The bells and gongs begin to sound for dinner, and these two causes tend to lessen the crowd in the streets for an hour or two. Two o'clock is the usual dinner-time for business men, but some of the old and successful merchants have adopted the fashionable hour of five. Where shall we dine to-day? the restaurants display their signs invitingly on all sides; we have choice of the United States, Tortoni's, the Alhambra, and many other equally classic resorts, but Delmonico's, like its distinguished original in New York, has the highest prices and the greatest variety of dishes. We go down Kearney street to a two-story wooden house on the corner of Jackson. The lower story is a market; the walls are garnished with quarters of beef and mutton; a huge pile of Sandwich Island squashes fills one corner, and several cabbage-heads, valued at $2 each, show themselves in the window. We enter a little door at the end of the building, ascend a dark, narrow flight of steps and find ourselves in a long, low room, with ceiling and walls of white muslin and a floor covered with oil-cloth.

There are about twenty tables disposed in two rows, all of them so well filled that we have some difficulty in finding places. Taking up the written bill of fare, we find such items as the following:

SOUPS.		ENTREES.	
Mock Turtle	$0 75	Fillet of Beef, mushroom sauce	$1 75
St. Julien	1 00	Veal Cutlets, breaded	1 00
FISH.		Mutton Chop	1 00
Boiled Salmon Trout, Anchovy		Lobster Salad	2 00
sauce	1 75	Sirloin of Venison	1 50
BOILED.		Baked Maccaroni	0 75
Leg Mutton, caper sauce	1 00	Beef Tongue, sauce piquante	1 00
Corned Beef, Cabbage	1 00		
Ham and Tongues	0 75		

So that, with but a moderate appetite, the dinner will cost us $5, if we are at all epicurean in our tastes. There are cries of "steward!" from all parts of the room—the word "waiter" is not considered sufficiently respectful, seeing that the waiter may have been a lawyer or merchant's clerk a few months before. The dishes look very small as they are placed on the table, but they are skilfully cooked and very palatable to men that have ridden in from the diggings. The appetite one acquires in California is something remarkable. For two months after my arrival, my sensations were like those of a famished wolf.

In the matter of dining, the tastes of all nations can be gratified here. There are French restaurants on the plaza and on Dupont street; an extensive German establishment on Pacific street; the *Fonda Peruana;* the Italian Confectionary; and three Chinese houses, denoted by their long three-cornered flags of yellow silk. The latter are much frequented by Americans, on account of their excellent cookery, and the fact that meals are $1 each, without regard to quantity. Kong-Sung's house is near the water; Whang-Tong's in Sacramento Street, and Tong-Ling's in Jackson street. There the grave Celestials serve up their chow-chow and curry, besides many genuine English dishes; their tea and coffee cannot be surpassed.

The afternoon is less noisy and active than the forenoon. Merchants keep within-doors, and the gambling-rooms are crowded with persons who step in to escape the wind and dust. The sky takes a cold gray cast, and the hills over the bay are barely visible in the dense, dusty air. Now and then a watcher, who has been stationed on the hill above Fort Montgomery, comes down and reports an inward-bound vessel, which occasions a little excitement among the boatmen and the merchants who are awaiting consignments. Toward sunset, the plaza is nearly deserted; the wind is merciless in its force, and a heavy overcoat is not found unpleasantly warm. As it grows dark, there is a lull, though occasional gusts blow down the hill and carry the dust of the city out among the shipping.

The appearance of San Francisco at night, from the water, is unlike anything I ever beheld. The houses are mostly of canvas, which is made transparent by the lamps within, and transforms them, in the darkness, to dwellings of solid light. Seated on the slopes of its three hills, the tents pitched among the chapparal to the very summits, it gleams like an amphitheatre of fire. Here and there shine out brilliant points, from the decoy-lamps of the gaming-houses; and through the indistinct murmur of the streets comes by fits the sound of music from their hot and crowded precincts. The picture has in its something unreal and fantastic; it impresses one like

GAMBLING SCENE AT SAN FRANCISCO

the cities of the magic lantern, which a motion of the hand can build or annihilate.

The only objects left for us to visit are the gaming-tables, whose day has just fairly dawned. We need not wander far in search of one. Denison's Exchange, the Parker House and Eldorado stand side by side; across the way are the Verandah and Aguila de Oro; higher up the plaza the St. Charles and Bella Union; while dozens of second-rate establishments are scattered through the less frequented streets. The greatest crowd is about the Eldorado; we find it difficult to effect an entrance. There are about eight tables in the room, all of which are thronged; copper-hued Kanakas, Mexicans rolled in their sarapes and Peruvians thrust through their ponchos, stand shoulder to shoulder with the brown and bearded American miners. The stakes are generally small, though when the bettor gets into "a streak of luck," as it is called, they are allowed to double until all is lost or the bank breaks. Along the end of the room is a spacious bar, supplied with all kinds of bad liquors, and in a sort of gallery, suspended under the ceiling, a female violinist tasks her talent and strength of muscle to minister to the excitement of play.

The Verandah, opposite, is smaller, but boasts an equal attraction in a musician who has a set of Pandean pipes fastened at his chin, a drum on his back, which he beats with sticks at his elbows, and cymbals in his hands. The piles of coin on the monte tables clink merrily to his playing, and the throng of spectators, jammed together in a sweltering mass, walk up to the bar between the tunes and drink out of sympathy with his dry and breathless throat. At the Aguila de Oro there is a full band of Ethiopian serenaders, and at the other hells, violins, guitars or wheezy accordeans, as the case may be. The atmosphere of these places is rank with tobacco-smoke, and filled with a feverish, stifling heat, which communicates an unhealthy glow to the faces of the players.

We shall not be deterred from entering by the heat and smoke, or the motley characters into whose company we shall be thrown. There are rare chances here for seeing human nature in one of its most dark and exciting phases. Note the variety of expression in the faces gathered around this table! They are playing monte, the favorite game in California, since the chances are considered more equal and the opportunity of false play very slight. The dealer throws out his cards with a cool, nonchalant air; indeed, the gradual increase of the hollow square of dollars at his left hand is not calculated to disturb his equanimity. The two Mexicans in front, muffled in their dirty sarapes, put down their half-dollars and dollars and see them lost, without changing a muscle. Gambling is a born habit with them, and they would lose thousands with the same indifference. Very different is the demeanor of the Americans who are playing; their good or ill luck is betrayed at once by involuntary exclamations and changes of countenance, unless the stake should be very large and absorbing, when their anxiety, though silent, may be read with no less certainty. They have no power to resist the fascination of the game. Now counting their winnings by thousands, now dependent on the kindness of a friend for a few dollars to commence anew, they pass hour after hour in those hot, unwholesome dens. There is no appearance of arms, but let one of the players, impatient with his losses and maddened by the poisonous fluids he has drank, threaten one of the profession, and there will be no scarcity of knives and revolvers. Frequently, in the absorbing interest of some desperate game the night goes by unheeded and morning breaks upon haggard faces and reckless hearts. Here are lost, in a few turns of a card or rolls of a ball, the product of fortunate ventures by sea or months of racking labor on land.

There had been a vast improvement in the means of living since my previous visit to San Francisco. Several large hotels had been opened, which were equal in almost every respect to houses of the second class in the Atlantic cities. The Ward House, the Graham House, imported bodily from Baltimore, and the St. Francis Hotel, completely threw into the shade all former establishments. The rooms were furnished with comfort and even luxury, and the tables lacked few of the essentials of good living, according to a "home" taste. The sleeping apartments of the St. Francis were the best in California. The cost of board and lodging was $150 per month—which was considered unusually cheap. A room at the Ward House cost $250 monthly, without board. The principal restaurants charged $35 a week for board, and there were lodging houses where a berth or "bunk"—one out of fifty in the same room—might be had for $6 a week. The model of these establishments —which were far from being "model lodging-houses"—was that of a ship. A number of state-rooms, containing six berths each, ran around the sides of a large room, or cabin, where the lodgers resorted to read, write, smoke and drink at their leisure. The state-rooms were consequently filled with foul and unwholesome air, and the noises in the cabin prevented the passengers from sleeping, except between midnight and four o'clock.

The great want of San Francisco was society. Think of a city of thirty thousand inhabitants, peopled by men alone! The like of this was never seen before. Every man was his own housekeeper, doing, in many instances, his own sweeping, cooking, washing and mending. Many home-arts, learned rather by observation than experience, came conveniently into play. He who cannot make a bed, cook a beefsteak, or sew up his own rips and rents, is unfit to be a citizen of California. Nevertheless, since the town began to assume a permanent shape, very many of the comforts of life in the East were attainable. A family may now live there without suffering any material privations; and if every married man, who intends spending some time in California, would take his family with him, a social influence would soon be created to which we might look for the happiest results.

Towards the close of my stay, the city was as dismal a place as could well be imagined. The glimpse of bright, warm, serene weather passed away, leaving in its stead a raw, cheerless, southeast storm. The wind now and then blew a heavy gale, and the cold, steady fall of rain, was varied by claps of thunder and sudden blasts of hail. The mud in the streets became little short of fathomless, and it was with difficulty that the mules could drag their

empty wagons through. A powerful London dray-horse, a very giant in harness, was the only animal able to pull a good load; and I was told that he earned his master $100 daily. I saw occasionally a company of Chinese work-men, carrying bricks and mortar, slung by ropes to long bamboo poles. The plank sidewalks, in the lower part of the city, ran along the brink of pools and quicksands, which the Street Inspector and his men vainly endeavored to fill by hauling cart-loads of chapparal and throwing sand on the top; in a day or two the gulf was as deep as ever. The side-walks, which were made at the cost of $5 per foot, bridged over the worst spots, but I was frequently obliged to go the whole length of a block in order to get on the other side. One could not walk any distance, without getting at least ancle-deep, and although the thermometer rarely sank below 50°, it was impossible to stand still for even a short time without a death-like chill taking hold of the feet. As a consequence of this, coughs and bronchial affections were innumerable. The universal custom of wearing the pantaloons inside the boots threatened to restore the knee-breeches of our grandfathers' times. Even women were obliged to shorten their skirts, and wear high-topped boots. The population seemed to be composed entirely of dismounted hussars. All this will be remedied when the city is two years older, and Portsmouth Square boasts a pavé as elegant as that on the dollar side of Broadway.

The effect of a growing prosperity and some little taste of luxury was readily seen in the appearance of the business community of San Francisco. The slouched felt hats gave way to narrow-brimmed black beavers; flannel shirts were laid aside, and white linen, though indifferently washed, appeared instead; dress and frock coats, of the fashion of the previous year in the At-lantic side, came forth from trunks and sea-chests; in short, a San Francisco merchant was almost as smooth and spruce in his outward appearance as a merchant anywhere else. The hussar boot, however, was obliged to be worn, and a variation of the Mexican sombrero—a very convenient and becoming headpiece—came into fashion among the younger class.

The steamers which arrived at this time, brought large quantities of newspapers from all parts of the Atlantic States. The speculation which had been so successful at first, was completely overdone; there was a glut in the market, in consequence whereof newspapers came down to fifty and twenty-five cents apiece. The leading journals of New-York, New-Orleans and Boston were cried at every street-corner. The two papers established in the place issued editions "for the Atlantic Coasts," at the sailing of every steamer for Panama. The offices were invaded by crowds of purchasers, and the slow hand-presses in use could not keep pace with the demand. The profits of these journals were almost incredible, when contrasted with their size and the amount of their circulation. Neither of them failed to count their gains at the rate of $75,000 a year, clear profit.

My preparations for leaving San Francisco, were made with the regret that I could not remain longer and see more of the wonderful growth of the Empire of the West. Yet I was fortunate in witnessing the most peculiar and interesting stages of its progress, and I took my departure in the hope of returning at some future day to view the completion of these magnificent beginnings. The world's history had no page so marvellous as that which has just been turned in California.

41

An Editor Goes West, 1859

*H*orace Greeley was born in 1811 in Amherst, New Hampshire. Though *his career was varied, he is today chiefly associated with the* New York Tribune. *Under his skillful guidance, that newspaper, in the twenty years after 1841, became the best known and perhaps most influential publication in the United States. Nor are the causes hard to find. Greeley was a man of exceptional integrity and the warm champion of all kinds of "causes." He held strong convictions and possessed a sturdy American sense of his right to express them, whether they were popular or not. Consequently, his news-paper was not, like the majority of them today, a namby-pamby effort to conciliate all shades of interests. It relied, too, for its popularity not upon* *scandalous sensation but rather upon a strong sense of public and social responsibility.*

His Overland Journey, *made in 1859, was typical of such an editor. He was accompanied by Henry Villard and Albert D. Richardson, the latter of whom has left us a parallel account of the journey. Greeley pried into odd corners for interesting material; he looked below the surface to discover the truth; and his observations are stated with all the candor expected of such an author. Greeley did not like proslavery Democrats, and ridiculed them; he did not like land speculators, and exposed them; he thought the Mormons less vicious than they were painted, and justified their works if not their theology; he had no mawkish sentiment about Indians; and he thought young men better advised to dig the soil for crops than for gold, and said so. One has little difficulty in following his trail across the continent to Denver, Salt Lake City, through Nevada, to San Francisco. The observations are interesting, for they come in the years between the first discoveries of gold and the building of the transcontinental railways.*

In 1872 Greeley was the unhappy presidential candidate of the Liberal Republicans and, ironically, of the Democrats. He would probably not have made a successful President, though it is hard to believe that he would have made a worse one than the Republican victor in that election. He died shortly after his defeat.

CORN AND KANSAS

I like Kansas—that is, natural Kansas—better than I had expected to. The soil is richer and deeper; the timber is more generally diffused; the country more rolling, than I had supposed them. There are of course heavy drawbacks in remoteness from the seaboard, heavy charges for bulky goods, low prices for produce, Indian reserves, and the high price of good lumber. For instance, pine boards used in building at this place, Manhattan, came from Alleghany County, N.Y., and were rafted down some mill-stream to the Alleghany, thence down the Alleghany to Pittsburgh, and the Ohio to Cario; were thence taken up the Mississippi to St. Louis, the Missouri to Kansas City, and the Kansas to this place, which has but twice or thrice been reached by steamboat. When here, they were dog cheap at one hundred dollars per thousand superficial feet, or ten cents for every square foot. In the absence of steamboat navigation on the Kansas, they must here be richly worth one hundred and twenty-five dollars per thousand feet. And, while there is pretty good timber here for other purposes, there is little—and that mainly black-walnut—that will make good boards. The ready cotton wood along the banks of the streams cuts easily, but warps so when seasoned that it will draw the nails out of the side of a house.

No doubt, the timber of Kansas increases each year, and will increase still faster as roads and improvements are multiplied, limiting the sweep of the prairie-fires; but it will always cost more to build a decent house of wood in the interior of Kansas than in any part of New York or New England—I think twice as much. This is a heavy tax on a new country, where not only houses but barns are a general, primary, and pressing need. I rejoice to see the new timber creeping up the bluffs of the streams; I note with pleasure that much of this is hickory and some of it white-ash; and I doubt not that there will always be wood enough here for fencing and fuel.

I judge that Indian corn can be grown here as cheaply as anywhere on earth. Thousands of acres last year produced their hundred bushels of shelled grain per acre, at a very moderate cost for labor and none at all for manure. An extensive farmer, who grew many thousands of bushels near Leavenworth, assured me that the cost of his corn, crib-bed in the ear, was just six cents per bushel of ears, equal to nine cents per bushel of grain—three half bushels of ears of the great Ohio kind here cultivated making a bushel of grain. Of course, this estimate excludes the cost of land, breaking, and fencing; but, making a fair allowance for these, the net cost of that corn cannot have exceeded twenty cents per bushel. I presume it would now sell in his crib for forty cents, while here in the interior it is worth from twenty-five to thirty-five cents per bushel.

I met at Osawatamie an old Whig and now Republican friend who left New York City (where he had been an industrious mechanic) and settled between Lawrence and Topeka two years ago. He had last year eighty acres in corn, which yielded four thousand bushels, worth to him thirty-five or forty cents per bushel. His clear profit on this corn, above the immediate cost of growing it, can hardly have been less than one thousand dollars. He will grow more this year, with wheat, potatoes, etc.; yet he is one of a class who are popularly supposed incapable of making money by farming. I suspect few life-long farmers of similar means will have good buildings over their heads and fruit-trees and other elements of material comfort around them sooner than my friend.

But an unpleasant truth must be stated: There are too many idle, shiftless people in Kansas. I speak not here of lawyers, gentlemen speculators, and other non-producers, who are in excess here as elsewhere; I allude directly to those who call themselves settlers, and who would be farmers if they were anything. To see a man squatted on a quarter-section in a cabin which would make a fair hog-pen, but is unfit for human habitation, and there living from hand to mouth by a little of this and a little of that, with hardly an acre of Prairie broken (sometimes without a fence up), with no garden, no fruit-trees, "no nothing"—waiting for someone to come along and buy out his "claim" and let him move on to repeat the operation somewhere else—this is enough to give a cheerful man the horrors. Ask the squatter what he means, and he can give you a hundred good excuses for his miserable condition: he has no breaking-team; he has little or no good rail-timber; he has had the "shakes"; his family have been sick; he lost two years and some stock by the border-ruffians, etc. But all this don't overbear the facts that, if *he* has no good timber, some of his neighbors have it in abundance, and would be very glad to have him work part of it into rails on shares at a fair rate; and if he has no breaking-team, he can hire out in haying and harvest, and get nearly or quite two acres broken next month for every faithful week's work he chooses to give at that busy season. The poorest man ought thus to be able to get ten acres broken, fenced, and into crop, each year. For poor men gradually hew farms out of heavy timber, where every fenced and cultivated acre has cost twice or thrice the work it does here.

And it is sad to note that hardly half the settlers make any sort of provision for wintering their cattle, even by cutting a stack of prairie-hay, when every good day's work will put up a ton of it. If he has a corn-field, the squatter's cattle are welcome to pick at that all winter; if he has none, they must go into the bottoms and browse through as best they can. Hence his calves are miserable affairs; his cows unfit to make butter from till the best of the season is over; his oxen, should he have a pair, must be recruiting from their winter's famine just when he most urgently needs their work. And this exposing cattle all winter to these fierce prairie-winds, is alike inhuman and wasteful. I asked a settler the other day how he *could* do it? "I had no time to make a shelter for them." "But had you no Sundays?—did you not have these at your disposal?" "O, yes? I don't work Sundays." "Well, you *should* have worked every one of them, rather than let your cattle shiver in the cold blasts all winter—it would have been a work of humanity and mercy to cut and haul logs, get up a cattle-stall, and cover it with prairie-hay, which I will warrant to be more religious than any thing you did on those Sundays." But the squatter was of a different opinion.

How a man located in a little squalid cabin on one of these rich "claims" can sleep moonlit nights under the average circumstances of his class, passes my comprehension. I should want to work moderately but resolutely, at least fourteen hours of each secular day, until I had made myself comfortable, with a fence around at least eighty acres, a quarter of this partitioned off for my working cattle, a decent, warm shelter to cover them in cold or stormy weather, a tolerable habitation for my family, at least forty acres in crop, and a young orchard growing. For one commencing with next to nothing, I estimate this as the work of five years; after which, he might take things more easily, awaiting the fruit from his orchard and the coming up of his boys to help him. But for the first four or five years, the poor pioneer should work every hour that he does not absolutely need for rest. Every hour's work then will save him many hours in after life.

As to the infernal spirit of land speculation and monopoly, I think no state ever suffered from it more severely than this. The speculators in broadcloth are not one whit more rapacious or pernicious than the speculators in rags, while the latter are forty times the more numerous. Land speculation here is about the only business in which a man can embark with no other capital than an easy conscience. For example: I rode up the bluffs back of Atchison, and out three or four miles on the high rolling prairie, so as to have some fifteen to twenty square miles in view at one glance. On all this inviting area, there were perhaps half a dozen poor or middling habitations, while not one acre in each hundred was fenced or broken. My friend informed me that every rood I saw was "preëmpted," and held at thirty up to a hundred dollars or more per acre. "Preëmpted!" I exclaimed; how preempted? by living or lying?" "Well," he responded, "they live a little and lie a little." I could see abundant evidence of the lying, none at all of the living. To obtain a preëmption, the squatter must swear that he actually resides on the quarter-section he applies for, has built a habitation and made other improvements there, and wants the land for his own use and that of his family. The squatters who took possession of these lands must every one have committed gross perjury in obtaining preëmption—and so it is all over the territory, wherever a lot is supposed likely to sell soon for more than the minimum price. I heard of one case in which a squatter carried a martin-box on to a quarter-section, and on the strength of that martin-box, swore that he had a house there "eighteen by twenty"—he left the officer to presume the feet. So it is all over; the wretched little slab shanty which has sufficed to swear by on one "claim," is now moved off and serves to swear by on another, when the first swearing is done. I am confident there is not at this hour any kind of a house or other sign of improvement on one-fourth of the quarter-sections throughout Kansas which have been secured by preëmption. The squatter who thus establishes a "claim" sells it out, so soon as practicable, to some speculator, who follows in his wake, getting from $50 to $300 for that which the future bona-fide settler will be required to pay $250 to $1,500 for. Such, in practical operation, is the system designed and ostensibly calculated to shield the poor and industrious settlers from rapacity and extortion; but which, in fact, operates to oppress and plunder the real settler—to pay a premium on perjury—to foster and extend speculation—to demoralize the people, paralyze industry and impoverish the country.

THE HOME OF THE BUFFALO

We are near the heart of the buffalo region. The stages from the west that met us here this evening report the sight of millions within the last two days. Their trails chequer the prairie in every direction. A company of Pike's Peakers killed thirteen near this point a few days since. Eight were killed yesterday at the next station west of this by simply stampeding a herd and driving them over a high creek-bank, where so many broke their necks. Buffalo-meat is hanging or lying all around us, and a calf two or three months old is tied to a stake just beside our wagons. He was taken by rushing a herd up a steep creek-bank; which so many could not possibly climb at once; this one was picked out in the melee as most worth having, and taken with a rope. Though fast tied and with but a short tether, he is true game, and makes at whoever goes near him with desperate intent to butt the intruder over. We met or passed to-day two parties of Pike's Peakers who had respectively lost three oxen or steers, stampeded last night by herds of buffalo. The mules at the express stations have to be carefully watched to preserve them from a similar catastrophe—to their owners.

I do not like the flesh of this wild ox. It is tough and not juicy. I do not forget that our cookery is of the most unsophisticated pattern—carrying us back to the age of the building of the Pyramids, at least—but I would much rather see an immense herd of buffalo on the prairie than eat the best of them.

The herbage hereabout is nearly all the short, strong grass known as the buffalo-grass, and is closely fed down; we are far beyond the stakes of the land-surveyor—beyond the usual haunts of white men. The Santa Fé trail is far south of us; the California is considerably north. Very probably, the buffalo on Solomon's Fork were never hunted by white men till this spring. Should one of these countless herds take a fancy for a man-hunt, our riflemen would find even the express-wagons no protection.

All day yesterday, they darkened the earth around us, often seeming to be drawn up like an army in battle array on the ridges and adown their slopes a mile or so south of us—often on the north as well. They are rather shy of the little screens of straggling timber on the creek-bottoms—doubtless from their sore experience of Indians lurking therein to discharge arrows at them as they went down to drink. If they feed in the grass of the narrow valleys and ravines, they are careful to have a part of the herd on the ridges which overlook them, and with them the surrounding country for miles. And, when an alarm is given, they all rush furiously off in the direction which the leaders presume that of safety.

This is what gives us such excellent opportunities for regarding them to the best advantage. They are moving northward, and are still mainly south of our track. Whenever alarmed, they set off on their awkward but effective canter to the great herds still south, or to haunts with which they are comparatively familiar, and wherein they have hitherto found safety. This necessarily sends those north of us across our roads often but a few rods in front of us, even when they had started a mile away. Then a herd will commence running across a hundred rods ahead of us, and, the whole blindly following their leader, we will be close upon them before the last will have cleared the track. Of course, they sometimes stop and tack, or, seeing us, sheer off and cross further ahead, or split into two lines; but the general impulse, when alarmed, is to follow blindly and at full speed, seeming not to inquire or consider from what quarter danger is to be apprehended.

What strikes the stranger with most amazement is their immense numbers. I know a million is a great many, but I am confident we saw that number yesterday. Certainly, all we saw could not have stood on ten square miles of ground. Often, the country for miles on either hand seemed quite black with them. The soil is rich, and well matted with their favorite grass. Yet it is all (except a very little on the creek-bottoms, near to timber) eaten down like an overtaxed sheep-pasture in a dry August. Consider that we have traversed more than one hundred miles in width since we first struck them, and that for most of this distance the buffalo have been constantly in sight, and that they continue for some twenty-five miles further on—this being the breadth of their present range, which has a length of perhaps a thousand miles—and you have some approach to an idea of their countless myriads. I doubt whether the domesticated horned cattle of the United States equal the numbers, while they must fall considerably short in weight, of these wild ones.

I shall pass lightly over the hunting exploits of our party. A good many shots have been fired—certainly not by me; even were I in the habit of making war on nature's children, I would as soon think of shooting my neighbor's oxen as these great, clumsy, harmless, creatures. If they were scarce, I might comprehend the idea of hunting them for sport; here, they are so abundant that you might as well hunt your neighbor's geese. And, while there have been several shots fired by our party at point-blank distance, I have reason for my hope that no buffalo has experienced any personal inconvenience therefrom. For this impunity, the foulness of the rifle has had to answer in part; the greenness of the sportsmen is perhaps equally responsible for it. But then we have had no horse or mule out of our regular teams, and the candid will admit that a coach-and-four is not precisely the fittest turn-out for a hunting party.

I write in the station-tent (having been driven from our wagon by the operation of greasing its wheels, which was found to interfere with the steadiness of my hastily-improvised table), with the buffalo visible on the ridges south and every way but north of us. They were very close down to us at daylight, and, till the increasing light revealed distinctly our position, since which they have kept a respectful distance. But a party of our drivers, who went back seven miles on mules last evening, to help get our rear wagon out of a gully in which it had mired and stuck fast, from which expedition they returned at midnight, report that they found the road absolutely dangerous from the crowds of buffalo feeding on either side, and running across it—that, the night being quite dark, they were often in great danger of being run over and run down by the headlong brutes. They were obliged to stand still for minutes, and fire their revolvers right and left, to save their lives and their mules.

The superintendent of this division, Mr. Fuller, had a narrow escape day before yesterday. He was riding his mule along our road, utterly unconscious of danger, when a herd of buffalo north of the road were stampeded by an emigrant train, and set off full gallop in a south-westerly direction, as usual. A slight ridge hid them from Mr. F.'s sight till their leader came full tilt against his mule, knocking him down, and going over him at full speed. Mr. F. of course fell with the dying mule, and I presume lay very snug by his side while the buffaloes made a clear sweep over the concern—he firing his revolver rapidly, and thus inducing many of the herd to shear off on one side or the other. He rose stunned and bruised, but still able to make his way to the station—with an increased respect for buffalo, I fancy, and a disposition to give them a reasonably wide berth hereafter. But he has gone out this morning in quest of the mired coach, and our waiting for his return gives me this chance to write without encroaching on the hours due to sleep.

LO! THE POOR INDIAN

The Indians are children. Their arts, wars, treaties, alliances, habitations, crafts, properties, commerce, comforts, all belong to the very lowest and rudest ages of human existence. Some few of the chiefs have a narrow and short-sighted shrewdness, and very rarely in their history, a really great man, like Pontiac or Tecumseh, has arisen among them; but this does not shake the general truth that they are utterly incompetent to cope in any way with the Caucasian race. Any band of schoolboys, from ten to fifteen years of age, are quite as capable of ruling their appetites, devising and upholding a public policy, constituting and conducting a state or community, as an average Indian tribe. And, unless they shall be treated as a truly Christian community would treat a band of orphan children providentially thrown on its

APACHES

hands, the aborigines of this country will be practically extinct within the next fifty years.

I have learned to appreciate better than hitherto, and to make more allowance for, the dislike, aversion, contempt, wherewith Indians are usually regarded by their white neighbors. It needs but little familiarity with the actual, palpable aborigines to convince any one that the poetic Indian of Cooper and Longfellow—is only visible to the poet's eye. To the prosaic observer, the average Indian of the woods and prairies is a being who does little credit to human nature—a slave of appetite and sloth, never emancipated from the tyranny of one animal passion save by the more ravenous demands of another. As I passed over those magnificent bottoms of the Kansas which form the reservations of the Delawares, Potawatamies, etc., constituting the very best corn-lands on earth, and saw their owners sitting around the doors of their lodges at the height of the planting season and in as good, bright planting weather as sun and soil ever made, I could not help saying, "These people must die out—there is no help for them. God has given this earth to those who will subdue and cultivate it, and it is vain to struggle against His righteous decree." And I yesterday tried my powers of persuasion on Left-Hand—the only Arapaho chief who talks English—in favor of an Arapaho tribal farm—say of two hundred acres for a beginning—to be broken and fenced by the common efforts of the tribe, and a patch therein allotted to each head of a family who would agree to plant and till it—I apprehend to very little purpose. For Left-Hand, though shrewd in his way, is an Indian, and every whit as conservative as Boston's Beacon street or our Fifth Avenue. He knows that there is a certain way in which his people have lived from time immemorial, and in which they are content still to live, knowing and seeking no better. He may or may not have heard that it is the common lot of prophets to be stoned and of reformers to be crucified; but he probably comprehends that squaws cannot fence and plow, and that "braves" are disinclined to any such steady, monotonous exercise of their muscles. I believe there is no essential difference in this respect between "braves" of the red and those of the white race, since even our country's bold defenders have not been accustomed to manifest their intrepidity in the corn-fields along their line of march, save in the season of roasting-ears; and the verb "to soldier" has acquired, throughout Christendom in all its moods and tenses, a significance beyond the need of a glossary. Briefly, the "brave," whether civilized or savage, is not a worker, a producer; and where the men are all "braves," with a war always on hand, the prospect for productive industry is gloomy indeed. If, then, the hope of Indian renovation rested mainly on the men, it would be slender enough. There is little probability that the present generation of "braves" can be weaned from the traditions and the habits in which they find a certain personal consequence and immunity from daily toil, which stand them instead of intelligence and comfort. Squalid and conceited, proud and worthless, lazy and lousy, they will strut out or drink out their miserable existence, and at length afford the world a sensible relief by dying out of it.

But it is otherwise with the women. Degraded and filthy as they are, beyond description or belief, they bear the germ of renovation for their race, in that they are neither too proud nor too indolent to labor. The squaw accepts work as her destiny from childhood. In her father's lodge, as in that wherein she comes in turn to hold a fifth or sixth interest in a husband—(for all Indians are polygamists in theory, and all who have means or energy become such in practice)—she comprehends and dutifully accepts drudgery as her "peculiar institution." She pitches and strikes the tent, carries it from one encampment to another, gathers and chops the wood, and not only dresses and cooks the game which forms the family's food (when they have any) but goes into the woods and backs it home, when her lord returns with the tidings that he has killed something. Tanning or dressing hides, making tents, clothing, moccasins, etc., all devolve on her. Under such a dispensation, it is not difficult to believe that she often willingly accepts a rival in the affections of her sullen master, as promising a mitigation rather than an aggravation of the hardships of her lot.

And yet even the Indian women are idle half their time, from sheer want of any thing to do. They will fetch water for their white neighbors, or do anything else whereby a piece of bread may be honestly earned; and they would do ten times more than they do, if they could find work and be reasonably sure of even a meagre reward for it.

WESTERN CHARACTERISTICS AND LIFE IN DENVER

I know it is not quite correct to speak of Colorado as "Western," seeing that it is in fact the centre of North America and very close to its backbone. Still, as the terms "Eastern" and "Western" are conventional and relative, I take the responsibility of grouping certain characters I have noted on the plains and in or about the mountains as "Western," begging that most respectable region which lies east of the buffalo-range—also that portion which lies west of the Colorado—to excuse the liberty.

The first circumstance that strikes a stranger traversing this wild country is the vagrant instincts and habits of the great majority of its denizens—perhaps I should say, of the American people generally, as exhibited here. Among any ten whom you successively meet, there will be natives of New England, New York, Pennsylvania, Virginia or Georgia, Ohio or Indiana, Kentucky or Missouri, France, Germany, and perhaps Ireland. But, worse than this; you cannot enter a circle of a dozen persons of whom at least three will not have spent some years in California, two or three have made claims and built cabins in Kansas or Nebraska, and at least one spent a year or so in Texas. Boston, New York, Philadelphia, New Orleans, St. Louis, Cincinnati, have all contributed their quota toward peopling the new gold region. The next man you meet driving an ox-team, and white as a miller with dust, is probably an ex-banker or doctor, a broken merchant or manufacturer from the old states, who has scraped together the candle-ends charitably or contemptuously allowed him by his creditors on settlement, and risked them on a last desperate cast of the dice by coming thither. Ex-editors, ex-printers, ex-clerks, ex-steamboat men, are here in abundance—all on the keen hunt for the gold which only a few will secure. One of the stations at which we slept on our way up—a rough tent with a cheering hope (since blasted) of a log house in the near future—was kept by an ex-lawyer of Cincinnati and his wife, an ex-actress from our New York Bowery—she being cook. Omnibus-drivers from Broadway repeatedly handled the ribbons; ex-border ruffians from civilized Kansas—some of them of unblessed memory—were encountered on our way, at intervals none too long. All these, blended with veteran Mountain men, Indians of all grades from the tamest to the wildest, half-breeds, French trappers and *voyageurs* (who have generally two or three Indian wives apiece) and an occasional negro, compose a medley such as hardly another region can parallel. Honolulu, or some other port of the South Sea Islands, could probably match it most nearly.

The old mountaineers form a caste by themselves, and they prize the distinction. Some of them are Frenchmen, or Franco-Americans, who have been trapping or trading in and around these mountains for a quarter of a century, have wives and children here, and here expect to live and die. Some of these have accumulated property and cash to the value of two hundred thousand dollars, which amount will not easily be reduced, as they are frugal in everything (liquor sometimes excepted), spend but a pittance on the clothing of their families, trust little, keep small stocks of goods, and sell at large profits. Others came years ago from the states, some of them on account each of a "difficulty" wherein they severally killed or savagely maimed their respective antagonists under circumstances on which the law refuses to look leniently; whence their pilgrimage to and prolonged sojourn here, despite enticing placards offering five hundred dollars or perhaps one thousand dollars for their safe return to the places that knew them once, but shall know them no more. This class is not numerous, but is more influential than it should be in giving tone to the society of which its members form a part. Prone to deep drinking, soured in temper, always armed, bristling at a word, ready with the rifle, revolver or bowie-knife, they give law and set fashions which, in a country where the regular administration of justice is yet a matter of prophecy, it seems difficult to overrule or disregard. I apprehend that there have been, during my two weeks sojourn, more brawls, more fights, more pistol-shots with criminal intent in this log city of one hundred and fifty dwellings, not three-fourths completed nor two-thirds inhabited, nor one-third fit to be, than in any community of no greater numbers on earth. This will be changed in time—I trust within a year, for the empty houses are steadily finding tenants from the two streams of emigration rolling in daily up the Platte on the one hand, down Cherry Creek on the other, including some scores of women and children, who generally stop here, as all of them should; for life in the mountains is yet horribly rough. Public religious worship, a regular mail and other civilizing influences, are being established; there is a gleam of hope that the Arapahoes—who have made the last two or three nights indescribably hideous by their infernal war-whoops, songs and dances—will at last clear out on the foray against the Utes they have so long threatened, diminishing largely the aggregate of drunkenness and riot, and justifying expectations of comparative peace. So let me close up my jottings from this point—which circumstances beyond my control have rendered so voluminous—with a rough ambrotype of life in Denver.

The rival cities of Denver and Auraria front on each from either bank of Cherry Creek, just before it is lost in the South Platte. The Platte has its sources in and around the South Park of the Rocky Mountains, a hundred miles south-west of this pont; but Cherry Creek is headed off from them by that river, and, winding its northward course of forty or fifty miles over the plains, with its sources barely touching the Mountains, is a capricious stream, running quite smartly when we came here, but whose broad and thirsty sands have since drank it all up at this point, leaving the log foot-bridges which connect the two cities as useless as an ice-house in November. The Platte, aided by the melting of the snows on the higher mountains, runs nearly full-banked, though the constant succession of hot suns and dry winds begins to tell upon it; while Clear Creek (properly Vasquer's Fork), which issues directly from the Mountains just above its crossing on the way to the Gregory diggings, is nearly at its highest, and will so remain till the inner mountains are mainly denuded of their snowy mantles. But, within a few days, a foot-bridge has been completed over the Platte, virtually abolishing the ferry and saving considerably time and money to gold-seekers and travelers; while another over Clear Creek precludes not only delay but danger— several wagons having been wrecked and two or three men all but drowned in attempts to ford its rapid, rocky current. Thus the ways of the adventurous grow daily smoother; and they who visit this region ten years hence, will regard as idle tales the stories of privation, impediment, and "hair-breadth 'scapes" which are told, or might be, by the gold-seekers of 1859.

Of these rival cities, Auraria is by far the more venerable—some of its structures being, I think, fully a year old, if not more. Denver, on the other hand, can boast of no antiquity beyond September or October last. In the architecture of the two cities there is, notwithstanding, a striking similarity— cotton-wood logs, cut from the adjacent bottom of the Platte, roughly hewed on the upper and under sides, and chinked with billets of split cotton-wood on the inner, and with mud on the outer side, forming the walls of nearly or quite every edifice which adorns either city. Across the center of the interior, from shorter wall to wall, stretches a sturdy ridge-pole, usually in a state of nature, from which "shooks," or split saplings of cotton-wood, their split sides down, incline gently to the transverse or longer sides; on these (in the more finished structures) a coating of earth is laid; and, with a chimney of mud-daubed sticks in one corner, a door nearly opposite, and a hole beside it representing or prefiguring a window, the edifice is complete. Of course, many have no earth on their covering of shooks, and so are liable to gentle inundation in the rainy season; but, though we have had thunder and lightning almost daily, with a brisk gale in most instance, there has been no rain worth naming such here for weeks, and the unchinked, barely shook-covered houses, through whose sides and roofs you may see the stars as you lie awake nights, are decidedly the cooler and airier. There is a new hotel nearly finished in Auraria, which has a second story (but no first story) floor; beside this, mine eyes have never yet been blessed with the sight of any floor whatever in either Denver or Auraria. The last time I slept or ate with a floor under me (our wagon-box and mother earth excepted) was at Junction-City, nearly four weeks ago. The "Denver House," which is the Astor House of the gold region, has walls of logs, a floor of earth, with windows and roof of rather flimsy cotton-sheeting; while every guest is allowed as good a bed as his blankets will make. The charges are no higher than at the Astor and other first-class hotels, except for liquor—twenty-five cents a drink for dubious whiskey, colored and nicknamed to suit the taste of customers—being the regular rate throughout this region. I had the honor to be shaved there by a nephew (so he assured me) of Murat, Bonaparte's king of Naples—the honor and the shave together costing but a paltry dollar. Still, a few days of such luxury surfeited me, mainly because the main or drinking-room was also occupied by several black legs as a gambling hall, and their incessant clamor of "Who'll go me twenty? The ace of hearts is the winning card. Whoever turns the ace of hearts wins the twenty dollars," etc., persisted in at all hours up to midnight, became at length a nuisance, from which I craved deliverance at any price. Then the visitors of that drinking and gambling-room had a careless way, when drunk, of firing revolvers, sometimes at each other, at other times quite miscellaneously, which struck me as inconvenient for a quiet guest with only a leg and a half, hence in poor condition for dodging bullets. So I left.[1]

1. [A. D. Richardson, in his account of the scene in *Our New States and Territories* (New York, 1866), adds: "Of course we took lodging at the first-class hotel—an enormous wooden structure with walls of logs, a floor of mother earth, and windows and roof of cotton cloth. True to the national instinct, the *habitués* of its great drinking and gambling saloon, which occupied nearly the whole building, demanded a speech. On one side the tipplers at the bar silently sipped their grog; on the other, the gamblers respectfully suspended the shuffling of cards and the

"How do you live in Denver?" I inquired of a New York friend some weeks domiciled here, in whose company I visited the mines. "O, I've jumped a cabin," was his cool, matter-of-course reply. As jumping a cabin was rather beyond my experience, I inquired further, and learned that, finding an uninhabited cabin that suited him, he had quietly entered and spread his blankets, eating at home or abroad as opportunity might suggest. I found, on further inquiry, that at least one-third of the habitations in Denver and Auraria were desolate when we came here, some of the owners having gone

LAYING TRACK FOR THE PACIFIC RAILROAD

into the mountains, digging or prospecting, and taken their limited supply of household goods along with them; while others, discouraged by the poor show of mining six weeks ago, when even the nearer mountains were still covered with snow and ice, rushed pell-mell down the Platte with the wild reflux of the spring emigration, abandoning all but what they could carry away. It is said that lots and cabins together sold for twenty-five dollars—so long as there were purchasers; but these soon failing, they were left behind like camp-fires in the morning, and have since been at the service of all comers.

So, in company with a journalizing friend, I, too, have "jumped a cabin," and have kept to it quite closely, under a doctor's care, for the last week or ten days. It is about ten feet square, and eight feet high, rather too well

counting of money from their huge piles of gold and silver coin, while Mr. Greeley, standing between them, made a strong anti-drinking and anti-gambling speech, which was received with perfect good humour."—ED.]

chinked for summer, considering that it lacks a window, but must be a capital house for this country in winter. I board with the nearest neighbor; and it is not my landlady's fault that the edible resources of Denver are decidedly limited. But even these are improving. To the bread, bacon, and beans, which formed the staple of every meal a short time ago, there have been several recent additions; milk, which was last week twenty-five cents per quart, is now down to ten, and I hear a rumor that eggs, owing to a recent increase in the number of hens, within five hundred miles, from four or five to twelve or fifteen, are about to fall from a dollar a dozen to fifty cents per dozen. On every side, I note signs of progress—improvements—manifest destiny:—there was a man about the city yesterday with lettuce to sell—and I am credibly assured that there will be green peas next month—actually peas!—provided it should rain soakingly meantime—whereof a hazy, lowering sky would seem just now to afford some hope. (P. S. The hope has vanished.) But I—already sadly behind, and nearly able to travel again—must turn my back on this promise of luxuries, and take the road to Laramie to-day, or at furthest tomorrow.

SALT LAKE CITY AND THE MORMONS

Salt Lake City wears a pleasant aspect to the emigrant or traveler, weary, dusty, and browned with a thousand miles of jolting, fording, camping, through the scorched and naked American Desert. It is located mainly on the bench of hard gravel that slopes southward from the foot of the mountains toward the lake valley; the houses—generally small and of one story—are all built of adobe (sun-hardened brick), and have a neat and quiet look; while the uniform breadth of the streets (eight rods) and the "magnificent distances" usually preserved by the buildings (each block containing ten acres, divided into eight lots, giving a quarter of an acre for buildings and an acre for garden, fruit, etc., to each householder), make up an *ensemble* seldom equaled. Then the rills of bright, sparkling, leaping water which, diverted from the streams issuing from several adjacent mountain cañons, flow through each street and are conducted at will into every garden, diffuse an air of freshness and coolness which none can fail to enjoy, but which only a traveler in summer across the Plains can fully appreciate. On a single business street, the post-office, principal stores, etc., are set pretty near each other, though not so close as in other cities; everywhere else, I believe, the original plan of the city has been wisely and happily preserved. Southward from the city, the soil is softer and richer, and there are farms of (I judge) ten to forty or sixty acres; but I am told that the lowest portion of the valley, nearly on a level with the lake, is so impregnated with salt, soda, etc., as to yield but a grudging return for the husbandman's labor. I believe, however, that even this region is available as a stock-range—thousands on thousands of cattle, mainly owned in the city, being pastured here in winter as well as summer, and said to do well in all seasons. For, though snow is never absent from the mountain-chains which shut in this valley, it seldom lies long in the valley itself.

The pass over the Wahsatch is, if I mistake not, eight thousand three hundred feet above the sea-level; this valley about four thousand nine hundred. The atmosphere is so pure that the mountains across the valley to the south seem but ten or fifteen miles off; they are really from twenty to thirty. The lake is some twenty miles westward; but we see only the rugged mountain known as "Antelope Island" which rises in its center, and seems to bound the valley in that direction. Both the lake and valley wind away to the north-west for a distance of some ninety miles—the lake receiving the waters of Weber and Bear Rivers behind the mountains in that direction. And then there are other valleys like this, nested among the mountains south and west to the very base of the Sierra Nevada. So there will be room enough here for all this strange people for many years.

My friend Dr. Bernhisel, late delegate in Congress, took me this afternoon, by appointment, to meet Brigham Young, President of the Mormon Church, who had expressed a willingness to receive me at two P.M. We were very cordially welcomed at the door by the president, who led us into the second-story parlor of the largest of his houses (he has three), where I was introduced to Heber C. Kimball, General Wells, General Ferguson, Albert Carrington, Elias Smith, and several other leading men in the church, with two full-grown sons of the President. After some unimportant conversation on general topics, I stated that I had come in quest of fuller knowledge respecting the doctrines and polity of the Mormon Church, and would like to ask some questions bearing directly on these, if there were no objection. President Young avowing his willingness to respond to all pertinent inquiries, the conversation proceeded substantially as follows:

H. G.—Am I to regard Mormonism (so-called) as a new religion, or as simply a new development of Christianity?

B. Y.—We hold that there can be no true Christian Church without a priesthood directly commissioned by, and in immediate communication with the Son of God and Saviour of mankind. Such a church is that of the Latter-Day Saints, called by their enemies Mormons; we know no other that even pretends to have present and direct revelations of God's will.

H. G.—Then I am to understand that you regard all other churches professing to be christian as the Church of Rome regards all churches not in communion with itself—as schismatic, heretical, and out of the way of salvation?

B. Y.—Yes, substantially.

G. H.—Apart from this, in what respect do your doctrines differ essentially from those of our Orthodox Protestant Churches—the Baptist or Methodist, for example?

B. Y.—We hold the doctrines of christianity, as revealed in the Old and New Testaments—also in the Book of Mormon, which teaches the same cardinal truths and those only.

H. G.—Do you believe in the doctrine of the Trinity?

B. Y.—We do; but not exactly as it is held by other churches. We believe in the Father, the Son, and the Holy Ghost, as equal, but not identical—not as one person [being].[2] We believe in all the bible teaches on this subject.

H. G.—Do you believe in a personal devil—a distinct, conscious, spiritual being, whose nature and acts are essentially malignant and evil?

B. Y.—We do.

H. G.—Do you hold the doctrine of eternal punishment?

B. Y.—We do; though perhaps not exactly as other churches do. We believe it as the bible teaches it.

H. G.—I understand that you regard baptism by immersion as essential?

B. Y.—We do.

H. G.—Do you practice infant baptism?

B. Y.—No.

H. G.—Do you make removal to these valleys obligatory on your converts?

B. Y.—They would consider themselves greatly aggrieved if they were not invited hither. We hold to such a gathering together of God's people, as the bible foretells, and that this is the place, and now is the time appointed for its consummation.

H. G.—What is the position of your church with respect to slavery?

B. Y.—We consider it of divine institution, and not to be abolished until the curse pronounced on Ham shall have been removed from his descendants.

H. G.—Are any slaves now held in this territory?

B. Y.—There are.

H. G.—Do your territorial laws uphold slavery?

2. I am quite sure that President Young used here the word "person" as I have it; but I am not aware that christians of any denomination do regard the Father, Son and Holy Spirit, as one person.

B. Y.—Those laws are printed—you can read for yourself. If slaves are brought here by those who owned them in the states, we do not favor their escape from the service of those owners.

H. G.—Am I to infer that Utah, if admitted as a member of the Federal Union, will be a slave state?

B. Y.—No; she will be a free state. Slavery here would prove useless and unprofitable. I regard it generally as a curse to the masters. I myself hire many laborers, and pay them fair wages; I could not afford to own them. I can do better than subject myself to an obligation to feed and clothe their families, to provide and care for them in sickness and health. Utah is not adapted to slave-labor.

H. G.—Let me now be enlightened with regard more especially to your church polity: I understand that you require each member to pay over one-tenth of all he produces or earns to the church.

B. Y.—That is a requirement of our faith. There is no compulsion as to the payment. Each member acts in the premises according to his pleasure, under the dictates of his own conscience.

H. G.—What is done with the proceeds of this tithing?

B. Y.—Part of it is devoted to building temples, and other places of worship; part to helping the poor and needy converts on their way to this country; and the largest portion to the support of the poor among the saints.

H. G.—Is none of it paid to bishops, and other dignitaries of the church?

B. Y.—Not one penny. No bishop, no elder, no deacon, nor other church officer, receives any compensation for his official services. A bishop is often required to put his hand into his own pocket, and provide therefrom for the poor of his charge; but he never receives anything for his services.

H. G.—How, then, do your ministers live?

B. Y.—By the labor of their own hands, like the first apostles. Every bishop, every elder, may be daily seen at work in the field or the shop, like his neighbors; every minister of the church has his proper calling, by which he earns the bread of his family; he who cannot, or will not do the church's work for nothing is not wanted in her service; even our lawyers (pointing to General Ferguson and another present, who are the regular lawyers of the church), are paid nothing for their services; I am the only person in the church who has not a regular calling apart from the church's service, and I never received one farthing from her treasury; if I obtain anything from the tithing-house, I am charged with, and pay for it, just as any one else would; the clerks in the tithing-store are paid like other clerks; but no one is ever paid for any service pertaining to the ministry. We think a man who cannot make his living aside from the ministry of Christ unsuited to that office. I am called rich, and consider myself worth two hundred and fifty thousand dollars; but no dollar of it was ever paid me by the church, nor for any service as a minister of the ever-lasting Gospel. I lost nearly all I had when we were broken up in Missouri, and driven from that state. I was nearly stripped again, when Joseph Smith was murdered, and we were driven from Illinois; but nothing was ever made up to me by the church, nor by any one. I believe I know how to acquire property, and how to take care of it.

H. G.—Can you give me any rational explanation of the aversion and hatred with which your people are generally regarded by those among whom they have lived and with whom they have been brought directly in contact?

B. Y.—No other explanation than is afforded by the crucifixion of Christ and the kindred treatment of God's ministers, prophets and saints, in all ages.

H. G.—I know that a new sect is always decried and traduced—that it is hardly ever deemed respectable to belong to one—that the Baptists, Quakers, Methodists, Universalists, etc., have each in their turn been regarded in the infancy of their sect as the offscouring of the earth; yet I cannot remember that either of them were ever generally represented and regarded by the older sects of their early days as thieves, robbers, murderers.

B. Y.—If you will consult the contemporary Jewish account of the life and acts of Jesus Christ, you will find that he and his disciples were accused of every abominable deed and purpose—robbery and murder included. Such a work is still extant, and may be found by those who seek it.

H. G.—With regard, then, to the grave question on which your doctrines and practices are avowedly at war with those of the Christian world—that of a plurality of wives—is the system of your church acceptable to the majority of its women?

B. Y.—They could not be more averse to it than I was when it was first revealed to us as the Divine will. I think they generally accept it, as I do, as the will of God.

H. G.—How general is polygamy among you?

B. Y.—I could not say. Some of those present (heads of the church) have each but one wife; others have more: each determines what is his individual duty.

H. G.—What is the largest number of wives belonging to any one man?

B. Y.—I have fifteen; I know no one who has more; but some of those sealed to me are old ladies whom I regard rather as mothers than wives, but whom I have taken home to cherish and support.

H. G.—Does not the Apostle Paul say that a bishop should be "the husband of one wife"?

B. Y.—So we hold. We do not regard any but a married man as fitted for the office of bishop. But the apostle does not forbid a bishop having more wives than one.

H. G.—Does not Christ say that he who puts away his wife, or marries one whom another has put away, commits adultery!

B. Y.—Yes; and I hold that no man should ever put away his wife except for adultery—not always even for that. Such is *my* individual view of the matter. I do not say that wives have never been put away in our church, but that I do not approve of the practice.

H. G.—How do you regard what is commonly termed the Christian Sabbath?

B. Y.—As a divinely appointed day of rest. We enjoin all to rest from secular labor on that day. We would have no man enslaved to the Sabbath, but we enjoin all to respect and enjoy it.

Such is, as nearly as I can recollect, the substance of nearly two hours' conversation, wherein much was said incidentally that would not be worth reporting, even if I could remember and reproduce it, and wherein others bore a part; but as President Young is the first minister of the Mormon Church, and bore the principal part in the conversation, I have reported his answers alone to my questions and observations. The others appeared uniformly to defer to his views, and to acquiesce fully in his responses and explanations. He spoke readily, and not always with grammatical accuracy, but with no appearance of hesitation or reserve, and with no apparent desire to conceal anything, nor did he repel any of my questions as impertinent. He was very plainly dressed in thin summer clothing, and with no air of sanctimony or fanaticism. In appearance, he is a portly, frank, good-natured, rather thick-set man of fifty-five, seeming to enjoy life, and to be in no particular hurry to get to heaven.

His associates are plain men, evidently born and reared to a life of labor, and looking as little like crafty hypocrites or swindlers as any body of men I ever met. The absence of cant or snuffle from their manner was marked and general; yet, I think I may fairly say that their Mormonism has not impoverished them—that they were generally poor men when they embraced it, and are now in very comfortable circumstances—as men averaging three or four wives apiece certainly need to be.

The degradation (or, if you please, the restriction) of woman to the single office of child-bearing and its accessories, is an inevitable consequence of the system here paramount. I have not observed a sign in the streets, an advertisement in the journals, of this Mormon metropolis, whereby a woman proposes to do anything whatever. No Mormon has ever cited to me his wife's

or any woman's opinion on any subject; no Mormon woman has been introduced or has spoken to me; and, though I have been asked to visit Mormons
in their houses, no one has spoken of his wife (or wives) desiring to see me,
or his desiring me to make her (or their) acquaintance, or voluntarily indicated the existence of such a being or beings. I will not attempt to report
our talk on this subject; because, unlike what I have given above, it assumed
somewhat the character of a disputation, and I could hardly give it impartially; but one remark made by President Young I think I can give accurately,
and it may serve as a sample of all that was offered on that side. It was in
these words, I think exactly: "If I did not consider myself competent to
transact a certain business without taking my wife's or any woman's counsel with regard to it, I think I ought to let that business alone." Another
feature of President Young's remarks on this topic strikes me on revi-
sion. He assumed as undeniable that outside of the Mormon church, married men usually keep mistresses—that incontinence is the general rule,
and continence the rare exception. This assumption was habitual with the
Mormons, who, at various times, discussed with me the subject of polygamy.

Since my interview with Brigham Young, I have enjoyed opportunities
for studying the Mormons in their social or festive and in their devotional
assemblies. Of private social intercourse—that is, intercourse between family
and family—I judge that there is comparatively little here; between Mormons and Gentiles or strangers, of course still less. Their religious services
(in the tabernacle) are much like those that may be shared or witnessed in
the churches of most of our popular sects; the music rather better than you
will hear in an average worshiping assemblage in the states; the prayers
pertinent and full of unction; the sermons adapted to tastes or needs different from mine. They seemed to me rambling, dogmatic, and ill-digested; in
fact, Elder Orson Pratt, who preached last Sunday morning, prefaced his
harangue by a statement that he had been hard at work on his farm throughout the week, and labored under consequent physical exhaustion. Elder John
Taylor (a high dignitary in the church) spoke likewise in the afternoon with
little or no pre-meditation. Now, I believe that every preacher should be also
a worker; I like to see one mowing or pitching hay in his shirt-sleeves; and
I hear with edification an unlettered but devout and earnest evangelist who,
having worked a part of the week for the subsistence of his family, devotes
the rest of it to preaching the gospel to small school-house or wayside gather-
ings of hearers, simply for the good of their souls. Let him only be sure to
talk good sense, and I will excuse some bad grammar. But when a preacher

is to address a congregation of one to three thousand persons, like that which assembles twice each sabbath in the Salt Lake City Tabernacle, I insist that a due regard for the economy of time requires that he should prepare himself, by study and reflection, if not by writing, to speak directly to the point. This mortal life is too short and precious to be wasted in listening to rambling, loose-jointed harangues, or even to those which severally consume an hour in the utterance, when they might be boiled down and clarified until they were brought within the compass of half an hour each.

The two discourses to which I listened were each intensely and exclusively Mormon. That is, they assumed that the Mormons were God's peculiar, chosen, beloved people, and that all the rest of mankind are out of the ark of safety and floundering in heathen darkness. I am not edified by this sort of preaching.[3]

The spirit of the Mormon religion appears to me Judiac rather than Christian; and I am well assured that Heber C. Kimball, one of the great lights of the church, once said in conversation with a Gentile—"I *do* pray for my enemies: I pray that they may all go to hell." Neither from the pulpit nor elsewhere have I heard from a Mormon one spontaneous, hearty recognition of the essential brotherhood of the human race—one generous prayer for the enlightenment and salvation of all mankind. On the other hand, I have been distinctly given to understand that my interlocuters expect to sit

3. [Six years later, Samuel Bowles (see p. 746), editor of the *Springfield Republican,* made the following report verbatim of a sermon by Heber C. Kimball, first vice-president and chief prophet of the church:

"Ladies and gentlemen, good morning. I am going to talk to you by revelation. I never study my sermons, and when I get up to speak, I never know what I am going to say only as it is revealed to me from on high; then all I say is true; could it help but be so, when God communicates to you through me? The Gentiles are our enemies; they are damned forever; they are theives and murderers, and if they don't like what I say they can go to hell, damn them! They want to come here in large numbers and decoy our women. I have introduced some Gentiles to my wives, but I will not do it again, because if I do, I will have to take them to my houses and introduce them to Mrs. Kimball at one house, and Mrs. Kimball at another house, and so on; and they will say Mrs. Kimball such, and Mrs. Kimball such, and so on, are whores. They are taking some of our fairest daughters from us now in Salt Lake City, damn them. If I catch any of them running after my wives I will send them to hell! and ladies you must not keep their company, you sin if you do, and you will be damned and go to hell. What do you think of such people? They hunt after our fairest and prettiest women, and it is a lamentable fact that they would rather go with them damned scoundrels than stay with us. If Brother Brigham comes to me, and says he wants one of my daughters, he has a right to take her, and I have the exclusive right to give her to who I please, and she has no right to refuse; if she does, she will be damned forever and ever, because she belongs to me. She is part of my flesh, and no one has a right to take her unless I say so, any more than he has a right to take one of my horses or cows.

"We have our apostolic government. Brigham Young is our leader, our President, our Governor. I am Lieutenant-Governor. Aint I a terrible feller? Why, it has taken the hair all off my head. At least it would, if I hadn't lost it before. I lost it in my hardships, while going out to preach the kingdom of God, without purse or script."—ED.]

on thrones and to bear rule over multitudes in the approaching kingdom of God. In fact, one sincere, devout man has to-day assigned that to me as a reason for polygamy; he wants to qualify himself, by ruling a large and diversified family here, for bearing rule over his principality in the "new earth," that he knows to be at hand. I think he might far better devote a few years to pondering Christ's saying to this effect, "He who would be least in the kingdom of heaven, the same shall be greatest."

I was undeceived with regard to the Book of Mormon. I had understood that it is now virtually discarded, or at least neglected, by the church in its services and ministrations. But Elder Pratt gave us a synopsis of its contents, and treated it throughout as of equal authority and importance with the Old and New Testaments. He did not read from it, however, but from Malachi, and quoted text after text from the prophets, which he cited as predictions of the writing and discovery of this book.

The congregation consisted, at either service of some fifteen hundred to two thousand persons—more in the morning than the afternoon. A large majority of them (not including the elders and chief men, of whom a dozen or so were present) were evidently of European birth; I think a majority of the males were past the meridian of life. All gave earnest heed to the exercises throughout; in fact, I have seldom seen a more devout and intent assemblage. I had been told that the Mormons were remarkably ignorant, superstitious, and brutalized; but the aspects of these congregations did not sustain the assertion. Very few rural congregations would exhibit more heads evincing decided ability; and I doubt whether any assemblage, so largely European in its composition, would make a better appearance. Not that Europeans are less intellectual or comely than Americans; but our emigrants are mainly of the poorer classes; and poverty, privation, and rugged toil plow hard forbidding lines in the human countenance elsewhere than in Utah. Brigham Young was not present at either service.

Do I regard the great body of these Mormons as knaves and hypocrites? Assuredly not. I do not believe there was ever a religion whereof the great mass of the adherents were not honest and sincere. Hypocrites and knaves there are in all sects; it is quite possible that some of the magnates of the Mormon Church regard this so-called religion (with all others) as a contrivance for the enslavement and fleecing of the many, and the aggrandizement of the few; but I cannot believe that a sect, so considerable and so vigorous as the Mormons, was ever founded in conscious imposture, or built up on any other basis than that of earnest conviction. If the projector, and two or three of his chief confederates are knaves, the great body of their followers were dupes.

A party of us visited the lake on Saturday. It is not visible from this city, though it must be from the mountains which rise directly north of it; Antelope, Stansbury, and perhaps other islands in the lake, are in plain sight from every part of the valley. The best of these islands is possessed by "the church," (Mormon) as a herd ground, or *ranche,* for its numerous cattle, and is probably the best tract for that purpose in the whole territory. That portion of the lake between it and the valley is so shallow, that cattle may, at most seasons, be safely driven over to the island; while it is so deep (between three and four feet) that none will stray back again, and it would be difficult and dangerous to steal cattle thence in the night, when that business is mainly carried on. So the church has a large and capital pasture, and her cattle multiply and wax fat at the least possible expense. The best cañon for wood near this city is likewise owned by "the church"—*how* owned, I can't pretend to say—but whoever draws wood from it must deposit every third load in the church's capacious yard. (On further inquiry, I learn that Brigham Young personally is the owner; but, as he is practically the church, the correction was hardly worth making.) These are but specimens of the management whereby, though the saints are generally poor, often quite poor, so that a saint who has three wives can sometimes hardly afford to keep two beds—"the church" has a comfortable allowance of treasures laid up on earth. And her leading apostles and dignitaries also, by a curious coincidence, seem to be in thriving circumstances. It looks to me as though neither they nor the Church could afford to have the world burnt up for a while yet.

Crossing, just west of the city, the Jordan (which drains the fresh waters of Lake Utah into Salt Lake, and is a large, sluggish creek), we are at once out of the reach of irrigation from the northern hills—the river intercepting all streams from that quarter—and are once more on a parched clay-plain, covered mainly with our old acquaintance, sage-brush and grease-wood; though there are wet, springy tracts, especially toward the southern mountains and near the lake, which produce rank, coarse grass. Yet this seeming desert has naturally a better soil than the hard, pebbly gravel on which the city stands, and which irrigation has converted into bounteous gardens and orchards.

I rejoice to perceive that a dam over the Jordan is in progress, whereby a considerable section of the valley of that river (which valley is forty miles long, by an average of twenty broad) is to be irrigated. There are serious obstacles to the full success of this enterprise in the scarcity of timber and the inequality of the plain, which is gouged and cut up by numerous (now dry) water-courses; but, if this project is well-engineered, it will double the productive capacity of this valley.

In the absence of judicious and systematic irrigation, there are far too many cattle and sheep on this great common, as the gaunt look of most of the cattle abundantly testifies. Water is also scarce and bad here; we tried several of the springs which are found at the bases of the southern mountains, and found them all brackish, while not a single stream flows from those mountains in the five or six miles that we skirted them, and I am told that they afford but one or two scanty rivulets through the whole extent of this valley. In the absence of irrigation, nothing is grown or attempted but wild grass; of the half-dozen cabins we have passed between the Jordan and the lake, not one had even the semblance of a garden, or of any cultivation whatever. A shrewd woman, who had lived seven years near the lake, assured me that it would do no good to attempt cultivation there; "too much alkali" was her reason. I learn that, on the city side of the Jordan, when irrigation was first introduced, and cultivation attempted, the soil, whenever allowed to become dry, was covered, for the first year or two, with some whitish alkaline substance; but this was soon washed out and washed off by the water, so that no alkali now exhibits itself, and this tract produces handsomely.

That this lake should be salt, is no anomaly. All large bodies of water into which streams discharge themselves, while they have severally no outlet, are or should be salt. I am told that three barrels of this water yield a barrel of salt; that seems rather strong, yet its intense saltness, no one who has not had it in his eyes, his mouth, his nostrils, can realize. You can no more sink in it than in a clay-bank, but a very little of it in your lungs would suffice to strangle you. You make your way in from a hot, rocky beach over a chaos of volcanic basalt that is trying to the feet; but, at a depth of a yard or more, you have a fine sand bottom, and here the bathing is delightful.

The water is of a light green color for ten or twenty rods; then "deeply, darkly, beautifully blue." No fish can live in it; no frog abides it; few birds are ever seen dipping into it. The rugged mountains in and about it have a little fir and cotton-wood or quaking-asp in their deeper ravines or behind their taller cliffs, but look bare and desolate to the casual observer; and these cut the lake into sections and hide most of it from view. Probably, less than a third of it is visible from any single point.

These Mormons are in the main an industrious, frugal, hard-working people. Few of them are habitual idlers; few live by professions or pursuits that require no physical exertion. They make work for but few lawyers—I know but four among them—their differences and disputes are usually settled in and by the church; they have no female outcasts, few doctors, and pay no salaries to their preachers—at least the leaders say so. But a small portion of them use tea and coffee. Formerly they drank little or no liquor; but, since the army came in last year, money and whiskey have both been more abundant, and now they drink considerably. More than a thousand barrels of whiskey have been sold in this city within the last year, at an average of not less than eight dollars per gallon, making the total cost to consumers over two hundred and fifty thousand dollars, whereof the Mormons have paid at least half. If they had thrown instead, one hundred and fifty thousand dollars in hard cash into the deepest part of Salt Lake, it would have been far better for them. The appetite they are acquiring, or renewing will cling to them after the army and its influx of cash shall have departed; and Saints who now drink a little will find themselves as thirsty as their valley, before they suspect that they care anything for liquor. And yet, I believe, they have few or no drunkards.

Utah has not a single export of any kind; the army now supplies her with cash; when that is gone, her people will see harder times. She ought to manufacture almost everything she consumes, or foreign debt will overwhelm her. Yet, up to this hour, her manufacturing energies have been most unhappily directed. Some two hundred thousand dollars was expended in preparations for iron making at a place called Cedar City; but the ore, though rich, would not flux, and the enterprise had to be totally abandoned, leaving the capital a dead loss. Wool and flax can be grown here cheaply and abundantly; yet, owing to the troubles last year, no spinning and weaving machinery has yet been put in operation; I believe some is now coming up from St. Louis. An attempt to grow cotton is likely to prove a failure. The winters are long and cold here for the latitude, and the Saints must make cloth or shiver.

Sugar is another necessary of life which they have had bad luck with. They can grow the beet very well, but it is said to yield little or no sugar— because, it is supposed, of an excess of alkali in the soil. The sorghum has not yet been turned to much account, but it is to be. Common brown sugar sells here at sixty cents per pound; coffee about the same; in the newer settlements, they are of course still higher. All sorts of imported goods cost twice to six or eight times their prices in the states; even quack medicines (so-called) and yellow-covered novels are sold at double the prices borne on their labels or covers.

Doubtless this city is far ahead of any rival, being the spiritual metropolis and the earliest settled. Its broad, regular streets, refreshed by rivulets of bright, sparkling, dancing water, and shaded by rows of young but thrifty trees, mainly locust and bitter cotton-wood, are already more attractive to the eye than those of an average city of like size in the states. The houses (of *adobe* or merely sun-dried brick) are uniformly low and generally too small; but there is seldom more than one family to a dwelling, and rarely but one dwelling on a lot of an acre and a quarter. The gardens are well filled with peach, apple, and other fruit trees, whereof the peach already bears profusely, and the others begin to follow the example. Apricots and grapes are grown, through not yet abundant; so of strawberries. Plums are in profusion, and the mountain currants are large, abundant and very good. Many of the lots are fenced with cobble-stones laid in clay mortar, which seems to stand very well. The wall of Brigham Young's garden and grounds is nine or ten feet high, three feet thick at the base, and cost some sixty dollars per rod. Undoubtedly, this people are steadily increasing in wealth and comfort.

Still the average life in Utah is a hard one. Many more days' faithful labor are required to support a family here than in Kansas, or in any of the states. The climate is severe and capricious—now intensely hot and dry; in winter cold and stormy; and, though cattle are usually allowed to shirk for themselves in the valleys, they are apt to resent the insult by dying. Crickets and grasshoppers swarm in myriads, and often devour all before them. Wood is scarce and poor. Irrigation is laborious and expensive; as yet, it has not been found practicable to irrigate one-fourth of the arable land at all. Ultimately, the valleys will be generally irrigated, so far as water for the purpose can be obtained; but this will require very costly dams and canals. Frost is very destructive here; Indian corn rarely escapes it wholly, and wheat often suffers from it. Wheat, oats, corn, barley, rye, are grown at about equal cost per bushel—two dollars may be taken as their average price; the wheat crop is usually heavy, though this year it threatens to be relatively light. I estimate that one hundred and fifty days' faithful labor in Kansas will produce as large an aggregate of the neccessaries of life—food, clothing, fuel—as three hundred just such days' work in Utah. Hence, the adults here generally wear a toil-worn, anxious look, and many of them are older in frame than in years.

I do not believe the plural-wife system can long endure; yet almost every man with whom I converse on the subject, seems intensely, fanatically devoted to it, deeming this the choicest of his earthly blessings. With the women, I am confident it is otherwise; and I watched their faces as Elder Taylor, at a social gathering on Saturday night, was expatiating humorously on this feature of the Mormon system, to the great delight of the men; but not one responsive smile did I see on the face of a woman. On the contrary, I thought they seemed generally to wish the subject passed over in silence.

Fanaticism, and a belief that we are God's especial, exclusive favorites, will carry most of us a great way; but the natural instinct in every woman's breast must teach her that to be some man's third or fourth wife is to be no wife at all. I asked my neighbor the name of a fair, young girl who sat some distance from us with a babe on her knee. "That is *one* of Judge Smith's ladies," was his quiet, matter-of-course answer. I need hardly say that no woman spoke publically on that occasion—I believe none ever speaks in a Mormon assemblage—and I shall not ask any one her private opinion of polygamy; but I think I can read an unfavorable one on many faces.

Yet polygamy is one main pillar of the Mormon church. He who has two or more wives rarely apostatizes, as he could hardly remain here in safety and comfort as an apostate, and dare not take his wives elsewhere. I have heard of but a single instance in which a man with three wives renounced Mormonism and left for California, where he experienced no difficulty; "for" said my informant (a woman, no longer a Mormon,) "he introduced his two younger wives (girls of nineteen and fourteen) as his daughters, and married them both off in the course of six weeks."

I am assured by Gentiles that there is a large business done here in *un*-marrying as well as in marrying; some of them assure me that the church exacts a fee of ten dollars on the marriage of each wife after the first, but charges a still heavier fee for divorcing. I do not know that this is true, and I suspect my informants were no wiser in the premises than I am. But it certainly looks to me as though a rich dignitary in the church has a freer and fuller range for the selection of his sixth or eight wife than a poor young man of ordinary standing has for choosing his first. And I infer that the more sharp-sighted young men will not always be content with this.

Since the foregoing was written, I have enjoyed opportunities for visiting Mormons, and studying Mormonism, in the home of its votaries, and of discussing with them in the freedom of social intercourse, what the outside world regards as the distinguishing feature of their faith and polity. In one instance, a veteran apostle of the faith, having first introduced to me, a worthy matron of fifty-five or sixty—the wife of his youth, and the mother of his grown-up sons—as Mrs. T., soon after introduced a young and winning lady of perhaps twenty-five summers, in these words: "Here is another Mrs. T." This lady is a recent emigrant from our state, of more than average powers of mind and graces of person, who came here with her father, as a convert, a little over a year ago, and has been the sixth wife of Mr. T. since a few weeks after her arrival. (The intermediate four wives of Elder T. live on a farm or farms some miles distant.) The manner of the husband was perfectly unconstrained and off-hand throughout; but I could not well be mistaken in my conviction that both ladies failed to conceal dissatisfaction with their position in the eyes of their visitor, and of the world. They seemed to feel that it needed vindication. Their manner toward each other was most cordial and sisterly—sincerely so, I doubt not—but this is by no means the rule. A Gentile friend, whose duties require him to travel widely over the territory, informs me that he has repeatedly stopped with a bishop, some hundred miles south of this, whose two wives he has never known to address each other, nor evince the slightest cordiality, during the hours he has spent in their society. The bishop's house consists of two rooms; and when my informant staid there with a Gentile friend, the bishop being absent, one wife slept in the same apartment with them rather than in that occupied by her double. I presume that an extreme case, but the spirit which impels it is not unusual. I met this evening a large party of young people, consisting in nearly equal numbers of husbands and wives; but no husband was attended by more than one wife, and no gentleman admitted or implied, in our repeated and animated discussions of polygamy, that *he* had more than one wife. And I was again struck by the circumstance that here, as heretofore, no woman indicated, by word or look, her approval of any arguments in favor of polygamy. That many women acquiesce in it as an ordinance of God, and have been drilled into a mechanical assent of the logic by which it is upheld, I believe; but that there is not a woman in Utah who does not in her heart wish that God had *not* ordained it, I am confident. And quite a number of the young men treat it in conversation as a temporary or experimental arrangement, which is to be sustained or put aside as experience shall demonstrate its utility or mischief. One old Mormon farmer, with whom I discussed the matter privately, admitted that it was impossible for a poor working-man to have a well-ordered, well-governed household, where his children had two or more living mothers occupying the same ordinary dwelling.

Though Brigham has buried eight sons and two daughters, he has fifty surviving children and several grandchildren.[4] His wives number about thirty; he increases the list by one or two additions yearly. The first and eldest is matronly and well-looking; all the later ones I saw are exceedingly plain and unattractive, though some of their daughters are pretty, winning and graceful. Among the present generation of Mormons, the men are far more intelligent and cultivated than the women.

The Gentiles relate many stories at the expense of the leading patriarch of the church. He is the grand Supreme Court of all his people; to him they

4. [These concluding paragraphs are taken from the account of Greeley's companion, A. D. Richardson.—ED.]

carry their troubles for relief, and their difficulties for adjustment. There is a legend that one day a woman went to Brigham for counsel touching some alleged oppression by an officer of the church. Brigham, like a true politician, assumed to know her; but when it became necessary to record her case, hesitated and said:

"Let me see, sister—I forget your name."

"My name!" was the indignant reply; "Why, I am your wife!"

"When did I marry you?"

The woman informed the "President," who referred to an account-book in his desk, and then said:

"Well, I believe you are right. I *knew* your face was familiar!"

The Gentile women recognize and visit only the first wives. The first wife deems herself superior to the rest, sometimes refusing to associate or speak with them, or to recognize the legitimacy of their marriage.

"Are you Mr. ———'s only wife?" asked a Gentile of a Mormon sister.

"I am," was the reply; "though several other women call themselves his wives!"

We are told of one poor fellow, with a pair of wives in a single house containing two rooms. When he brought home his second wife, the first indignantly repudiated him, and would no longer even speak with him. Soon after, the second wife also refused to serve him further; and there the poor wretch was, sleeping alone upon the floor of his cabin, and doing his own cooking, washing and mending, while his consorts were at least agreed in hating him cordially.

But the wives are sometimes very amiable, even toward each other. We dined at the house of a leading Saint, whose two consorts, present at the board, but only as waiters, were dressed precisely alike, and seemed to regard each other as sisters. One portly brother has a wife in nearly every village; so whenever he makes the annual tour of the territory, with Brigham, he can always stay in his own house and with his own family! Polygamy is at least self-sustaining; the women are expected to support themselves.

The Saints' theatre is the grand material wonder of Salt Lake City. It was built by Brigham, and will cost, when completed, a quarter of a million dollars. Its walls are of brick and rough stone, to be covered with stucco. It will seat eighteen hundred persons, and is the largest building of the kind west of New York, except the Cincinnati and Chicago opera houses. The proscenium is sixty feet deep. In the middle of the parquette is an armed rocking-chair, which Brigham sometimes occupies, though his usual place is one of the two private boxes. It is open three nights in the week, when the parquette is filled almost entirely by the families of the leading polygamists. One often sees a dozen of Brigham's wives side by side, and long seats quite filled with his children. The scenery, all painted in Salt Lake, and the costumes, all made there, are exquisite. The wardrobe is very large and rich, varied enough for the standard and minor drama, from the sables of Hamlet to the drapery of the *ballet* girl. With two exceptions, the company are all amateurs—Mormons, who perform gratuitously, and with whom it is a labor of love and piety. It is a novel way of increasing one's chances of heaven; but Brigham is the church, and they do unquestioningly whatever the church requires.

On the whole the theatre is the rarest feature of the rare city, in view of its location, twelve hundred miles from the steamboat and the railroad. During the day the performers are engaged in their regular pursuits, as clerks, mechanics, etc.; and they rehearse only in the evening. Last season the receipts averaged eight hundred dollars per night, and once, thirteen hundred dollars were taken at the box-office. Mrs. Julia Deane Hayne, who was playing a most successful star engagement, had trained the amateurs until they played exceedingly well, producing entertainments in all respects better than one finds anywhere else in the Union, save at three or four leading metropolitan theatres. It was a novel place for the best actress in the United States.

At first she found the audiences curiously excitable, and inexperienced, composed very generally of persons who had never seen a theatre before. When she played the last act of Camille, one old lady left her seat, passed through the private entrance and rushed upon the stage with a glass of water for the dying girl. Another declared, in a voice audible throughout the house: "It is a shame for President Young to let that poor lady play when she has such a terrible cough!"

Brigham shows unequalled sagacity in strengthening the church and putting money in his purse, by the same operation. He says: "The people must have amusement; human nature demands it. If healthy and harmless diversions are not attainable, they will seek those which are vicious and degrading." Therefore he built this Thespian temple, which spiritually refreshed all the Saints of Utah, and increases his personal income fifty thousand dollars annually.

42

The American Desert, 1865

The name of Samuel Bowles (1826–78) is connected indissolubly with the newspaper which he raised to the rank of one of America's leading journals, the Springfield Republican. *Like a good editor, he took time off to see for himself what he was often writing about, and, in 1865, accompanied by Schuyler Colfax, speaker of the House of Representatives, and Albert D. Richardson, who had gone out in 1859 with Horace Greeley, he journeyed westward across the continent to California. His itinerary was much the same as Greeley's; his account is less eloquent, his opinions less arbitrary. If he was less inspired than Greeley, he was also less gullible.*

The Great Desert Basin,—but desert only because comparatively waterless, —lies on the very central and commercial line of the Republic,—the line of greatest population and thrift and wealth both east and west of it,—stretches three hundred miles from north to south and six hundred miles from east to west, is about equally divided between the two states of Utah and Nevada, and is walled in on the one side by the Rocky Mountains and on the other by the Sierra Nevadas. Not a wide, unbroken plain, however, is this vast basin desert of the West. Through it, north and south, run subsidiary ranges of mountains, averaging at least one to every fifty miles, and the intervening valleys or plains all dip, though almost imperceptibly, to the center, which gratefully suggests that they were once not altogether so tearless as now. Mountain and plain alike are above dew point; rain is a rarity,—near neighbor to absolute stranger; and only an occasional range of hills mounts so high as to hold its winter snows into the summer suns, and yield the summer streams that give, at rare intervals, sweet lines of green, affording forage for cattle and refreshment and rest for traveler. Springs are even more infrequent, but not altogether unknown, and water may sometimes, though very hardly, be got, when all else fails, by digging deep wells. Such streams as rise from springs or snow-banks in the mountains, begin to shrink as they reach the Plains, and end in salt lakes, or sink quietly into the famishing earth.

Humboldt River, the largest and longest of the basin, runs west and south from three hundred to five hundred miles, and then finds ignominious end in a "sink," or, in a very natural big disgust at the impossibility of the job it has undertaken, quietly "peters out." So of the Carson River, which comes from the Sierra Nevadas on the west, and finds its home on a lagoon within sight of its parent peaks. Reese River, now so famous as localizing the new and extensive silver mining operations about Austin, is but a sluggish brook that the shortest-legged man could step across at its widest, and yields itself up to the hot sands without greening but a narrow line in the broad plain in which it runs. And yet it is the largest and almost only stream that we met in traveling westward from the Jordan which waters the valley of Salt Lake; and the two are four hundred miles apart!

Through this wide stretch of treeless mountain and plain, at its center,—fifty to one hundred miles below the old and more fortunately watered emigrant route along the valley of the Humboldt,—on a nearly straight line west, we have made the most rapid stage ride yet achieved on the great overland line.

Our fast ride by the Overland Mail stages from Salt Lake will always be a chief feature in the history and memory of our grand journey across the Continent. The stations of the company are ten to fifteen miles apart; at every station fresh horses, ready harnessed, took the places of the old, with a delay of from two to four minutes only; every fifty miles a new driver took his place on the box; wherever meals were to be eaten, they were ready to serve on arrival; and so, with horses ever fresh and fat, and gamey, and with drivers, gentlemanly, intelligent and better dressed than their passengers, and a division superintendent, who had planned the ride and came along to see it executed, for each two hundred miles,—we were whirled over the rough mountains and through the dry and dusty plains of this uninhabited and uninhabitable region, rarely passing a house except for stage stations, never seeing wild bird or beast, for there were none to see, as rapidly and as regularly as we could have been over macadamized roads amid a complete civilization. The speed rarely fell below eight miles an hour, and often ran up to twelve.

But the passengers are content that it should be a single experience for them. The alkali dust, dry with a season's sun, fine with the grinding of a season's stages and freight trains, was thick and constant and penetrating beyond experience and comparison. It filled the air,—it was the air; it covered our bodies,—it penetrated them; and finding its way into bags and trunks, begrimed all our clean clothes and reduced everything and everybody to a common plane of dirt, with a soda, soapy flavor to all.

This alkali element in the soil of all this region, as of much of the country on the other side of the Rocky Mountains, I have heard no explanation of. In some spots it prevails to such a degree as to clean the ground of all, even the most barren vegetation; and wide, smooth, bare alkali plains stretch out before the eye sometimes for miles, and white in the distance like a snowbank. Yet I find no evidence of any general unhealthy effect from its presence; animals eat the grass and drink the water flavored with it; and though the dust chokes all pores and makes the nose and lips sore, the inconvenience and annoyance seems to be but temporary from even large doses of it.

Then the jolts of the rocks and the "chuck holes" of the road, to which the drivers in their rapid progress could give no heed, kept us in a somewhat perpetual and not altogether graceful motion. There was certainly small sleep to be enjoyed during this memorable ride of three days and nights; and though we made the best of it with joke and felicitation at each other's discomfort, there was none not glad when it was over.

Do not think such a country is altogether without beauty or interest for a traveler. Mountains are always beautiful; and here they are ever in sight, wearing every variety of shape, and even in their hard and bare surfaces presenting many a fascination of form,—running up into sharp peaks; rising up and rounding out into innumerable fat mammillas, exquisitely shapen, and inviting possibly to auriferous feasts; sloping down into faint foot-hills, and mingling with the plain to which they are all destined; and now and then offering the silvery streak of snow, that is the sign of water for man and the promise of grass for ox. Add to the mountains the clear, pure, rare atmosphere, bringing remote objects close, giving new size and distinctness to moon and stars, offering sunsets and sunrises of indescribable richness and reach of color, and accompanied with cloudless skies and a south wind, refreshing at all times, and cool and exhilarating ever in the afternoon and evening; and you have large compensations even for the lack of vegetation and color in the landscape.

Coming west out of the barren plains of the great interior basin,—even in their midst,—we strike the first wave of Pacific coast life at Austin. In middle Nevada, huddled and incoherent along the steep hill-sides of a close canyon, running sharply up from the Reese River valley, lies the eastern-most and freshest mining town of the State and section.

Two years old, Austin has already had a population of six or eight thousand, cast one thousand nine hundred votes at the presidential election, and, now, experiencing its first reaction, falls back to four thousand inhabitants. Houses are built anywhere and everywhere, and streets are then made to reach them; one side of a house will be four stories and the other but two, —such is the lay of the land; not a tree nor a flower, nor a grass plot does the whole town boast,—not one; but it has the best French restaurant I have met since New York, a daily newspaper, and the boot-blacks and barbers and baths are luxurious and aristocratic to the continental degree; —while one of the finest specimens of feminine physical beauty and grace presides over a lager beer saloon; gambling riots openly in the large area of every drinking shop,—miners risking to this chance at night the proceeds of the scarcely less doubtful chance of the day; and weak-minded and curious strangers are tempted by such advertisements as this:—

Mammoth Lager Beer Saloon, in the basement, corner Main and Virginia streets, Austin, Nevada. Choice liquors, wines, lager beer and cigars, served by pretty girls, who understand their business and attend to it. Votaries of Bacchus, Gambrinus, Venus or Cupid can spend an evening agreeably at the Mammoth Saloon.

Both inquisitive and classical, we went in search of this bower of the senses; and we found a cellar, whitewashed and sawdusted; two fiddles and a clarionet in one corner; a bar of liquors glaring in another; and a fat, coarse girl proved the sole embodiment and representative of all these proclaimed gods and goddesses. We blushingly apologized, and retired with our faces to Mistress Venus, Cupid, etc., as guests retire from mortal monarchs,—lest our pockets should be picked; and we shall take our mythology out of the dictionaries hereafter.

All up the Austin hill-sides, among the houses, and beyond them, are the big ant-hills that denote mines or the hopes of such. Down in the valley are the mills for crushing and separating the ore. The main Austin belt has been successfully traced for but five miles, and one in width. The veins of ore lie thick in the rotten granite of the hills, like the spread fingers of some mineral giant. They are also comparatively small, sometimes as inches, rarely widening to more than three or four feet. But to compensate for this disadvantage, they are exceeding rich and generally reliable. But then again, the metal is so compounded with sulpheretts of other metals, with antimony and arsenic, that it is hard to extract, and requires a roasting, burning, or smelting process, in addition and intermediate to those of crushing and amalgamating, to successful operation. About fifty veins are now being worked successfully, and as many more have been satisfactorily prospected, and are being put in condition for operating, or are awaiting the coming of capital and its machinery. Water flows into all the veins freely, and much labor is required to pump it out. The first necessity of every mine, indeed, is a steam engine and hoisting apparatus, to draw up water and ore from the bottom of the shaft or tunnel. But few of the mines have mills connected with them. The mills are located with regard to wood and water, rather than to the ore, and the latter is carted sometimes for miles to be worked. Half a dozen mills, working some seventy-five stamps in all, are already put up in the Austin and neighboring canyons; but only about fifty stamps are now at work. The ore yields from one hundred to four hundred dollars in silver and gold per ton; but at present prices, it costs nearly or quite one hundred dollars to mine and work it, so that which yields only one hundred dollars cannot be profitably worked.

New discoveries of valuable ore are constantly making both in the immediate neighborhood of Austin, and far south and north on the same range of mountains. In both directions veins equally rich and much larger have been found; and many parties are busy prospecting. But Austin is the chief point of mining population and development in central Nevada, as Virginia is in western; and the two are by far the most conspicuous and representative points of the silver mining interest on the Pacific Coast.

But Virginia presents many contrasts to Austin. It is three or four years older; it puts its gambling behind an extra door; it is beginning to recognize the Sabbath, has many churches open, and closes part of its stores on that day; it is exceedingly well built, in large proportion with solid brick stores and warehouses; and though the fast and fascinating times of 1862–63 are over, when it held from fifteen thousand to twenty thousand people, and Broadway and Wall street were not more crowded than its streets, it has a thrifty and enterprising air, and contains a population of ten thousand, besides the adjoining town or extension of Gold Hill, which has about three thousand more.

The situation of Virginia is very picturesque; above the canyon or ravine, it is spread along the mountain side, like the roof of a house, about half way to the top. Right above rises a noble peak, fifteen hundred feet higher than the town, itself about six thousand feet high; below stretches the foot-hill, bisected by the ravine; around on all sides, sister hills rise in varying heights, rich in roundness and other forms of beauty, but brown in barrenness, as if shorn for a prize fight, and fading out into a distant plain, with a sweet green spot to mark the rare presence of water and verdure.

Different, too, in its mines is Virginia from Austin. Instead of numerous little veins, the wealth of Virginia lies in one grand ledge of ore, running along the mountain side, just within the upper line of the town, for three miles; of width, from fifty to one hundred feet, and of depth incalculable. This is the famous Comstock Ledge; and no silver mines worth working have yet been found off from it, in the neighborhood of Virginia; though thousands of dollars and years of labor have been spent in the search. Nor has the working of this ledge at its various points been attended with uniform success. At least as many companies have failed upon it as have succeeded. Only fourteen out of about thirty companies formed and still at work upon the Comstock Ledge have paid dividends. One company has spent over a million dollars in the vain pursuit of "pay ore"; the vein it has, the ore it finds, but the latter is not rich enough to pay for milling. But it still goes on, seduced by the hope of finding the valuable streak which its neighbor had yesterday, but may have lost to-day.

The Gould & Curry is the largest and most famous enterprise here. It has twelve hundred feet in length on the surface of the ledge, has dug down six hundred to eight hundred feet in depth, and back and forth on its line twenty or thirty times; its whole excavations foot up five millions of cubic feet, and afford some two miles of underground travel, and it has consumed more lumber to brace up the walls of its tunnels than the entire city of Virginia above ground has used for all its buildings. This company owns the largest and finest mill probably in the world, costing nearly a million of dollars, and running eighty stamps. This mammoth enterprise has only drawn one hundred and eighty thousand dollars from its stockholders, and has paid them back four millions in dividends. Altogether, it has produced twelve millions of bullion, and but for extravagance in management and the necessity for many a blind and expensive experiment, its profit share of this sum would have been at least fifty, instead of thirty-three per cent.

This immense development was secured under the energetic superintendence of Mr. Charles L. Strong, a native of Easthampton, Massachusetts. Mr. Strong took charge of the Gould & Curry mine in its infancy, and carried it on to its perfection and triumph, when, about a year and a half ago, his constitution gave way under its great responsibility and work, and he was forced to retire. At one time, the mine sold at the rate of six thousand dollars a foot, but now it is down to about eighteen hundred; for, though it is producing bullion at the rate of two millions a year, and pays handsome monthly dividends uninterruptedly, it has about exhausted all the valuable ore in its mine at the present depth, and is working up mainly the poorer ore that it rejected in its first progress through the vein. The company is now making an important experiment to find richer ore at a lower depth; and by means of a tunnel, started half a mile off down the hill, and a shaft one thousand feet deep, will soon open the mine that distance down. The future fortunes of the company hang mainly upon the result of this enterprise. Not only, indeed, that of Gould & Curry, but of most of the enterprises upon the Comstock Ledge.

The Ophir Company is another of the mammoth enterprises. That, too, has taken out twelve millions of bullion, but the stockholders have not got much as their share, in consequence of extravagant and fickle management, and experiments that proved expensive failures. The Savage Company, owning another large and successful mine, has taken out six millions bullion.

The Empire Company's claim has sold as high as eighteen thousand dollars per foot, the highest price ever obtained for any mine here; but it has grown less profitable and interrupted its dividends since, and has fallen to from three thousand to four thousand dollars a foot. Another successful and now popular company in Gold Hill is the Yellow Jacket, which has taken out about two millions of bullion, and paid its stockholders three hundred and thirty thousand dollars, or thirty-five thousand dollars more than all their assessments. But among its heavy expenditures, which suggests one cause of the ruin of many of these mining companies, is an item of two hundred and seventy thousand dollars for "legal services and quieting title."

The Comstock Ledge ore is, with small exceptions, much more simple in its combinations than that at Austin, and requires only to be crushed and amalgamated to extract the bullion. These two processes will produce from sixty to eighty per cent. of all the precious metal. It is also less rich than the Austin ore; fifty dollars is a good average per ton, and is about what the Gould & Curry claims for what it works of its own ore. But the average of all mines is even less than that; one mine reports an average yield for the year of but $30.26 per ton; and the product of the whole ledge for the first three months of the present year is given to me as about one hundred thousand tons, yielding nearly four million dollars, and averaging a fraction less than forty dollars. To meet this lower yield per ton, however, is a greatly decreased cost of working the ore, which does not need the roasting or smelting process, and the whole expense of mining and reducing does not exceed twenty-five dollars a ton, and is even brought as low as eighteen and twenty dollars by the Gould & Curry company.

The present product of the whole State is probably nearly twenty million dollars a year, of which Austin is sending forward a million and a quarter, and Virginia and Gold Hill fifteen to sixteen millions. Though the bullion, as perfected here, looks like pure silver, nearly or quite one-third of it in value is really gold; and this is extracted after it gets to market, in England, or by the United States mints at San Francisco and in the East.

Our last day in Nevada was passed among its pleasantest and richest valleys, under the shadows of the Sierra Nevada mountains, and rejoicing in the fertilizing streams from their springs and snows. Here in the valleys of the Truckee, the Washoe, and the Carson, is the garden of the State; here .were a few agricultural settlers, fifteen and twenty years ago, colonists from Utah, to which all this region was originally attached. Now, the Mormons are displaced by a more vigorous and varied population, prosperous with farming, with lumbering among the rich pines of the Sierras, and with quartz mills, seeking proximity here to wood and water, and fed by the mines in Virginia and Gold Hill.

Skirting the hill-sides from Virginia at early morning, on a capital toll road, that runs from mountain to mountain on a common level, we breakfasted at Steamboat Springs, where the phenomenon of an immense natural tea-kettle is in operation. For a mile or more along a little stream, underneath a thin crust of earth, water immeasurable is seething and boiling, and occasionally breaking through in columns of steam and in bubbling spouts too hot to bear the hand in. In winter the vapor fills the valley, and from this and the rumbling, bubbling noise of the seething waters, comes the name of Steamboat Springs. Down the valleys we drove to Washoe Village and Lake, and then farther on to Carson City, the capital of the young State.

Here we confronted the long-looked-for, the even long-seen Sierra Nevadas, pathway to the Golden Gate.

The ride over the mountains, down their western valleys, on to the ocean, was a succession of delights and surprises. The surging and soughing of the wind among the tall pines of the Sierras came like sweetest music. The pines of these mountains are indeed monsters,—three, four, five feet through, and running up to heaven for light, straight and clear as an arrow by the hundred feet,—suggestive forerunners of *the* "big trees" of Calaveras and Mariposa. Rich green-yellow mosses cling to many a trunk; and firs and balsams fill up the vacant spots between the kingly pines; while laughing waters sport lustily before our unaccustomed eyes, among the rocks in the deep ravines, along and far below the road on which our horses gallop up hill and down at a fearful pace.

The initial trip of the little steamer upon Lake Tahoe was among the novelties of our mountain experience. This is one of the beautiful lakes of the world, richly ranking with those of Scotland and Swiss-Italy, and destined to arouse as wide enthusiasm. It is located up among the mountains, itself six thousand five hundred feet high, overlooked by snow-capped peaks, bordered by luscious forests; stretches wide for eight to fourteen miles in extent, with waters clear and rare almost as air,—so rare, indeed, that not even a sheet of paper can float, but quickly sinks, and swimming is nearly impossible; and abounds in trout. Already, though far from heavy populations, it has its mountain and lake hotel, and draws many summer visitors from California and Nevada.

From Lake Tahoe to Placerville, the first considerable town in California, is seventy-five miles of well-graded road, up to the mountain summits, and down on the western side; and the drive over it, made in less than seven hours, even surpassed any that had gone before in rapidity and brilliancy of execution. With six horses, fresh and fast, we swept up the hill at a trot, and rolled down again at their sharpest gallop, turning abrupt corners without a pull-up, twisting among and by the loaded teams of freight toiling over into Nevada, and running along the edge of high precipices, all as deftly as the skater flies or the steam car runs; though for many a moment we held our fainting breath at what seemed great risks or dare-devil performances. The road is excellent, hard and macadamized, constructed by private enterprise and imposing heavy tolls.

At Placerville, among vineyards and orchards and flower gardens, a night, at Sacramento, sixty miles hence by a railroad, which is seeking the mountains,—a superb breakfast, and thence by steamboat, large and elegant as the best of Sound and North River boats, and all built in San Francisco, through wide grain fields, we came to a refreshing halt in the luxurious halls of the Occidental Hotel, of famous Leland creation.

43

Northwest and Southwest 1866

*T**hough he was not a professional man of letters, James F. Rusling deserves better to be remembered than some who were. He was born in Washington, New Jersey, in 1834, graduated from Dickinson College in 1854, and earned his living as a lawyer. His career was moderately distinguished—at least he was a trustee of several educational institutions. He apparently harbored a taste for creative writing. He wrote for the most distinguished periodicals in America—Harper's, the Atlantic, and Century—and published a variety of books, mostly on occasional topics. He served with distinction in the Civil War and was breveted a brigadier general before its conclusion. In his military capacity he was sent, soon after the close of the conflict, on a tour of inspection through the West, and the result was embodied in his one outstanding volume, Across America.*

He covered an amazing amount of ground, and all that he saw he recorded faithfully, with much humor, with discernment, and with perspicacity. It is hard to discover in his professional career of the law the background which could produce so humane a work; and one certainly does not associate with the army the cultivated tone and objectivity with which he wrote. However inexplicable it may be, he achieved one of the most graphic travel accounts of mid-nineteenth-century America.

THE MINING TOWN OF BOISE

Idaho, one of the latest of our new Territories, was formed by lopping off the eastern prolongations of Oregon and Washington, and calling the incipient state by that euphonious name. Lewiston, the head of navigation then, *via* the Columbia, was originally its capital; but the "shrieks of locality" demanded a more central position, and so Boisè City secured the honor. We found it a mushroom town of log and frame buildings, but thoroughly alive in every way. Three years before, there was nothing there but the Boisè bottoms, and a scattered ranch or two. Now she boasted three thousand inhabitants, two daily newspapers, stage-lines in all directions, and ebullient prosperity. A hotel, of large capacity, that was to "take the shine" out of all the rest, was just being completed. The Episcopalians and Presbyterians already had their churches up, and the Methodists were expecting soon to build theirs, though then worshipping temporarily in the Court House. Excellent free-schools, to accommodate all the children and more, abounded, and the sermon we heard on Sunday was chiefly a "pitching into" Brigham Young, largely for the want of these. The preacher had been down to Salt Lake, spying out the land for missionary purposes, and had returned filled with hearty unction against the whole system of Mormonism.

Boisè City was then the centre of the mining regions of Idaho, though not *of* them—like Denver, as related to Colorado. The mines were chiefly miles away, at Owyhee, Ruby, Idaho City, and Silver City; but all business sprang from and converged here at Boisè, as the most central point, all things considered, and most of the "bricks" dropped first into her lap. Mining operations were mostly over for that season, and the streets and saloons of Boisè were thronged with rough miners, *en route* from the Columbia, or even California, to winter and return. They claimed they could save money by this temporary exodus—the price of living was so high in Idaho—and at the same time escape the rigor of the climate. With expensive hats, clad chiefly in red-shirts, and "bearded like a pard," every man carried his bowie-knife and revolver, and seemed ready for any emergency. They were evidently a rougher crowd, than the Colorado miners, and in talking with them proved to be from California, Arizona, Nevada, Oregon, Frazer's River, Montana, and about everywhere else, except Alaska. Your true miner is a cosmopolite who has "prospected" everywhere, from the British Dominion to Mexico, and he is all ready to depart for any new "diggings," that promise better than where he is, on half a day's notice, no matter how far. His possessions are small, soon bundled up or disposed of, and he mocks at the old maxim, "A rolling stone gathers no moss," though usually he is a good exemplification of it.

The chief business of Boisè, just then, seemed to be drinking whiskey and gambling. The saloons were the handsomest buildings in town, and were thronged at all hours of the day and night. The gamblers occupied corners of these, and drove a brisk trade unmolested by anybody. The restaurants were also important points of interest, and gave excellent meals at not unreasonable prices, all things considered. Here at Boisè, our U.S. greenbacks for the first ceased to be "currency," and the precious metals became the only circulating medium. It did one's eyes good to see our old gold and silver coins in use once more, though gold and silver "dust" was also recognized as a medium of exchange. All the stores, restaurants, and saloons kept a delicate pair of scales, and their customers carried buck-skin or leather bags of "dust," from which they made payment, and into which they returned their change. Disputes now and then arose, from the "dust" offered not being up to standard, but these were usually settled amicably, unless the "dust" proved basely counterfeit, and then the saloons sometimes flashed with bowie-knives, or rung with revolvers.

Here, also at Boisè, for the first time, we met John China-man. Quite a number of the Celestials had already reached Idaho from California, *via* the Columbia, and were scattered through the towns, as waiters, cooks, launderers, etc. A few had sought the mines, but not many, as they preferred the protection of the towns. Along with the rest, these Chinese miners were migrating to the Columbia and beyond; and as they paid their stage-fare and rode, while many others footed it to the "River," of course, we augured well of them.

The imbecile, brutal, and barbarous laws of the whole Pacific Coast, where Chinamen are concerned, it appeared, however were still in force in Idaho. A good illustration of their practical workings had just occurred over in Owyhee, or somewhere there, and should be recorded here. Three or four ruffians over there, it appears, had set upon an unoffending Chinaman at work in the mines, and had first abused and insulted him, and then robbed and killed him. Other miners, hearing of the circumstances, arrested the murderers and took them before an Idaho Dogberry, who promptly liberated them on the ground, that no Anglo-Saxon was present at the transaction, and that the Chinamen (who were) were incompetent as witnesses, as against white men! This was good Idaho law and justice, no doubt. But it was too strong for the indignant miners, and the same day Judge Lynch amended it by *hanging* all the miscreants in the nearest gulch. This was rude law, and rough justice, no doubt; but was it not infinitely better, than the absurd and inhuman code of the Pacific Coast?

PORTLAND, OREGON

A ride of six miles down the Columbia, on the little steamer *Fanny Troup,* and then twelve miles up the Willamette, landed us at Portland, the metropolis of all that region. Here we found a thrifty busy town, of eight or ten thousand people, with all the eastern evidences of substantial wealth and prosperity. Much of the town was well built, and the rest was rapidly changing for the better. Long rows of noble warehouses lined the wharves, many of the stores were large and even elegant, and off in the suburbs handsome residences were already springing up, notwithstanding the abounding stumps nearly everywhere. The town seemed unfortunately located, the river-plateau was so narrow there; but just across the Willamette was East Portland, a growing suburb, with room plenty and to spare. A ferry-boat, plying constantly, connected the two places, and made them substantially one. Portland already boasted water, gas, and Nicholson pavements; and had more of a solid air and tone, than any city we had seen since leaving the Missouri. The rich black soil, on which she stands, makes her streets in the rainy season sloughs or quagmires; but she was at work on these, and they promised soon to be in good condition. Several daily papers, two weekly religious ones, and a fine Mercantile Library, all spoke well for her intelligence and culture, while her Public School buildings and her Court-House would have been creditable anywhere. The New England element was noticeable in many of her citizens, and Sunday came here once a week, as regularly as in Boston or Bangor. The Methodists and Presbyterians both worshipped in goodly edifices, and the attendance at each the Sunday we were there was large and respectable.

Being the first city of importance north of San Francisco, and the brain of our northwest coast, Portland was full of energy and vigor, and believed thoroughly in her future. The great Oregon Steam Navigation Company had their headquarters here, and poured into her lap all the rich trade of the Columbia and its far-reaching tributaries, that tap Idaho, Montana, and even British America itself. So, also, the coastwide steamers, from San Francisco up, all made Portland their terminus, and added largely to her commerce. Back of her lay the valley of the Willamette, and the rich heart of Oregon; and her wharves, indeed, were the gateways to thousands of miles of territory and trade, in all directions. Nearer to the Sandwich Island and China, by several hundred miles, than California, she had already opened a brisk trade with both, and boasted that she could sell sugars, teas, silks, rice, etc., cheaper than San Francisco. Victoria, the British city up on Puget Sound, had once been a dangerous rival; but Portland had managed to beat her out of sight, and claimed now she would keep her beaten. It was Yankee Doodle against John Bull; and, of course, in such a contest, Victoria went to the wall!

It seemed singular, however, that the chief city of the northwest coast should be located there—a hundred miles from the sea, and even then twelve miles up the little Willamette. Your first thought is, Portland has no right *to be* at all, where she now is. But, it appears, she originally got a start, from absorbing and controlling the large trade of the Willamette, and when the Columbia was opened up to navigation rapidly grew into importance, by her heavy dealings in flour, wool, cattle, lumber, etc. The discovery of mines in Idaho and Montana greatly invigorated her, and now she had got so much ahead, and so much capital and brains were concentrated here, that it seemed hard for any new place to compete with her successfully. Moreover, we were told, there are no good locations for a town along the Columbia from the ocean up to the Willamette, nor on the Willamette up to Portland. Along the Columbia, from the ocean up, wooded hills and bluffs come quite down to the water, and the whole back country, as a rule, is still a wilderness of pines and firs; while the Willamette up to Portland, they said, was apt to overflow its banks in high water. Hence, Portland seemed secure in her supremacy, at least for years to come, though no doubt at no distant day a great city will rise on Puget Sound, that will dominate all that coast, up to Sitka and down to San Francisco. From want of time, we failed to reach the Posts on Puget's Sound; but all accounts agreed, that—land-locked by Vancouver's and San Juan islands—we there have one of the largest and most magnificent harbors in the world. With the Northern Pacific Railroad linking it to Duluth and the great lakes, commerce will yet seek its great advantages; and the Boston, if not the New York, of the Pacific will yet flourish where now are only the wilds of Washington. The Sound already abounded in saw-mills, and the ship-timber and lumber of Washington we subsequently found famed in San Francisco, and throughout California. She was then putting lumber down in San Francisco, cheaper than the Californians could bring it from their own foothills, and her magnificent forests of fir and pine promised yet to be a rare blessing to all the Pacific Coast.

The Portlanders, of course, were energetic, go-ahead men, from all parts of the North, with a good sprinkling from the South. Outside of Portland, however, the Oregonians appeared to be largely from Missouri, and to have retained many of their old Missouri and so-called "conservative" ideas still. All through our Territories, indeed, Missouri seemed to have been fruitful of emigrants. Kentucky, Indiana, Illinois, were everywhere well represented; but Missouri led, especially in Idaho and Oregon. This fact struck us repeatedly, and was well accounted for by friend Meacham's remark (top of the Blue Mountains), "the left wing of Price's army is still encamped in this region."[1] The tone of society, in too many places, seemed to be of the Nasby

1. [An allusion, probably, to the Confederate raider in Missouri, Sterling Price.—ED.]

order, if not worse.[2] No doubt hundreds of deserters and draft-sneaks, from both armies, had made their way into those distant regions; and then, besides, the influence of our old officials, both civil and military, had long been pro-slavery, and this still lingered among communities, whom the war had not touched, and among whom school-houses and churches were still far too few. Of course, we met some right noble and devoted Union men everywhere, especially in Colorado; but elsewhere, and as a rule, they did not strike us as numerous, nor as very potential. In saying this, I hope I am not doing the Territories injustice; but this is how their average public opinion impressed a passing traveller, and other tourists we met *enroute* remarked the same thing.

Here at Portland, John Chinaman turned up again, and seemed to be behaving thoroughly well. At Boisè, we found these heathen paying their stage-fare, and riding down to the Columbia, while many Caucasians were walking, and here at Portland they appeared alike thrifty and prosperous. Their advent here had been comparatively recent, and there was still much prejudice against them, especially among the lower classes; but they were steadily winning their way to public favor by their sobriety, their intelligence and thrift, and good conduct generally. Washing and ironing, and household service generally, seemed to be their chief occupations, and nearly everybody gave them credit for industry and integrity. Mr. Arrigoni, the proprietor of our hotel (and he was one of the rare men, who know how to "keep a hotel"), spoke highly of their capacity and honesty, and said he wanted no better servants anywhere. One of them, not over twenty-one, had a contract to do the washing and ironing for the Arrigoni House, at a hundred dollars per month, and was executing it with marked fidelity. He certainly did his work well, judging by what we saw of the hotel linen. In walking about the town, we occasionally came upon their signs, over the door of some humble dwelling, as for example, "Ling & Ching, Laundry"; "Hop Kee, washing and ironing"; "Ching Wing, shoemaker"; "Chow Pooch, doctor"; etc. As far as we could see, they appeared to be intent only on minding their own business, and as a class were doing more hearty honest work by far, than most of their bigoted defamers. We could not refrain from wishing them well, they were so industrious, and orderly; for, after all, are not these the first qualities of good citizenship the world over?

THE CALIFORNIA CHINESE

We found the Chinese everywhere on the street and in the houses, in pretty much all occupations except the highest, and were constantly amazed

2. [I.e., Petroleum V. Nasby, the American humorist.—ED.]

at their general thrift and intelligence. Out of the hundred thousand or so on the Coast, perhaps half were massed in San Francisco and its suburbs.

All wore the collarless Chinese blouse, looped across the breast, not buttoned—that of the poorer classes of coarse blue stuff, but of the richer of broadcloth. Otherwise, they dressed outwardly chiefly as Americans. Here and there a Chinese hat, such as you see in the tea-prints, appeared, but not often—the American felt-hat being the rule, stove-pipes never. A good many still wore the Chinese shoe, wooden-soled, with cotton uppers; but the American boot and shoe were fast supplanting this, especially among the out-door classes, such as mechanics and laborers. Pig-tails were universal, generally hanging down, but often coiled about the head, under the hat, so as to be out of the way and attract less attention. In features, of course, they were all true Mongolians; but here and there were grand faces, worthy of humanity anywhere. Their food consists chiefly of fish and rice; but the wealthier classes indulge freely in poultry and beef, and the Chinese taste for these was constantly on the increase. The old stories of their dog and rat diet are evidently myths, at least here in America. Intelligent Californians laugh at such reports as antediluvian, and say their Chinese neighbors are only too glad to eat the very best, if they can only get it.

Everybody gave them credit for sobriety, intelligence, and thrift, the three great master qualities of mankind, practically speaking; and without them the industry of the Pacific Coast, it was conceded, would soon come to a stand-still. All are expert at figures, all read and write their own tongue, and nearly all seemed intent on mastering English, as quickly and thoroughly as possible. When not at work or otherwise occupied, they were usually seen with a book in their hands, and seemed much given to reading and study.

Their chief vices were gambling, and opium-smoking; but these did not seem to prevail to the extent we had heard, and appeared really less injurious, than the current vices of other races on the Coast, all things considered. The statistics of the city and Coast somehow were remarkably in their favor, showing a less percentage of vagrancy and crime among these heathens, than any other part of the population, notwithstanding the absurd prejudices and barbarous discriminations against them.

Their quickness to learn all American ways, even when not able to speak our tongue, was very surprising. They engaged in all household duties, ran errands, worked at trades, performed all kinds of manual labor, and yet as a rule, their only dialect was a sort of chow-chow or "Pigeon English." "Pigeon" is said to be the nearest approach a Chinaman can make to "*business*," and hence "Pigeon English" really means *business* English. Most of the words are English, more or less distorted; a few, however, are Chinese Anglicized. They always use *l* for *r*—thus *lice* for "rice"; *mi* for "I," and abound in terminal "ee's." *Chop-chop* means "very fast"; *maskee,* "don't mind." If you call on a lady, and inquire of her Chinese servant, "Missee have got?" he will reply, if she be up and about, "Missee hab got topside"; or if she be still asleep, "Missee hab got, wakee sleepee." Not wishing to disturb her, you hand him your card, and go away with, "maskee, maskee; no makee bobbery!"

We had seen a good deal of the Chinese generally, but on the evening of Dec. 31st were so fortunate as to meet most of their leading men together. The occasion was a grand banquet at the *Occidental,* given by the merchants of San Francisco, in honor of the sailing of the *Colorado,* the first steamer of the new monthly line to Hong-Kong. All the chief men of the city—merchants, lawyers, clergymen, politicians—were present, and among the rest some twenty or more Chinese merchants and bankers. The Governor of the State presided, and the military and civil dignitaries most eminent on the Coast were all there. The magnificent Dining-Room of the *Occidental* was handsomely decorated with festoons and flowers, and tastefully draped with the flags of all nations—chief among which, of course, were our own Stars and Stripes, and the Yellow-Dragon of the Flowery Empire. A peculiar feature was an infinity of bird-cages all about the room, from which hundreds of canaries and mocking-birds discoursed exquisite music the livelong evening. The creature comforts disposed of, there were eloquent addresses by everybody, and among the rest one by Mr. Fung Tang, a young Chinese merchant, who made one of the briefest and most sensible of them all. It was in fair English, and vastly better than the average of post-prandial discourses. This was the only set speech by a Chinaman, but the rest conversed freely in tolerable English, and in deportment were certainly perfect Chesterfields of courtesy and propriety. They were mostly large, dignified, fine-looking men, and two of them—Mr. Hop Kee, a leading tea-merchant, and Mr. Chy Lung, a noted silk-factor—had superb heads and faces, that would have attracted attention anywhere. They sat by themselves; but several San Franciscans of note shared their table, and everybody hob-nobbed with them, more or less, throughout the evening. These were the representatives of the great Chinese Emigration and Banking Companies, whose checks pass current on 'Change in San Francisco, for a hundred thousand dollars or more any day, and whose commercial integrity so far was unstained. There are five of these Companies in all, the Yung-Wo, the Sze-Yap, the Sam-Yap, the Yan-Wo, and the Ning-Yung. They contract with their countrymen in China to transport them to America, insure them constant work while here at fixed wages, and at the expiration of their contract return them to China again, dead or alive, if so desired. They each have a large and comfortable building in San Francisco, where they board and lodge their members, when they first arrive, or when sick, or out of work, or on a visit from the interior. Chinese beggars are rare on the Coast, and our public hospitals contain no Chinese patients, although John before landing has always to pay a "hospital-tax" of ten dollars. This is what it is called out there; but, of course, it is a robbery and swindle, which the Golden State ought promptly to repeal. These great Companies also act, as express-agents and bankers, all over the Coast. In all the chief towns and mining districts, wherever you enter a Chinese quarter or camp, you will find a representative of one or more of them, who will procure anything a Chinaman needs, from home or elsewhere; and faithfully remit to the Flowery Kingdom whatever he wants to send, even his own dead body. Both parties appear to keep their contracts well—a breach of faith being seldom recorded. Here, surely, is evidence of fine talent for organization and management—the best tests of human intellect and capacity—and a hint at the existence of sterling qualities, which the English-speaking nations are slow to credit other races with. Such gigantic schemes, such far-reaching plans, such harmonious workings, and exact results, imply a genius for affairs, that not even the Anglo-Saxon can afford to despise, and which all others may ponder with profit. A race that can plan and execute such things as these, must have some vigor and virility in it, whatever its other peculiarities.

Some days after the Banquet, we were driven out to the Mission Woolen Mills, where Donald McLennan, a Massachusetts Scotch-Yankee, was converting California wool into gold. The climate being so favorable to sheep, the wool-product of the coast was already large, and everywhere rapidly increasing. I mention all these things in order to emphasize the fact, that out of the 450 persons then employed about these Mills, 350 were Chinamen. For the heavier work, Americans or Europeans were preferred; but the more delicate processes, we were assured, Chinamen learned more quickly and performed more deftly, besides never becoming drunk, or disorderly, or going on a "strike." We saw them at the looms, engaged in the most painstaking and superb pieces of workmanship, and they could not have been more attentive and exact, if they had been a part of the machinery itself. And yet, these one hundred Anglo-Saxons were paid $2,95 per day, coin, while the three hundred and fifty Chinamen received only $1,10 per day, coin, though the average work of each was about the same. Without this cheap labor of John Chinaman, these Mills would have had to close up; with it, they were run at a profit, and at the same time were a great blessing and credit to the Pacific Coast in every way. So, also, the Central Pacific Railroad was then being pushed through and over the Sierra Nevadas, by some ten thousand Chinamen, working for one dollar per day each, in coin, and finding themselves, when no other labor could be had for less than two dollars and a half per day, coin. It was simply a question with the Central directors, whether to build the road or not. Without John, it was useless to attempt it, as the expense would have bankrupted the company, even if other labor could have been had, which was problematical. With him, the road is already a fact accomplished; and in view of possible contingencies, nationally and politically, who shall say we have completed it an hour too soon? Here are practical results, not shadowy theories—of such a character, too, as should give one pause, however anti-Chinese, and ought to outweigh a world of prejudices.

Not long afterwards, we were invited to join a party of gentlemen, and make a tour of the Chinese quarter. Part were from the East, like ourselves, bent on information, and the rest Pacific-Coasters. We started early in the evening, escorted by two policemen, who were familiar with the ins and outs of Chinadom, and did not reach the *Occidental* again until long after midnight. We went first to the Chinese Theatre, an old hotel on the corner of Jackson and Dupont streets, that had recently been metamorphosed into an Oriental playhouse. We found two or three hundred Chinese here, of both sexes, but mainly males, listening to a play, that required eighty weeks or months—our informants were not certain which—to complete its performance. Here was drama for you, surely, and devotion to it! It was a history of the Flowery Kingdom, by some Chinese Shakespeare—half-tragedy, half-comedy, like most human history—and altogether was a curious medly. The actors appeared to be of both sexes, but we were told were only men and boys. Their dresses were usually very rich, the finest of embroidered silks, and their acting quite surprised us. Their pantomime was excellent, their humor irresistible, and their love-passages a good reproduction of the grand passion, that in all ages "makes the world go round." But it is to be doubted, if the Anglo-Saxon ear will ever become quite reconciled to John's orchestra. This consisted of a rough drum, a rude banjo or guitar, and a sort of violin, over whose triple clamors a barbarous clarionet squeaked and squealed continually. Japanese music, as rendered by Risley's troupe of "Jugglers," is much similar to it; only John's orchestra is louder, and more hideous. Much of the play was pantomime, and much opera; some, however, was common dialogue, and when this occurred, the clash and clang of the Chinese consonants was something fearful. Every word seemed to end in "ng," as Chang, Ling, Hong, Wung; and when the parts became animated, their voices roared and rumbled about the stage, like Chinese gongs in miniature. The general behavior of the audience was good; everybody, however, smoked —the majority cigars and cigarritos, a very few opium. Over the theatre was a Chinese lottery-office, on entering which the Proprietor tendered you wine and cigars, like a genuine Californian. He himself was whiffing away at a cigarrito, and was as polite and politic, as a noted New York ex-M.C. in the same lucrative business. Several Chinamen dropped in to buy tickets, while we were there; and the business seemed to be conducted on the same principle, as among Anglo-Saxons elsewhere.

Next we explored the famous Barbary Coast, and witnessed scenes that Charles Dickens never dreamed of, with all his studies of the dens and slums of London and Paris. Here in narrow, noisome alleys are congregated the wretched Chinese women, that are imported by the ship-load, mainly for infamous purposes. As a class, they are small in stature, scarcely larger than an American girl of fourteen, and usually quite plain. Some venture on hoops and crinoline, but the greater part retain the Chinese wadded gown and trousers. Their chignons are purely Chinese—huge, unique, indescribable— and would excite the envy even of a Broadway belle. They may be seen on the street any day in San Francisco, bonnet-less, fan in hand, hobbling along in their queer little shoes, perfect fac-similes of the figures you see on lacquered ware imported from the Orient. They are not more immodest, than those of our own race, who ply the same vocation in Philadelphia and New York; and their fellow-countrymen, it seemed, behaved decently well even here. But here is the great resort of sailors, miners, 'long-shoremen, and the floating population generally of San Francisco, and the brutality and bestiality of the Saxon and the Celt here all comes suddenly to the surface, as if we were fiends incarnate. Here are the St. Giles of London and the Five Points of New York, magnified and intensified (if possible), both crowded into one, and what a hideous example it is for Christendom to set to Heathendom! San Francisco owes it to herself, and to our boasted civilization, to cleanse this Augean stable—to obliterate, to stamp out this plague-spot—to purge it, if need be, by fire—and she has not a day to lose in doing it. It is the shameful spectacle, shocking alike to gods and men, of a strong race trampling a weaker one remorselessly in the mud; and justice will not sleep forever, confronted by such enormities.

The same evening we took a turn through the Chinese gambling-houses, but did not find them worse than similar institutions elsewhere. Indeed, they were rather more quiet and respectable, than the average of such "hells" in San Francisco. They were frequented solely by Chinamen, and though John is not averse to "fighting the tiger," he proposes to do it in his own *dolce far niente* way. They seemed to have only one game, which consisted in betting whether in diminishing steadily a given pile of perforated brass-coins, an odd or even number of them would at last be left. The banker with a little rod, drew the coins, two at a time, rapidly out of the pile towards himself, and when the game was ended all parties cheerfully paid up their losses or pocketed their gains. The stakes were small, seldom more than twenty-five or fifty cents each, and disputes infrequent. A rude idol or image of Josh, with a lamp constantly burning before it, appeared in all these dens, and indeed was universal throughout the Chinese quarter.

The Chinese New Year comes in February, and is an occasion of rare festivities. It began at midnight on the 4th that year, and was ushered in with a lavish discharge of fire-crackers and rockets, to which our usual Fourth of July bears about the same comparison as a minnow to a whale. The fusilade of crackers continued, more or less, for a day or two, until the whole Chinese quarter was littered with the remains. It takes them three days to celebrate this holiday, and during all this period there was a general suspension of business, and every Chinaman kept open house. Their leading merchants welcomed all "Melican" men who called upon them, and the Celestials themselves were constantly passing from house to house, exchanging the compliments of the season. I dropped in upon several, whom I had met at the Banquet, and now have lying before me the unique cards of Mr. Hop Kee, Mr. Chy Lung, Mr. Fung Tang, Messrs. Tung Fu and Co., Messrs. Kwoy Hing and Co., Messrs. Sun Chung Kee and Co., etc. Several of these understood and spoke English very well, and all bore themselves becomingly, like well-to-do gentlemen. Like the majority of their countrymen, many were small; but some were full-sized, athletic men, scarcely inferior, if at all, to our average American. Their residences were usually back of their stores, and here we everywhere found refreshments set out, and all invited to partake, with a truly Knickerbocker hospitality. Tea, sherry, champagne, cakes, sweetmeats, cigars, all were offered without stint, but never pressed unduly. For three days the whole Chinese quarter was thus given up to wholesale rejoicing, and hundreds of Americans flocked thither, to witness the festivity and fun. John everywhere appeared in his best bib and tucker, if not with a smile on his face, yet with a look of satisfaction and content; for this was the end of his debts, as well as the beginning of a new year. At this period, by Chinese custom or law, a general settlement takes place among them, a balance is struck between debtor and creditor, and everything starts afresh. If unable to pay up, the debtor surrenders his assets for the equal benefit of his creditors, his debts are sponged out, and then with a new ledger and a clean conscience he "picks his flint and tries it again." This is the merciful, if not sensible, Bankrupt Law of the Chinese, in force among these heathen for thousands of years—"for a time whereof the memory of man runneth not to the contrary"—and its humane and wise provisions suggest, whether our Christian legislators, after all, may not have something to learn, even from Pagan Codes.

The Chinese temple, synagogue, or "Josh House," of which we had heard such conflicting reports, stands near the corner of Kearney and Pine streets, in the heart of the city. It is a simple structure of brick, two or three stories high, and would attract little or no attention, were it not for a plain marble slab over the entrance, with "Sze-Yap Asylum" carved upon it, in gilt letters, and the same repeated in Chinese characters. It was spoken of as a "Heathen Synagogue," a "Pagan Temple," etc., and we had heard much ado about it, from people of the William Nye school chiefly,[3] long before reaching San Francisco. But, in reality, it appeared to be only an asylum or hospital, for the unemployed and infirm of the Sze-Yap Emigration Company; with a small "upper chamber," set apart for such religious services, as to them seemed meet. The other companies all have similar hospitals or asylums, but we visited only this one. The first room on the ground-floor seemed to be the business-room or council-chamber of the company, and this was adorned very richly with crimson and gold. Silk-hangings were on the walls, arm-chairs elaborately carved along the sides, and at the end on a raised platform stood a table and chair, as if ready for business. The room adjoining seemed to be the general smoking and lounging room of the members of the company. Here several Chinamen lay stretched out, on rude but comfortable lounges, two smoking opium, all the rest only cigarritos— taking their afternoon siesta. Back of this were the dining-room, kitchen, etc., but we did not penetrate thither. A winding stairs brought us to the second floor, and here was the place reserved for religious purposes,—an "upper chamber" perhaps twenty by thirty feet, or even less. Its walls and ceiling were hung with silk, and here and there were placards, inscribed with moral maxims from Confucius and other writers, much as we suspend the same on the walls of our Sunday-school rooms, with verses on them from *our* Sacred writings. These mottoes, of course, were in Chinese; but they were said to exhort John to virtue, fidelity, integrity, the veneration of ancestors, and especially to admonish the young men not to forget, that they were away from home, and to do nothing to prejudice the character of their country in the eyes of foreigners. A few gilded spears and battle-axes adorned either side, while overhead hung clusters of Chinese lanterns, unique and

3. [A reference to the American humorist, Edgar Wilson Nye, whose writings were published under the name of "Bill" Nye.—ED.]

beautiful. Flowers were scattered about quite profusely, both natural and artificial—the latter perfect in their way. At the farther end of the room, in "a dim religious light," amid a barbaric array of bannerets and battle-axes, stood their sacred Josh—simply a Representative Chinaman, perhaps half life-size, with patient pensive eyes, long drooping moustaches, and an expression doubtless meant for sublime repose or philosophic indifference. Here all orthodox Chinamen in San Francisco, connected with the Sze-Yap company, were expected to come at least once a year, and propitiate the deity by burning a slip of paper before his image. There was also some praying to be done, but this was accomplished by putting printed prayers in a machine run by clock-work. Tithes there were none—at least worth mentioning. Altogether, this seemed to be a very easy and cheap religion; and yet, easy as it was, John did not seem to trouble himself much about it. The place looked much neglected, as if worshippers were scarce, and devotees infrequent. A priest or acolyte, who came in and trimmed the ever-burning lamp, without even a bow or genuflection to Josh, was the only person about the "Temple," while we were there. The dormitories and apartments for the sick and infirm, we were told, were on this same floor and above; but we did not visit them. This Josh-worship, such as it is, seemed to be general among the Chinese, except the handful gathered into the various Christian churches; but it did not appear to be more than a ceremony. The truth is, John is a very practical creature, and was already beginning to understand, that he is in a new land and among new ideas. Surely, our vigorous, aggressive California Christians stand in no danger from such Pagan "Temples," and our all-embracing nationality can well afford to tolerate them, as China in turn tolerates ours.

LATINS AND GERMANS IN SOUTHERN CALIFORNIA

We anchored off the old wharf, then fallen to decay, at San Diego, where in other days the Panama steamers had floated proudly, and after rowing well in, were carried ashore on the shoulders of Mexican peons. San Diego was three miles off up the bay. Formerly numbering two or three thousand inhabitants, and a pretty stirring place, it now had only about two or three hundred. Its buildings, of course, were all one-story adobe, but partly inhabited, and these were grouped about a squalid Plaza, that reminded one of Mexico or Spain, rather than the United States. Being the county-seat, of course, it had a court-house and a jail, the one, a tumble-down adobe, the other, literally a cage, made of boiler-iron, six or seven feet square at the farthest. The day we were there three men were brought in, arrested for horse-stealing, or something of the sort; but as the jail would accommodate only two—and crowded at that—the judge discharged the third, with an appropriate reprimand. At least, we supposed it "appropriate"; but as it was in Californicé, and the judge a native, we could make nothing of it. In hot weather, this iron jail-cage must be a miniature tophet; but, no doubt, it remains generally empty. On a hill just back of the town, commanding it and the harbor, were the remains of Fort Stockton, which our Jersey commodore of that name built and garrisoned with his gallant Jack-Tars, during the Mexican war, and held against all comers. Beyond it still, were the ruins of the old Mexico Presidio, with palm and olive trees scattered here and there, but all now desolate and forsaken. The general broken-down, dilapidated, "played out" appearance of the town, was certainly most forlorn. And yet, the San Diegoans, like all good Californians, had still a profound faith in their future, and swore by their handsome bay as stoutly as ever. All united in pronouncing the climate simply perfect, though a little warm in summer; and, I must say, it really seemed so, when we were there. They declared the thermometer never varied more than twenty degrees the year round, and maintained people never died there, except from the knife or bullet. When reminded of a Mr. S. who had died that morning, they replied, he came there too late—a confirmed consumptive; otherwise, he would have got well, and in the end have shrivelled up and evaporated, like the rest of their aged people.

As to business, the town really seemed to have none, except a little merchandising and whiskey-drinking, and these only gave signs of life, because it was "steamer-day." The country immediately about the town was dull and barren, from want of water to irrigate and cultivate it. The great ranches were at a distance, and these depended on streams from the Coast Range, that mostly disappeared before reaching the harbor. Here horses, cattle, and sheep were raised in considerable numbers; but the breadth of valuable land was not considered large, and the population of the section seemed to be on the stand-still, if not decrease. The splendid harbor, however, is there—the second as I have said, on the California Coast—and it will be passing strange, if the future does not evolve something, that will give it vitality and importance.

Los Angelos itself proved to be a brisk and thriving town. It is the county-seat of a large county of the same name, and probably contained then some five thousand inhabitants—about one-third Americans and Europeans, and the balance native Californians and Indians. The Americans seemed to own most of the houses and lands, the Europeans—chiefly Jews—to do the business, the native Californians to do the loafing, and the Indians to perform the labor. It had mail communication with San Francisco twice a week by stage, and twice a month by steamer *via* San Pedro, and telegraphic communication *via* San Francisco with the whole coast and country. It boasted two or three very fair hotels, a fine old Spanish church, and quite a number of brick and frame residences, that would have been called creditable anywhere. The town seemed steadily increasing in wealth and population, as more and more of the surrounding Plains were brought under cultivation, and already had a substantial basis for prosperity in its vineyards and fruit-orchards, aside from its flocks and herds. It was also doing a considerable business with Utah, Arizona, and Southern California, for all which regions it was then largely a mart and entrepôt. Its climate was mild and equable, reminded one more of Italy and the Levant, than America, and already it was quite a resort for invalids from all parts of the Coast. Then in February, and again in May, when we returned there from Arizona, the air really seemed like the elixer of life, and quickened every sense into new life and power of enjoyment. As in all Spanish Americans towns, however, Sunday seemed to be the chief day for business and pleasure. A few stores and shops were closed; but the majority kept open, the same as any other day. The native Californian and Indian population of the surrounding country flocked into town that day, in holiday attire and, after a brief service at the old church (dedicated "To the Queen of the Angels,") assembled in the Plaza, to witness their customary cock-fights. There were several of these, which men and women, priests and people—alike eager and excited—all seemed to enjoy; but to us, Eastern-bred, they seemed cruel and barbarous. The poor fowls pecked away at each other, until some fell dead, and others dropped exhausted, when the survivors were borne away in triumph.

A ride across the breezy Plains, ten miles to the south, brought us to the ranch and vineyard of Mr. Ben. D. Wilson. His noble ranch lies at the foot of the Coast Range of mountains, with their snow-clad summits towering above, the Los Angelos plains in front stretching away to the ocean, while an intervening roll of hills shuts out the raw winds and fogs of the summer and autumn. Two or three dashing rivulets, that issue from the mountains like threads of silver, have been caught up and carried by *acequias* all along the slopes, whence they are distributed wherever the thirsty soil in summer needs them. Here he has orange, lemon, peach, olive, almond, and English walnut groves, by the many acres, while beyond are his vineyards by the hundred acres—part planted by himself, but many a half century ago by the Jesuit Fathers. Just now, his vineyards, trimmed closely as they were, looked for all the world like a Delaware or Jersey field of old peach-trees, with the tops sawn off, as we sometimes see them here. Without trellis or support of any kind, these aged vines stood stiff and gnarled, in rows five or six feet apart, themselves about as many inches thick; but in summer, they throw out runners, that form a leafy wilderness, loaded down with the purpling clusters. In addition, he had great herds of horses, and cattle, and flocks of sheep by the thousand, that roamed over his outlying broad acres and the Los Angelos plains at will. In sauntering through his orange-groves, he showed us trees, from which he had gathered twenty-five dollars' worth of the golden fruit each that season, and one that yielded him forty dollars' worth. In his wine-cellars, back of the mansion, he showed us two hundred thousand gallons of wine, the product of that year's vintage alone, and it hadn't been much of a year for wine either. This he reported to be worth only fifty cents a gallon then, but as increasing in price, of course, with age. He made both white and red wine, of a superior brand, and had branch houses in San Francisco and New York, that disposed of the bulk of it at fair figures. It all had the peculiar sharpness and alcoholic qualities of the California wines generally; but, he thought, with more careful culture, and increasing age, their wines would improve in this respect. He computed the wine-product of California then, at not less than three millions of gallons annually, and rapidly increasing. He said at the end of a year and a half, the wine usually became clear and less alcoholic; but it continued to mellow and soften with age for twenty years, when its delicacy of flavor and oiliness of consistency culminated. Brandy was made from indifferent or miscellaneous grapes, skins and all, and from what we saw of its effects, was as fierce and fiery a liquid, surely, as Jersey lightning, or Nebraska needle-gun.

Land just about Los Angelos, and adjacent to the acequias, was held at a good figure; but a few miles from town, it was selling at only five and ten dollars per acre, and a great stock or fruit ranch, it would seem, could be built up here, at small expense, in a few years. The soil and climate are certainly all anybody could desire; the chief drawbacks seemed to be the absence of good schools and churches. These, however, will come with time and sufficient Yankees; and it is not too much to say, that the Plains and City of the Angels will yet become widely known, and well-peopled. California, rich in so many things, may yet well be vain of them.

At Anaheim, we found quite a settlement of Germans, fresh from the Rhineland, engaged chiefly in wine-making. It appears, they had clubbed together in San Francisco, and bought a thousand acres of the Los Angelos Plains, bordering on the Santa Anna river, whose waters they now used for irrigating purposes. This they divided into twenty-acre lots, with a town-plot in the centre and convenient streets, each lot-holder being also owner of a town-lot of half an acre besides. Here were some five hundred or more Germans, all industriously engaged, and exhibiting of course their usual sagacity and thrift. They had constructed acequias, and carried the hitherto useless Santa Anna river everywhere—around and through their lots, and past every door; they had hedged their little farms with willows, and planted them with vines, orange, lemon, and olive trees; and the once barren plains in summer were now alive with perpetual foliage and verdure. Of course, there had consequently been a great rise in values. The land had cost them only two dollars per acre in 1857; but now in 1867, it was rated at one hundred and fifty dollars, with none to sell. We drove through the clean and well-kept avenues and streets, scenting Rhineland on every side; and, indeed, this Anaheim itself is nothing but a bit of Germany, dropped down on the Pacific Coast. It has little in common with Los Angelos the dirty, but the glorious climate and soil, and was an agreeable surprise every way. We halted at the village-inn, which would have passed very well for a Wein-Haus in the Fatherland, and were entertained very nicely. The proprietor was also the village-schoolmaster, and his frau was one of the brightest and neatest little house-keepers, we had seen on the Coast. They gave us bologna sausage and native wine for supper, as well as excellent tea; and when bed time came, we were conducted to apartments unimpeachable every way. In the course of the evening, half the village seemed to drop in for a sip of wine or glass of beer (they kept both, of course), and the guest-room became so thick with smoke, you could have cut it with a knife. The next morning they gave us some wine for our trip.

ARMY POSTS AND ARIZONA SAND

At Anaheim we bade good-bye to civilization, and at last were fairly off for Arizona. The distance from Wilmington to Yuma is about three hundred miles, and we hoped to make it in ten days at the farthest. We got an early start from Anaheim, and crossing the Santa Anna river through a congeries of quicksands rode all day (by ambulance), with the Coast Range to the right of us, and another serrated ridge ten or twelve miles off to the left, through what was mostly arid and sterile plain, though here and there it was broken up into ravines and "arroyas," or dry water-courses, abounding in cottonwood and live-oaks. Just at sunset, we crossed a divide, and before us lay a sheet of water, five miles long by two wide, reposing like a sea of silver, skirted by wide plateaus, and these in turn flanked by outlying ranges of mountains. This was Laguna Grande, the pet lake of all that region. Draining a wide extent of country, it always remains a large body of water, though in summer much of it disappears, and the balance becomes brackish from alkali. It continues palatable, however, for horses and cattle, and accordingly here we found a great hacienda, one of the largest south of Los Angelos.

The proprietors were two brothers Machado, who here owned leagues square of land, from the summit of one mountain range to the other, including the Laguna. They lived in a rude adobe hut, with three rooms, that no common laborer East would think of inhabiting; but they numbered their live-stock by the thousand, and esteemed their rude home a second paradise. They raised a little barley and some beans on a few acres, bordering on the lagoon; but devoted the great bulk of their broad acres to stock-raising. Señor Delores Machado met us at the door, as we drove up; but as he could speak no English, and we no Spanish, there seemed to be a predicament. Before leaving Los Angelos, we had anticipated this, knowing the old Mexican or Spanish-speaking population still prevailed over most of Southern California and Arizona, and had provided ourselves with "Butler's method of learning to speak Spanish quickly," accordingly. We had conned this over several days, selecting the phrases that would apparently be more useful, and now assailed Señor Machado with everything we could summon. Imagine our disgust, when he looked wild at our attempted Spanish, and responded to every phrase, "No sabe, Señors!" Our driver, Worth, at last came to our rescue, with some mongrel Spanish he had picked up, when soldiering formerly down in Arizona; and when Señor M. understood we only wanted entertainment for the night, he smilingly replied, "O, Si! Señors! Si! Si!" "Yes! Yes!" with true Castilian grace, and invited us into his abode. He gave us a rough but substantial meal, of coffee, frejoles, and mutton; and when bedtime came, allowed us the privilege of spreading our blankets on the softest part of the only board floor in the house. He and his wife occupied a rude bed in one corner of the same room, while his brother slept on one in another. There was not, and never had been, a pane of glass in the house, notwithstanding they were such large-landed proprietors. The breeze stole in at the broken shutter, that closed the only window in the room, and all night long we could count the stars through the dilapidated roof.

Thence to Buena Vista, we passed through a succession of small valleys, between the same general mountain ranges before mentioned. Though wanting in water, yet these all had small streams of some sort flowing through them, which if carefully husbanded could be made to irrigate thousands of fertile acres all through here. We were detained here a day, by a severe rain that set in at nightfall, just after our arrival, and continued for twenty-four hours; but as it gave us and our team a bit of rest, we did not greatly regret it. Thence to Villacito, the valley opened broader and wider, and the grand San Bernardino peak—which day after day had dominated the landscape off to the right—its outlines sharply defined against that exquisite sky—dropped gradually out of sight.

Here we struck the southern California or great Colorado Desert, and thence on to Yuma—one hundred and fifty miles—we might as well have been adrift on the Great Sahara itself. Until we reached this point, the country consisted chiefly of arid plains, it is true; but broken, more or less, into ravines or valleys, with some semblance of life, or at least capacity for supporting life hereafter, should sufficient intelligence and labor ever drift that way. But as we approached the Desert, all this ceased, and the very genius of desolation seemed to brood over the landscape. We descended into it through a narrow rocky cañon, so rough and precipitous, that T. and I both got out and walked down, leaving the driver to navigate the empty ambulance to the foot, the best he could. Jolting and jumping from rock to gully, now half upset, with wheels spinning in the air, and now all right again, he got down safe and whole at last, and we augured well of our wheels and springs, after such a rugged experience.

Quitting Villacito, we found the road sandy and heavy, the air sultry and hot, and the nearest water eighteen miles off at Carissa Creek. The country was one dreary succession of sand and gravel, barren peaks and rocky ridges, with arroyas now and then, but no signs of humidity anywhere. It was not, however, such a perfect desert, as we had anticipated; for here and there were clumps of chemisal, mescal and cactus, and these somewhat relieved the general dreariness of the landscape, poor apologies as they were for trees and shrubbery. The flora, as we proceeded southward, constantly became sparcer and thornier; but the fauna continued about the same—the chief species being jack-rabbits and California quails—the latter a very handsome variety, with top-knots, never seen east. The rabbits were numerous, and the quails whirred across our road in coveys quite frequently, until we were well into the Desert, when both mainly disappeared. We reached Carissa Creek, with its welcome though brackish water, about 2 P.M.; but as it was thirty-three miles yet to the next certain water at Laguna, with only uncertain wells between (dug by the Government), concerning which we could get no definite information, we concluded to halt there till morning.

From there on, the first few miles were about the same as the day before. Then we ascended an abrupt bluff, that looked in the distance like an impassable castellated wall, and suddenly found ourselves on an elevated *mesa* or table-land, the very embodiment of dreariness and desolation. On all sides, it was a vast, outstretched plain, of coarse sand and gravel, without tree, or shrub, or living thing—even the inevitable mescal and cactus here disappeared. Behind us, to the north and east, there was a weird succession of grand terraces and castellated mountains, reminding one of portions of Wyoming. On our right, to the west, the ever present Coast Range loomed along the landscape, barren and ghostly. To the south, all was a dead level, panting and quivering beneath the sun, as he neared the zenith, except where here and there a heavy mirage obscured the view, or vast whirlwinds careered over the desert, miles away—their immense spirals circling upward to the very sky. These last, on first sight, we took for columns of smoke, so erect and vast were they. But soon they rose all along the southwestern horizon, one after another, like mighty genii on the march, and our driver bade us look out for a Yuma sand-storm. We had already here and there found the sand drifted into ridges, like snow-banks, where sand-storms had preceded us, and had heard ugly accounts of them before leaving Wilmington; but, fortunately, we escaped this one—the whirlwinds keeping away to the southwest, where they hugged the Coast Range, and in the course of the afternoon obscured the whole landscape there. This was now the Colorado or Yuma Desert in earnest, without bird, or beast, or bush, or sign of life anywhere—nothing, in fact, but barrenness and desolation, as much as any region could well be. A large portion of it is so low, that the overflow of the Colorado often reaches it during spring freshets, and remains for weeks. In travelling over this portion, now baked dry and hard beneath the sun, we had frequent exhibitions of mirage, on a magnificent scale. One day in particular, we had been driving since early morning, over a heavy sandy road, with the sun blazing down upon us like a ball of fire, with no water since starting, our poor mules panting with heat and thirst, when long after noon we observed—apparently a mile or so ahead—what seemed like a great outspread pond or lake, with little islands here and there, their edges fringed with bushes, whose very images appeared reflected in the water. The scene was so perfect, that the driver and T. both insisted it must be water; however, I inclined to believe it mirage, as it afterwards turned out, but the optical illusion was so complete in this and other instances, that when later in the day we really did approach a veritable sheet of water at Laguna, we all of us mistook this for a mirage also. Here, however, we found a body of water a mile long by half a mile wide, surrounded by a rank growth of coarse grass, and covered with water-fowl—a perfect oasis in the desert. This was also a part of the overflow of the Colorado, there being a depression in the Desert just here, which holds the water like a cup. The quantity is so large, that it lasts for two seasons; but after that, is apt to dry up, if the overflow does not come. But as this usually happens every year, this Laguna (Spanish for *lagoon* or *lake*) becomes a perfect god-send to the traveller here. On its southern margin, a Mr. Ganow from Illinois had established a ranch, and already was acquiring a comfortable home. His horses and cattle found ample subsistence in the brakes, on the borders of the lagoon, and the passing travel to and from California and Arizona made him considerable patronage in the course of the year.

Thence past Alamo to Pilot Knob, where we rounded the corner of the mountains, and struck the valley proper of the Colorado, the country continued more or less an unbroken desert. The roads were heavy and dusty, the air hot and stifling, the landscape barren and monotonous; and when, at last, we made Pilot Knob, and struck the river, eight or ten miles below Fort Yuma, we rejoiced heartily, that the first stage of our tour was so nearly over. The Colorado flowed by our side, red and sluggish, but of goodly volume; the breeze came to us cool and moist across its broad bosom; and as we neared the post, the garrison-flag floating high in the air seemed to beckon us onward, and welcome us beneath its folds. Starting long before daylight, and lying by in the middle of the day, we had driven fifty-three miles that day, over a country that equals, if it does not surpass Bitter Creek itself; and when at last we drew rein at Fort Yuma, we were thoroughly jaded ourselves, and our poor animals quite fagged out. We had made the distance from Wilmington in nine driving days, instead of ten; but they seemed the longest we had ever driven.

Fort Yuma is popularly believed to be in Arizona, but is in reality in the extreme southeastern corner of California. The fort itself stands on a high bluff, on the west bank of the Rio Colorado, which alone separates it from Arizona, and is usually occupied by two or three companies of U.S. troops. Directly opposite, on the east bank of the Colorado, stands Arizona City, a straggling collection of adobe houses, containing then perhaps five hundred inhabitants all told. Here and at Yuma are located the government storehouses, shops, corrals, etc., as the grand depot for all the posts in Arizona. Hence, considerable business centres here; but it is chiefly of a military nature, and if the post and depot were removed, the "City" as such would speedily subside into its original sand-hills. Being at the junction of the Gila and Colorado, where the main route of travel east and west crosses the latter, it is also the first place of any importance on the Colorado itself; and hence would seem to be well located for business, if Arizona had any business to speak of. The distance to the mouth of the Colorado is one hundred and fifty miles, whence a line of schooners then connected with San Francisco two thousand miles away *via* the Gulf of California. From the head of the Gulf, light-draught stern-wheel steamers ascend the Colorado to Yuma, and occasionally to La Paz, and Fort Mojave or Hardyville—one hundred and fifty, and three hundred miles, farther up respectively. Sometimes they had even reached Callville, some six hundred miles from the Gulf, but this was chiefly by way of adventure, as there was no population or business sufficient to justify such risks ordinarily.

March 2d, while still at Arizona City, inspecting the depot there, we saw something of a Yuma sand-storm. The whirlwinds we had observed in the distance, when crossing the Colorado Desert a day or two before, seemed to have been only its precursers. It struck Yuma on the 2d, and promised to be only a passing blow, lulling away at eventide; but on the 3d, it resumed its course, with increased violence, and all day long rolled and roared onward furiously. We had heard much of these Yuma sand-storms, and on the whole were rather glad to see one, disagreeable as it proved. The morning dawned, hot and sultry, without a breath of air anywhere. Along about 9 A.M., the wind commenced sweeping in from the Desert, and as it increased in power uplifted and whirled along vast masses of sand, that seemed to trail as curtains of tawny gossamer from the very sky. As yet, it was comparatively clear at Yuma, and we could see the sweep and whirl of the storm off on the Desert, as distinctly as the outlines of a distant summer shower. But, subsequently, the Desert itself seemed to be literally upborne, and sweeping in, on the wings of the wind. The heavens became lurid and threatening. The sun disappeared, as in a coppery fog. The landscape took on a yellowish, fiery glare. The atmosphere became suffocating and oppressive. Towards noon, the wind rose to a hurricane; the sand, if possible, came thicker and faster, penetrating into every nook and cranny; the air became absolutely stifling, until neither man nor beast could endure it passably. People kept within doors, with every window closed, and animals huddled in groups with their noses to the ground, as if the only place to breathe. As night approached, the tempest ceased, as if it had blown itself out; but it followed us on a minor scale, for a day or two afterwards, as we journeyed up the Gila. The ill-defined horror, and actual suffering of such a day, must be experienced to be appreciated. Out on the Desert, in the midst of the storm, the phenomenon no doubt would amount much to the same thing as the simoons of the Sahara. Travellers or troops caught in these sand-storms have to stop still, and instances are not rare where persons have lost their lives, in attempting to battle with them. They obliterate all sign of a road, whirling the sand into heaps and ridges, like New England snow-drifts; and the next travellers, who chance along, have either to go by compass, or employ a guide, who understands the lay of the mountains, and country generally.

These sand-storms, it appears, are pretty much the only *storms* they ever get at Yuma, and they would not be unwilling there to dispense with even these. In the spring and summer, they frequently prevail there, sweeping in from the south and southwest, and they are simply execrable. They have done much to make the name of Fort Yuma proverbial on the Pacific Coast, as the hottest place in the Union.[4]

The Post stands on a high gravel bluff, facing to the east and south, exposed to the blazing sun throughout the day; and, subsequently, becoming saturated through and through with heat, retains it for months together. Hence, in the summer months, for weeks together, the thermometer there ranges from 100° to 125° in the shade, and the chief end of the garrison becomes an effort to keep cool, or even tolerably so. A tour of duty there was commonly regarded on the Coast, as a kind of banishment to Botany Bay; and yet we found the officers a very clever set of gentlemen, and spent some days there quite delightfully.

The Post here was established about 1857 to overawe the Yumas, then a stalwart and numerous tribe of Indians, occupying both banks of the Colorado for a few hundred miles or more. Though much reduced, they still numbered over a thousand souls; and physically speaking, were the finest specimens of aborigines we had seen yet. They cultivate the river-bottoms to some extent, and raise barley, wheat, beans, melons, etc.—for their surplus of which, when any, they find a ready market at Fort Yuma and Arizona City. Some chop wood for the river-steamers, and others indeed we found employed on the steamers themselves, as deck-hands, firemen, etc. Altogether, these Yumas seemed to have more of the practical about them, than any savages we had met yet, and no doubt they might be saved to the

4. [James F. Meline, in his *Two Thousand Miles on Horseback* (New York, 1867), pp. 53–54, tells the following story of Fort Yuma's heat:

"I listened to a discussion, last evening, on the comparative merits, or rather demerits, of the various military posts.

" 'Boys, did ever any of you hear of Fort Yuma?'

"Not one of them.

" 'Well, Fort Yuma is clear over beyond Arizona, where nothing lives, nor grows, nor flies, nor runs. It's the hottest post, not only in the United States, but in all creation, and I'll prove it to you.

" 'You see I was ordered to Fort Yuma six years ago, and hadn't been on duty two weeks in the month of August, when two corporals took sick. Well, they both died, and where do you think they went?'

"No one could possibly imagine.

" 'Why, I'll tell you; they both went straight to hell!'

"Profound astonishment in the auditory.

" 'Yes, but they hadn't been gone forty-eight hours—hardly time to have their descriptive-lists examined and put on fatigue duty down below—when, one night at twelve o'clock, the hospital steward at the Fort was waked up in a hurry, and there he saw the two corporals standing by his bedside.'

" ' "What do you want?" says he. You know them hospital stewards always get out of temper at a soldier's ever wanting any thing. "What do you want?" says he.'

" ' "We want our blankets," says they!'

" 'After that, you needn't talk to me about any post being hot as Yuma!' "—ED.]

race for generations to come, were proper efforts made to protect and care for them. They had been peaceable for years, and scores of them thronged the Post and the depot, every day we were there.

The men wore only a breech-cloth, with long ends fluttering fore and aft; the women but little more, though some of them affected a rude petticoat. Both sexes, as a rule, were naked from the waist up, and many of each were superb specimens of humanity; but all seemed corrupted and depraved, by contact with the nobler white race. The open and unblushing looseness and licentiousness of the riff-raff of Arizona City, with these poor Indians, was simply disgusting, and it is a disgrace to a Christian government to tolerate such orgies, as frequently occur there, under the very shadow of its flag. Great blame attaches to the army, in former years, for ever admitting these poor creatures within the precincts of the Post at all. Some time before, it was said, the commanding officer sent for Pasquol, their head-chief, and bade him order his squaws away.

"*My* squaws?" he indignantly responded; "no *my* squaws now! White man's squaws. Before white man come, squaws good—stay in wigwam—cook—fish—work in field—gather barley—heap good. But now squaws about Fort all day—City all night—and Yumas no want 'em. White man made squaws a heap bad. White man keep 'em!"

And with this, old Pasquol, a stately savage, wrapped his blanket about his shoulders, and strode haughtily away.

With a host of "adios" and "good-byes," from our Yuma friends, we swung out of Arizona City late that morning, through knee-deep sand, and thus were fairly off for Tucson. The roads proved heavy all that day, and the remains of the sand-storm kept us company; yet we succeeded in making thirty-one miles, and went into camp before night-fall on the banks of the Gila. Some twenty miles out we passed Gila City, consisting of two adobe huts and an abandoned mine. Thence on to Maricopa Wells, indeed all the way from Arizona City, the road ascends the south bank of the Gila, and confines itself pretty closely to it, except here and there where it strikes across the mesas, to avoid some bend in this most tortuous of streams.

The Gila itself ordinarily is an insignificant river, apparently famed more for quicksands than water; but just now its banks were full with the spring freshet, and its usual fords dangerous if not impassable. Its valley is of uncertain breadth, from one to five miles, though its river-bottoms—its only really valuable land—are of course much narrower.

Beyond the valley, on either side, are high mesas or plateaus, covered often with barren volcanic rocks, like the table-lands of Idaho; and, beyond these still, are substantial mountain-ranges. The range on the north, day after day, was a constant wonder and delight. Instead of ridges and peaks, it seemed to be rather a succession of domes, and towers, and castellated ramparts, sharp and well-defined against a peerless sky, chief among which was Castle Dome—a superb domelike mountain, that dominated the landscape for two or three days together. The dome-shaped mountains are a feature of Arizona, and abound everywhere in the Territory, especially in the northern part of it.

A few miles west of Gila Bend, we passed a group of rocks, that interest everybody, but which nobody seemed to know much about. They stand near the roadside, and consist of smooth red porphyry, or some such stone, curiously carved with figures of men, birds, beasts, fishes, etc. Many of the figures are now quite indistinct, but sufficient remain to show what they were, and their very indistinctness—coupled with the hardness of the stone— proves their great antiquity. The rocks themselves, when struck, ring like genuine clink-stones; and, it would seem, only the sharpest and hardest of instruments could make much impression on them. The place is called "Painted Rocks," and we had only time for a cursory examination; but the sculpturing seemed too remote for Spanish times, and was generally attributed to the days of the Aztecs. However this may be, they appeared to be there as a species of hieroglyphics, and doubtless have a story to tell, that some future Champollion may unfold. It may be that the ancient travel for Mexico left the Gila here, or about here, and struck across the country for the Santa Cruz and so south, flanking the Maricopa Desert, and that these sculptured rocks record the place as the starting point—as a sort of finger-board or milestone. This is only a conjecture; but here, at least, is work for the archaeologist and antiquarian, as well as at so many points in Arizona.

At Maricopa Wells, and thence up the Gila, we found a large settlement of the Maricopa and Pimo Indians. The Maricopas, it seems, are an offshoot of the Yumas, and number less than a thousand souls. The Pimos foot up five or six thousand, and from them are sprung the Papagos—a great tribe dominating all southern Arizona. The Maricopas and Pimos have a Reservation here together, some twenty-five miles long by four or five wide, embracing both sides of the Gila, and live in twelve different villages scattered over it. Two of these are occupied by Maricopas—the rest, by Pimos.

Both tribes are a healthy, athletic, vigorous-looking people, and they were decidedly the most well-to-do aborigines we had yet seen. Unlike most Indians elsewhere, these two tribes are steadily on the increase; and this is not to be wondered at, when one sees how they have abandoned a vagabond condition, and settled down to regular farming and grazing. They have constructed great acequias up and down the Gila, and by means of these take out and carry water for irrigating purposes, over thousands of acres of as fine land as anybody owns. Their fields were well-fenced with willows, they had been scratched a little with rude plows, and already (March 9th) they were green with the fast springing wheat and barley. In addition, they raise corn, beans, melons, etc., and have horses and cattle in considerable numbers. One drove of their live stock, over two thousand head, passed down the road just ahead of us, subsequently when *en route* to Tucson, and we were told they had many more. The year before, these Indians had raised and sold a surplus of wheat and corn, amounting to two millions of pounds, besides a large surplus of barley, beans, etc.

Their wigwams are oval-shaped, wicker-work lodges, made of poles, thatched with willows and straw, and this in turn overlaid with earth. An inverted wash-bowl, on an exaggerated scale, would not be a bad representation of one of them. They are usually five or six feet high in the centre, by fifteen or twenty in diameter, and would be very comfortable dwellings, were it not for their absurd doors. These are only about thirty inches high, by perhaps twenty wide, and consequently the only mode of entrance is on your hands and knees. While halting at the Pimo villages for a day, we managed to crawl into one, for the sake of the experience; but the smoke and the dirt soon drove us out. There was a dull fire in the centre, but with no means of exit for the smoke, except the low doorway. Rush or willow mats covered the rest of the floor, and on these three or four Pimos lay snoozing, wrapped in hides and blankets. Various articles of rude pottery, made by themselves, were stowed away under the eaves of the roof; and at the farther side, suspended from a roof-pole in a primitive cradle, was a pretty papoose sound asleep.

These Indians had long been quiet and peaceable, and it would seem are already on the road to civilization. What they need is school-houses and religious teachers.

Tucson we found to be a sleepy old town, of a thousand or so inhabitants, that appeared to be trying its best to take things easy, and succeeds in doing so. It was formerly, and is now again, the capital of Arizona, and the largest town in the territory. It is reputed to be some two hundred years old, and its appearance certainly justifies its reputation.

The town itself is built wholly of adobe, in thorough Mexican or Spanish style, and its population fluctuated. It was then only about a thousand or so, as above stated, of whom fully two-thirds or more were Mexicans, originally or by descent. Its streets are unpaved, and all slope to the middle as a common sewer, as in Spain. It boasted several saloons, one rather imposing, and some good stores; but had no bank, newspaper, school-house, or church, except a rude adobe structure, where a Mexican padre officiated on Sunday to a small audience, with much array of lights, images, drums and violins, and afterwards presided at the customary cock-fight.

As specimens of ruling prices, grain (barley and wheat) sold at $3 per bushel, hay at $40 per ton, lumber at $250 per thousand, all coin, and other things in proportion. The lumber came from the Santa Rita Mountains, fifty miles away, and was poor and scarce at that.

The basis of Tucson's existence, it appears, is the little Santa Cruz river, which flows along just at the edge of the town, and irrigates some hundreds of surrounding acres. There is a good breadth of fine land here, and near here, and the river ought to be made to irrigate the whole valley. No doubt with proper husbanding and utilizing of the little stream, thousands of acres might be cultivated, and the whole region, both above and below Tucson, be made to produce largely. Peach-trees were in bloom down by the river side when we were there; the grape, the orange, and the olive appeared in many gardens; and both climate and soil seemed all the most fastidious could wish. But Tucson lacks energy and capital, and besides, it seemed, the Apaches claim original, and pretty much undisputed, jurisdiction over most of the country there. Merchants complained that the Apaches raided their teams and trains *en route,* and ranchmen that the wily rascals levied contributions regularly on their live stock, as soon as it was worth anything, and did not hesitate to scalp and kill, as well as steal. Farming or grazing under such circumstances, it must be conceded, could hardly be called very lucrative or enticing, and the Tucsonians are entitled to the benefit of this explanation.

The liveliest and most energetic things, however, that we saw about Tucson were its innumerable blackbirds, that thronged the few trees about the streets, and awoke us every monring with their multitudinous twittering and chattering. What a relief they were to the dull and prosy old town! The men and women, wrapped in their serapes or blankets, sunned themselves by the hour in the doorways. The dogs and cats, the goats and pigs, slept on in the streets, or strolled about lazily at will. But these plucky birds sung on and on, with all the heartiness and abandon of the robin or mocking-bird in the East; and Tucson should emulate their intrepidity, and zeal. She should shake off somewhat of the spirit of Rip Van Winkle, and remember she is under Yankee government now, and in the latter half of the nineteenth century.

A Bibliographical Note

There is no general bibliography of books of travel in America. Though one such was projected by the American Historical Association, and some progress made on it, work has long since been suspended. An account of this plan, and the problems inherent in it, is to be found in Solon J. Buck, "The Bibliography of American Travel: A Project," in the *Papers of the Bibliographical Society of America,* XXII, Part I (1928), 52–59.

In lieu of any complete, general bibliographical guide for the whole United States, there exist a few lists, varying in degree of completeness and value, which are nonetheless useful. None of them, however, relates solely to American travelers in America, intermixing foreign accounts with native; and very few of them make any rigid distinction between books of travel and books of description. The great bibliographical compilations of books printed in America by Evans, Sabin, and Roorbach are rewarding but, by their very nature, unwieldy. For travel accounts specifically, the most complete are in the *Literary History of the United States,* edited by Robert E. Spiller *et al.,* Volume III: *Bibliography* (New York: Macmillan Co., 1948), pages 245–83; the *Cambridge History of American Literature,* edited by William P. Trent *et al.* (New York: G. P. Putnam's Sons, 1917–21), Volume I: *Travellers and Observers, 1763–1846,* pages 468–90; Volume IV: *Travellers and Explorers, 1846–1900,* pages 681–728; and Seymour Dunbar, *A History of Travel in America* (Indianapolis: Bobbs-Merrill Co., 1915), IV, 1447–81. Within its special field, William Matthews, *American Diaries: An Annotated Bibliography of American Diaries Written Prior to the Year 1861* (Berkeley and Los Angeles: University of California Press, 1945), is of special value. Helpful, too, are Edward G. Cox, *A Reference Guide to the Literature of Travel* (Seattle: University of Washington, 1938), Volume II: *The New World,* though the listings go only to the year 1800 with any completeness; Charles W. Plympton, "Select Bibliography on Travel in North America," in the *New York State Library Bulletin,* Bibliography No. 3 (May, 1897), pages 35–60, which describes as well as lists; and Joseph P. Ryan, "Travel Literature as Source Material for American Catholic History," in the *Illinois Catholic Historical Review,* Volume X, No. 3 (January, 1928), and No. 4 (April, 1928). More limited in value are Edward Channing, Albert B. Hart, and Frederick J. Turner, *Guide to the Study and Reading of American History* (Boston: Ginn & Co., 1912), pages 89–102; Josephus N. Larned (ed.), *The Literature of American History: A Bibliographical Guide* (Boston: Houghton Mifflin & Co., 1902), the Index of which lists works of travel; and Justin Winsor (ed.), *Narrative and Critical History of America* (Boston: Houghton Mifflin & Co., 1884–89), VIII, 489–94, which lists travel accounts only to 1820.

Unique, and written entertainingly, is Henry T. Tuckerman's *America and Her Commentators: With a Critical Sketch of Travel in the United States* (New York: Charles Scribner, 1864). Not only is the work a valuable bibliographical contribution, but the discussion of the travelers is pertinent and penetrating. Chapter x is devoted entirely to American travelers.

For the separate geographic sections of the United States the amount of bibliographical matter is uneven. For the Northeastern States no bibliography exists, though the guides for the entire United States noted above offer considerable aid. For travel in the Southern States, for its limited period, E. Merle Coulter, *Travel in the Confederate States: A Bibliography* (Norman: University of Oklahoma Press, 1948), is a model work, compiled with scholarly competence and furnished with critical and descriptive notes. The Middle West has four bibliographies of use: Solon J. Buck, "Travel and Description, 1765–1865," in the *Illinois State Historical Library Collections,* Volume IX ("Bibliographical Series," Vol. II [1914]), relates specifically only to Illinois, but, since travelers in that state usually went beyond its borders, the work has a larger value than its place of publication would suggest; Dorothy A. Dondore, *The Prairie and the Making of Middle America* (Cedar Rapids, Iowa: Torch Press, 1926), offers an interpretive text as well as bibliographical aid; Ralph L. Rusk, *The Literature of the Middle Western Frontier* (New York: Columbia University Press, 1925), gives an extended bibliography in Volume II (pp. 96–144); and R. W. G. Vail, *The Voice of the Old Frontier* (Philadelphia: University of Pennsylvania Press, 1949), whose lists extend, however, only to the year 1800. The Southwest and the Pacific West have two bibliographical guides to their travel literature of surpassing excellence: Jesse L. Rader, *South of Forty: From the Mississippi to the Rio Grande. A Bibliography* (Norman: University of Oklahoma

Press, 1947), and Henry R. Wagner, *The Plains and the Rockies: A Bibliography of Original Narratives of Travel and Adventure, 1800–1865. Revised and Extended by Charles L. Camp* (San Francisco: Grabhorn Press, 1937).

The number of works by American travelers in the United States is so extensive that only a highly selective list is possible here. The following are included because of some special value in the book itself or because they offer parallel or contrasting accounts to the selections contained in this volume. Starred titles are those from which the extracts for the present work have been taken.

Unless otherwise noted, it is always the first edition of a work which has been listed.

I

*[Bobo, William M.] *Glimpses of New-York City. By a South Carolinian.* Charleston: J. J. McCarter, 1852.

Child, Lydia M. *Letters from New-York.* New York: Charles S. Francis & Co., 1843. Though largely a vehicle for Mrs. Child's moral and humanitarian interests, there are many unusual and amusing observations on the metropolis.

[Clinton, DeWitt.] *Letters on the Natural History and Internal Resources of the State of New-York. By Hibernicus.* New York, 1822. A highly diverting account of the flora and fauna, the manners and customs, of Upstate New York, with special attention to the Erie Canal.

*Crockett, Davy[?]. *An Account of Col. Crockett's Tour to the North and Down East . . . in 1834 . . . Written by Himself.* Philadelphia: E. L. Carey & A. Hart, 1835.

Davidson, Gideon M. *The Fashionable Tour: Or, a Trip to the Springs, Niagara, Quebeck, and Boston . . . in 1821.* Saratoga Springs, N.Y., 1822. No better and no worse than many similar works, Baedeker-like, on one of the most-visited places of the United States.

*Drayton, John. *Letters Written during a Tour through the Northern and Eastern States of America.* Charleston, 1794.

*[Dwight, Theodore.] *Things as They Are. . . .* New York: Harper & Bros., 1834. A second edition, entitled *Summer Tours,* was issued in 1847.

*Dwight, Timothy. *Travels in New-England and New-York.* 4 vols. New Haven, 1821.

Foster, Lillian. *Way-side Glimpses, North and South.* New York: Rudd & Carleton, 1860. Superficial, but there are good accounts of hotel life, of railway journeys, and of Chicago.

*[Greene, Asa.] *A Glance at New York. . . .* New York, 1837.

*[Ingersoll, Charles J.] *Inchiquin, the Jesuit's Letters . . . Containing a Favourable View of the Manners, Literature, and State of Society, of the United States. . . .* New York: I. Riley, 1810.

*Lieber, Francis. *The Stranger in America: Or, Letters to a Gentleman in Germany. . . .* Philadelphia: Carey, Lea & Blanchard, 1835.

*[Nicklin, Philip H.] *A Pleasant Peregrination through the Prettiest Parts of Pennsylvania. Performed by Peregrine Prolix. Philadelphia:* Grigg & Elliot, 1836.

"Notes on a Tour through the Western Part of the State of New York," *The Ariel,* Vol. III, Nos. 14–20 (October 31, 1829—January 23, 1830). There is also a limited edition, reprinted for George P. Humphrey, Rochester, N.Y., 1916.

OGDEN, JOHN C. *An Excursion into Bethlehem & Nazareth in Pennsylvania, in the Year 1799: With a Succinct History of the Society of United Brethren, Commonly Called Moravians.* Philadelphia, 1805. Somewhat matter of fact and without literary style, but a friendly account of the Moravians.

*[PAULDING, JAMES K.] *The New Mirror for Travellers: And Guide to the Springs. By an Amateur.* New York: G. & C. Carvill, 1828.

Prominent Features of a Northern Tour: Written from a Brief Diary, Kept in Travelling from Charleston, S.C. . . . in . . . 1821. Charleston, 1822. Very brief and hardly more than jottings, yet it contains some unique and highly illuminating observations.

ROYALL, ANNE. *The Black Book: Or, Continuation of Travels in the United States.* 2 vols. Washington, D.C., 1828. Like all of Mrs. Royall's works, this is weak in punctuation and strong in personal invective. Nonetheless, it is a most valuable travel work by an American.

———. *Mrs. Royall's Pennsylvania: Or Travels Continued in the United States.* 2 vols. in 1. Washington, D.C., 1829.

*[———.] *Sketches of History, Life, and Manners in the United States.* New Haven, 1826.

SCHULTZ, CHRISTIAN. *Travels on an Inland Voyage . . . Performed in 1807 and 1808.* New York: Isaac Riley, 1810. A series of letters to a friend describing a journey across New York to St. Louis and New Orleans. No better account exists of the precanal, presteamboat, prerailway era.

*[SILLIMAN, BENJAMIN.] *Remarks Made on a Short Tour, between Hartford and Quebec in the Autumn of 1819.* New Haven: S. Converse, 1820.

*[THOMPSON, WILLIAM T.] *Major Jones's Sketches of Travel . . . from Georgia to Canada.* Philadelphia: T. B. Peterson, 1848.

WILLIAMSON, CHARLES. *Description of the Settlement of the Genessee Country in the State of New-York. . . .* New York, 1799. A good account of early Upper New York State.

[WINES, ENOCH C.] *A Trip to Boston. . . .* Boston: Charles C. Little & James Brown, 1838. A slender volume but amusing and especially good on the railway just completed.

II

*ABBOTT, JOHN S. C. *South and North: Or Impressions Received during a Trip to Cuba and the South.* New York: Abbey & Abbot, 1860.

ADAMS, NEHEMIAH. *A South-Side View of Slavery: Or, Three Months at the South, in 1854.* Boston: T. R. Marvin, 1854. A friendly view of the South by a Boston clergyman.

*ANDREWS, SIDNEY. *The South since the War: As Shown by Fourteen Weeks of Travel and Observation in Georgia and the Carolinas.* Boston: Ticknor & Fields, 1866.

BARTRAM, WILLIAM. *Travels through North and South Carolina, Georgia, East and West Florida. . . .* Philadelphia: James & Johnson, 1791. The actual travels took place over fifteen years before publication. They are comprised, as would be expected, of observations on the natural phenomena of the areas visited, but life and manners are not disregarded.

BLAKE, HENRY N. *Three Years in the Army of the Potomac.* Boston: Lee & Shepard, 1865. A wide range of comment on southern life by a soldier-traveler who did not like officers or army management.

BRYANT, WILLIAM C. *Letters of a Traveller: Or, Notes of Things Seen in Europe and America.* New York: George P. Putnam, 1850. By the distinguished poet and editor of the *New York Evening Post.* An excellent account of the South in 1843, of Illinois in 1841, and of the steamboat trip from Buffalo to Chicago in 1846.

COFFIN, CHARLES C. *Four Years of Fighting.* . . . Boston: Ticknor & Fields, 1866. A vivid, finely reported account of southern life during the war, though filled with a violent hatred of slavery and secession.

*CONYNGHAM, DAVID P. *Sherman's March through the South with Sketches and Incidents of the Campaign.* New York: Sheldon & Co., 1865.

COOK, JOEL. *The Siege of Richmond: A Narrative of the Military Operations . . . during . . . May and June, 1862.* Philadelphia: G. W. Childs, 1862. The author, a special correspondent of the *Philadelphia Press,* gives far more than his title indicates, surveying a wide aspect of Virginia life in the brief period of two months.

DUGANNE, AUGUSTINE J. H. *Camps and Prisons: Twenty Months in the Department of the Gulf.* New York: J. F. Robens, 1865. A Bostonian's observations of sugar plantations in Louisiana and life in Texas. Interesting and valuable.

HIGGINSON, THOMAS W. *Army Life in a Black Regiment.* Boston: Fields, Osgood & Co., 1870. A well-written account of southern plantations and towns.

*[INGRAHAM, JOSEPH H.] *The South-West. By a Yankee.* 2 vols. New York: Harper & Bros., 1835.

*[KNIGHT, HENRY C.] *Letters from the South and West.* Boston: Richardson & Lord, 1824.

KNOX, THOMAS W. *Camp-Fire and Cotton-Field: Southern Adventures in Time of War.* . . . New York: Blelock & Co., 1865. An outstanding account of confiscated plantations on the Lower Mississippi.

LANMAN, CHARLES. *Letters from the Alleghany Mountains.* New York: George P. Putnam, 1849. Less florid than the rest of Lanman's writings, this volume deals with the southern Appalachians.

[LONGSTREET, AUGUSTUS B.] *Georgia Scenes, Characters, Incidents, &c., in the First Half Century of the Republic.* 2d ed. New York: Harper & Bros., 1851. This is one of the minor classics of American literature. Descriptive rather than travel in character, its accounts of life and manners are realistic and often extraordinarily humorous.

*MACKIE, J. MILTON. *From Cape Cod to Dixie and the Tropics.* New York: G. P. Putnam, 1864.

[NASON, DANIEL.] *A Journal of a Tour from Boston to Savannah, Thence to Havana . . . Thence to New Orleans and Several Western Cities.* . . . Cambridge, Mass., 1849. An unvarnished account by a Cambridge carpenter. Without literary style, but shrewd and valuable for the details of everyday travel.

NICHOLS, GEORGE W. *The Story of the Great March.* New York: Harper & Bros., 1866. One of the most popular accounts of Sherman's march to the sea. Valuable but prejudiced against the South.

*OLMSTEAD, FREDERICK L. *A Journey in the Back Country.* New York: Mason Bros., 1860.

*———. *A Journey in the Seaboard Slave States: With Remarks on Their Economy.* New York: Dix & Edwards, 1856.

*———. *A Journey through Texas: Or, a Saddle-Trip on the Southwestern Frontier.* New York: Dix, Edwards & Co., 1857.

PARKER, AMOS A. *Trip to the West and Texas . . . in 1834-5.* . . . Concord, N.H.: White & Fisher, 1835. Matter-of-fact but useful account of a New Englander through New York State, the Middle West, to Texas and Louisiana.

PARKER, THOMAS H. *History of the 51st Regiment . . . from 1861 . . . to 1865.* Philadelphia: King & Baird, 1869. No better account of wartime conditions in the South exists than this apparent regimental history, whose author traveled widely and observed acutely.

*[PAULDING, JAMES K.] *Letters from the South, Written in . . . 1816.* 2 vols. New York: Jas. Eastburn & Co., 1817.

POPE, JOHN. *Tour through the Southern and Western Territories of the United States . . . the Spanish Dominions . . . and the Floridas. . . .* Richmond, 1792. Despite the grandiose title, the account is meager but written with considerable wit.

*[ROGERS, CARLTON H.(?)] *Incidents of Travel in the Southern States and Cuba: With a Description of the Mammoth Cave.* New York, 1862.

*ROYALL, ANNE. *Letters from Alabama. . . .* Washington, D.C., 1830.

*———. *Mrs. Royall's Southern Tour.* 2 vols. Washington, D.C., 1830, 1831.

*STODDARD, AMOS. *Sketches, Historical and Descriptive, of Louisiana.* Philadelphia: Matthew Carey, 1812.

Tour through Part of Virginia . . . in 1808, A. Belfast, Ireland: Smyth & Lyons, 1810. There was a New York edition in 1809.

*TICKNOR, GEORGE. *Life, Letters, and Journals.* Edited by Anna Ticknor and George S. Hilliard. 2 vols. Boston: James R. Osgood & Co., 1876.

TUNNARD, WILLIAM H. *A Southern Record: The History of the Third Regiment Louisiana Infantry. . . .* Baton Rouge, La., 1866. Far more than a regimental history, it is an account of scenery, backwoodsmen, and the life of the Confederacy in wartime. There are few southern accounts of description, and this has additional value on that account.

III

*ANDREWS, CHRISTOPHER C. *Minnesota and Dacotah: Or Letters Descriptive of a Tour through the North-West in . . . 1856. . . .* Washington, D.C.: Robert Farnham, 1857.

ATWATER, CALEB. *Remarks Made on a Tour to Prairie du Chien; Thence to Washington City, in 1829.* Columbus, Ohio: Isaac N. Whiting, 1831. A slightly different version may be found in his *Writings* (Columbus, Ohio, 1833).

AYERS, ELISHA. *A Journal of Travel, by Elisha Ayers, Esq., Formerly Gen. Taylor's School-Master, now of Preston, Conn. . . .* 1847. As illiterate an account of travel across Virginia to Ohio and Tennessee as one is likely to find.

BOND, J. WESLEY. *Minnesota and Its Resources to Which Are Appended . . . Notes of a Trip from St. Paul to . . . the Red River of the North.* New York: J. S. Redfield, 1853. A good account though more nearly akin to a gazetteer than a travel work.

*BRACKENRIDGE, HENRY M. *Journal of a Voyage up the River Missouri Performed in Eighteen Hundred and Eleven.* 2d ed. Baltimore: Coale & Maxwell, 1815. This account is reprinted from the author's *Views of Louisiana* (Pittsburgh: Cramer, Spear & Eichbaum, 1814) but greatly enlarged. The 1817 edition of *Views of Louisiana* does not contain the *Journal.*

———. *Recollections of Persons and Places in the West.* 2d ed. Philadelphia: J. B. Lippincott, 1868. The first edition was published in 1834. Autobiographical as well as descriptive. Especially vivid is a voyage down the Ohio River in 1810.

*CATLIN, GEORGE. *Letters and Notes on the Manners, Customs, and Conditions of the North American Indians. . . . Written during Eight Years' Travel amongst the . . . Indians . . . in 1832, 33, 34, 35, 36, 37, 38, and 39.* 2 vols. 2d ed. New York: Wiley & Putnam, 1842.

*DOW, LORENZO. *The Travels and Providential Experiences of Lorenzo Dow; Written by Himself.* 2 vols. 2d ed. Liverpool: H. Forshaw, 1806.

*[FLAGG, EDMUND.] *The Far-West: Or, a Tour beyond the Mountains.* 2 vols. New York: Harper & Bros., 1838.

FLINT, TIMOTHY. *Recollections of the Last Ten Years.* Boston: Cummings, Hilliard & Co., 1826. One of the most valuable and readable accounts of the middle western frontier. Republished, with an introduction by C. HARTLEY GRATTON, by Alfred A. Knopf, New York, 1932.

FULLER, MARGARET. *Summer on the Lakes.* Boston: Little & Brown, 1844. A superficial account, mostly of the Indians, by the famous Transcendentalist.

HALL, JAMES. *Letters from the West.* . . . London: Henry Colburn, 1828. Excellent account of a voyage down the Ohio River.

———. *Statistics of the West.* Cincinnati: J. A. James & Co., 1836. A valuable account published later under various titles: *Notes on the Western States* (Philadelphia, 1838) and *The West: Its Commerce and Navigation* (Cincinnati, 1848).

*HAWLEY, ZERAH. *A Journal of a Tour through Connecticut, Massachusetts, New-York . . . Including a Year's Residence in [the Northern] Part of . . . Ohio.* New Haven, 1822.

*HOFFMAN, CHARLES F. *A Winter in the West. By a New Yorker.* 2 vols. New York: Harper & Bros., 1835.

LANMAN, CHARLES. *A Summer in the Wilderness: Embracing a Canoe Voyage up the Mississippi and around Lake Superior.* New York: D. Appleton & Co., 1847. Flowery style but good descriptions of St. Louis and Nauvoo and of copper-mining at Lake Superior.

LINDLEY, HARLOW (ed.). *Indiana as Seen by Early Travellers.* Indianapolis: Indiana Historical Commission, 1916. A compilation of travel and descriptive material about Indiana. Not confined to American accounts alone.

*[LIPPINCOTT, SARA CLARKE ("GRACE GREENWOOD").] *New Life in New Lands.* New York: J. B. Ford & Co., 1873.

*MACKIE, J. MILTON. *From Cape Cod to Dixie.* . . . *See* Part II, "The Cotton Kingdom."

*OLMSTEAD, FREDERICK LAW. *A Journey through Texas.* . . . *See* Part II, "The Cotton Kingdom."

*PEYTON, JOHN L. *Over the Alleghanies and across the Prairies.* 2d ed. London: Simpkin, Marshall & Co., 1870.

PIERCE, BESSIE L. (comp. and ed.). *As Others See Chicago: Impressions of Visitors, 1673–1933.* . . . Chicago: University of Chicago Press, 1933. A model compilation of extracts from the works of travelers to Chicago.

PIKE, ZEBULON M. *An Account of Expeditions to the Sources of the Mississippi.* . . . Philadelphia, etc.: C. and C. Conrad, 1810. This classic account has been often reprinted. See ELLIOTT COUES (ed.), *The Expeditions of Zebulon Pike* (3 vols.; New York, 1895).

SCHULTZ, CHRISTIAN. *Travels on an Inland Voyage. See* Part I, "The Rising Cities of the Atlantic Northeast."

SCHOOLCRAFT, HENRY R. *A View of the Lead Mines of Missouri.* New York, 1819. The earliest of many valuable travel works, many of them reissued in later editions with different titles by this author. For example, *Journal of a Tour into the Interior of Missouri and Arkansaw* (London, 1821); *Narrative Journal of Travels through the Northwestern Regions of the United States* (Albany, 1821); *Narrative of an Expedition through the Upper Mississippi* (New York, 1834); and *Travels in the Central Portions of the Mississippi Valley* (New York, 1825).

THOMAS, DAVID. *Travels through the Western Country in the Summer of 1816.* Auburn, N.Y., 1819. A splendid account of early Pittsburgh and a voyage down the Ohio River.

THWAITES, REUBEN G. (ed.). *Early Western Travels, 1748–1846: A Series of Annotated Reprints of Some of the Best and Rarest Contemporary Volumes of Travel . . . in the Middle and Far West.* . . . 32 vols. Cleveland: A. H. Clarke Co.,

1904-7. Probably the finest collection, as it is the most ambitious, of travel accounts in America. The accounts of foreign observers are included as well as American.

IV

*BOWLES, SAMUEL. *Across the Continent.* Springfield: S. Bowles & Co.; New York: Hurd & Houghton, 1865.

BRYANT, EDWIN. *What I Saw in California.* . . . New York: D. Appleton & Co., 1848. An excellent account of the overland journey, vivid in recalling the slow monotony of the trip. Often reprinted.

[CLEMENS, SAMUEL L.] *Roughing It. By Mark Twain.* Hartford, Conn.: American Publishing Co., 1872.

COLTON, WALTER. *Three Years in California.* New York: A. S. Barnes & Co., 1850. Extremely interesting account of a clergyman who served as the alcalde of Monterey.

DAMAN, SAMUEL C. *A Trip from the Sandwich Islands to Lower Oregon, and Upper California.* Honolulu, 1849. An excellent account of the Pacific Northwest. Reprinted in the *Magazine of History,* Vol. XXV (1924).

DANA, RICHARD H., JR. *Two Years before the Mast.* New York: Harper & Bros., 1840. This great classic of the voyage around the Horn to California has been often reprinted.

DELANO, ALONZO. *Life on the Plains and among the Diggings.* . . . Auburn and Buffalo, N.Y.: Miller, Orton & Mulligan, 1854. The overland journey across the Plains and in the gold fields.

FRÉMONT, JOHN C. *Report of the Exploring Expedition to the Rocky Mountains . . . in 1842, and to Oregon and North California . . . in 1843–44.* Washington, D.C.: Blair & Rives, 1845. This famous account is more available in the 1846 edition of D. Appleton & Co., New York.

GASS, PATRICK. *A Journal of the Voyages and Travels of a Corps of Discovery, under . . . Captain Lewis and Captain Clark.* Pittsburgh, 1807. The first published account of the expedition. Often reprinted. See J. K. HOSMER (ed.), *Gass's Journal of the Lewis and Clark Expedition* (Chicago, 1904).

*GREELEY, HORACE. *An Overland Journey, from New York to San Francisco in . . . 1859.* New York: C. M. Saxton, Barker & Co., 1860.

*GREGG, JOSIAH. *Commerce of the Prairies.* 2 vols. New York: Henry G. Langley, 1844. The great classic of the Santa Fé trade. Often reprinted.

[IRVING, WASHINGTON.] *The Crayon Miscellany, No. 1: Containing a Tour on the Prairies.* Philadelphia: Carey, Lea & Blanchard, 1835. Beautifully written but possibly somewhat romanticized.

JOHNSON, OVERTON, and WINTER, WILLIAM H. *Route across the Rocky Mountains: With a Description of Oregon and California.* . . . Lafayette, Ind., 1846. Factual but interesting. Excessively rare and has been reprinted by Princeton University Press, Princeton, 1932, under the editorship of CARL L. CANNON.

LANGWORTHY, FRANKLIN. *Scenery of the Plains, Mountains and Mines.* . . . Ogdensburgh, N.Y.: J. C. Sprague, 1855. Vivid account of the transcontinental journey. Unfavorable to the Mormons.

MELINE, JAMES F. *Two Thousand Miles on Horseback: Santa Fé and Back . . . in 1866.* New York: Hurd & Houghton, 1867. Somewhat generalized but good on Santa Fé.

PARKER, SAMUEL. *Journal of an Exploring Tour beyond the Rocky Mountains . . . in 1835, '36, and '37.* . . . Ithaca, N.Y., 1838. Valuable descriptions of scenery, routes, and Indians, told entertainingly.

PARKMAN, FRANCIS, JR. *The California and Oregon Trail.* New York: G. P. Putnam,

1849. Perhaps the most reprinted of all the great classics dealing with the transcontinental journey.

POWERS, STEPHEN. *Afoot and Alone: A Walk from Sea to Sea.* . . . Hartford, Conn.: Columbian Book Co., 1872. An exceptionally interesting record of a journey across the Southern States through the Southwest.

*REVERE, JOSEPH W. *A Tour of Duty in California.* . . . New York: C. S. Francis & Co., 1849. Reprinted as *Naval Duty in California* (Oakland, Calif., 1947).

RICHARDSON, ALBERT D. *Our New States and Territories.* . . . New York: Beadle & Co., 1866. One of several accounts of the transcontinental tour by this author. Excellent descriptions of San Francisco.

*RUSLING, JAMES F. *Across America: Or, the Great West and the Pacific Coast.* New York: Sheldon & Co., 1874.

STANSBURY, HOWARD. *An Expedition to the Valley of the Great Salt Lake of Utah.* . . . Philadelphia: Lippincott, Grambo & Co., 1855. Valuable and straightforward account of Utah. Friendly to the Mormons.

*TAYLOR, BAYARD. *Eldorado: Or, Adventures in the Path of Empire: Comprising a Voyage to California; Life in San Francisco and Monterey; Pictures of the Gold Fields.* . . . 2 vols. in 1. 4th ed. New York: George P. Putnam & Co., 1854.

WINTHROP, THEODORE. *The Canoe and the Saddle.* Boston: Ticknor & Fields, 1863. A charming account of the Pacific Northwest.

*WISE, HENRY A. *Los Gringos: Or, an Inside View of Mexico and California.* . . . New York: Baker & Scribner, 1849.

WOODS, DANIEL B. *Sixteen Months at the Gold Diggings.* New York: Harper & Bros., 1851. An excellent factual account which does much to dispel the "glamour" of the gold fields.

Index of Illustrations

The illustrations chosen for these volumes have been found in a variety of sources. Many of the small illustrations at the heads of chapters were reproduced from the type catalogues of Bruce's New York Type Foundry and the Caslon Letter Foundry (Stephenson Blake): others were found in *The Loyal West in the Times of the Rebellion*, by John Barber and Henry Lowe (1865); *A General View of the World*, by S. Augustus Mitchell (1845); *America, Historical, Statistic, and Descriptive*, by James S. Buckingham (1841); *Wood-Engravings by Thomas Bewick* (privately published, 1951); *Our Country*, by B. J. Lossing (1843); and *Commerce of the Prairies*, by Josiah Gregg (1845). There follows a detailed list of sources for the other illustrations.

I

Frontispiece. The Yorke Family at Home, 1837. An anonymous primitive watercolor in the collection of the Museum of Modern Art, New York.

P. 6. A View of New York. *A General View of the World*, by S. Augustus Mitchell. 1845.

P. 13. Harvard Square in 1776. A print in the collection of the Max Epstein Library of Reproductions, University of Chicago.

P. 36. Excursion to the Beach. *Appleton's Journal*, Vol. 1. 1869.

P. 39. Boston before 1845. Mitchell, *op. cit.*

P. 51. The Capitol. Mitchell, *op. cit.*

P. 72. Germantown, Pa., in 1793. From the Epstein Library, University of Chicago.

P. 102. May Day in New York. *Harper's Weekly*, Vol. III, 1859.

P. 109. Steamboat, 1835. Anonymous print from the Seymour Dunbar Collection, Museum of Science and Industry, Chicago.

P. 132. Philadelphia in 1834. Mitchell, *op. cit.*

P. 134. Girard College in 1834. Mitchell, *op. cit.*

P. 147. Fairmount Park, Philadelphia. *Scribner's Monthly Magazine*, Vol. I. 1870.

P. 148. An Early Sleeping Car. *Frank Leslie's Illustrated Newspaper*, Vol. VII. 1859.

P. 164. Fashions for June, 1856. *Harper's New Monthly Magazine*, Vol. XIII. 1856.

P. 183. A Fish Vendor. *Scribner's*, Vol. I. 1870.

P. 172. Central Park, New York. *Appleton's*, Vol. I. 1869.

P. 196. Baltimore in 1834. Mitchell, *op. cit.*

P. 214. Sunday on Fifth Avenue. *Appleton's*, Vol. I. 1869.

P. 219. Hints for Celebrating the Fourth of July. *Harper's New Monthly Magazine*, Vol. XIII. 1856.

II

Frontispiece. Cotton Plantation. A painting by C. Giroux in the Boston Museum of Fine Arts. Probably painted in 1850. From the M. and M. Karolik Collection.

P. 256. Cable Ferry. From the Dunbar Collection, Museum of Science and Industry, Chicago.

P. 263. Natural Bridge, Virginia. Mitchell, *op. cit.*

P. 286. Charleston in 1837. *The Family Magazine; or, Monthly Abstract of General Knowledge.* 1837.

P. 302. The Levee at New Orleans. From the Dunbar Collection, Museum of Science and Industry, Chicago.

P. 318. Riverboat at a "Wooding Station." From the Dunbar Collection, Museum of Science and Industry, Chicago.

P. 365. Two Slave Drivers and a Backwoodsman. From *Forty Etchings, etc.*, by Basil Hall. 1829.

P. 379. King Cotton. Mitchell, *op. cit.*

P. 401. Stage Coach and Team. *Harper's Magazine*, Vol. XXXV. 1867.

III

III

P. 331. *Across the Great Plains.* From the Bisbee Collection, Museum of Science and Industry, Chicago.

P. 335. Nahuatza, Sea Life. The Journey of a Salmon. *Harper's Weekly*, Vol. IV, No. 8.

INDEX

Index

Index

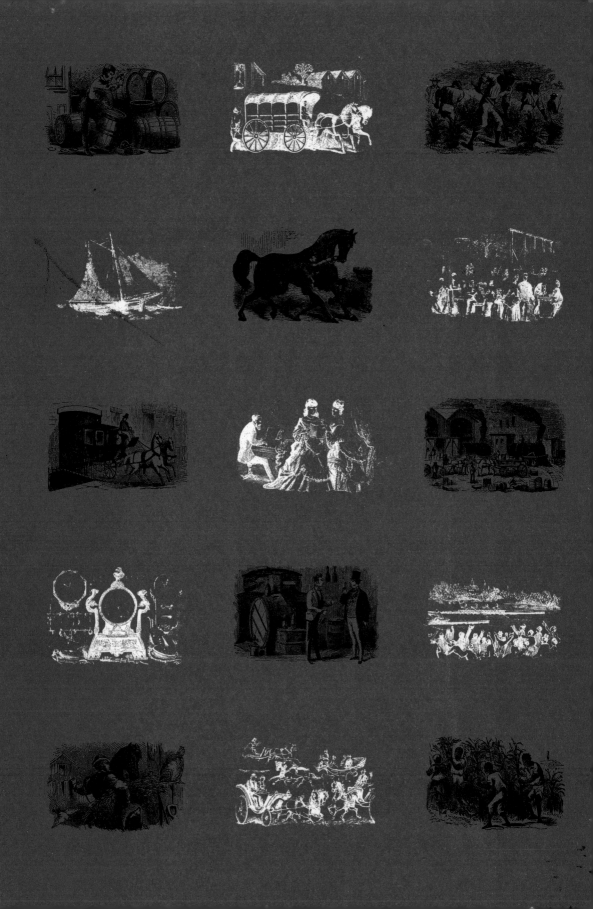